Stalinism and the Seeds of Soviet Reform

Stalinism and the Seeds of Soviet Reform

The Debates of the 1960s

MOSHE LEWIN

Pluto Press
LONDON, ENGLAND

M.E. Sharpe, Inc.
ARMONK, NEW YORK

Note about this edition:

This work is a reprint of a 1974 publication by Princeton University Press, New Jersey, and Pluto Press (1975), London, which was titled *Political Undercurrents in Soviet Economic Debates: from Bukharin to the Modern Reformers*. Except for a few corrections of errors, no changes have been made in the text. We have changed only the title. At the time of original publication, 'political undercurrents', as well as the subtitle mentioning Bukharin, were new themes. These themes still preserve their importance in the book and as features of today's Soviet scene; but the title can now be changed. As the book anticipated, 'undercurrents' have become 'currents' and Bukharin is not only fully rehabilitated and his works published but he is even surpassed by numerous other rehabilitations and newer ideas and preoccupations. On the other hand, it is more important today to point to the earlier, unsuccessful effort to reform the system and underline the continuing validity of the thinking of 'the men of the sixties' – a whole generation of them – whose ideas are still potent and a number of whom are still active on the political stage.

This edition published in 1991 by Pluto Press,
345 Archway Road, London N6 5AA and
M.E. Sharpe, Inc.
80 Business Park Drive, Armonk, New York 10504
Copyright © 1974,1991 Moshe Lewin

British Library Cataloguing-in-Publication Data
Lewin, Moshe *1921*–
    Stalinism and the Seeds of Soviet Reform:
    The Debates of the 1960s
    1. Soviet union. Economic development. Political aspects
    I. Title
    330.9470853

    ISBN 0–7453–0427–3 (UK)

Library of Congress Cataloging-in-Publication Data
Lewin, Moshe.
    Political Undercurrents in Soviet
    Economic Debates.

    1. Economics–History–Russia.   2. Bukharin, Nikolai

Ivanovich, 1888–1938. I. Title.
HB113.A2L46   330.9'47   73-2477
ISBN 0-87332-858-2

Printed and bound in the UK by Billing and Sons Ltd, Worcester

CONTENTS

THE economic debates that provided the canvas for this book took place in the Soviet Union in the relatively relaxed atmosphere of the early and mid-1960s. We know from subsequent events that the reformers failed to achieve their aims because the modest reforms actually put in place with the support of A. Kosygin, Politbureau member and Premier in those years, were sabotaged and finally put to rest under the pressure of a conservative coalition led by Brezhnev. This failure of projects into which went the creativity and hopes of a generation of intellectuals, technicians and enlightened bureaucrats who came to be known as 'the men of the sixties' was a very costly affair for the Soviet Union. There were many more of those critics and dreamers than the ones mentioned in this book and this fine cohort did not, to my knowledge, receive enough attention, although a good monograph would certainly be of great interest. The dashed hopes of this generation of presumed losers created a deep-seated pessimism, inside and outside the USSR, about prospects for any serious reforms in that country. But less than 20 years later – 20 years recklessly wasted, according to some – a new wave of reforms is being attempted there, on a scale and scope 'the sixties' were not free to preach openly. It turned out that the men of the sixties may not have been such losers after all.

It is not easy to give a full assessment of the historical importance of the earlier reformers as long as we do not yet know what fate is reserved for the reforms under Gorbachev. We will know better some years from now – but it is clear already that what is being attempted today, not only in the sphere of the economy but also, to a large extent, in the sphere of politics, follows most of the desiderata of the pioneering debaters. Therefore, even if the final result of the Gorbachevian efforts is not yet known, a book about the 1960s is not just history. It is still relevant to what is going on currently – a measure both of the validity of the ideas in question as well as testimony to the barrenness of a system that seemed to have destroyed all internal mechanisms of change – in an apparent effort, as it were, to achieve immunity from history.

On the face of it, everything in these debates revolved around economics. Markets and prices, methods of planning, ways of motivating labor, ways of achieving balanced growth were, of course, economic problems. But they also had an added historical dimension in that these ideas were clearly inspired by the experience of the New Economic Policy (NEP) – by then some 30 years in the past – finally culminating in the programmatic slogan of equally 'nepian' vintage calling to link the plan and the market in the new, creative combination. The old Stalinist planning system was deemed so damaging that it had to be scrapped and replaced by an entirely different concept of 'planning' – such was the unanimous verdict of a whole class of critics.

Readers will, of course, see for themselves what exactly the reforming economists contributed. But it is worth underscoring the fact that the economists did not just produce an impressive and alarming indictment of the economic system that fettered economic development. They also proposed ideas which amounted to a whole program of change. Among them the late academician Nemchinov was particularly convincing. He castigated 'an ossified, mechanical system' and sounded a dramatic *memento mori:* 'An economic system, so fettered from top to bottom, will put a brake on social and technological progress, and will break down, sooner or later, under the pressure of real processes of economic life.' He then went on to propose a thoughtful program of 'a cost-accounting planning system', containing features such as freely entered contracts between producers, suppliers and consumers, including the state among the latter, on the basis of a price and quality of goods acceptable to the contracting parties. Nemchinov insisted on the importance of juridical norms and legislative regulation of economic life, instead of the prevailing administrative commands by a high-handed and economically inept bureaucracy.

This kind of reasoning, interested in stopping 'administrative methods' and switching to economic and legal ones, was already transcending the sphere of 'strictly economic' matters. Whether they wanted it or not, whether they were cautious or bold, politics with a capital P was peeping through every possible economic curtain. When Venzher demanded that *kolkhozy* be freed of bureaucratic tutelage and be allowed to regain their autonomy and their cooperative character, he also clearly stated that the essence of socialism resided precisely in the principles of self-management and cooperation. These principles were – according to him – 'higher' on the scale of socialist values than the official dogma, which extolled the *sovkhoz,* or state-run farms, as the superior socialist form. In Venzher's statement about socialism and property, amplified by others, notably and conspicuously Shkredov, the property system was submitted for the first time in many years to a serious scrutiny. Predictably, state-owned property was denied the claim to being socialist *per se,* as long as 'nationalization' did not turn into 'socialization', i.e. did not transform all the producers into real co-owners of national productive assets.

This problem is sufficient in itself to illustrate an important feature of the debates: in scrutinizing the ways the economy was run, it was impossible not to inquire about the ways the polity was structured. Consequently, economic debates could not but be political ones. And they had also to spill over into the taboo area of ideology: the official definition of socialism could not withstand free inquiry and only censorship could save it – temporarily. Such was, in substance, the message of the three well-known future dissidents – academician Sakharov, the physicist Turchin and the historian Medvedev – who together wrote a 'letter to the Central Committee'. But their text wasn't about economics. It was directly political and dealt with the political system. It was not intended initially for publication and the authors did not bother about censors. Here again we heard stern warnings and proposals about how to change things: the chasm between state and society and, in particular, between the state and the intelligentsia is growing. The way out consisted of adopting a program of a broad and deep democratization of political life. Without it, Russia was doomed to become a second-rate provincial power – to say the least.

By spelling out such demands the three authors added an indispensable and clearly stated cap to what was more implied than explicit in the writings of economists. Together, the reasoning of the economists and of the political writers allowed a common conclusion: the main culprit was not arbitrary planning *per se* – but an arbitrary state. When another economist involved in the debates, Birman, raised the question as to why the reforms of 1965 hadn't managed to solve problems (he certainly wanted simply to ask why they failed), the answer was only thinly veiled: because there were no changes 'in the ways the social system was functioning' – a formula that obviously included the whole existing soviet state system.

The logic of the situation was clear: it was not just the case that the theoretical debate on the economy had to deal with the state. The problem was that the reform of the economy had to change the character of the state too, and quite profoundly at that. No wonder conservatives, as long as they had the power to do it, scuppered these reforms to avoid changing the system. They offered themselves an additional lease of life for some 15 years – proving convincingly that the ruling apparatus was too sclerotic to be able to do much more than to try to perpetuate itself while the system simply ossified.

The salutary programs devised by reformers had to wait for another chance.

An Unmentioned Presence

When studying the problems besetting the system as the debaters saw and interpreted them, we divined the existence of some very special features in the discussion. One has already been alluded to: the problem of the state was, mostly, implicit or self-censored although some authors pushed near to the limits of the permissible. But there were also two important themes that were conspicuously present – without ever being mentioned. One was a person. The other – an institution.

The person in question was Nikolai Bukharin. The institution was the party. Bukharin was, as I argued, the unsung hero of the reformers. The whole 'plan and market' approach that interested him was also the central plank in the thinking of the reformers. And behind this kind of reasoning was the socioeconomic model of the NEP that loomed so large, as inspiration, in the reformist writings. Bukharin's most interesting ideas evolved during the last years of the NEP when he, together with Rykov and Tomskii, two other politburo members, tried to save the framework of the NEP, without forgoing a reasonable rate of economic development.

The introduction of the NEP at the lowest ebb of the civil-war and war-communism was characterized by a deliberate effort – followed by an appropriate ideological backing – to dismantle the centralist-bureaucratic system of war-communism and to introduce a model of economic and social activity based on quite different principles. The slogans that reverberated all over the country, like 'down with war-communist methods', and 'down with the *glavkokratiia*', referred to powerful, centralized agencies using predominantly administrative-coercive methods.

But no more than about seven years later, even before this job of dismantling was fully completed, the bewildered Bukharin – and many others with him – realized that the predominant Stalin faction in the leadership of the party was taking the country back to the coercive mode that was rather solemnly condemned shortly before. No other leader was as outspoken and as far-sighted as Bukharin was during his battle against the specter of an ominous 'leviathan-state' that he anticipated almost with a sense of panic. But his most important ideas and criticisms were hurled on the party leadership behind closed doors. The reading and politically sophisticated public of the late 1920s was aware of Bukharin's economic ideas about planning and industrial development, but they knew nothing then about the quite prophetic political accusations that he launched against the leadership in internal, unpublicized meetings. It was Western scholarship that unearthed these facts, showing thereby the much deeper and more radical face of Bukharin's program – the program of an anti-Stalinist bolshevik.[1]

The path taken by the Stalinist leadership at the end of the NEP led to a radical transformation of the whole system and of the party and led the country, to believe the official claims, to all kinds of credible and incredible achievements. When the debaters of the 1960s looked for ways to dismantle the Stalinist model, they were not yet free – maybe still unprepared conceptually – to deal with the problem of the party, even if they showed convincingly that the system was declining dangerously and its leading institution could not have been exempt from responsibility for the trouble. This is why I found it indispensable to add some chapters on the party although this was not part of the economic debates the book was concentrated on.

In doing so, one could discern a situation in the party not unlike the one Nemchinov deplored in the sphere of the country's economy: 'some kind of an entirely fettered system' that would, according to him, break down one day if deep and timely reforms were put off.

So the party was in a similar position. It was a political party only by name. It was a hierarchical, basically administrative organization where almost everyone, from just under the very top to the bottom of the pyramid, was no more than a subordinate, without much chance of meaningful political participation. Despite a semblance of 'a membership' and an abundance of different 'party bodies', it was basically an *apparat*. Moreover, it was a bureaucratic organization that was an intricate part of the broader state apparatus, albeit a very influential one. This kind of organization was denying the citizens political rights, even if they were party members, and was quite successful in depoliticizing the country so thoroughly that many could not imagine that such a system could be toppled.

[1] But we in the West probably erred when we thought that Bukharin continued, at least in private, his anti-Stalinism during the 1930s. As his widow A. Larina showed in her recently published memoirs, Bukharin succumbed to the Stalinist myths and allowed himself to be demolished as a person before being eliminated by Stalin physically.

An authentically political party might have played the role of a counter-balancing force to the bureaucratic phenomenon that went deeper in the Soviet Union than in most other countries. In the Soviet case – as we said – the party found itself instead in the position of being an intricate part of the phenomenon and therefore also part of the mechanism of gradual sclerotic decline. It was logical to assume that it was only a matter of time before an organization of this type would reach the limits of its ability to rule. Sooner or later, it had to lose effective control over the country, notably because powerful, sometimes spontaneous developments in society, economy and culture would inevitably render obsolete the ruling institutional grid.

Pointer to the Future – Civil Society

Among the topics that I introduced, in order to offer a historical and sociological perspective to the ideas of the reforming wing of the intelligentsia, was the notion of 'civil society' to which a chapter is dedicated in the book. An idea that is today, simply and obviously, manifesting itself in the streets all over the Soviet Union, was not yet part of the vocabulary of Western thinking about Russia at that time. 'Political Undercurrents', which no longer need to be proven, were also a novelty in the early 1970s. The emerging pluralism of an urbanizing society had to be urgently introduced into the conceptual wherewithal in order to grasp the trends that soviet leaders kept disregarding so stubbornly. The book pointed therefore not only to a growing 'spectrum of cultural life' but also to 'a gamut of political opinions that worked their way through the maze of groups and social classes, kept penetrating the party'. Disregarding this social and political reality was extremely dangerous for the party – and yet its very character pushed to claiming and insisting on 'monolithism', and on such red herrings as 'the growing homogeneity of soviet society', when, in fact, soviet politics was not responding any more to a monolithic model of any kind. Not even inside the party. 'So much – I wrote in the book – is, in fact, happening in the depth of society, so much is brewing and maturing that the existing façade of political unanimity and apparent simplicity is no longer identical with "soviet politics".'

The book was therefore clearly built on an anticipation that those 'undercurrents' would unavoidably become 'currents' one day. Existing data made it possible to argue that 'public interests and opinion had their ways of finding an expression, in word and deed in many roundabout ways, and refusal to see the subterranean political reality meant a deepening of the social crisis and an ever-expanding crisis of values and ideology'.

There was also enough material to allow the reader to discern the axis around which problems will keep accumulating and festering, and therefore 'the struggle – I believed – will grow fiercer' to force the party to shed its obsolete methods. If not, one did not need to be a prophet to foresee that 'the malfunctions will continue unabated ... more conflict and even considerable tremors can be expected to haunt soviet political life in the coming years'.

Consequently, even a seemingly improbable 'democratization', that many of the reformers preached, and a new wave of reforms, much more important than anything attempted earlier, had to be seen as a reasonable prospect. There was no way of knowing, in the years when a rather timid reform was just throttled, when such a new wave would appear and what it would consist of. But there was a new society, a new reality in the making in Russia – and the old institutions, products, mostly, of the 1930s, were aging quickly and becoming quite improbable carriers of important changes in the way they worked. In fact the system was fast rotting away.

Perestroika – Between Gloom and Hope

Since Gorbachev came to power and initiated his new policy of *perestroika,* the term 'wave' became inadequate. In the 1960s, there was only one periodical, *Novyi Mir,* which, under the able and courageous editorship of the poet Tvardovskii, could raise important issues and vent some criticisms. Today *glasnost* is producing a press and a periodic literature that is pouring out enormous quantities of information, criticism, political and social thinking which an observer can no longer grasp without the services of compilers and indexers. The political changes – notably the election of a new style 'parliament', as it is generally called inside and outside the USSR – are astonishing, and many spheres of life are touched upon by revisions, reforms, public action, in an atmosphere of a vast improvement in the whole range of human rights and the virtual disappearance of terror and other, lesser forms of repression of which the soviet system was an accomplished master.

The list can be prolonged – the expected 'wave' has become a flood that the whole world is keenly observing even now – but at the same time the switch to a liberal, consensus-seeking policy stumbled over powerful, conservative and centrifugal forces that surfaced and keep surfacing, allowing opponents of the changes to accuse the liberalization itself of being the source of all the evils that beset the country. These accusations – and the strength of different, especially nationalist stirrings – are made more strident by the deteriorating economic situation. The new regime has, thus far, been unsuccessful in this crucial sphere. The leaders have committed a number of errors and, as of the time of writing, the economy does not seem to be working. Predictably, voices of gloom prophesying the coming collapse of the Gorbachev experiment are persistent and some Russian intellectuals are even trumpeting it with a dose of masochistic glee.

They may be wrong, notably because the term 'experiment', to my mind, does not apply to the Gorbachev reforms anymore. But the situation in the USSR is of incredible complexity and warrants a brief elaboration here, to explain the difference between events and ideas of the 1960s and those of the late 1980s and 1990s.

There is no doubt that Gorbachev's policies have weakened considerably the mainstays of the old power structure. Bureaucracy, the party and the economic administrators have had many of their practices and dogmas considerably shaken. As a result of *perestroika* policies, many institutions were forced into feverish but chaotic reorganizations that, at first, couldn't but disorganize them, causing the whole state machinery to shiver and perform quite poorly. Considering that new institutions, methods and leaders are slow in coming, the central government is in danger of losing the levers of control and management without which its policies cannot be implemented.

It all amounts to an extremely complicated situation where the government and the whole system find themselves, in a sense, 'nowhere' – if one assumes that the old system is still there but does not work. Or, seen from a different angle, 'in-between' two systems, where the old does not work properly and the new is still too weak to replace it. Such is the impression and it is awesome. One can understand why so many in the USSR are saying that actually nothing has changed and 'the old' will have no difficulty in staging a comeback with a vengeance at any moment. Not too many dare to say that those changes that have already taken place are irreversible.

Being suspended in between the old and the new does not sound too reassuring to many citizens, since the new, even if it exists, may not really function. The atmosphere this creates explains the widespread disorientation and despondency in the public, and the panicky talk and rumors about some imprecise but menacing forces, either coming from the apparatus or from an often talked-about mass uprising of the people. The new regime and its leader look to be walking a tightrope between the prospect of a conventional failure and loss of power or, much worse, some catastrophic and resounding collapse. A less bumpy road with steady advances is a prospect that is more rarely discussed. The prevailing opinion among all kinds of observers and among the people maintains that if some tangible results are not obtained soon in the performance of the economy, a drastic worsening of an already tense situation is to be expected, with disquietingly unpredictable results.

An apparently dangerous impasse like that is not easy to analyse and makes it difficult for leaders to formulate policies. It is 'a moment of truth' for the people and most certainly for the politicians who have to devise the next steps, some of which will certainly bring more trouble. No wonder voices are being heard calling for a new dictator, or for Gorbachev to assume this role

himself and, concurrently, regrets are proffered that too many
political freedoms were offered prematurely instead of the
economy being handled first. Markets, so the argument runs, can
be introduced by authoritarian regimes; they do not have to be
preceded by democratization of political life.

That is not entirely untrue and it might have worked,
eventually, in the 1960s. By now, however, after a lengthy period
of further petrification, Gorbachev's liberalization of the system,
preceding the battle for a new economic model, was essential. A
rotten branch cannot revive a tree. Even if he didn't think in
precisely these terms, Gorbachev knew and said that the country
was on the brink of a dangerous precipice and that his *glasnost*
was actually a shock treatment – not without its dangers for an
enfeebled body. That another shock treatment is still ahead – with
'the brink' still menacingly near – is a likely prospect.

Having quoted so far, quite liberally, gloomy terms such as
'menaces' and 'brinks', 'catastrophes' and 'an all-out popular
rebellion', let me now try a more sober approach. Amidst all
those, often very exaggerated, laments in the Soviet and some
Western pronouncements, one can point to a set of different
facts and arguments. First, let us note that despite all the
turmoil, the government of the Soviet Union is pretty stable and
hard-working. Nothing has 'fallen apart' so far – unless dumping
the mechanical and useless Stalinist empire, or getting out from
Afghanistan are to be seen as signs of decomposition or sell-outs,
as nostalgic militarists certainly do. Even an eventual restitution
of independence (or some form of it) to the Baltic states would
not be too crucial – though it would be very tough on a leader who
hasn't yet succeeded in bringing about the hoped for upswing and
too many retreats could weaken him. It would simply be part of
the whole process of finally 'finishing the Second World War' and
eliminating some more of the pernicious legacy of Joseph Stalin.
This could only help and would be not unlike a painful but
courageous restructuring of an ailing corporation.

In this spirit, a more positive and pragmatic light can be cast
on the very anguishing 'in between' situation in which the USSR
finds itself. Dangers exist; but if there were no elements of a

counter-model in the economic and political system, hopelessness would be justified. Talking about 'in between' two (or more) models would not make sense. But my argument here is that the new seeds, forms, adumbrations of a new model (or models) that are emerging and will mature in the near future were already, in part, there before, and many more were created by *perestroika* itself. Let us take the sphere of politics first. The big novelty here is the new character and role of the media that has both stirred up and also educated the public for the elections to the new Supreme Soviet. This is a key innovation that may soon, in conjunction with the coming elections to local governments, produce the basis for a new political system, – acting in parallel with, and soon, quite probably, independent of the party. (As this text is being edited, such phenomena are already unfolding, under the baton of the newly established presidency assumed by Gorbachev and with the elections to local governments already over.)

The party itself is also 'in between', with its old authoritarians locked in a complex and uneasy coexistence with the party reformers. But the parliamentary principles, which are already quite popular with the soviet public, may help 'repoliticize' the party, curtail or destroy its administrative proclivities and force it to integrate in a renovated political system. Or face a split or, simply, extinction.

It is true that the internal *perestroika* of the party and of its apparatus was lagging far behind changes elsewhere, too long for its own good. But this is why Gorbachev's people themselves began to float the idea they tried to contain until recently, namely the one of legalizing independent political parties. This could, in fact, serve as a powerful whip over the party's head to become a political party, i.e. a political organization that faces a pluralist society and acts accordingly.

A coup against Gorbachev, from the military or even from inside the party, is by now improbable. Even if a party congress (improbably) tells Gorbachev to step down, parliament will certainly refuse to take orders from the party and keep him as its president. The probability of such an outcome testifies to the contours of a powerful novelty in the political landscape. We do remember also that the country is now teeming with social and political organizations and that the leadership demands from its political nominees that they learn to conduct a dialogue with these informal groups and fronts. The official line is that society is 'pluralist' and that the party must learn to handle this and prove to the public that it deserves to stay in power. This means, clearly, that such proof has to be obtained at the polls.

The emergence of these new traits, among many others, in the sphere of politics – in particular the well-known new role of the media – is relevant also for the situation in the economy. Here too we can point to important elements of a counter-model: many economic institutions have begun to learn different principles of action, notably in foreign trade but, more importantly, the new laws granting autonomy to enterprises and to their voluntary business associations have created an eager constituency for economic change. The difficulty – maybe drama – is because this part of the economic reform is, so far, stalemated, if not directly sabotaged. Granting independence to enterprises without changing the pricing system and the supply system of inputs, and without redefining the relationship between the ministries and the factories amount to a frustrating and demoralizing mockery.

Why this has happened, thus causing considerable discredit to the image of the reforming government, demands the testimony of specialists and special research. It may well be that the initial reforms were based on inadequate knowledge of economic realities and hence on exaggerated optimism. The very first steps taken in the direction of changing over to market methods stumbled on the reality of enormous deficits, inflationary pressures, dangers of massive bankruptcies and huge unemployment, and this forced the leadership to pause, probably in a state of bewilderment, and to rethink its strategies. It is a fact though, that the newly granted rights, even if still frustratingly muzzled, have produced enormous pressures in the economic sphere for going forward into a new model, and accepting that the old one has already proved to be unworkable.

We may add, in this brief survey, that the existing cooperatives, private but already official services, and even sectors of the huge black markets, are all elements that can be expanded or legalized, and can be used in the building of a renovated economic system. The pressure from the public facing empty shelves in the stores and other miseries is also a powerful spur, and the existence of an elected parliament is of great importance here. A renewed drive for changing the economic system, even if most judiciously executed, cannot but be a crisis-maker. The party does not have enough prestige to launch the tough measures and supervise their execution. The parliament will have to do it, and it may eventually succeed.

Contrary to the prevailing impressions of political fragmentation and just plain massive cynicism and despondency, there exists already, in sufficiently broad layers of the population, a number of shared opinions that will allow the emergence of enough of a consensus for a successful national policy of crisis management and revolutionary change. This point should not be overlooked. The press is a key factor responsible for this: millions of people are fully aware of and ready to do whatever is necessary to stop the ecological depletion of the country; and to discard an administrative system (now quite hated) that is characterized by enormous waste and destruction of national resources. Majorities can certainly be found, for changing the property system, notably to allow different property forms in agriculture – *kolkhoz, sovkhoz*, cooperative, or even a de facto private ownership of farmland – in order to save Soviet agriculture. There is a craving in the public for a work-ethic to overcome the crisis of values and the state of political disarray the country has been plunged into, but still to preserve *glasnost* and develop the new parliamentary institutions.

These and other popular aspirations are a good basis for a broad politico-economic program of action. But powder-kegs and minefields are visible. Among them the national, nationalistic and other centrifugal forces, for example the problem of the legitimacy of the party, and the vexing, extremely complicated ideological problem: whether Russia is or should be socialist or go over to a capitalist system. It is true that in the broader working masses the latter problem is not formulated in this way, as many want, first of all, to see the provision of basic necessities of life. But the problem of restoring some ideological vision or, at least, some clearly formulated ideological schools, in cooperation or competition with each other, is on the agenda, notably because many of the old formulae, being discredited or extremely suspect, do not stand much of a chance of being accepted.

In the unusual situation we are describing, with its many ambiguities – an excellent ground for writers with a sense for the surreal but an ordeal for all but the most steadfast reporters – the personal role of Gorbachev is remarkable. He is the object of criticism, even wrath, from those who accuse him of having betrayed the Marxist-Leninist heritage and selling out Russia's empire, and from those who see in him the servant of the apparatus who is deliberately stalling the reforms he himself has initiated. These two extreme interpretations do not seem to bother about the complexity of the situation, the devilishly skilful maneuvring it entails and the sometimes masterly and steady breakthroughs Gorbachev and his supporters keep making to circumvent one obstacle after another. Between the hopes of dawn and the menaces of dusk, he is the catalyst of change and a stabilizing factor. The need to continue reforms and at the same time preserve the integrity of the state demands, for instance, reshaping the apparatus, yet temporarily keeping it afloat by making compromises with some of the older apparatchiks. If not, the central government risks losing all levers of control in mid–stream. Obviously, too many compromises may produce too much procrastination and this too is fraught with dangers for the reformers. This is why the whole thing is a risky game with the outcome still in doubt.

Adding to the anxieties is the fact that even in the best of the cases, no one can predict with any certainty what kind of new system will emerge, even taking into account the new elements of the counter-model we have discussed. In other words, change may be unstoppable and reforms will succeed, but what they may produce is an open question.

Nothing that complicated was envisaged in the writings of the thinkers who reflected upon the state of the economy in the

1960s and how to mend it. The actual reforms undertaken in the
1960s under prime-minister Kosygin, later nipped in the bud, were
quite modest. But the debate this book described and the ideas
they contained were certainly the forerunners of *perestroika*.
There is no doubt that Gorbachev's program stems, basically, from
this earlier school of thinking and draws its inspiration from there,
without being able, so far, to complete the job. But to the many
who keep complaining that Gorbachev has *already* been several
years in power but has so far failed to deliver, one can argue that
his job is without precedent in scope and complexity. A period of
one *piatiletka*, much of which has been taken up with working
out what could and had to be done, is very short indeed. It is
doubtful that expectations for a quick-fix make sense. *Perestroika*
is a process, not just a set of political or administrative measures
and the changes in question will certainly demand a more
substantial period of time and there is quite a bumpy road ahead.

Nevertheless, chances of success are no less realistic a prospect
than the much proffered prophecies of doom. In addition to some
favorable factors already mentioned and others we could not
analyse here, it is worth repeating the statement that may not
be amenable to rigorous proof but is convincing nonetheless: the
old system had already proven its inadequacies. It was a living
corpse that was additionally shaken up and further weakened
by reforms, by *glasnost* and by the changes of personnel. It has
no positions to return to. Therefore the present problem is how
to find a way forward. Moving backward – despite cravings in
many quarters to do just that – would mean but one thing: back
to the precipice ...

Socialism – Back to the Drawing Board

Two more points remain to be treated briefly. It is clear that the
reformers of the earlier period wanted to change the content of
'planning' and to reformulate the meaning of 'socialism'. There
is no doubt that our authors, in most cases, did not do this openly
because of censorship. They were, however, sincere in their
quest. Right or wrong, they were actually searching for a 'socialist

market', indirect, 'parametric, not administrative planning', 'a socialist, not just nationalized and bureaucratized property'.

This is interesting and worth underlining because one hears an outcry from both East and West nowadays about the definitive bankruptcy of these concepts. Such an approach is both shallow and misleading. Methods of planning will not only continue to be an important problem everywhere; they will actually become ever more indispensable. As to 'socialism' as an ideology and a series of programs for action, it is not going to vanish. Not unlike the Soviet society that has become unmanageable under its 'command-administrative methods', as soviet critics keep calling them, the contemporary world has become too much for the current grand-capitalist economic, political and administrative ways and means. Though one should not commit the error of talking about 'bankruptcy', the prevailing world system keeps creating menacing and cumulative imbalances and there are clear signs of a coming planetary crisis. But there is not much talk of how to deal with it. Without the formulation of the interests of societal survival and the imposition of an adequate response from the economic mechanisms that squander human and material capital, the current worries will become nightmares. Whatever the name that will be found for such policies and strategies of action, they will be, very probably, socialist in inspiration. Whatever a Stalin or a Suslov might have said about this term is irrelevant and there is no glory at all in hiding behind such prophets or behind the demise of their 'real socialism'. The misnomer can be tolerated as long as it does not become a fraud.

There was effectively no planning in the Soviet system. What they had was a way of producing a more or less arbitrary assortment of targets, couched in figures, rarely if at all achieved, and these kept accumulating imbalances and inconsistencies of a type that serious planning would not have allowed. It was an administrative act of task-setting, administratively supervised and imposed and it kept producing an economy that sooner or later had to come almost to a standstill because of fatal, even ridiculous, squandering and finally exhaustion of resources. It is not possible

to use terms like 'planning' and 'economic' for such an activity –
even if it could claim important achievements and some sort of
rationale for a time.[2]

There was not and there could not have been any 'socialism'
in the Soviet Union, even if its founders were genuine socialists
and many believed that this was what they were building and
getting. But although it did not take the road of a capitalist
economy, the socialist claims of the regime, especially as it
evolved over the next few decades, were no more than a fig-leaf
and the fact that such claims were largely accepted is, in itself,
puzzling.

It is also worth reminding ourselves of the largely forgotten
fact – this forgetfulness is equally puzzling – that the best
Marxist minds and other socialist thinkers, as well as the major
socialist organizations, not only questioned but altogether
repudiated the claim that the Soviet regime was socialist. No time
should be wasted to prove that *it was not soviet either*.

Those who stuck and keep sticking to these labels did a lot of
damage to the thinking about the Soviet system, but also to the
analysis of the capitalist reality, its critique by socialists and the
socialist ideology in general.

NEP was eliminated by Stalin's government and this was
presented by Stalinist ideologues as the elimination of capitalism;
but Russia during the period of the NEP was not capitalist, even
if it had private sectors and markets, and Stalin's Russia could
not be called socialist just because it did not have a market
economy. The identification of the terms in question with 'markets'
was one of the fallacies of Bolshevik (and some other socialist)
thinking which they had begun to cure themselves of during the
NEP. Even an impetuous industrializer like Trotsky, in his
proposals to the politburo about industrial policies, spoke about
'plan and market' and this in 1923, well before Bukharin began
to think in these terms. Hence, the anti-market obsession was
not an incurable disease.

[2] I was not the only one to argue this point, but I do allow myself to
refer to a comment in a discussion of the first five-year plan, in *Slavic
Review*, vol. 32, June 1973, pp. 271–87. Its title: 'The Disappearance of
Planning in the Plan'.

More important, however, was the other fallacy of 'nationalization' that came to be widely accepted as a socialist measure *par excellence* and made into a center-piece of soviet ideology. It was significant that some of the thinkers of the 1960s refuted the idea that 'nationalization' equalled socialism. It was, or could be, a measure to help transform capitalist into socialist property relations, but it was supposed to be a transitional measure. The reader studying Shkredov's opinion in the book discovers that although nationalization as practised by the Soviet government was imposed by circumstances, he still maintained that much of it was premature since it contributed to the emergence of a system that centered on the state and its bureaucracy, and transformed society into a mere cog, powerless in both the polity and the economy.

However vague, the concept of socialism is not a dustbin into which any tyrant or ignorant can throw any thoughts. It is a complicated but very serious reflection about lifting political democracy to a higher level by allowing the citizenry to master not just the political but also the economic environment and to eliminate the glaring disparities of economic power between social classes, allowing equal rights to such classes, (in this sense 'eliminating' them). It is also a tool to loosen or break the power of too rigid structures such as classes, bureaucracies and oppressive dogmas, and to open up a larger space for individual freedom and creativity. This definition can be challenged, changed or expanded, but without such features, and especially in an environment that is practising exactly the opposite, the term is an abuse or a plain fraud.

Be that as it may, if one thinks that this ideology is just utopian, then the Soviets, quite obviously, did not have it. If it is a viable ideology – then an oppressive mechanism of Stalinist or post-Stalinist Russia, characterized by an unprecedented accumulation of political and economic power at the narrow apex of a pyramid (and where its own lower echelons were deprived of rights, even if enjoying some perks), cannot withstand examination by socialist criteria, whenever such examination is conducted by serious people whether socialist themselves or not.

Using this term in regard to Russia was too easy a boon for propagandists and an escape from realities and requirements of scholarship in both the East and the West.

What will Russia choose? Which ideologies will emerge there in the near future? Or does it actually have to choose between 'capitalism' or 'socialism'? It may well be that these familiar terms will not or do not reflect any more the alternatives Russia or, maybe, the rest of the world are facing. I mention this only as yet another feature that characterizes the fast changing sociopolitical and ideological scene of the contemporary Soviet Union. Its latest developments have opened up all these questions and allow all kind of hypotheses, including the one a historian may be tempted to consider: namely that politicians, governments, ideologues, writers can say or decide to do one thing, but real life may spontaneously follow a different track and simply move 'elsewhere'.

This has happened before, most certainly to Lenin, to Stalin, to Khrushchev. My own support for Gorbachev's policies cannot prevent me from saying that whatever his role, we have to talk about Russia moving somewhere and not just of Gorbachev leading them somewhere. We can claim we understand what created their national agenda, produced a crisis and made them want to solve their problems by reforms, but the outcome of this endeavour, the shape of things to come, is still open-ended. The past can teach a lot, though not everything, about the present but little about the future, so we had better stop here and let unfolding events speak for themselves.

Philadelphia, June 1990

Author's corrections to 1991 edition:

p. 25, addition to footnote 35: I should mention here that Bukharin's widow, who was with him in Paris, denied in her recent memoirs that such conversations, including with Lydia Dan (see note 38) took place at all. The reader should view these sources with a dose of scepticism.

p. 32, addition to footnote 45: Again, I remind the reader that the conversation with Nicolaevsky might never have taken place. But Bukharin did participate in the work of the drafting committee.

p. 67, footnote 23: See also note 45 on page 32 and amendment above.

p. 68, line 8 continues: [But we learned from the memoirs of his widow Anna M. Larina that Bukharin actually adapted himself in the 1930s to Stalin's rule and did not continue any serious theoretical rethinking, even in private.]

p. 79, line 10: *for* 'war' *read* 'war-time'.

p. 79, addition to footnote 5: It is worth reminding the reader that the term war-communism was not used during the events but was applied by Lenin after the civil war. But other similar terms, expressing the same content, were current.

p. 165, line 26: *for* 'microeconomic' *read* 'macroeconomic'.

p. 171, final paragraph: *for* 'Soviet economists, and no doubt politicians as well, split problems ... of the economy.' *read* 'Soviet economists, and no doubt politicians as well, dealing with problems of value, markets and the commodity character of the products, split into several groups or schools in their approach.'

p. 219, subheading: *for* (Venzher) *read* (V. G. Venzher).

p. 254, third paragraph, line 8: *for* 'from outside agriculture to some 20 percent today' *read* 'from outside agriculture, to some 20 percent today'.

p. 286, fourth paragraph, line 3: *for* '*raikom*?' *read* '*rai-ispolkom*?'.

p. 324, fourth paragraph, starting line 7: *for* 'The economic reforms tried to change it but the reforms are still in their initial stages, and even may be frozen entirely at this stage.' *read* 'The economic reforms tried to change it but these reforms are almost entirely frozen at this stage.'

ACKNOWLEDGMENTS

I owe a debt of gratitude to the following scholars who generously agreed to read the whole manuscript, or substantial parts of it and provided me with detailed comments: Stephen Cohen, R. W. Davies, Alexander Erlich, Michael Kaser, Jack Miller, and Peter Wiles. E. H. Carr read the part dealing with Bukharin and sent an encouraging note. It goes without saying that listing here these colleagues and acknowledging my gratitude does not, in any way, engage their responsibility for what is said in this book.

I had the privilege of staying at the Institute for Advanced Study, Princeton, N. J., during the academic year 1972–1973 (on a grant partly financed by the National Endowment for the Humanities), and it was there that I prepared the definitive draft of my book. I express my thanks to the staff of the Institute for their friendliness and help, in particular to the librarians and to Mrs. Peggy Van Sent, who typed the manuscript and helped, as secretary, in many technical matters.

Birmingham,
Autumn, 1973.

THE Soviet Union, its society and polity, has undergone a considerable transformation since it began to accelerate its industrialization some four decades ago. But even during the shorter period since Stalin's death, the country has made big strides forward in many fields. Its economy and social structure are now urban-industrial, although a very substantial agricultural sector and relative underdevelopment still remain. Many traits in the political system have also changed, and the list of innovations and modifications in the ways the country is governed, as compared to Stalin's time, is long and significant.

Nevertheless, however spectacular the changes in many walks of life, institutions created under Stalin's rule—some date even further back—and bequested to his heirs persist in the political system, in the economy, and significantly in the system's crucial link, the ruling party.

The assumption underlying this study is that, in the opinion of many politically literate Soviet citizens, in the process of modernization the development of the society was not matched by a corresponding overhaul of the institutions that run the state and the economy. The debate among Soviet economists, which is the concern of this book, illustrates the lag between the new society as it evolved and continues to unfold in the post-Stalinist period and the institutional setting of the polity. If such a statement is true, then it will be taken as a diagnosis of the nation's state, a general condition that is accountable for tensions throughout the system, and will help explain the emergence and persistence of reforming and dissenting tendencies.

In fact, many observers of the Soviet Union agree on such a diagnosis and are aware of those tendencies, although their scope and depth are, as yet, a matter of speculation. Historians can quite easily and precisely point to phenomena like "inadequacy of institutions," "tensions," "alienation from the system" or "dissent" in some society when they enjoy the advantages of hindsight. But this is much more difficult to do when dealing with current events in a complex society run by a state embracing a whole continent. This is even more true in the case of the Soviet Union, where information is more difficult to obtain than elsewhere and where so much that is happening is new, still in the making, and genuinely unknown to the leaders and censors themselves.

The very awareness by the Soviet elites of the complexity of the problems they are facing and the admission of a sense of bewilderment they experience are new and important phenomena in Soviet politics; they are acknowledged by the promotion of several social sciences that were banned as "reactionary" until at least the mid-1950s. However, political science is not among officially allowed disciplines. Also many aspects of Soviet history are still heavily censored, and this has something to do with habits of thought and ways of ruling inherited from the past. Nevertheless, in many ways, both such fields of inquiry—politics and history—are irrepressible. Study and research in politics are conducted in the Soviet Union, against or for the government, under headings other than "political science." No less important, if not ominous to some Soviet vigilantes, was the burst of historical inquiry, and analysis of many important spheres of life, both in the past as well as in the present which occurred during the 1960s. When a country has had such a short and dramatic history, its past and present are still inextricably meshed, so that history is directly part of politics and looks frightening to some powerholders; but, at the same time, politics raises historical questions which are attracting and fascinating many minds engaged in a study of their country's problems.

The curious blend of the present and of the not too distant past, so pertinent to Soviet political life, is one of the main themes of this study. The relevance of many dramatic events of the past, with their yet unextinguished heat, becomes apparent every time we observe some important turn of events or big debate in the Soviet Union. The latter occurred in post-Stalinist Soviet Russia in the domains of literature, history, politics, and economics, and offered each time a unique occasion to learn more about the Soviet Union. Like small seismic movements, they lay bare some hitherto hidden geological layers, and allowed an insight into the social system at large.

We chose for our survey the debates on economics and economic reforms that began in the late 1950s, flourished in the 1960s, and are still being pursued in the early 1970s, although with somewhat less verbal and analytical vigor. These debates were an important phenomenon in Soviet intellectual life. They accompanied and fostered the emergence of a new scholarly discipline in the Soviet Union—economics, and simultaneously testified to a considerable intellectual fermentation among a particular group of Soviet intellectuals—the economists.

The sources we used consisted of writings of economists talking about economic theory and about the day-to-day economic problems in the Soviet Union. But the strictly professional side of the debate (the validity of the ideas, for example, on pricing or techniques of planning, and the details of the economic reforms as they were actually enacted and how exactly they fare today) is not the concern here. The reader will find these themes amply studied by professional economists. Rather, this study focuses on social and political problems of the Soviet Union as revealed in debates on economics. Of special interest to us are the following phenomena: the pressure for change in the economic system; the onslaught on many dogmas and their revision; the emergence of new ideas and schools of thinking in spheres much larger than just economics; and finally the social, political, and historical connotations of the debate among one important group of social scientists. The development of a critical political thought, the cleavages and plurality of opinion, and different views of the past—these are the new phenomena, which the economic debates produced, as will be shown in our study. They point to a more general pattern in Soviet intellectual and political life, which is not yet sufficiently understood: a gamut of political opinion that works its way through the maze of groups and social classes, penetrates the party, and participates in shaping opinions of policy makers and political realities alike.

The existence of such a spectrum in cultural life has already been sufficiently proven by students of the cultural and literary scene, using the abundant *samizdat* output as evidence. In fact, the apparently monolithic and dull political scene is, in fact, much richer and more colorful than appearances suggest, and at least two texts from the *samizdat* production—one by Amalric and the more recent one by Roy Medvedev—offer analyses of existing political trends inside and outside the party.[1]

Moreover, the literature pertinent to the economic debates of the 1960s and later, the evaluations of the performance of the economic model in the past and present, and the criticisms and proposals for change, show an amazing parallelism, even similarity, to the debates of the 1920s in theme, wording, and phraseology. As the intellectual map of the present controversy unfolded, it became entirely clear that it contained hints, allusions, plagiarized quotations, unnamed authorities, and direct and indirect use of ideas of personalities of the 1920s, who were apparently irrelevant

---

[1] See A. Amalric, *Will the Soviet Union Survive until 1984?* (New York, 1970); R. Medvedev, *Kniga O Sotsialisticheskoi Demokratii* (Amsterdam, 1972), chaps. 3 and 4; trans. S. Geoffroy, *De la Democratie socialiste* (Paris, 1972).

and long forgotten and some of whom were executed and buried in infamy in the 1930s. It was not difficult to find the missing pieces in this jigsaw puzzle: central among them is N. I. Bukharin, the leader of the last important opposition to Stalin. However, the impact of a personality like him cannot be freely acknowledged, either because of political restraints that today are stronger than those under Khrushchev or because of the lack of political and historical training among the debaters, who sometime do not know much about such affinities.

It was astonishing to discover how many ideas of Bukharin's anti-Stalinist program of 1928–1929 were adopted by current reformers as their own and how much of their critique of past practices followed his strictures and prophecies even in their expression; this is the main reason why this study begins with a historical excursus on Bukharin and on the old debate conducted by the "rightists," under his leadership, against Stalin's policies.

It will be heavily emphasized that Bukharin's role is singled out because he was the foremost political leader opposed to Stalin. He was not the only one involved, of course, nor was he the author of all those ideas out of which his arguments and programs were woven. But he was the chief spokesman of the New Economic Policy (NEP) and became identified with the struggle for the preservation of its framework; it is this role that explains many of his ideas as well as the reappearance of analogous ones thirty years later, in quite different circumstances, it is true, but also at some sort of crossroads in the development of the country.

Bukharin, an exceedingly interesting figure in Soviet history and one of the most popular leaders of the party until he was defeated by Stalin and his faction, has not attracted in Western scholarship the same amount of attention as has been devoted to Lenin, Trotsky, and later, to Stalin. Partly at least, the reason is obvious: he was much younger and certainly a man of a different and lesser caliber than the others. They theorized, acted in a vast arena, and displayed a variety of intellectual, political, and administrative talents. Bukharin, though he served on the Central Committee and the Politbureau from their inception, never held important administrative or military posts. His field was predominantly political theory and ideology, a mixture of scholarship and propaganda, which denote basically a political intellectual. The party and Lenin thought of him as the youngest and the ablest party theoretician. In general, he was not an infighter, political strategy was not his forte, and his record in this regard was often very poor. A highly intelligent book devourer, an art lover, a collector of butterflies, and a man with highly cultivated habits, Bukharin was a typical Russian intellectual. If the strictly political animal in him was too much restrained by moral and artistic qualms, the vivacity of his mind and his moral and intellectual stature are best illustrated by the fact that he did not hesitate to clash, often with fiery ardor, with all three of the top figures of the Soviet revolutionary scene—Lenin, Trotsky, and Stalin. He also contributed in an important way to the development of Bolshevik theory—sometimes before Lenin, other times in polemics with him—and added many original ideas. Some of these ideas survived him and have come to play a role today, even if their authorship is not acknowledged. But his eclipse in the West can be explained partly by his shortsightedness in helping Stalin to destroy the left-wingers led by Trotsky and later by his defeat by Stalin, which appeared to render irrelevant his and his associates' ideas. Had not Russia become what Stalin wanted it to be, and not what the defeated factions wanted it to become? This seemed to seal the verdict. Trotsky, moreover, had ample opportunities to put forward his views himself, and his talented biographer, Deutscher, later helped to restore Trotsky to the place he deserved in Soviet history, at least in Western literature.

Bukharin still awaits a fair judgment. But the ruler who pulled the strings behind Vyshinsky, the prosecutor in Bukharin's and other trumped-up trials, has gone, and his role and personality have been seriously questioned. The phenomenon of "liberal communism" in Eastern Europe, the economic reforms in all these countries, polycentrism, economic difficulties, reforms, and new ways of thinking in the Soviet Union, especially among many of the intellectuals there—all rested on the critique of the system created under the aegis of Stalin. New studies and interpretations of Soviet history began to appear in the wake of the so-called de-Stalinization which pointed to the brewing of new rehabilitations of the shadows of the past, first tacit and next official. Although this process is now arrested, our biographical sketch of Bukharin, which opens this book, rests on the assumption that the issues involved in the activities of party oppositions, led by Bolshevik "old guard" figures who were annihilated by Stalin's purges, in the first place the Bukharinites, continue to be highly relevant for the current Soviet political stage. This implies that "the ideas of the twenties are far from dead in our days."[2] It is common knowledge that in the Soviet Union condemnation, rehabilitation, and reevaluation of personalities acquired a deep political meaning. The attitude toward Stalin is a case in point. Bukharin most likely is the next candidate for reconsideration. If such occurs and this opposition leader is one day readmitted to official history, many more will then be resurrected.

For the moment the whole issue seems frozen in an uneasy stalemate, due to the conservative line in the current internal Soviet policy. But in the West a biography has become available,[3] and in the Soviet Union—as already noted—indirect, veiled, or even entirely unintentional pronouncements and disclosures in the economic debate point to an ongoing reevaluation.

[2] This is how A. Erlich saw it already in 1960 in *The Soviet Industrialization Debate* (Cambridge, Mass., 1960), p. xxii.

[3] S. Cohen, *Bukharin and the Bolshevik Revolution: A Political Biography* (New York, 1973). It was not yet available to me at the moment of finishing the final draft of my book.

In the case of some scholars, especially the older ones, this reassessment is not an unconscious exercise. From personal experience or from studies, some of these economists know very well the writings of the main scholarly and political figures of the 1920s. Were it not for censorship or self-censorship, the names of Bazarov and Groman; Preobrazhensky and Piatakov; Bukharin, Rykov, and Tomsky— to mention only some—would immediately fill out many pages in a heated debate. Was Stalin unavoidable? Did Bukharin's plan have a chance? Who can doubt that the Russian intellectuals, who are deeply interested in studying these problems, would adopt, in such a debate, positions often far apart from the official ones?

But for the moment the recurrence of themes from the past, including opinions very similar to Bukharin's on many points, is even more remarkable because for the majority of those engaged in the recent economic debates, it is a broad coincidence, a genuine discovery, in reaction to present realities; this, in some cases at least, subsequently can lead to a study of older authors and to a realization of the similarity.

But whether or not such an intellectual process takes place in the mind of each scholar involved, the very coincidence of themes and arguments is in itself revealing, and there are certainly cogent reasons for this. First, the axis around which many worries, problems, and theories are revolving is to be found in the specific power nexus that the Soviet Union was first to create in our century: an entirely, or almost entirely, nationalized economy run by a highly centralized state bureaucracy, and a political system run by a unique state-party making the whole system into a *sui generis* party-state. Essentially, the debate of the 1920s, in particular the Bukharin-Stalin controversy, was a battle for or against the installment of this particular model. Bukharin and those thinking like him preferred the NEP system as a long-term prospect and framework for continuing industrialization, whereas the group around Stalin intended to shed the NEP framework and to build, even if they did not immediately fully realize where they were going, their new system. A quarter of a century or so later a new debate began that was still deeply concerned with the same model, the one that the right-wingers and others were anticipating and trying to prevent in the 1920s, and that their heirs now observed with hindsight and wanted to change.

One can then dare say that the object of the criticism in many ways is the same in both debates. This is why, after a prolonged hiatus, the modern controversy appears to revert to previous arguments, then continues, with many refinements, applying itself to new circumstances. Quite obviously, in the present situation, the question is no longer how to industrialize a peasant country but how to run an industrial giant. The environment of the 1960s and the 1970s is very different from that of the 1920s, and the experience and tools of analysis available to the participants today are superior to what the 1920s could offer. Naturally enough, the current debates have ramifications beyond the ones put forth by those originally advocating the NEP. However, the actual arguments used in both periods coincide astonishingly.

The reader, one hopes, will realize that the author does not seek to idealize Bukharin or to exaggerate his importance. This would be of no interest to the author or to the study at hand. The sought-after phenomena are independent of the precise evaluation of both Bukharin's personality and the depth of his thinking. Numerous weaknesses in his actions and policies will be pointed out. But, once again, it is to be stressed that Bukharin was an intelligent spokesman for a body of opinion, a trend in society, and a political faction in the party. He formulated opinions and criticisms, a warning and an alternative, at a time when the system was at a crossroads. When at a later stage, though in very different circumstances, another crossroad was reached, the ideas of the losers in the previous stage suddenly emerged, even if some of the new discussants were not aware that quite similar ideas had been the center of a dramatic debate a generation earlier.

The structure of this text is a direct outcome of the preceding considerations. Part I, "The Historical Record," gives a short biography and a relatively detailed examination of the ideas that were incorporated into, or explain, the "Bukharinist" thinking at the last stage of his political activity as a member of the top leadership. While the earlier periods are touched upon briefly, this stage is stressed because some of the issues debated during the NEP reveal the convergence of the programs of Left and Right in the face of the emerging Leviathan and lend more weight to the relevance for future development of the only counterprogram then in existence. A more general inquiry into what we call "models," or stages through which Soviet history moved from the 1917 revolution to the end of Stalin's rule, follows.

While Part I is a somewhat independent, self-contained entity, serving as background to Part II, "Economics and the State," the latter delves into the next chronological stage and basically centers on problems as they were argued during the 1960s. This part examines the problems and critical thought that emerged in the modern economic debates, and their political connotations. In the course of the debate on economics and planning, the search for new blueprints and models for the economy begot a phenomenon that is striking in Soviet intellectual history: the emergence of a critical analysis of the state.

Part III, "Society and Party," concentrates on the party, in order to check the assumption implicit in reformist thinking and in numerous analyses done outside the USSR that this institution, the lynchpin of the political system, is showing signs of strain or inadequacy in its function as the leading organization in the system. This part sketches problems as they emerge from an examination of the rank and file and of the lower ranks of the party apparatus. Finally, Part III also attempts to integrate the historical debates and the current ones on economics, the implications of which concern the Soviet system at large.

Many political trends in the Soviet Union are still in an embryonic state, others are more mature but remain underground or below the surface and do not lend themselves to systematic study, and this book is not a treatise on the Soviet system as a whole. By weaving together strands from the past and present, from biography and history, from economics and politics, it merely adumbrates a complex set of problems, makes tentative conclusions, and offers information for further debate and reflection.

PART ONE

THE HISTORICAL RECORD

CHAPTER ONE

Bukharin's Life

BUKHARIN's story, from his underground activities, through his role in the leadership of the party as a young theoretician and Politbureau member, until the ignominy of the 1938 trial, is certainly worthy of the pen of a novelist or playwright. The presence of the prince pulling the strings behind the scenes and enjoying the show of his rivals confessing to an unbelievable list of crimes they never committed, adds a Kafkaesque flavor to the plot. But this chapter constitutes only a short biography and a historical sketch of a personal fate that epitomized much of the history of Bolshevism and the Soviet system. The personal and the historical are inextricably enmeshed in Bukharin's life, so that the exploration of his political and ideological preoccupations may serve as an introduction to further chapters dealing with problems without the personal-biographical ingredient.

Nikolai Ivanovitch Bukharin was born on 27 September 1888 in Moscow to parents who were both highly cultivated teachers.[1] His father was a gentle, impractical man, and this probably accounts for their less than modest situation. From childhood, they encouraged their son to plunge into the world of letters. As E. H. Carr noted, "Bukharin was thus more distinctively intellectual by origin than any of the other leading Bolsheviks."[2] The urge to read and to learn

[1] This biographical account will stress only some aspects of Bukharin's life that are relevant to the focus of this book. It is based mainly, unless stated otherwise, on S. Heitman and P. Knirsch, *N. I. Bukharin* (Berlin, 1959).

[2] E. H. Carr, ed., *ABC of Communism* (London, 1969), p. 18.

remained a constant feature of his life, but at school revolutionary politics intruded and led him, a lad of eighteen, to join (in 1906) the Bolshevik wing of the Russian Social Democratic Party. The next stages of his life were very similar to those of many Russian revolutionary intellectuals: university, several arrests, exile, and flight abroad.

The years of exile from 1911 to 1917 were a very creative period in his life, one full of feverish activity. He lived first in Austria, whence he was expelled to Switzerland at the outbreak of World War I; he was next exiled to Sweden, later to Norway. The next expulsion brought him, after a short stay spent mainly in detention in England, to the United States. In all these countries Bukharin participated in the international and Russian socialist movements, and engaged in intensive studies, especially in economics in Vienna under Böhm-Bawerk and Von Wieser, and in mathematical economics in Switzerland. During his exile, three fateful meetings occurred: first with Lenin in Cracow; then with Stalin in Vienna, whom Bukharin probably helped in his research for a pamphlet on the national question; and, finally, with Trotsky in New York, where the two men collaborated for a short time on the review *Novyi Mir*. However, news about the outbreak of the February (March) 1917 revolution in Russia made him rush home.

Bukharin's relations and disputes with Lenin are significant.[3] At first relations between Lenin and the promising young economist were rather cordial, but they soon deteriorated, became punctuated by sharp disputes, and were followed by strained personal feelings, caused by Lenin's intransigence rather than by the respectful and loyal Bukharin. As always with Lenin, political issues dictated his personal relations, and the points on which the young newcomer clashed with the older authority were by no means trivial.

[3] On Bukharin's disputes with Lenin at that time, see S. Cohen, "Bukharin, Lenin and the Theoretical Foundations of Bolshevism," *Soviet Studies*, 1970, no. 4.

At the beginning, though, Bukharin's collaboration with Lenin in the theoretical field met with the latter's approval. In Switzerland Bukharin wrote his *Imperialism and World Economy*, which preceded and influenced Lenin's own book on imperialism. Lenin openly acknowledged his debt to the young Bukharin. Like Lenin, Bukharin followed the trail of Hilferding's idea of "finance capital," but developed in his work the particular concept of "state capitalist trust" and "state capitalism." According to Bukharin the main characteristic of contemporary capitalism was a new interventionist role of the state culminating in a new phase of economic development in which, contrary to the previous *laissez-faire* principles, the economy was organized and planned by the capitalist state. The German war economy served, then and later, as corroboration for such statements and was seen by Bukharin as indicating a new and frightening tendency toward the emergence of a Leviathan of unprecedented strength, capable of more tightly controlling the economy and the masses than any previous state organization. National economies were becoming "regulated," and the imperialist states underwent a transformation that forced a revision of Marx: "organized capitalism" seemed able to overcome the chaos of market economies and to master the anarchic tendencies that should have led to an internal breakdown as expected by Marx. The breakdown of capitalism and transition to socialism were now to be expected, not so much from internal contradictions but from clashes and wars between competing imperialist states.

Bukharin did not always draw all these conclusions specifically, but they were implicit in his writings; and he developed his thought further in an article that deepened his insight into the new role of the state. This article, "Towards a Theory of the Imperialist State,"[4] while adding to the

[4] This text was published in book form for the first time in the Soviet Union as "K Teorii Imperialisticheskogo Gosudarstva" in *Revolutsiia Prava, Sbornik pervyi* (Moscow, 1925). The previous book entitled *Mirovaia Ekonomika i Imperializm* appeared in Russia with

analysis of "state capitalism," attempted to revive the basically anarchistic attitude of Marx toward the state and affirmed that the revolution had to destroy the capitalist state apparatus and create a new proletarian state, which, after some transition period, had to wither away promptly.

Lenin at first reacted angrily to this "semianarchism" and refused to publish the article, but several months later, when working himself on the problems of the state, he adopted Bukharin's theses on the state and underlined in his *State and Revolution* the basic agreement of Marxism and anarchism on the future of the state.

S. Cohen, reviewing the story of these disagreements, noted that on this point it was Bukharin who won, although both "lost to history" for their excessive utopianism. In a further point of disagreement, the role of nationalism and nationalist movements, it was Lenin's understanding that was vindicated by history rather than the concepts of Rosa Luxembourg and Bukharin, who followed her in this field.[5]

The third controversy between the two, one in which no accommodation was ever reached, concerned the capacity of the capitalist state to overcome internal conflicts and organize its economy within state boundaries. Since the young Bukharin first wrote on this topic, history seems to vindicate his insight, although such judgments cannot be taken as being forever valid.

The discussions on imperialism, state capitalism, and the future of the state, topics about which Bukharin contributed solidly to Marxist and especially Leninist doctrines, are important for us here. The capacity of "organized capitalism" to overcome its internal crises and the

---

a foreword by Lenin. Both texts were accepted as good party doctrine up to 1929. Yet another book, written in 1912–1914, *Politicheskaia Ekonomia Rant'e* (Moscow, 1919), should be mentioned. In this book Bukharin studied the Austrian marginalism. For a bibliography of Bukharin's work, see Heitman and Knirsch, *N. I. Bukharin*, and a more recent and complete one by S. Heitman, *Nikolai I. Bukharin, A Bibliography* (Stanford, Calif., 1969).

[5] See Cohen, "Bukharin, Lenin."

realization of the frightful might of the state apparatus persisted in Bukharin's thought and explains much of his later thinking; the need for the socialist state to assure and enhance liberty by moving as quickly as possible toward the "commune-state,"[6] which would inaugurate the dwindling of the "state" and the growth of the "commune" elements, was a postulate ever present in his mind and which was strengthened by his gloomy vision of the potential of modern states. This anarchistic and humanistic tendency of Bukharin and this streak of hostility to state power common to many socialists, including many of the Bolshevik "old guard," are indispensable for an understanding of his subsequent actions; paradoxically, they contribute to an explanation of some of his and of his party's apparently spectacular swings from extreme left to extreme right in the Soviet period. As Cohen correctly notes, "the spectre of the Leviathan state was to be a factor both in his left-communism of early 1918 and his gradualist policies of the twenties."[7]

After a long journey from America to the now republican Russia (through Siberia), he immediately became active in the party, and its highest body, the Central Committee, in August 1917. Thus he became involved in the decisions that triggered the October coup. The coup itself found him at the head of the Bolshevik organization in Moscow, where he soon found considerable backing in his next dramatic and heated opposition to Lenin over the Brest-Litovsk issue. In this debate the first strictly "Soviet" motive of opposition to Lenin appeared: the defense of the original concepts of direct workers' democracy—the workers' councils' (and trade unions') administration of the economy—against the apparent tendencies of the new state to supersede workers'

[6] *Gosudarstvo-Kommuna* meaning a "commune-state" is a term inspired by Engels and used by Lenin in *State and Revolution* (Petersburg, 1918), chap. 4, para. 3. This book can be found in English in Lenin's *Collected Works*, vol. 25 (Moscow, 1960–1969), 1964.

[7] Cohen, "Bukharin, Lenin," p. 445.

control by that of administrators in collaboration with former capitalist owners and experts.[8] On this occasion Bukharin lost his job as editor of *Pravda*, a position that he had held since December 1917, but he regained this post a few months later when the Brest-Litovsk issue lost is acuity and new, grave problems faced the young regime. The most serious was the outbreak of the civil war, which lasted for more than two-and-a-half years and from which policies emerged that were later called "war communism." Under the pressure of a devastating civil war, unavoidable measures for total mobilization of material and human resources for a life-and-death struggle—including rationing, centralization, and mass terror—merged peculiarly with an ideological construct that mistook the egalitarianism of poverty and wartime brotherhood not only for that of socialism, but also for that of communism, although the "proletarian dictatorship" of the transitional period remained. There was enough strain in the life of the country and of the party to explain the need to mobilize energies and to prop up commitment by appealing to the most utopian hopes. There was no tactical subterfuge here: the leaders needed the ideological drug no less than the rank and file. The majority of party leaders, among them Bukharin and Lenin, held the utopian belief that the militarization of an economy and a society at war produced the features of the higher communist system. It took Lenin some time to abandon "war communism" and to turn to more realistic policies. Clinging to illusions produced a near-disastrous situation, and it taught a lesson much more efficiently than theoretical treatises. To

[8] He thus clashed here with Lenin's controversial concept concerning transition strategies toward socialism, which Lenin called (Soviet) "state capitalism." On this concept, see Lenin's polemics against Bukharin in 1918, in "O Levom Rebiachestve," *Polnoe Sobranie Sochinenii*, 36 (5th ed., Moscow, 1962), 283–314. This edition of Lenin's works (Moscow, 1958–1965), hereafter will be cited *Sochineniia*.

8

be sure, the lack of realism was not evident in the conduct of the war, but rather in the implementation of social policies. Relations with the peasants, the central strategic problem of the revolution, were deeply influenced not only by the wartime food shortage but also by the view that market phenomena were basically capitalist (or bourgeois), whereas the direct distribution of resources through central-command methods was essentially communist. Thus toward the end of the period, when rethinking would have been in order, "war-communist" practices were enhanced and the full abolition of money was being prepared. As procrastination about abandoning these policies culminated in an incipient jacquerie, Lenin changed course and introduced the New Economic Policy (NEP).[9]

During the civil war period Bukharin was no more left-wing, except in the Brest-Litovsk episode, than Trotsky or Lenin. Since March 1919, together with Lenin, Trotsky, Stalin, and Kamenev, he served on the Politbureau. At the end of 1920 and the beginning of 1921, he moved toward an alliance with Trotsky and a new clash with Lenin in the famous "trade-union debate." (Whether this alliance resulted from his clinging to "war communism" longer than Lenin, or from Trotsky's personal influence, is a problem for a biographer.) The idea of the militarization of the trade unions very quickly became irrelevant and was forgotten, to be revived only during the industrialization period and then in a different form and under a changed leadership. Still, it cost the insubordinate Bukharin his place in the Politbureau, and he did not regain full membership until 1924, after Lenin's death. Bukharin's theoretical and propagandist activities during the civil war period were rather amazing in their scope and variety, especially since, like

[9] For Lenin's obstinate adherence to "war communism" policies in 1920, in contrast to his own previous, more cautious pronouncements, see A. Nove, *An Economic History of the USSR* (London, 1969), p. 81.

other leaders, he was not exempt from carrying out other assignments.

His capacity for work was apparently limitless, and he probably read the bibliographical sources for his writings, including the latest Western literature on economics and sociology, at night after completing his other tasks. In 1919, he published with Preobrazhensky, then a personal friend, a popular explanation of the party's doctrine and policies, *The ABC of Communism.* A year later, he finished the first volume of the incomplete theoretical work, *The Economics of the Transition Period* (one chapter was drafted by another personal friend, Y. Piatakov), of which Lenin approved.[10] In 1921, *The Theory of Historical Materialism,* which became popular and controversial, appeared.[11]

In the meantime the NEP was inaugurated—an astonishing new chapter in Soviet history that was soon to open a very different period in Bukharin's life. At the end of 1923 he began attacking Trotsky for his industrialist policies, among other things, and he did it with a considerable amount of fury, until some three years later he saw the Trotsky-Zinoviev opposition banned from political life, exiled, and imprisoned. From 1924 onward he became identified with the NEP policies as the policy *par excellence* for the transition period, very different indeed from the program for transition that he had outlined some years before. The official line was by now seen as a Bukharin-Stalin product, with Bukharin its chief theorist. In the eyes of the Left oppositionists of the day, he became the defender of peasants, an agent of kulaks in the party, and the bearer, together with Stalin, of the Thermidorian danger of a capitalist restoration.

[10] With some misgivings on the unpopular form and criticisms against terms that Bukharin borrowed from A. Bogdanov. Lenin's annotations are in *Leninskii Sbornik,* 11 (2d ed., Moscow, 1931), 348–403.

[11] *Teoriia Istoricheskogo Materializma* (Moscow, 1921); *Historical Materialism: A System of Sociology,* introd. A. Meyer (Ann Arbor, Mich., 1969).

The Rightist

The *volte-face* was unmistakable. Not only did Bukharin become, in Carr's words, "Stalin's willing henchman,"[12] but he also moved to the right wing of the political spectrum, became identified with the interests of the peasants, and, according to the same author, replaced his previous extreme utopian convictions with no less a devotion to "administrative prudence."[13] When Stalin later made a so-called left turn toward speedy and violent industrialization, Bukharin, it has been argued, "true to his role as a defender of the peasant, resisted Stalin, as he had formerly resisted Trotsky."[14] Using a similar interpretation to explain subsequent events, Deutscher adds: "The alpha and omega of Bukharinism has been its approach to the peasantry; in this it had become pointless (after the beginning of Stalin's collectivization).

"From the moment the smallholder vanished, the right opposition had no ground to stand on."[15]

Thus, on Bukharin's role these two authors accept the Left-Right dichotomy and definition, as it had been expressed in the views of the left-wing opposition in the 1920s and by its exiled leader later. There is some truth in this evaluation, but it is also one-sided and on some points incorrect.

Although in 1925 Bukharin formulated for the peasants the slogan "enrich yourself," an apparent switch from his position in *The ABC of Communism* and one that exacerbated the controversy between the left-wing opposition and the Bukharin-Stalin line over a wide range of questions, it is important to note that in 1926 Bukharin's views underwent important and specific modifications, a point that Carr and Deutscher fail to observe. But Bukharin and his associates adjusted their views to the new stage of "reconstruc-

[12] Carr, ed., *ABC of Communism*, p. 24.
[13] *Ibid.*, p. 50.　　　　　[14] *Ibid.*, p. 25.
[15] I. Deutscher, *The Prophet Outcast* (London, 1963), p. 123.

11

tion" (which will be examined in more detail in Chapter 2). However, even during the period before this adjustment, which contributed to an image of Bukharin that stuck to him for longer than he deserved, the following qualifications are warranted.

"Stalin's faithful henchman" is correct as a description of Bukharin's role, but mainly insofar as he helped Stalin and was used by him to destroy the left-wing opposition. There are no laurels to be granted him for this performance, but it is important to emphasize that in the fields of theory and political strategy Bukharin was never Stalin's mouthpiece. Insofar as thinking on internal and general policies was concerned, the theoretical basis for the strategies he defended were his own. He may have been deceiving himself about the actual influence that he had on practical policies, but even in such a concept as "socialism in one country," which he shared with Stalin, the elaboration of the argument was his and so were the conclusions. In fact, Bukharin formulated his own theory about the road to socialism through the methods of the NEP. When Stalin later openly challenged his conceptions, Bukharin reasserted his views and countered Stalin in the name of his own theories and strategies. There was, therefore, a distinct Bukharin line during the NEP, which did much more than just echo Stalin's position.

There was enough controversy between the Left and the Right over industrialization, kulaks, the Comintern, "socialism in one country," party regime, and workers' and party democracy to have created two hostile political parties. However, both factions moved within a common programmatic framework that would allow them to compromise if they wished and worked toward one. Since the factions were blind to the need for accommodation, a heavy toll was exacted on both sides.

After the proclamation of the NEP, the party accepted the new framework; Bukharin supported the new stage with more vigor than others, and showed some political naïveté in the crossing of "t's." Everybody acquiesced to the NEP as an unavoidable step, even though there were misgivings or considerations about its prospects and desirability in the future. Despite reservations about the NEP's future or its opinions on the ways to industrialize, even the Left did not want forcible collectivization of peasants, did not advocate expropriation of kulaks' property (not even an immediate brake on their growth as a class), nor did they intend to eliminate markets and the private sector in commerce and small industries. The move to the NEP, the concern to preserve the alliance with the peasants, and the concomitant conclusions Bukharin drew as to the pace of Russia's progress toward both industrialization and socialism were clearly Lenin's legacy. Bukharin's dictum that the country will move at a "snail's pace" but will move nevertheless might have been a tactical error (and he later changed this view), but one should remember that this was said in 1925, less than two years after Lenin exhorted the party to move cautiously and slowly in pace with the peasants' understanding and acceptance of the state's policies.[16] When Bukharin later advocated this approach, the Left derided him as tying the country to "peasant limitedness." But the term was Lenin's, who stated categorically that his gradualist propeasant policies would "not amount to peasant limitedness" because every free penny would be ploughed back into industry.[17] It is well enough known that the main lines of the *volte-face* were Lenin's and not Bukharin's. In 1921–1923, it was Lenin who redefined the relations with the peasantry and proposed a new "propeas-

[16] For Lenin's insistence in his last writings on moving cautiously and slowly, in pace with the peasants' readiness to follow, see *Sochineniia*, 45 (Moscow, 1964), 45, 137, 330, 370–372. See "On Cooperation" and "Better Fewer but Better" in Lenin, *Collected Works* (4th ed., Moscow, 1966), p. 330.

[17] Lenin, 45 *Sochineniia*, 405.

13

ant" strategy, including the concept of socialism as a system of "civilized cooperators" on which Bukharin built his platform.

Of course, nobody knows what Lenin would have said later. The history of the Soviet Revolution and of its policies is one of dramatic and frequent reversals on all sides. The Trotskyite opposition clearly deserves credit for having pushed the rethinking of the tasks of industrialization, the need to accelerate this process, and for their insight, especially Preobrazhensky's, into the strains and problems that the accelerated rate of investment was bound to produce. Bukharin's blatant weakness during the 1924–1926 period was that he had no serious program for industrial development to offer at this stage. His concept of "accumulation through commercial circulation" between the state and the peasantry made sense only so long as industry was speedily moving ahead as a result of the relative ease of restoring unused prewar capacities. But this recovery was nearing completion, and the "reconstruction period" was about to begin.

This was an important threshold in the country's economic development. The restored industry and communications were a good but quite narrow basis for further growth, particularly because the equipment in the plants was old and considerably worn out. The next stage would require a discontinuous spurt in the form of a steep increase of investment to renovate old and especially to build new plants and whole industries. A. Gerschenkron, summing up the experience of several countries, stated that successful industrialization processes can begin "only if the industrialization movement can proceed, as it were, along a broad front, starting simultaneously along many lines of economic activity. This is partly the result of the existence of complementarity and indivisibilities in economic processes."[18] Russia was entering a situation of this kind, in which many

[18] A. Gerschenkron, *Economic Backwardness in Historical Perspective* (New York, 1965), p. 10.

factors converged to necessitate a large addition to capital stock, as Preobrazhensky forcefully pointed out.

In order to reach the technological level of other countries during this period, essential in view of the country's precarious military position, new industries had to be equipped with costly and complicated machinery, and to accommodate this machinery plants of a considerable size had to be constructed; the population surplus, especially in the countryside, had to be absorbed; and in order to increase the peasants' productivity and their willingness to sell food to the growing industrial labor force, their needs for producer and consumer goods had to be met.[19] It could be added as well that modern armaments, like other technology, needed a more developed industry than had existed before the war.

The gradual process of accumulating profits from exchanges with peasants and ploughing them back into industry, as Bukharin maintained, was not suitable for obtaining quickly large amounts of capital for rapid industrialization. Unquestionably his opponents' plan was superior, and his strongly propeasant program unaccompanied by a clear and realistic assessment of the industrialization problems seems to justify the view of him as a mere spokesman of peasant interests. However, if a broader perspective and a larger set of problems are examined, a different picture emerges. The Left correctly anticipated the tensions that accelerated industrialization would create, especially among the peasantry. Yet they continued to profess their fidelity, for the time being at least, to the principles of the NEP; their analysis of the peasantry was rather influenced by many of the "pretestament" pronouncements of Lenin, in which he spoke of the peasantry as a bearer of capitalism and an enemy to be fought. But Lenin's analysis of the peasantry in class terms was not firm, hence the whole attitude toward

[19] See the discussion of Preobrazhensky's views on these points in A. Erlich, *The Soviet Industrialization Debate* (Cambridge, Mass., 1960), pp. 32–42.

the peasantry was ambivalent; they appeared to him, in different contexts, sometimes as the "main enemy," other times as the "main support" and "ally." There was, of course, enough complexity in the situation to warrant uncertainties on this matter, but this does not change the following facts: some on the Left understood that "primitive accumulation" would be strenuous, but they did not state clearly how the problem would be tackled during the critical period. They envisaged the continuation of the NEP and therefore, logically enough, they stated that although they intended to exercise greater control over the kulaks and private entrepreneurs, to tax them more efficiently, and to promote more collectivization in the countryside, the liquidation of kulaks and of private sectors (businessmen, traders, and other small property holders), or a large-scale administrative drive against peasants, was out of the question. This was exactly Bukharin's position, but he also formulated a coherent program for the peasantry, which differed from the Left's. In fact, the Left had an industrialization program but lacked clear answers concerning the peasants, whereas Bukharin had no adequate blueprint for industrialization but offered a plan to the peasantry. His approach was a gradualist one, with an outspoken warning against a "third revolution," and he firmly believed that the core of this program was faithful to Lenin's bequest. If the Left had in Preobrazhensky's *New Economics* a memorable document about accumulation and industrialization, the Left had nothing on the peasantry comparable to Bukharin's *The Road to Socialism and the Worker-Peasant Alliance*.[20] Trotsky, too, as Deutscher maintained, adhered to gradualism and was a "reformist" so far as internal policies were concerned;[21] such a "dreadful" Bukharinist sin as the appeal

[20] This article can be found in Russian in N. Bukharin, *Path to Socialism in Russia*, introd. S. Heitman (New York, 1967).

[21] Deutscher, in *The Prophet Outcast*, p. 110, stated: "In his approach to domestic Soviet issues the author of *Permanent Revolution* was in a sense a reformist."

to "enrich yourself" looks less "rightist" when compared with what Trotsky had to say on the same topic in August 1925 in a widely distributed brochure. Trotsky argued there that if the key sectors in industry, cooperation, and circulation are growing at a satisfactory rate, there is no disaster if private sectors are also growing to some extent including, in agriculture, the " 'strong,' i.e., capitalist farmers."

He also stated that so far as internal factors were concerned, there was no reason "to fear any surprises whatsoever."[22] In substance, this was exactly what Bukharin believed, although he not only saw no disaster in some growth of kulaks but actually thought that this would be beneficial. Also, Bukharin was no less adamant than the Left that the state preserve the "strategic key positions." Nor did he renounce Bolshevik doctrine on the "dictatorship of the proletariat" or the political monopoly of the party. These points of common ground must be added in order to establish the real scope of divergence between the extremes of the spectrum. In turn it can be reasserted that the protagonists often held complementary positions, which resulted from viewing the same problems from different angles or from providing insight that was lacking in the other side's argument.[23]

Thus both factions moved ever closer to performing within the party the vital function of debate, which in other conditions is performed by a bipartisan system. The drama consisted in the inability to understand this and to accept such a function as a legitimate principle of party structure. Instead, there was on all sides an adherence to the concept of a monolithic party. This assisted the forces inside the party pushing toward its transformation to a different type

[22] Bukharin launched his awkward "enrich yourself" slogan in *Bol'-shevik*, nos. 9–10 (1925), p. 5. Trotsky's opinion is in his brochure *K Kapitalizmu ili k Sotsializmu* (Moscow, 1925), p. 23.

[23] See M. Lewin, *Russian Peasant and Soviet Power* (London, 1968), p. 14.

of a social organization, one in which any faction was soon to be annihilated.

Rethinking

In 1925 Bukharin, now a well-known theoretician and ideologist of the official line, labored for the transformation of the NEP into a firmly established reality and an ideologically consecrated framework for a peaceful evolution into a socialist society. In order to achieve this he undoubtedly dotted too many "i's," with considerable tactical imprudence. Industrialization was as important to him as to anybody else in the party, but at this stage he lacked insight into the complexity and urgency of this problem and, committed as he was to fighting the Left, did not have much to offer against their arguments on this issue. At the same time, with a naive optimism he counterattacked the Left who accused the party of fostering bureaucratization, stifling inner-party life, and tolerating tendencies toward "degeneration of the workers' state." The Russian term used by the Left to epitomize all such phenomena was *pererozhdenie*, degeneracy or decay. Bukharin's reaction to such an accusation was as natural for one in power as it was uncritical and shortsighted. In the following years he changed his view on industrialization and on "*pererozhdenie*-cum-democratization," but he stuck to a certain number of other concepts which he developed during the first years in his new role as principal theoretical spokesman, and they remained permanent and valuable parts of his thinking. They focused mainly on the role of the peasantry, cooperation as their road to socialism, the social nature of this class, and party strategy toward it. In *Road to Socialism and the Worker-Peasant Alliance*, which he later described as his most important programmatic formulation about the NEP, Bukharin argued that there should be "no mass coercion against the peasantry in building socialism!"[24] He also wrote

[24] During his visit to Paris in spring 1936, Bukharin told B. Nicolaevsky, a former Menshevik leader, that "Road to Socialism" ex-

there about the role of the market and market categories in a mixed economy on its road to socialism.

Until 1927 Bukharin primarily wrote polemics against the Left and treatises on political strategy and tactics, almost neglecting general Marxist or sociological theory.[25] In addition to his duties as editor of *Pravda* and coeditor of Lenin's works and of the *Great Soviet Encyclopedia*, he produced an amazing number of articles, speeches, and brochures. In 1926, after Zinoviev and Kamenev joined Trotsky in opposition, Bukharin inherited Zinoviev's post as chairman of the executive of the Comintern. In 1926, the last relatively prosperous year of the NEP of which Bukharin was then such an active spokesman, the regime embarked upon the first stage of a program to accelerate industrialization after years devoted mainly to restoration. On the other hand, control measures and checks on the growth of private sectors also appeared. Although they were not too stringent, they pointed unmistakably to a hardening of policy in which Bukharin and Rykov participated. A. Erlich was the first to draw attention to signs of Bukharin's rethinking of the complex interrelations between industry and agriculture, and of the industrialization process, that became more pronounced during 1927.[26] Left-wing criticism and such disturbing phenomena as the growing "goods famine" certainly played their role in influencing the decisions of the Fifteenth Party Congress at the end of 1927 on collectivization, industrialization, and economic policies, which ex-

---

pressed not only what Lenin actually wrote but also what he told Bukharin in private before his death. On this, as well as on this visit to Paris in general, see the interview given by Nicolaevsky to J. Zagoria, ed., in B. Nicolaevsky, *Power and the Soviet Elite* (London, 1966), pp. 3–25.

[25] *Imperialism and Accumulation of Capital* (Moscow, 1925).

[26] "Preobrazhensky and the Economics of Soviet Industrialization," *Quarterly Journal of Economics*, 64, 1 (1950), 81–83; and *Industrialization Debate*, pp. 78–89. I took the lead from him and explored the theme in the fields of politics and ideology.

pressed to a large extent the opinions of the moderate leaders.[27]

In the course of the next important reversal of roles soon after the Fifteenth Congress, Bukharin further developed these kinds of arguments. With the Left either exiled or jailed as a result of the combined efforts of Stalin and Bukharin, the alliance turned overnight into a battle over the interpretation of the "grain crisis" that shook the country in the winter and spring of 1927–1928.

Within a few months after the late spring of 1928, a new opposition, the last important opposition in the party and in Soviet history, headed by the three Politbureau members, Bukharin, Rykov (head of the Council of Commissars), and Tomsky (chairman of the trade unions), coalesced. The battle the trio waged was heated. It lasted for over a year and ended in their defeat.[28] It was fought mainly inside the higher party bodies, although of course larger circles, especially in the governmental apparatus, were informed and involved. The country learned about the Right opposition only from official, fiercely venomous propaganda statements. During this controversy some events occurred of crucial importance for our argument here. The first was Bukharin's risky and rather bold initiative to contact the left-wing opposition to warn it about Stalin's designs and to propose some kind of common front. He met with Kamenev three times, who reported to the other opposition leaders. This initiative had no practical results and added to Bukharin's subsequent troubles because the Left refused the offer with contempt.[29] Besides this significant event,

[27] This was how Erlich saw the industrialization program of the Fifteenth Congress in *Industrialization Debate*, p. 84.

[28] For an account of this struggle, see R. Daniels, *The Conscience of the Revolution* (Cambridge, Mass., 1960) from which I drew myself and added more material in Lewin, "The Last Opposition," *Russian Peasant*, chap. 8. The grain crisis is described in *ibid.*, chap. 9.

[29] Not Trotsky, though. He proposed to strike a limited agreement with the Right, but his troops, scattered over detention places but

other developments occurred mainly in the field of political thinking: during these months Bukharin, still editor of *Pravda* (he lost the editorship in April 1929), published a series of articles in which, together with his proposals and criticisms launched during the infighting in Politbureau meetings in January–February 1929, he developed a set of theses that amounted to a full-fledged counterprogram for Russia's road to socialism as opposed to the one the majority leaders were embarking upon. Among the remarkable features of this program were the warnings he gave about what would happen if Stalin's line was pursued. These warnings have turned out to be quite accurate forecasts.

The most remarkable of these articles was published in *Pravda* on 30 September 1928 under the title "Notes of an Economist." Both Stalin and Trotsky immediately counterattacked, though not yet publicly, dismissing and deriding it.[30] In two other significant articles, published at the beginning of the following year,[31] Bukharin presented to the public, which was completely unaware of Bukharin's role as the head of the opposition and of the fierce fight between the two factions within the Politbureau, what he thought was Lenin's testament and the program he bequeathed to the party. The exercise was simple, but only the initiated understood that this very faithful, almost dull, presentation of Lenin's bequest was, in the new situation, a rather explosive thing. The leadership was taking the party and the

---

still very ardent, were indignant and forced Trotsky to drop his proposals. On this see I. Deutscher, *The Prophet Unarmed* (London, 1959), pp. 448–450.

[30] Stalin said that this was "a muddled anti-Party article" and Trotsky spoke about its "theoretical nullity." See Stalin, *Sochineniia*, 11 (Moscow, 1949), 324; Trotsky is quoted from the Trotsky Archives in Harvard by E. H. Carr and R. Davies, *Foundations of a Planned Economy*, 1 (London, 1970), 90, 112.

[31] They were "Lenin i Zadachi Nauki," *Pravda*, 20 January 1929, and, more important, "Politicheskoe Zaveshchanie Lenina," *Pravda*, 24 January 1929.

country on a new path, and the repetition of the contents of the articles Lenin wrote before his death was about to become a heretical, if not immediately criminal, program of a deviator.

One more text by Bukharin is worth mentioning for its content and implied meaning: an ideologically "innocent" review in *Pravda* (30 June 1929) of Western writings about trends in capitalism, curiously entitled "The Theory of Organized Chaos," was in fact an exercise in "Aesopian language," a way of saying things about Soviet affairs in a roundabout, camouflaged fashion. Undoubtedly, the story of "organized chaos" dealt with trends in Western industrial organization, but it was also criticism of the bureaucratized industrial organization in Russia itself. "Aesopian language" remained the only way in which in later years one could convey ideas to another who would be able to decode them. The last and most dramatic instance of the use of such a code, not easy to decipher even today, occurred during Bukharin's trial in 1938.

But before the denouement in March 1938, Bukharin suffered several more unexpected turnabouts and reversals. After his first recantation at the end of 1929, when he lost his position on the Politbureau (but was at the same time elected an academician), he was not allowed either to play any direct political role or to publish anything of importance on party theory or politics. The attacks against the "rightist danger," the "agency of kulaks inside the party," and so on, would continue unabated for some years. But for a while Stalin was forced to contend with members of his own caucus, and he met, as some sources record, with rather stubborn opposition from them when he prepared to annihilate some former, current, or suspected critics. Personal attacks of the more vicious kind against Bukharin stopped in 1931 (but not against Rykov and Tomsky, probably the result of a high-level deal), and he was allowed, together with his former companions and many members of the left-wing opposition who had rallied to Stalin during

1929–1930, to keep nonpolitical but important administrative and research jobs.

With the campaign toward rapid industrialization, Bukharin, as head of the Academy's Institute of History of Science and Technology, and head of a similar institute in the Council of the National Economy (VSNKh), was allowed to direct his attention to the study of industrial organization, technological innovation, and the planning of science. In this field Bukharin proved to be innovating and pioneering. In 1931 he presented his ideas on this subject inside Russia and accompanied a delegation of Soviet scientists to the first international conference in London devoted to scientific policy. According to recent Western research, Bukharin's ideas left an impact in the West, although he has had none in his own country.[32]

Biographical data on Bukharin for the subsequent years are scanty. His name kept appearing in the press, in which he published various nonpolitical articles, and he even wrote one long work on Marxism in 1933 which has, however, only minor theoretical importance.[33] Although he himself was under constant suspicion, he often tried to help people in trouble, especially writers; one such case is documented by Nadezhda Mandelshtam. Bukharin had already

[32] See L. Graham, "Bukharin and the Planning of Soviet Science," *Russian Review*, no. 2 (1964), pp. 134–148. Studies into planning of science were soon to be discontinued in the Soviet Union, like many other sophisticated beginnings in the field of planning.

[33] "Uchenie Marksa i Ee Teoreticheskoe Znachenie" in *Sotsialisticheskaia Rekonstruktsiia i Nauka*, nos. 3, 4, 5, 6 (1933), is still worth mentioning, not so much for its intrinsic as for its biographical value. In the prevailing anti-intellectual atmosphere, with the growing adulation of Stalin, nobody wrote anymore, in such length and tone, about the importance of Marx and of Marxism without the already obligatory liturgical incantations on Leninism-Stalinism. Moreover, he quoted an impressive number of Western works on economics and sociology, critically but without the usual invectives—a very significant fact in itself. Sycophants immediately attacked him on this and many other points, including the things he failed to say but should have—according to their taste.

helped her husband during the NEP and tried to interfere on his behalf when the poet was arrested in 1933.[34]

Articles and malicious stories about him never stopped, but they were controlled and major outbursts were clearly prohibited. But soon another important change occurred: some time between mid-1933 and the assassination of Kirov in December 1934, the leadership effected an important change of policy with the aim of appeasing the country and uniting the party—mass terror was stopped and a new line began to be followed with regard to relations between the party and society.

This change of policy, which occurred almost concurrently with the Seventeenth Party Congress, offered the former opponents a measure of reconciliation, readmission to party life without further harassment, and new hope. The rationale and argument of the new line countered Stalin's and stated that the former class enemies, including the numerous kulaks, had been irreversibly defeated; that the *kolkhoz* system had been established and needed only consolidation; that industrialization had been enormously successful; that socialism and the party had definitively won the historical battle inside the country; and that mass terror had lost its usefulness since no significant opposition remained. Stalin, on the contrary, maintained that the opposition of class enemies would grow in pace with the victories of socialism, and that it would only take on ever new, more pernicious, and better masked forms.

Although not very much is known about the "Kirov faction," which was supposedly associated with the new course and which aimed at perpetuating and expanding it, its existence is very plausible.[35] However, there is no doubt about

[34] N. Mandelshtam, *Hope Against Hope* (London, 1971), pp. 22–23, 250, 254.

[35] Our main source on the Kirov line still remains Nicolaevsky, who got it from his conversations with Bukharin in 1936. Nicolaevsky published the information he gathered from conversing with Bukharin as "Pis'mo Starogo Bol'shevika" [Letter from an old Bolshevik], *Sot-*

the very significant change in internal policies paralleled by a switch to a pro-Western, anti-German, and "popular front" orientation in foreign policy. As a result of the shift in orientation, the pathological hunt for the mythical opposition and its agents, blind mass oppression (especially in the countryside), the relentless pressure for impossible quotas for industrial growth, and many other governmental practices were discontinued. Whatever the details of the new policies, they found more than symbolic expression in the readmission of numerous opponents, who, heretofore, had been savagely attacked and persecuted, not only to party ranks, but also to respectable positions and jobs, and even to seats on the Central Committee. In the wake of these changes, Bukharin was now allowed a high degree of public prominence and even regained a minor position in the Central Committee. With some other former leaders of the opposition, he was invited to speak to the Seventeenth Party Congress, and his speeches on industrial and technological questions were now published with due reverence and under headlines befitting a personality of first rank. In February 1934 he became editor-in-chief of *Izvestiia*. Much publicity was given to his speech, occupying several full pages of *Pravda* (3 August 1934), on the National Writers Congress, where he expressed many unorthodox thoughts about life and literature. But the murder of Kirov in December 1934 put an end to whatever hopes for the cessation of terror there had been among many groups in the country during the year-long interlude. An unprecedented witch hunt began, and from the beginning of 1935 trainloads of "Kirov's assassins" were jailed and executed and opponents of Stalin were reaccused and rearrested with a murderous fierceness.

No doubt Bukharin's expectations were once again shattered, since the former purge still haunted his memory and

---

sialisticheskii Vestnik, nos. 23–24 (December 1936), and nos. 1–2 (January 1937), reproduced in English in Nicolaevsky, *Power and the Soviet Elite*.

conscience. Since his first recantation and forced admission of the correctness of Stalin's line in 1929, he had known that his life was in danger and that he was kept inside the Central Committee (stripped of all positions of importance) as a captive to serve as scapegoat in case of trouble. During the years of the demential "big drive," the Stalinist faction, though victorious inside the party, knew that it was sitting on a volcano in a country seething with deep discontent. They clung to Stalin, the architect of the drive, as a lynchpin of the whole structure, but some of them hoped that one day, after the storm, Stalin's personal position would be changed and life in the party would be normalized as they understood it. This is why majorities in the Central Committee could be found to resist Stalin's demands to inflict capital punishment on some opponents who criticized him during the early 1930s.[36] This may also explain their unwillingness to expel from the party and even from the Central Committee Bukharin and Rykov, the only surviving colleagues of Lenin who still served on this body, although they endorsed decisions castigating these men as dreadful deviators. As long as it seemed useful to him, Stalin preferred to keep critics formally inside the official ruling body, although outside the actual ruling caucus, so that he could force them publicly to endorse policies that they had severely criticized in the past. It was a tactic designed to prevent people who were natural pretenders to leadership from heading a movement of popular discontent which might oust Stalin from power when the evils of the majority's line became apparent. Stalin used it on several occasions after 1929, when mounting dissatisfaction within the party created new centers of opposition. When the security

[36] The best example of such resistance or reluctance was the refusal of the Central Committee to inflict capital punishment on a party official, Riutin, an author of a long manuscript against Stalin, circulated sometime in 1932, that depicted Stalin as "the evil demon of the revolution." On Riutin see Nicolaevsky, *ibid.*, pp. 11, 28–30, 71–72.

police unearthed such a new real or imaginary opposition, Stalin would submit the former top leaders of Left or Right oppositions to new investigations, even if charges of direct involvement in new plots were not pressed against them. The procedure just consisted in bringing them before the Central Committee plenum and pressing them to prove that they had had nothing to do with the new deviation, that they condemned it, and that they faithfully adhered to official doctrine. The majority's, or Stalin's, procedure normally conformed to the following scenario: although former critics (e.g., Bukharin, Rykov, Zinoviev, and Kamenev) formally recanted and proclaimed their loyalty to the party line, the inquisitor maintained that they had not really proved their sincerity. While they may not have been directly involved with those now on trial, their previous behavior encouraged new detractors who sensed their lack of sincerity. Therefore, they were morally responsible for all treacherous opponents. Finally, and almost ritually, to prove that their loyalty was above suspicion, they had to reiterate how wrong they were in their earlier role as critics, and had to promise that they would fight hard all new critics.

The exdeviators, Bukharin among them, were forced to submit to such humiliating procedures time and again. Stalin's political and psychological need to have the former leaders' images rendered abject by this ritual seemed insatiable. In fact, he did not regain his composure until such people were physically eliminated. Bukharin knew Stalin well, and already realized what his aims were when he told the still rather incredulous Kamenev in July 1928 that "this Genghis Khan" would destroy anybody standing in his way.[37]

---

[37] The transcript of this conversation was published in the Menshevik journal *Sotsialisticheskii Vestnik*, no. 6 (1929), pp. 10–11, and no. 9 (1929), pp. 9–11. They obtained it originally from a Trotskyite source.

The Trial

Although Bukharin was not immediately harassed after Kirov's death he well knew that he faced death, and he had the chance to state this feeling on a rather puzzling trip to Paris in the spring of 1936 with a delegation of the party to negotiate with the German Social Democrats and some Mensheviks for the purchase of Marx's Archive for the Marx-Engels Institute in Moscow. It still remains a mystery why permission was granted to Bukharin to go abroad with his young wife at a time when his liquidation was already probably envisaged by the G.P.U. (secret police). Whether someone tried to give him a chance or whether it was a trap, posterity at least learned something from this trip. One of the negotiators for the Social Democrats happened to be Borys Nicolaevsky, Rykov's brother-in-law, and Bukharin saw him often in Paris and spoke to him relatively frankly. But Bukharin dared to do even more than that. He paid a sudden, totally unexpected visit to the Menshevik leaders Lydia and Fëdor Dan. He told them that he was driven by an irresistible urge to see them whatever the risks.[38] He left no doubt that he considered himself doomed, but did not wish to remain abroad as an émigré. Life was inconceivable for him outside his country. But he frankly told his hosts what he thought about Stalin: "This is a small, wicked man . . . no, not a man, a devil." Questioned as to how it happened that the country's fate was in such hands, he answered that the party somehow believed Stalin: "He is something like the symbol of the party, the rank-and-file workers, the people believe him. We are probably responsible for it ourselves, but this is how it happened and this is why we are all . . . crawling into his jaws knowing for sure that he will devour us."[39]

[38] For Nicolaevsky's recollections, see *Power and Soviet Elite*, pp. 3–25. Lydia Dan's "Bukharin o Staline" was published posthumously in *Novyi Zhurnal*, no. 75 (March 1965), pp. 176–186.

[39] Dan, *ibid.*, p. 182.

Back in Moscow Bukharin was soon to learn how he would be "devoured." In August 1936 the first batch of ex-opponents, Zinoviev and Kamenev among them, stood on trial and recited by heart all the monstrosities they had been forced to learn by rote during long rehearsals in the G.P.U. cellars. Bukharin's name was frequently mentioned at the trial, and half a year after these first executions he was arrested. Some sources state that his fate was discussed at a session of the Central Committee in his presence. The chief accusation against his presumed "plot against the party" was presented by the new head of the secret police Yezhov, and Bukharin was said to have counterattacked by charging his detractors with themselves plotting the destruction of the party and of transforming it into a branch of the G.P.U. After a secret vote was taken, Yezhov and Stalin were allegedly defeated by a majority of two-thirds.[40] Whatever the reliability of this account, two facts remain: an announcement appeared in *Pravda* in September 1936 that Bukharin and Rykov had been released for lack of sufficient evidence to instigate a criminal prosecution; but during the next year or so, the majority of this Central Committee that had allegedly defended Bukharin were themselves liquidated (see Khrushchev's secret speech in 1956). Once Stalin felt that the last obstacles had been removed, Bukharin was arrested, probably in February 1937. For at least three months, he refused to cooperate in the frame-up. It is not known what made him change his mind. The G.P.U. certainly did not lack either determination or ruthlessness to force this change. Bukharin may not have been tortured personally, but he may have been blackmailed by threats to kill his wife and child. Whatever the explanation,[11] he was finally the only one, with the notable excep-

---

[40] For these events, see "Introduction" in R. Tucker and S. Cohen, eds., *The Great Purge Trial* (New York, 1965), p. xx, based on A. Uralov, *Reign of Stalin* (London, 1955). The bulk of the book contains the minutes of the trial.

[41] R. Tucker's interpretation influenced my own reading of the

tion of A. Krestinsky,[42] to behave very differently from the others accused in these trials—dozens of people, among them former top political leaders of the country, mechanically repeating any nonsense put into their mouths, although the verdict had been predetermined. Ostensibly Bukharin "cooperated," too; he justified his death sentence in advance and even asked for it because, as he declared, of the immensity of his treason. In fact, however odd this might sound, he feverishly labored to wreck the show. In order to execute such a design Bukharin showed much ingenuity and no doubt courage against the prosecutor Vyshinsky. During the interrogation at the trial, his strategy seemed rather clear: he admitted all the charges that had a flavor of "monstrosity" to them. These were so exaggerated that he could assume them to be in fact self-defeating; on the other hand, he heatedly denied any specific criminal charge of wrecking, plotting, spying, assassination, and so on. How and why he forced the G.P.U. to put up with this is an enigma. The fact remains that in his last plea before the verdict he did even more. Into the mass of self-accusations that he agreed to repeat, he interjected several statements that challenged the trial and in fact demolished the whole crust of lies. First, he stated that the trial proved nothing and that the codefendants were not at all members of the "wrecking center," under Bukharin's and Trotsky's leadership, that they were accused to have been.

He also suddenly appeared to assert (as if unintentionally) that "the confession of the accused is not essential. The confession of the accused is a medieval principle of

---

trial's transcript. See his introduction, *ibid.*, and the minutes of the trial, in particular Bukharin's final plea, in order to form a personal opinion.

[42] Krestinsky, the former Soviet diplomat (and earlier one of the first Central Committee secretaries), suddenly denied the charges and declared that his pretrial testimony was false. But after a short break in the proceedings, the trial resumed and Krestinsky continued to "cooperate." See, for this episode, Tucker and Cohen, *The Great Purge Trial*, pp. 59–66, esp. p. 53.

jurisprudence"—and this was said at a trial based exclusively on confessions! Next came another more ambiguous sentence, not easy to interpret: "But here we also have the internal demolition of the forces of the counter-revolution.
And one has to be a Trotsky not to lay down one's arms."[43]
If one accepts the view that Bukharin was trying desperately not only to demolish the trial by making it burst at the
seams but also to communicate some message, one will
agree with R. Tucker, who believed Bukharin was trying
to say the following: the confessions were lies, but the
"counter-revolution" (Bukharin's term for "opposition")
was demolished, and therefore only somebody abroad
(Trotsky) could still continue to do something.

The risks involved in accepting this and other interpretations[44] are obvious, but Bukharin's testimony, especially his
performance in the last plea, is so clearly loaded with deliberate ambiguities, unfinished or loosely connected sentences
and ideas, that the very fact of an effort to convey some
message different from anything the authorities intended
to achieve is beyond doubt. He fought for his past and his
soul, using all the subtleties of his intellect in this peculiar
role of one confessing that he was a monster and implying
that he was neither confessing nor that he was a monster.

All this was futile in the final analysis, and nobody read
these messages. At that time not many even abroad tried to
decode this most enigmatic and stirring last plea in the history of trials. Here was Soviet Russia's most popular revolutionary leader, the party's pet, one of the few heirs of
Lenin (designated by him as such *expressis verbis*), now a

[43] *Ibid.*, pp. 653–667. See also p. 671 where another defendant
reacted to the assertion about confessions, in order to prove to the
court his own "full repentance."

[44] G. Katkov in his *The Trial of Bukharin* (New York, 1969), pp.
190–192, also shows that Bukharin resisted Vyshinsky with courage
but "scored only a partial success" and failed on another essential
point. We will return to Katkov's text in Chapter 12, especially to his
interesting assumption about the political sense of the trial from
Stalin's point of view.

lonely, desperate, vilified defendant who smeared his own reputation, who asked for death but still tried to rescue something of his human dignity using the only weapon still left to him: his dialectical wit.

It was an historical irony that the author of a highly democratic constitution,[45] was crushed together with a multitude of others—victims of Stalin's purges—in one of the most revolting assaults against human rights in modern history, while students in every school of the country memorized that same constitution, which expressed the humanistic creed of the executed "archcriminal."

The date of Bukharin's execution—15 March 1938—may safely be given as the date on which the remains of the revolutionary Bolshevik Party in Russia were ingloriously buried. It is not implausible that this was in fact the pessimistic message that the chief defendant in the trial against "the criminal anti-Soviet bloc of Rights and Trotskyists" had endeavored to broadcast.

[45] When in Paris, Bukharin full of pride raised his pen and told Nicolaevsky that with the pen he had written the entire Soviet Constitution. Only Radek helped him a little. Both of them had tried to introduce competing candidates in elections. See Nicolaevsky, *Power and Soviet Elite*, p. 22.

CHAPTER TWO

Left and Right in Perspective

THE preceding biographical sketch has already alluded to
the differences of approach of the warring factions—Left
and Right—and has implied that the differences between
them were sometimes less sharp than they seemed to be.
However, it is necessary to detail these differences before
discussing Bukharin's approach in more depth.

The story of the Left-Right-Center debates during the
1920s is complex. The positions of the protagonists sometimes clashed: for example, in economics the "primitive accumulation" thesis versus the "accumulation through market exchanges" proposition; or, in ideology, the possibility
versus impossibility of building socialism in one country.
But at the same time, as arguments kept shifting and positions changed, matter-of-fact discussions on practical issues
became inflamed by the growing hostility of factions and
other political factors, which were extraneous to the problem at hand, whereas themes of ideological character,
seemingly matters of principle hotly debated with dogmatic intransigence, turned out to be of no great consequence when translated into practical policy proposals. In
addition to the continuous shifting of respective positions,
sometimes brought about by the antagonists' influence and
pressure on each other, a further complication in evaluating
them was introduced by the fact that any theme of importance, or proposal for policies, or formulation of larger objectives—as well as almost any important criticism of the
regime—was also frequently voiced by the other side. Demagogy and tactical maneuvering was one reason for this; but
sincere commitment was often another. The differences

were also often ones of emphasis and arrangement of priorities. Although such determinants did in fact often amount to serious variations in policy, they always left possibilities for reshifting the arguments in order either to outflank the opponent or to find a way of compromising or moderating one's position. These phenomena can be observed in the great economic debate, at least insofar as political demagogy did not interfere. For instance, during the remarkable discussion in the Socialist Academy in September 1926 under the chairmanship of the historian Pokrovsky, chief spokesmen for the opposition—Preobrazhensky, Piatakov, Smilga, Radek—could still frankly and seriously discuss with party-line defenders all the controversial economic problems of the country.

On this occasion both sides of the debate displayed a considerable moderation in tone, and it was notably Preobrazhensky who made the appeal not to exacerbate unnecessarily the differences and not to introduce ideological problems, such as "socialism in one country," when practical economic questions were on the agenda. On these practical matters in the main fields of economic policy, the spokesmen of the Left, although advancing their argument for the redistribution of resources in favor of industrial growth, proposed quite moderate, businesslike targets for investment, taxation, and commercial policy.[1] This was proof that in a more rational atmosphere, with the fierce debate over theoretical issues kept under control, compromise on policy could be achieved. As long as Bukharin (and this is true of the political line of the whole Politbureau) held his overoptimistic views on the accumulation of capital and the rate of industrial growth, the Left's arguments displayed more insight than the official position, and it correctly predicted a gathering storm in the economic life of the country. But in 1926, as the "reconstruction" was setting in,

[1] This discussion was published in *Vestnik Kommunisticheskoi Akademii*, no. 18 (Moscow, 1926), pp. 208–217, 223–236.

the official line hardened with respect to industrialization targets and control and taxation measures, some of which were directed against private enterprise and richer peasants. The divergencies boiled down to bargaining over an additional 100 million rubles for investment, or over some additional 30 million rubles in taxes to be squeezed from the richer NEPmen. In propaganda texts, the majority's spokesmen accused the Left of planning to liquidate the NEP, to oppress the peasantry, to raise prices and lower the standard of living, and other sins. But the latter, no doubt sincerely, reasserted that it favored the NEP, did not intend to expropriate the property of kulaks, nor indeed, that of any other private entrepreneurs, and that it, in fact, even welcomed some growth of these elements provided the growth of the socialist sector, mainly industrial, was constantly assured. They opposed using the G.P.U. against the private sectors, as Pyatakov stated in the Academy, because it did not solve problems raised by basic economic imbalances. They pressed for a further stepping up of allocations in favor of industrial investments and opposed the premature lowering of industrial prices that the government had announced as its policy,[2] without protesting the lowering of prices of goods already in ample supply; they sought for further economies in government administrations and additional taxation of merchants and kulaks. However, all these plans were accompanied by the most moderating proviso as stated by the most "extremist" bible of "primitive accumulation": the pumping of the peasantry for capital in favor of industry was to be operated only in the limits "of what [was] economically possible, technically feasible, and rational." In addition, decisions to "pump" were limited by a long list of qualifications and restrictions. Thus, the quar-

---

[2] A policy that was economically unsound in a time of growing goods shortages. For a Western criticism of this policy see R. Davies, *The Development of the Soviet Budgetary System* (London, 1956), pp. 93–94.

rel with Bukharin could have been settled at a bargaining table at which practical policies might be formulated.[3] If only matters of grand theory had been left to be settled by further study. . . .

The same applied to such problems as collectivization and cooperation. The disagreements about them were centered only on the evaluation of the future of the cooperative movement and its prospects. Preobrazhensky, for example, avoided discussion of this subject because he felt the government had no money to put into cooperatives and collectives. The Left felt that collectivization had to follow industrial development and not precede it. The emphasis in the program of the Left on more *kolkhozy* in the countryside came later, in their 1927 platform, but this was an appeal that more attention be devoted to collectives in the future and was explicitly limited to existing means and to the peasants' consent. The Right, too, did not feel that the *kolkhozy* could become an important factor for the short term and believed that the future of the countryside and agriculture would depend for a long time on private farms, "growing into" socialism through a commercial cooperative movement. Bukharin, and others, emphasized that the main road to socialism was not through *kolkhozy*. While they mainly paved the route for the poor peasants, "the main road [would] go through the ordinary cooperation: marketing, purchasing, credit—in one word, through agricultural cooperatives."[4]

[3] E. Preobrazhenskii, *Novaia Ekonomika* (Moscow, 1926), p. 238, lists the conditions to be considered before deciding on the amount to the "pumped" over from peasants: "The relatively *slow* rate of accumulation on peasant farms, and the relatively slow growth of the peasant's purchasing power; the problem of balanced industrial development; the size of the harvest in the given year; the anticipated volume of exports; the world market prices for grain; the prices of exports, etc." Preobrazhenskii's important book is available in English, *The New Economics*, introd. A. Nove (Oxford, 1965).

[4] Quoted by F. Vaganov, *Pravyi Uklon v VKP (b) i Ego Razgrom, 1928–1930* (Moscow, 1970), p. 83. See Bukharin's *Put' k Sotsial-*

The complementarity of the competing theses in the sphere of economics, the fact that they often just stressed a different facet of the problem, was shown by researchers, such as Professors Erlich and Bobrowski, who explained much of the controversy by dissimilar points of focus: for Preobrazhensky dynamism and growth were important; for Bukharin, equilibrium. The former, although he understood the need for equilibrium in the long run, stressed the need to accelerate development; the latter, although he wanted a dynamic economy, was interested in applying brakes and establishing limits on growth so as not to lose control of the process.

One issue on which the contradiction was real and irreconcilable lay in the field of ideology. The controversy over the possibility of building "socialism in one country," seen on the Left as a "national-socialist" deviation from Marxism and Leninsim, had far-reaching implications for the development of the Soviet political mind; on this thesis the debate never subsided as long as the protagonists remained alive. The details of this controversy are beyond the scope of this essay,[5] the arguments were extremely complex,

---

izmu i Raboche-Krestianskii Soiuz (Moscow, 1926), p. 105; this passage, characteristically, is still used today to expose one of Bukharin's political sins.

[5] For some good texts representing the differing points of view, see the debate on the Fifteenth Party Conference at the end of 1926, in *Piatnadtsataia Konferentsiia VKP(b)* (Moscow, 1927), p. 463, and *passim.* A direct confrontation took place there between Stalin and other defenders of the "socialism in one country" thesis and their opponents, especially Kamenev and Trotsky who delivered impressive speeches and clearly carried the day. They would be given no other occasions to refute their opponents and to win the sympathy of the audience. Bukharin's most important statement is in *O Kharaktere Nashei Revoliutsii* (Leningrad, 1926). A short statement by Trotsky, among many others, is in "The Program of International Revolution or a Program of Socialism in One Country" in *The Third International After Lenin* (New York, 1957). For Stalin's arguments, see his speeches at the Fifteenth Conference and an earlier exposé in "Oktiabrskia Revoliutsia i Taktika Russikh Kommunistov" in *Sochineniia* (Moscow, 1947), 6, pp. 358–401.

and the balance sheet of rights and wrongs is not simple to establish; there were some correct insights on both sides, as well as many erroneous statements, emotional outbursts, and sham, which one could expect in an ideological battle of this size. And yet, even this debate over irreconcilable theoretical positions did not yield clear-cut differences in policy. The "internationalists," according to their opponents, were sowing confusion and disbelief in the ranks by denying the possibility of building socialism in Russia alone, but they did press hard for stepping up investments to bring about this "impossible" socialism. While it was possible to start building socialism in one country, its completion was dependent on its worldwide establishment. At the same time the internationalists accused the "one country" proponents of being narrow-minded nationalists and potential traitors to internationalism, an argument that did quite correctly anticipate changes toward a nationalist trend in Russia. But it was rash to keep repeating, as Trotsky often did, that if capitalism recovered from its crisis, Soviet Russia had no chance at all. Furthermore, the nationalist label could not be applied equally to Bukharin and Stalin. The argument that Russia had to build its socialism alone—quite a realistic statement in the face of the failure of revolutions to materialize elsewhere—did not have the same meaning to different people and did not lead at all to the same conclusions about policies. The quarrel between Stalin and Bukharin is the best illustration of this idea. For some time, they held similar policies with regard to the NEP, the peasantry, and industrial growth; but very soon they found themselves at antipodes on every one of these as well as other issues. The doctrinal thesis remained common, but it led to polarized conclusions. On the other hand, the adherence to antithetical doctrines would not prevent their proponents from formulating essentially similar policies on all the important issues, as will be demonstrated in the case of Bukharin and Trotsky after 1928.

Another irreconcilable difference involved the charge

made by consecutive oppositions, that the proletarian state and the party were "degenerating." The Russian term *pererozhdenie* (decay) was strongly pejorative and was extremely offensive to the majority leaders. Such an indictment against the system was seen as an act of treason, because it implied that the leadership itself was treasonable and presided over the job of liquidating the revolution.

The Left opposition during the 1920s, as had already been the case with the previous oppositions of the "Democratic Centralists" and the "Workers' Opposition," were trying to diagnose the trends in the state and the party that deeply worried them and drove them to fight the majority line. In order to account for the phenomena of bureaucratization of state and party, the estrangement of apparatuses from workers (although they were often composed of many ex-workers), and the loss of "real party spirit" and of devotion to socialist ideas, the opposition used terms such as "danger of Thermidorian restoration," "state capitalist [instead of socialist] character of the state-sector," or simply "bureaucratic degeneration" of what was still for them a "workers' state." For many years even after his deportation from Russia, Trotsky used this phrase, for he still hoped for a revival of socialist combativity in the working class and in some party cadres. The "United Opposition" of 1926 staged a major attack on the party, asserting, as Zinoviev did, that nationalized industry, as long as it offered its workers a very low standard of living and allowed them no say in running the affairs of enterprises and of the state, could not yet be called socialist. "State capitalism" was for him the appropriate term. At the same time, during a Central Committee session, Trotsky charged that the Soviet state was "far from a proletarian state," because the Soviets, allegedly organs of popular rule, were undergoing a process of bureaucratic degeneration.[6] The majority's spokes-

[6] For Zinoviev's statement on "state capitalism" see his *Leninism* (Moscow, 1925), pp. 101–110, 226. Trotsky's statement is quoted in Bukharin, *Partiia i Oppozitsionnyi Blok* (Leningrad, 1926), p. 44, but

men would react, naturally enough, with great fury against such accusations, and on this topic Bukharin delivered some of his more shallow and demagogic speeches. He vituperated with particular rage against the opposition's explicit or implied demand to allow factions and different platforms inside the party. He charged at that time that the opposition was "sliding towards a second party," abandoning the dictatorship of the proletariat "for political democracy," etc.[7] He undoubtedly bitterly regretted these opinions later. But in the same text and in many others, he admitted that *pererozhdenie* of the party and state was a possibility, and that party democracy had to be "strengthened." In the same vein, when facing attacks about dangers of kulak influence on other peasants, he denied that this did in fact take place but admitted that a danger of this kind existed. Again, such admissions were not always just tactical moves. Although he forcefully defended what seemed to him to be his own record in power, he did not ignore the issues raised by the opposition. Both sides of the debate shared the same basic ideas and ideals, and Bukharin could neither deny the existence of difficult problems nor maintain sincerely that the trends and shape of the state and party bureaucracies were not troublesome.

Although the common ground, especially the trend toward a compromise between the two sides, has been underlined, even if the sides themselves were unaware of this, there is no intention here to play down the range or depth of the dispute. The purpose is only to gauge independently of the exasperation of the adversaries, the real scope and depth of their differences. Hindsight offers the benefits of historical perspective. Once the thick smoke has cleared, the real fire can be described better. When the exaggerations and distortions engendered by polemic ardor are corrected, it is easier to pull from the tangle the specific con-

---

Bukharin himself admitted that "degeneration" is a real danger, *ibid.*, p. 34 ff.

[7] Bukharin, *O Kharaktere Nashei Revoliutsii*, pp. 60–64.

tributions and themes, especially those that displayed originality or insight into future developments and basic problems that had a potential for being unearthed and revived for subsequent use at another stage. In fact, Bukharin had put forward a set of themes that were distinctively his and to a large extent justified an "ism" of his own already before and during his partnership with Stalin. This does not mean that those themes and ideas were personal inventions. He had political associates, Rykov and Tomsky, and open or hidden followers in the party. Many of their proposals, especially in the field of economic policies, expressed ideas elaborated by experts, many of them non-Bolsheviks. Bukharin, a well-educated economist, was aware of the economic views among foreign and Russian experts. He synthesized these various conceptions with his own to develop a distinctly Bukharinist program, which encompassed more than economics and which countered Stalin's.

Some Key Ideas

Some of the ideas that Bukharin held during the NEP had antecedents in his prerevolutionary and civil war writings. His findings on state capitalism and the state's capacity for repression, which have already been mentioned, instilled in him an anarchistic distrust of state power and of bureaucracies, which shaped many of his views during the break with Stalin and his more or less clandestine thinking in subsequent years. During the NEP he stressed ideas on the role of cooperative principles in building a socialist society. For peasants cooperation was to be the "main road." Although he often stated that private entrepreneurs in the cities and the countryside were to be evicted in the long run, he did not see the deepening socialization as a process in which the evicted private sectors had to be replaced by an ever-growing, all-embracing state. Such a course was opposed to accepted socialist expectations. Bukharin's concept of state and cooperative socialism, similar to the one

41

sketched by Lenin in an article on cooperation, favored the cooperative principle of organization, which in the long run would contribute to the withering away of the state.[8] Without this "withering away," whatever its interpretations, socialism did not have much meaning for socialists, including Bolsheviks.

It is clear that this was a serious and deeply felt issue in Bukharin's thought, as his policy proposals for further socialist development by the party show. Once in power and once the illusions of "war communism"—"a caricature of socialism"[9]—had been shed, the party should adopt the strategy of "organic development." In 1924 Bukharin claimed that the formula of "organic development," although inherent in Lenin, was his own.[10] With this formula the NEP was definitively rescued from the ambiguous hesitations of the previous party doctrine ("a strategic retreat," or "a continuation of previous positions") and was adopted as a long-run strategy. Bukharin emphasized that there was no intention of ravaging (*razgrom*) shops or coercing peasants. Relations with the peasantry, with their strong commitment to family farming, might become strained at times, since peasants would not automatically become allies when facing certain unpopular policies applied to them. Likewise class warfare might remain and flare up temporarily, but, on the whole, it would not gain in intensity and would slowly disappear. Evolutionist, moderate policies would result from the lack of need, which exists in a revolution, to destroy the existing state.[11] Bukharin's position on the extinguishing of class warfare led him to the often-repeated slogan, "no third revolution," and was later presented in Stalin's propaganda, not without some reason, as the core of Bukharinism. Stalin's policies, on the other hand, appeared as direct counterpropositions to Bukharin's, and

[8] Cf. *Put' k Sotsializmu*, p. 58; *Bol'shevik*, no. 1 (1925), p. 27.

[9] *Bol'shevik*, no. 8 (1925), p. 8.

[10] *Vestnik Kommunisticheskoi Akademii*, no. 7 (1924), p. 58.

[11] See *Bol'shevik*, no. 1 (1925), p. 27.

were summarized in the Stalinist thesis of July 1928: an "ever growing exacerbation of class warfare" would accompany the victorious advance of socialism.

In view of their objectives, both were right. Bukharin's view of the process as an evolutionary one allowed him to promote his own "growing into" (*vrastanie*) thesis, an idea that was already present in his writings in 1920.[12] The entrepreneurial classes would be evicted but only through "overcoming" (*preodolenie*), only through the victory of the more efficient socialist (state and cooperative) enterprises in the market. Until then collaboration with the new bourgeoisie was necessary, and creaming off in favor of socialist accumulation would continue. But the problem with regard to the petite bourgeoisie, especially the peasantry, consisted not in "overcoming" (*preodolet'*) it, but in slowly transforming (*pererabotat'*) it, through cooperation.[13] While some form of coercion of peasants would be unavoidable, it was basically necessary to collaborate with them, to allow them to grow, and even to permit some class differentiation among them, which would not be politically dangerous so long as the socialist sector was actively expanding. A gradual transformation of society would be effected by helping peasants organize a voluntary cooperative movement as their road to socialism. With industry, banks, credit, legislation, etc. under the control of the socialist state, the peasantry—even the kulaks, convinced of its advantages, productivity, and cultural superiority—would be sucked into the growing industrial-cooperative complex, and would accept socialism.[14]

[12] See *Ekonomika Perekhodnogo Perioda* (Moscow, 1920), pp. 85–87, quoting from Kautsky. Lenin had no comment on this point in his notes to Bukharin's book.

[13] *Bol'shevik*, no. 1 (1925), p. 27, and *Put' k Sotsializmu*, p. 70. In another text Bukharin summed up this attitude as striving toward *uzhitsiia, peredelat' assimilirovat'* (to get along, transform, assimilate).

[14] See Bukharin's articles in *Bol'shevik*, no. 8 (1925), p. 14, and nos. 9–10, pp. 5–6, 10. On kulaks "growing into" socialism, see *Put' k Sotsializmu*, p. 49.

This relative optimism—relative because Bukharin did not unduly idealize the peasants, neither was he unaware of the dangerous potential of their more prosperous strata —was based on his class definition of the peasantry, which differed from the Leninist one, or rather came to differ from it substantially, sometime during the NEP period. Lenin's definitions of the peasants' class structure ranged from "the last capitalist class" to "a smallholder class breeding capitalism every hour," from "ally" to "petit-bourgeois anarchy [stikhiia]," and so on. They shifted according to the political situation, rather than following a firm theoretical principle. In 1926, however, Bukharin reached the conclusion that it was an error to confuse "the peasant economy with the capitalist economy."[15] In fact, this was obvious, and Lenin also employed the term "precapitalist class or stratum" in reference to the peasantry. In a search for a socio-theoretical basis both for his evolutionary policies and for his conceptions of a socialist society in Russia, Bukharin began to view the peasantry in a more positive, less ambiguous, light. He now fully recognized their revolutionary potential not only in Russia, where they seconded a proletarian revolution, but also as a revolutionary factor on a world scale. He looked forward to a time when the countryside, led by workers, would become "the great liberating power of our times," a slogan that anticipated later developments elsewhere.[16]

There was no self-complacency in Bukharin's conception of "socialism in one country," which in different hands became so heavily tinged with nationalism. If, as he believed, the peasants are not essentially a counterrevolutionary class, there was no important internal class left capable of operating a capitalist restoration in Russia. Their backwardness, on the other hand, was no obstacle to further progress, provided that it would be gradual.[17] This opinion

[15] *Pravda*, 3 August 1926.

[16] *Bol'shevik*, nos. 3–4 (1925), p. 8.

[17] He knew that external dangers can be such an obstacle, but a

formed the basis of his optimistic prospects for building socialism in backward Russia. The peasants would advance slowly to become a "backward part of the working class."[18] At the same time, the shape of such a socialism built without external help would be a kind of "backward socialism," an imprecise although rather prophetic term.[19]

At this juncture, Bukharin argued that different countries, according to their level of development, would choose different roads and ways to socialism.[20] With such a conception of "backward socialism," with the possibility of others doing better, one would not expect Bukharin to preach the superiority of the Soviet model all over the globe as later versions would have it.

Bukharin was as adamant as any other Bolshevik on the preservation of political supremacy in "proletarian hands" and on his opposition to sharing power in the state with anyone.[21] But the concept of monopoly of power was curiously mitigated by his assertion that peasants must be admitted "to the lower floors of proletarian dictatorship."[22] Whereas other leaders conceived such an alliance in terms of being patient with the peasantry, readily subscribed to the inadmissibility of using mass coercion against them (except in civil war situations), and expressed readiness to grant them important concessions, they never spoke in terms of granting them at least some political power. Furthermore, Bukharin did not interpret the granting of rights to peasants as "concessions," as purely tactical steps. For Lenin, as several of his (and his followers') pronouncements about the NEP indicate, the NEP was a concession to peasants, a deal in which the peasant was offered a meas-

---

peasantry ready to fight for the regime was the best possible guarantee, in the short run at least.

[18] *Bol'shevik*, no. 1 (1925), p. 30.

[19] *Put' k Sotsializmu*, p. 106.

[20] *Ibid.*, p. 105.

[21] *Ibid.*, p. 13.

[22] *Partiia i Oppozitsionnyi Blok*, p. 53. Peasants seldom have much more in any regime.

ure of "capitalism," of freedom to sell his surplus in markets, in return for not contesting the Bolsheviks' monopoly of political power.[23] But in Bukharin's implicit and explicit interpretations, both the NEP and the market ceased to be seen as tactical retreats; they were good strategy for the entire "transition period," if not longer. Moreover, they now became programmatic principles for the construction of socialism. At this juncture, his conception of markets appeared to be particularly "modern." He proclaimed: "We believed that it was possible to destroy the market relations by one stroke and immediately. It turned out that we shall reach socialism by no other ways than through market relations."[24] This meant for him that victory of socialist economic agencies over private merchants and entrepreneurs, as well as of socialist cooperatives in the countryside over kulak cooperatives, had to be achieved in open competition in the marketplace.

But this idea implied something more. There was a note of distrust of state monopolies, which was reinforced by the negative phenomena in the development of state enterprises whenever they were granted a privileged monopolistic position. Such a position was often justified on the grounds of the common identification of "state" with "socialist"; but Bukharin felt that monopolies tended toward bureaucratization, inefficiency, and the exhibition of phenomena of what he called "monopolistic putrefaction."[25] For him competition in the markets was a sure remedy against such trends. He never fully spelled out a concept of a "socialist market." If he had, he would have had to admit the preservation of market mechanisms even in a fully developed socialist economy. But he certainly did not need such a revision at this juncture: he could afford to dispense with another politically awkward dotting of an "i." As leader of

[23] Lenin, *Sochineniia*, vol. 45, p. 120.
[24] *Put' k Sotsializmu*, pp. 64–65.
[25] *Bol'shevik*, no. 1 (1925), pp. 43–51; *Partiia i Oppozitsionnyi Blok*, p. 34.

46

the ruling faction first, and as opposition leader next, he insisted upon the preservation of the NEP and its markets. This meant, in any case, that market mechanisms and much that goes with them were here to stay for the whole "transition period" (to socialism), that is, for quite some time. Nobody expected to have socialism in exactly ten years. But the term "socialist market" was used by other Bukharinites and paradoxically by "bourgeois specialists" like L. Yurovsky who was to be prosecuted later for these and related ideas.[26] Bukharin was attacked for having been influenced by such bourgeois sources.

It is quite clear that Bukharin's ideas were often similar to those of the so-called bourgeois specialists. For example, Molotov correctly pointed to the affinity between the ideas of Bukharin and those of Bazarov,[27] although who influenced whom is not always clear and is not very important in this context. The ideas concerning market mechanisms, dynamic equilibrium, and the related ideas of balanced growth were current in the social sciences at that time, and no one of the personalities involved really "invented" them. Bukharin was the first—probably the only party theorist at that time—who insisted on the notion of "dynamic equilibrium" of "social systems," already in his writings in 1920 and in which the influence of A. Bogdanov was apparent. In their writings during the NEP, Groman, Bazarov, and Yurovsky developed these ideas, and Preobrazhensky, in his last article published when still officially in opposition, spoke of "economic equilibrium in the Soviet system."[28] Bazarov, in particular, an excellent economist

[26] Yurovskii expressed ideas similiar to Bukharin's on market mechanisms in *Vestnik Finansov*, no. 12 (1926), p. 17 and *passim*.

[27] In *Bol'shevik*, no. 2 (1930), p. 11.

[28] See Bukharin, *Ekonomika Perekhodnogo Perioda*, pp. 87–88, 81–92, 127–129, and his *Teoria Istoricheskogo Materializma* (Moscow, 1921), where the idea of equilibrium between society and nature and among parts of the social system is discussed in chaps. 5, 6, and 7. Preobrazhensky's article is in *Vestnik Kommunisticheskoi Akademii*, no. 22 (1927), p. 19.

and a man with a good philosophical mind, played a conspicuous role during the NEP years in formulating conceptions on economic development and planning and came nearer than any other top planner to a synthesis between the opposing schools on Russia's economic development, notably between the "geneticists" and the "teleologists." He was outspoken in his belief in central planning by the state and at the same time argued that market categories, economic accounting (*khozraschët*), and the plan were one complex in which state action and checks offered by the prices created on private markets complemented each other. Economic equilibrium and balanced growth were as central to his reasoning[29] as they were to Bukharin's, and he certainly was the intellectual source of many of Bukharin's ideas. In the economics of planning they belonged to the same school of thought.

Thus, in both the social structure and in the economy, Bukharin discerned a tendency toward the formation of temporary equilibria, which were constantly, more or less violently, disrupted and restored. Ideas of this sort led him to endorse the NEP during the years 1924–1926 and to formulate his approach to the problems of Soviet sociopolitical development at that time, an approach quite distinctly "Bukharinist" but not yet a deviation.

From 1927 through 1929, additional ideas emerged from new experiences and strains in the country and the party, and they became interwoven into a new set of Bukharin's theoretical and practical proposals, though with different allies and against another adversary.

[29] On Bazarov and Groman, see A. Erlich, *The Soviet Industrialization Debate* (Cambridge, Mass., 1960), chap. 3; N. Jasny, *Soviet Economists of the Twenties* (Cambridge, Mass., 1972), chap. 6 on Groman and chap. 7 on Bazarov.

CHAPTER THREE

The Program of a Bolshevik Anti-Stalinist

THUS four themes, some of which dated back to the civil war or even to the prerevolutionary period, and which influenced his theory during the NEP, persistently appear in the writings of Bukharin: sometimes hidden and often open distrust of state power and administrative bureaucratic domination, reinforced by the symptoms of "monopolistic suppuration" of state enterprises discernible in the Soviet conditions; a perception of both social and economic systems in terms of a dynamic equilibrium periodically disturbed, especially and unavoidably during revolutionary transition, but subsequently restored during normalization when planned development become possible; the peasantry as neither socialist nor capitalist, and thus really more an ally and less a threat than assumed in many other Leninist formulas; and finally, with confidence stemming from an optimistic view of the peasantry's potential, a strong commitment to NEP forms and market mechanisms. (The NEP form was for Bukharin essentially a socio-economic framework best suited to the construction of a socialist society in a backward country, and probably in many ways for any country.)

These themes remained constant during the next stage of Bukharin's thought, which from 1926 to 1929 evolved into a new, larger program for socialist policies and strategies for development. With regard to industrialization the change in Bukharin's thought was patent and exhibited a more realistic approach to the problem of both accumulation of means and acceleration of industrial growth. Thus, he remedied a blatant weakness of his previous, untenable "accumulation through circulation" theory. A new, more acute awareness of both problems—"the pumping" and the "tempos," to use the Soviet terms of those days—can be documented from numerous texts, especially those published during 1927. His "new look" can be illustrated in a speech of 28 July 1926, where Bukharin declared: "It is absolutely clear that our socialist industry ought to grow not only at the expense of what is produced by the working class inside the state industry itself, but that we also have to pump resources from the nonindustrial reservoir into industry, including some means to be taken from the peasant economy; the peasantry too is obliged to help the state in building the socialist industry. . . ." He then lists the ways through which pumping is undertaken: "taxes, prices of industrial goods, and other incomes. . . ." (In fact, the state began to move more seriously toward an accelerated industrialization in 1926, and Bukharin's words expressed an awareness of this new practice.) But he added a significant qualification: "But the whole problem amounts to answering the question *how much* is to be taken from the peasantry for the purpose of building this industry."[1]

Once the principle of enhanced accumulation at the expense of peasants was accepted, it seemed essential to Bukharin to state the ways, methods, and limits of doing so. He accepted the industrial thrust as indispensable but constantly urged caution and the exercise of self-control by the state in this sensitive and dangerous sphere. As the predominant tone of Bukharin's developmental strategies, this approach found its expression first in the very balanced and considered industrialization policy recommended by the Fifteenth Party Congress in December 1927 and later in the "Notes of an Economist" published nine months after the Congress. Before and during the Congress, these strictures were directed against a supposed tendency on the Left to

[1] N. Bukharin, *Partia i Oppozitsionnyi Blok* (Leningrad, 1926), p. 38.

loot the peasants indiscriminately—an accusation that was, as can be amply documented, incorrect. In fact, very early in 1928, if not earlier, Bukharin realized that it was a leading group of the Politbureau rather than the demoted Trotskyists who displayed an eagerness for a head-on clash, which might, as he saw it, prove disastrous. Anticipating correctly the dangers of an overzealous "big drive," he and his associates managed to make the Congress adopt a resolution, couched in very general terms at this stage, that recommended the strategy of aiming at "a long run speedy rate of growth, rather than a maximum rate for the very next year. . . ." This document essentially warned against an overemphasis on heavy industry and stressed the development of light industries, which could serve not only as providers of consumer goods but also as a good source of accumulation for the benefit of further growth. In addition, small industries and the traditional handicrafts (*kustarnichestvo*) were encouraged, as convenient sources of supplies capable of mitigating shortages arising during a period of industrial expansion when resources became tied up in factory construction. The Congress' resolution lucidly warned against overinvestment—the danger of waste through unnecessary dispersal of means and bigness—and strongly emphasized the need to watch the market equilibrium. The priority to be given to heavy industry and the resulting stringencies and hardships were now better understood and expected, and provided Bukharin with the incentive to work out methods, to urge measures calculated to smooth crisis phenomena and strains, and to soften the political repercussions of the new line—with the overriding purpose of steering development to avoid too deep a split in the relations between the masses and the state.[2]

[2] The decisions of this Congress are in *KPSS v Rezoliutsiiakh i Resheniakh S'ezdov*, 2 (7th ed., Moscow, 1957), p. 454. Bukharin explained this line in a precongress speech published as "Partiia i Oppozitsiia na Poroge 15-togo part-s'ezda," which included his "new look"—a more radical anti-kulak and anti-nepmen stand, but he asked

51

He expanded these concepts into a full-fledged programmatic statement for balanced industrial development of Russia in his remarkable article, "Notes of an Economist."[3] Here, instead of the previous overcautious "snail's-pace" approach, so vulnerable to arguments of any "industrializer," he cogently argued for a high and steady rate of growth, for which today's term "optimal" would be appropriate. But he categorically rejected the emphasis on speed under the slogan "tempos decide everything," the unlimited squeezing of resources, and the one-sided concentration on heavy industry with utter disregard for other interests. For him neither "a unilateral interest in accumulation in a given lapse of time [nor] a unilateral interest in consumption" could help to shape correct strategies of growth.

In the conditions prevailing toward the end of 1928, Bukharin felt that there was no point in putting an even greater strain on the national economy by accelerating the rate of growth already achieved. In his opinion, this would cause disruption and become self-defeating, because a limit already existed and the Soviet economy was approaching it. The "tempos" achieved in 1928 were excellent—the rate of industrial growth was about 20 percent—and the problem consisted of devising methods for preserving this achievement. At a party meeting in 1928, the proceedings of which remained unpublished until 1946, Bukharin underlined his acceptance of a preferential treatment of heavy industry and of ambitious growth targets. But according to him, the upper limits had already been reached and "if

---

for nothing harsher than additional controls and taxation. This speech is included in *V Zashchitu Proletarskoi Revoliutsii* (Moscow, 1928), pp. 201–260, esp. pp. 210–215, 225. On the Bukharinist inspiration of the industrialization policies of the Congress, see A. Erlich, *The Soviet Industrialization Debate* (Cambridge, Mass., 1960), p. 87. See also "The Bukharin School Readjusts Its Views," ibid., pp. 78–89.

[3] "Zametki Ekonomista," *Pravda*, 30 September 1928. Much of the subsequent account is based on this article and will not be cited hereafter unless other sources are brought in.

somebody proposed now," he told the meeting, "to double the tempos, this would be a policy of madmen. . . ."[4]

This brought him the opprobrium of being an "enemy of industrialization," but it was clear that what he (and Rykov) clamored against were unattainable, therefore spurious "tempos," which would result, he felt, in enormous cost and finally in diminishing returns. This was an important, historically vindicated insight. A high rate of industrial development was necessary, heavy industry was an obvious and requisite priority, and the seizure of some peasants' resources was unavoidable. However, for Bukharin such measures were not complete in themselves, and it was necessary to implement them by devising actual policies. The question of "how much" resources and effort were to be expended on each of these objectives was a crucial and integral part of industrial development, which had to be resolved as thoughtfully as possible, by using all the scientific tools available. The problem of "tempos" was a case in point.

A very urgent political task consisted of stemming the transformation of "tempos" into an uncontrollable bogey. Rykov, Bukharin's ally, who engaged in numerous battles with overenthusiastic colleagues, stated quite bluntly: "We should not . . . create a fetish out of the tempos." In November 1928, he argued before the Plenum of the Central Committee: "It is incorrect to think that there is some law of the

---

[4] Quoted by Bogushevsky in Gorky, et al., eds., *Almanakh Vos'moi, god vosemnadsatyi* (Moscow, 1935), p. 473. The gross industrial output (in the "census industry") was expected by the control figures of the Gosplan to grow in 1927–1928 by 17.3 percent. The official fulfillment figure claimed 21.6 percent. The corresponding figures for the sole state industry were 13.4 percent (planned) and 16.9 percent (achieved). See *Kontrol'nye Tsifry Narodnogo Khoziaistva SSSR, 1928–1929 God* (Moscow, 1929), p. 25. Despite his anti-Bukharinist zeal Bogushevsky went on to quote the following from the same speech by Bukharin: "But we should not by any means cease to continue advancing our industrial construction with the same speed."

whole transition period according to which the tempo should constantly grow, or at least be kept on the same level year after year." When circumstances warrant, it is quite admissible "to lower the curve of investments." He warned that recklessness in this field might be disastrous and just "naked arithmetic." Pressing for ever-growing rates of budgetary allowances for industry was not sound policy.

Rykov feared that policies based upon "naked arithmetic" were ominous for the country since the objective of his opponents was to double the annual investment in capital construction and to reach an annual output growth rate of 30 percent. Such goals had been enunciated by Kuibyshev, a Politbureau member and head of the Gosplan.[5] However, for Bukharin such an approach was folly indeed, for he maintained that when dealing with complex matters of this sort the politician and planner should think in terms of correlations and proportions in the economic system as a whole in which all parts are interrelated. For example, it was impossible to base the taxation of peasants on the principle of "the more the better" without realizing that this would lead to the stagnation of agriculture, which, in turn, would create great difficulties for constant economic growth in the long run. In the final analysis, some accumulation must be allowed to occur in agriculture, in the very interests of industry itself.[6]

The same type of "balanced" approach was applicable to light industries in the developmental strategy. Here crude decisions in favor of a priority target could not replace the search for "the most favorable correlation" between the sectors of heavy and light industry, a goal recommended by

[5] Rykov is quoted in F. Vaganov, *Pravyi Uklon v VKP(b) i Ego Razgrom, 1928–1930* (Moscow, 1970), pp. 97–98; Kuibyshev is quoted from *Saratovskaia Partyinaia Organizatsiia v Period Nastuplenia Sotsializma po Vsemu Frontu* (Saratov, 1961), p. 155.

[6] Cf. Vaganov, *Pravyi Uklon*, p. 118, who brings another quotation from the party archives where Bukharin warned against disappointments awaiting industrialization if agriculture was not allowed some growth.

the Fifteenth Congress. Bukharin continued to ask: "Does everything, or almost, have to be invested in heavy industry —however desirable its growth? Will the desirable economic growth be achieved in fact by maximum investments in a short span of time?"

He advanced two reasons why such attitudes were erroneous. First, he believed that there was in the national income a ceiling for the share of accumulation and investments at the expense of consumption, and that when this ceiling was reached "overinvestment" set in; further acceleration would be followed by diminishing returns in terms of the growth of industry and of national income, and eventually would produce a great deal of waste. This idea was later elaborated by scholars in light of experience and theory.[7]

Second, the prescription concerning investment consisted of avoiding unnecessary dispersal of the "investment front." In 1927 Bukharin had already discerned the tendency toward such an "excessively dispersed front." For a long time, new building sites swallowed and froze enormous sums. Many of these projects dragged on because of the inability to do so much simultaneously. And he predicted that this "[would] not be accompanied by real growth" because many works already begun would be either constantly postponed, some even entirely abandoned, and, in any case, they would be inefficiently planned because of haste; at the same time many branches of the economy that needed resources would be starved for them. Such a policy contributed to the "goods famine," which had already become intolerable in 1928.

The negative results of overinvestment that Bukharin observed at the very beginning of the Five-Year Plan continued to manifest themselves more strongly in numerous

[7] For some modern Soviet studies on "ceilings" to the general norm of accumulation, see N. Pankratova (chap. 8) and V. Maevsky, Iu. Selivanov (chap. 9) in A. Notkin, ed., *Faktory Ekonomicheskogo Razvitiia SSSR* (Moscow, 1970).

ways during the next years and to plague the Soviet economy for decades. An unbalanced investment policy was creating a tangle of difficulties for the Soviet economy, and today's economic reforms have not yet managed to extricate the country from this inheritance.

Many of the pitfalls and incorrect answers in an enterprise of such magnitude could not be avoided, especially at the beginning of hasty industrializing and planning. But the refusal to ask the correct questions and to see the pitfalls were fatal. Bukharin's advice, like that of others, was rejected. He knew that many high-level decisions were made without any consideration of their repercussions and multiple effects throughout the economy. Thus he urged the strengthening of the role of science in economic planning and policy making and the study and mastery of management methods. He stated: "We shall win with the help of scientific economic management, or we shall not win at all." The art of "managing competently" (*kul'turno upravliat'*) was needed, especially at the highest level.[8]

Bukharin's ideas about scientific management and planning as well as those about the science of organization and the planning of science, fields to which he devoted his attention after he had been ousted from positions of political importance and to which he contributed pioneering concepts, were mostly neglected and abandoned sometime during the 1930s with the greatest prejudice to Soviet development. However, they were to become important once again in the 1960s.

Planning and the Market

Bukharin also said much about the specific activity of planning a national economy as a whole, an immensely complex activity on which the Soviet Union was then proudly embarking. The same considerations that guided him in for-

[8] "Lenin i Zadachi Nauki," *Pravda*, 20 January 1929. The Russian use of *kul'turno* is untranslatable. It denotes a way of behaving or of doing things that befits literate people.

mulating his approach to the problem of "tempos," as against what would become a "tempopathology," inspired his approach to the premises of general planning. He believed in the superiority of planning but did not think, as propaganda argued, that a planned economy was *ipso facto* superior to the unplanned (or less planned) economy. Planning, in its infancy—and in a country in the throes of a crisis—could ill afford to boast as yet. Everything depended on the quality of the plan and on its implementation. In a strongly centralized state, this powerful tool, if used incorrectly, could be potentially harmful.

Thus he often emphasized the limitations of a well-reasoned plan and the deleterious results of an ill-conceived one. Damages and chaos caused by incompetent but powerful planners could cause havoc worse than the unplanned spontaneity of capitalism. If planners ignored important correlations among areas and sectors of the economy for too long, "the crudest violation of basic proportions" could be committed by the state. In January 1929 he added: "With an incorrect policy the cost of the process as a whole might be no less than the cost of capitalist anarchy. . . ."[9]

Bukharin, then, correctly predicted the result of sloppy and inaccurate planning and of unbridled growth mindless of cost. For him planning was too important a function to be left to arbitrary, empirical guesswork. It had to be taken seriously and transformed "into a special applied science."[10] But he felt that such an approach had little chance to develop in a system that accumulates enormous power in the apex of a bureaucratic machinery with uncontrollable rulers at the top. Hence he constantly worried about the institutional side of the whole process. Overcentralization seemed to him to damage the very planning process, economic development as a whole, and its political aspects. The "Notes of an Economist" sounded the alarm on this crucial topic: "We have already overcentralized quite a bit!" and

[9] *Ibid.*   [10] *Ibid.*

57

he felt that this process deprived the system of many possibilities and energies. Such a regime would tend to indulge in whimsical utopias or narrow empiricism. Therefore, the whole system was in for immense trouble. Bukharin believed that he saw the signs of such planning already in the crisis-laden year 1928. According to him, the crisis was caused by a set of disproportions among basic branches of national economy, strongly aggravated by ill-conceived policies. One deficiency in planning, bound to become a constant practice (and even today still strongly criticized in the same terms as Bukharin's), consisted of allowing for a discrepancy between targets and resources. It seemed ludicrous to Bukharin that the current "control figures" predicted—therefore, in a sense, planned—a 20 percent gap between the building targets and the production of the necessary iron. Furthermore, he derided the idea that one could plan a number of houses without planning an adequate number of bricks. A plan "has to take into account real beams and iron, and not mythical ones. . . ." It looked very simple to him: "One does not build today's factories with future bricks."

Coordination among the various branches of the economy and the internal coherence of a plan were necessary to bring about the goals of the program. Planning should strive "to achieve as correct correlations of the basic elements of the national economy as possible (to balance them). . . ." This prescription retained its popularity among planners in the 1960s, as did the idea, strongly recommended by Bukharin, of the so-called balance of the national economy. From this idea grew the modern input-output table, a useful tool for better understanding economic interrelationships and for more precise planning. A modern Soviet scholar considers it "the most important tool for fixing tempos and proportions of the national economy."[11] The discontinuance of research and work on scien-

[11] See A. Efimov, regretting the abandoning of work on such "balance," in the book he edited, *Ekonomicheskoe Planirovanie v*

58

tific planning in the early 1930s meant that Soviet planning proceeded for a quarter of a century without a serious methodology for fixing its main targets.

Still, even when the plan possessed internal consistency on paper, such consistency was lacking in the process of its implementation; an overambitious claim to plan too much would lead, as it did, to a system of minutely detailed orders, with a potential for fettering people rather than really mastering essential trends. Anticipating these events, Bukharin's earlier assumption about reaching socialism "through market relations" and his planning concepts combined into a new view on the scope of programming. Market forces and relations, as well as other spontaneous factors outside economics, made an ideal, imperative plan impossible. Thus a plan, if it were to be effective, should be flexible enough to depart from the planners' objectives but should be adequately correlated with the best possible prediction of the inevitable inflections that would be introduced by market forces. In Bukharin's term the outcome of the plan should and would be corrected by "the spontaneous results" of social development, which could not be eliminated at this stage, if ever.

Such reasoning obviously corresponded to the realities of the NEP, but implied a long-term problem quite independent of the NEP framework. A combination of state action through plans and of "spontaneity," whatever forms both factors might assume in the future, was here to stay, and this was why Bukharin fought with such insistence to preserve the NEP. He believed that the basic traits of the NEP would remain valid for a long time, and that attempts to skip such a stage would be fatal. Therefore, the preservation of the NEP and market relations as an indispensable part of it, especially with regard to the peasants, became the central political point in a document, which he, Rykov,

---

SSSR (Moscow, 1967), p. 133; A. Nove regretted this too in *An Economic History of the USSR* (London, 1969), p. 134.

and Tomsky defended at an enlarged Politbureau meeting on 9 February 1929 and before the Central Committee in April of the same year. During these sessions, the trio argued in favor of market links and fought bitterly the new concept of the majority, the so-called "production link" with the peasants. Tomsky derided "these new forms of alliance with peasants. . . . There is nothing new here, but extraordinary [coercive] measures and rationing cards." And Bukharin opposed the new line as "monstrously unilateral." "The form of market relations," he insisted, "should remain for years the decisive form of economic relations." Some of the leaders, so the Central Committee heard from him, "blatantly overestimate the possibilities of influencing the peasant masses without market relations." Rykov supported this argument by pointing out that grain would have to be bought even from *kolkhozy*.

The NEP was a convenient framework for industrializing the country and the Bukharinian platform tried to avert the leap "into some further phase of economic development," which clearly could not be achieved in a five-year plan. For Bukharin a mixed economy was a long-term program. Hence a short-term project should not undermine it. "The five-year plan can be achieved, and should be achieved on the rails of the NEP."[12]

Ideas on planning reflected this basic viewpoint and quite unsurprisingly, implying an appeal for a more realistic and more sophisticated approach toward planning, the conclusion was reached that: "it [was] wrong to overestimate the planning principle and underestimate spontaneity." This fell within the tendency, best expressed by Bazarov, toward a "mixed plan" in which the ideas of the opposing schools of planning, the "geneticists" and "teleologists," could use-

[12] All the quotations are from the Central Party Archives reported in *16-aia Konferentsiia VKP(b)* (Moscow, 1962), pp. 803, 806. The last quotation, on the five-year plan, is reported in Vaganov, *Pravyi Uklon*, p. 209.

fully meet halfway. Both sides were already moving toward a common understanding—the latter of the realities and stringencies to be reckoned with in the existing pattern as it had been shaped by the past, the former toward the acceptance of the need and right for the planner to aim at shaping proportions in the economy according to some *a priori* principles and objectives. "Bukharin's 'Notes of an Economist' might have provided a platform and political blessing for a search of a planning capable of coming nearer to his dynamic equilibrium."[13]

However, political conditions made this impossible.

Planning and the State

Quite correctly, Bukharin felt that models of growth and ways of planning have an immense impact on the whole institutional setting, in fact, on the outlook of the state. His fear of the might of the modern state was largely evident in his thought from the time he reflected upon imperialism and the state capitalist organization during the war years. "Organized capitalism" was organized by the state, and this factor was powerful enough to help overcome internal anarchy of the market's forces, at least to a large degree, through the tools of organization and planning within the framework of the national state (although rivalry and clashes in the international arena were not lessened by these means).

In "Theory of Organized Chaos" in June 1929, he repeated this opinion and allegedly still defended the same position as late as December 1930, despite the chaos into which the economic crisis had plunged the whole Western world and in face of the ultraradical line of the Comintern, which at that time denied the capitalist countries the very

---

[13] This is the opinion of the Polish economist Cz. Bobrowski, *U Zródel Planowania Socjalistycznego* (Warsaw, 1967), pp. 117–124, and cf. W. Brus, *Ogólne Problemy Funkcjonowania Gospodarki Socjalistycznej* (Warsaw, 1964), pp. 98–101.

possibility of ever achieving a new stabilization.[14] This official line led eventually to the fatal policy of fighting "social-fascism" rather than fascism, with all the well-known and tragic results, especially in Germany.

Curiously enough, Molotov did not accuse Bukharin of hinting at internal Soviet problems in "Theory of Organized Chaos," especially since Bukharin did not attempt to conceal that the "organized chaos" in the West also alluded to the Soviet experience. "The Aesopian language" was not at all difficult to decipher, especially when one knew, as Molotov did, that Bukharin had criticized heavily the organization of the Soviet national economy and the central planners who were leading it on a path fraught with the dangers of disrupting the country's economic life. His conceptions, constantly fed by the shadow of the Leviathan, showed considerable insight into this problem in the Soviet context. His more cautious attitude to the possibilities of planning stemmed from the fear that overambitious plans might result in oppressing too many and suppressing too much. In a strong state planning was the main agency of change (an opinion common to all Bolsheviks). But Bukharin's insight into the complexities of industrialization that a strong-willed government imposed on a backward society led him to emphasize the dangers of such a process. In fact, wholesale statism and the concomitant phenomenon of "overadministering" were becoming reality very quickly. In order to avoid such a course, by favoring the NEP, Bukharin wanted the state to concentrate on what it realistically could do best, and not to engage in an overall drive to crush Russia's "small people"—the craftsmen, small merchants, small industrialists, and small agricultural producers. These social groups, as well as cooperative and governmental small-scale enterprises and services, were not only indis-

[14] This article "Teoria Organizovannoi Bezkhoziaistvennosti" was published in *Pravda*, 30 June 1929. For Molotov's attack against Bukharin's views on "organized capitalism" and for the official view on it, see *Bol'shevik*, no. 3 (1931), p. 20.

pensable but also complementary to industrialization, capable of mitigating current and future tensions generated by the investment effort that was largely directed toward large-scale projects. The neglect, or destruction, of such sectors would deprive the state of useful devices and possibilities for economic maneuvering in a period of strain, and, instead, would lead to the exacerbation of conflicts and crises.[15] The first Five-Year Plan and many subsequent events illustrated just that.

When warning against statism, Bukharin also feared that a sprawling officialdom (*chinovnichestvo*),[16] far from becoming a modern and efficient administration, might well create an obstacle to achieving this goal and would exact a heavy toll. Thus he warned on 12 September 1928 in *Pravda*: "If it [the state] takes too much upon itself, it is forced to create a colossal administrative apparatus." This meant that the premature elimination of "the small people" and their replacement by "*chinovniki*" would beget a swollen, costly, and inefficient apparatus, and "the expenditure for its maintenance [would be] incomparably more significant than the unproductive expenses which appear in consequence of the anarchistic conditions of small scale production. . . ."[17]

These ideas provided a good departure for a serious sociological and political analysis of the Soviet state, in fact, a basis for a genuine political sociology, which eliminated the nonsensical ascription of every unpalatable fact of life to "bourgeois survivals" or to "petit bourgeois pressures." The shape of the Soviet state and the character of its

[15] That the crisis was already here was Bukharin's argument in the "Notes of an Economist." A. Erlich elaborated the point that Bukharin's proposals could have had relaxing effects, in *Industrialization Debate*, pp. 84–89.

[16] *Chin* means grade, hence *chinovnichestvo* for "officialdom" but with a strong pejorative flavor as sum of all the evils bureaucratic inefficiency can cause.

[17] "Politicheskoe Zaveshchanie Lenina," *Pravda*, 24 January 1929.

bureaucracy were not "survivals," but creations of Soviet history, although powerful trends from the past were certainly important factors. Centralization of power in the process of running the national economy and the "administrative" character of the whole process were factors in the Russian environment, quite unprecedented in scope, whereas such important innovations as state ownership of all industrial assets and the transformation of a majority of the urban and a portion of the rural employed into state employees had no equivalents in the Russian past at all.

Brooding over the problems of the Soviet system in the late 1920s and during the 1930s, Bukharin did not need to repeat Lenin's statement that the trouble with "bureaucratization" stemmed from the Soviet government's reemployment of officials who had served the Tsars. It was too simple-minded. The centralized socialist economy, to consider only this crucial factor, created an immense administrative apparatus, and this, in turn, set in motion its own, self-sustaining dynamism. Class origin of the office holders was not the problem here. The sway of paper work over life, routine, and mechanical performance—bureaucratic stereotyping (*uravnilovka*)—was engendered by the way the state was acting and by its inherent tendency to castelike self-containment. Petit bourgeois influence—the other current scapegoat—could not but be a part of the story. All this seemed obvious to Bukharin, but such an analysis had already become heretical since it "slandered" the "dictatorship of the proletariat."[18]

Like all the other party leaders in those days, Bukharin adhered to the thesis of the "dictatorship of the proletariat" but was concerned with securing the eventual reduction of state power in the process of growing social development—an outcome promised repeatedly by every Bolshevik Party

[18] Most of the passage uses Bukharin's own words. The source is an attack against him by a former partisan E. Pashukanis, in *Sovetskaia Iustitsiia*, no. 17 (1934), p. 3. Pashukanis quoted Bukharin's article in *Izvestiia*, 1934, which could not be located.

program. But Bukharin really meant it, and this prompted him to insist on this slogan, which he took from Lenin's last writings: "no third revolution" in the conditions of Soviet power. Instead, according to him, the party leadership was embarking in 1928 on a course that could not be implemented without mass terror. Some pressures and elements of coercion were naturally inherent and unavoidable in the Soviet condition; Bukharin, an old Bolshevik, however "soft," would not forsake all use of force. But he felt that what had now been proposed was something different in kind, scope, and dimension. Molotov's attack in November 1929 before the Central Committee Plenum reveals Bukharin's meaning: ". . . they [the Right] cast a shadow on the party by accusing it of building socialism through policies of extraordinary measures, i.e. through a policy of administrative repression."

The accusation made by Bukharin, together with Rykov and Tomsky, which Molotov quoted in this context and violently denied, was launched against the application of "a system of extraordinary measures" as a long-term policy, based on mass coercion as its main method.[19]

The charge was rebutted then, as it still is by conservative writers today. At the end of 1929, Bukharin was already witnessing what it meant to enter the new Stalinist policy "through the gate of extraordinary measures." First, it led to an ever-expanding crisis in agriculture, with all the dire effects he had anticipated. The NEP was finished—"extraordinary measures are incompatible with NEP," he clamored at the Central Committee in April 1929, well in the spirit of *"Put' k Sotsializmu . . ." (The Road to Socialism and the Worker-Peasant Alliance)*, which demanded legality in all action and elimination of administrative arbitrariness, "be it revolutionary arbitrariness." As the Five-Year Plan unfolded, it was Vyshinsky, the new prophet of the Stalinist period, who reminded Bukharin of his 1926 text and all the "opportunism" involved in it, and who explained

[19] Molotov, *Bol'shevik*, no. 2 (1930), p. 17.

that "revolutionary legality" does not contradict but incorporates "revolutionary arbitrariness."[20]

For Bukharin, here was the crux of the matter. He wanted no revolution, no new civil war. Predominantly oppressive administrative methods could only lead to the creation of an *oppressive system*. This was why he fought for reasonable rates of growth, flexible methods of planning, including the question of "how much" accumulation and investment, and his peasant policies. During a closed session of the Politbureau in February 1929, Bukharin accused the leadership of installing a system of "a military feudal exploitation of the peasantry."[21] With this characterization he dramatized the problem and stressed the meaning of his appeal to remember and to achieve the "commune state" as outlined in "Notes of an Economist" and in "Lenin's Political Testament." This concept was taken from the utopian legacy of Marx and apparently flourished in revolutionary periods and among leaders of the opposition. In the prevailing context, however, such a position had a more practical political meaning. It summarized in an apparently quite orthodox terminology Bukharin's economic and political counterprogram: less centralization, more party democracy, more rationality and scientific approach to problems, no mass coercion, less reliance on strictly administrative state measures, priority to gradualism and persuasion.

Bukharin's critics correctly evaluated his use of "commune state" as a counterprogram for democratization, and they criticized him for proposing it as an alternative to the Soviet state.[22] But Bukharin never denied this concept that

[20] For a modern defense of "the extraordinary measures" see Vaganov, *Pravyi Uklon*, pp. 126–128. Vyshinskii is quoted here from *Sovetskaia Iustitsiia*, no. 19 (1932), p. 7, and he disputes Bukharin's passage in *Put' k Sotsializmu i Raboche-Krestianskii Soiuz* (Moscow, 1926), p. 79.

[21] Quoted by Rudzutak, *16-tyi S'ezd VKP(b), Stenotchet* (Moscow, 1930), p. 201.

[22] See, for example, the article by Ia. Berman, "Gosudarstvo-Kommuna," *Sovetskoe Gosudarstvo i Pravo*, nos. 5–6 (1930). Berman

inspired many Bolsheviks when the goals of the Bolshevik Revolution were becoming undermined.

Later, after several ritual recantations and although he had been temporarily readmitted to some measure of prominence but not power, Bukharin privately but not secretly continued to brood and dream of the destiny and needs of Soviet Russia. For the most part, sources about this period are lacking, and it is necessary to rely almost completely on the recollections of Borys Nicolaevsky about his conversations with Bukharin in the spring of 1936. According to Nicolaevsky, external affairs, the growing national-socialist danger, played an important role in Bukharin's thinking, and he believed it was crucial for the Soviet system to differentiate itself sufficiently from the Nazi state in order to become a real alternative for both Russians and other nations. The emphasis on the humanist value of socialism was indispensable, but this could not be effective without institutional changes in the conduct of the Soviet state. It seemed to him necessary to authorize a second party, composed predominantly of intellectuals who would be allowed to criticize the ruling party from the standpoint of general socialist principles. Presumably, Bukharin obtained the approval of Pavlov and Gorky for this project, and much of their common thinking on these topics was incorporated in the hopes and ideas expressed in the Soviet constitution of 1936. Nicolaevsky attributes the authorship of most of the constitution's text to Bukharin.[23]

Although no opponent of dictatorship, Bukharin was eager to see it perform only as a transition measure, which

---

spoke to a conference of "Marxist state-theorists." Dissertations on the "withering away of the state" are in full conformity with accepted party doctrine, today as well as 40 years ago, but they can serve also for the purpose of a quite genuine critique of an ubiquitous state machinery.

[23] B. Nicolaevsky, *Power and the Soviet Elite*, ed. J. Zagoria (London, 1966), p. 22.

would dissolve into a socialist community. But neither a "military-feudal exploitation of the peasantry" nor the rigors of "rapid socialism" could hasten the achievement of this goal. Socialism, if its humanist side were neglected for too long, could be lost entirely. No doubt, Bukharin reflected upon the metamorphosis of temporary and emergency measures into permanent ones and of new rulers accepting them as just routine.

The Convergence of Right and Left

When Bukharin fought the Left and helped Stalin to suppress them, he unwittingly contributed to the process of the party's metamorphosis and at the same time to his own demise. During 1928 and 1929, as he became engaged in a very different struggle in the course of which he developed his new program, he regained his lucidity. However, the Left was still blind to any danger from Stalin. A few months before Bukharin's rather bold visit to Kamenev to inform the Left of Stalin's plans and to offer them an alliance, Trotsky still saw the main danger on the Right. For him the Right was "a transmitting apparatus for the pressure of non-proletarian classes on the working class."[24] This was hardly different from the epithet "agent of kulaks," which soon became the official image of Bukharin. The same clichés prompted the Left to refuse Bukharin's offer, against Trotsky's advice who, in September of the same year, after having learned about the Bukharin-Kamenev talks, was for a moment inclined to strike a limited bargain with the Right. But he did not change his basic view about the "main danger," as Deutscher wrote, stressing that the Right repaid the Left with the same sentiments.[25] Since Stalin's left turn

[24] L. Trotsky, "What Now?" in *Third International After Lenin* (New York, 1951), p. 289

[25] I. Deutscher, *The Prophet Outcast* (London, 1963), pp. 448–450. It is true that the Right was afraid of the Left, but this has to be qualified by the new fact that Bukharin now decided with considerable risk to himself to approach Kamenev and to propose to the Left

in the spring of 1928, the Left, in fact, had expected a reconciliation with Stalin because they saw in his line the victory of their own views. Trotsky endorsed the support for Stalin, but very soon doubts about the very character of the new line led him to warn his followers that their support should be coupled with sharp criticism. He reasoned that their own left course did not at all imply as its main component brutal administrative pressure against the peasants.[26] This was the frame of mind that led him to envisage some limited alliance with the Right—limited indeed because his opinion of Bukharin's "Notes of an Economist" was as contemptuous as was Stalin's. But in a matter of months the bulk of his troops abandoned Trotsky and rallied to Stalin to save the revolution from the dreadful rightists, although most of them were promptly disappointed. Neither the Left militants nor their leader realized at that time that the program elaborated by Bukharin during his fight against Stalin was to become their own. The rightist dangers against which they were fighting were phantoms; Bukharin, paradoxical as this may sound, expressed at this stage better than anybody else the prospective common opinion of both the Left and the Right. But the quarrels of the past made both sides unaware of this basic convergence, and they continued to fight each other fiercely at a time when the right-wing program of 1928–1929 was the only counterprogram and alternative to Stalin's, which represented both wings inside the party.

Trotsky (Deutscher, too) never realized or at least never acknowledged that since the fall of 1928 he had been moving steadily toward a line that Bukharin formulated in

an alliance against Stalin. Deutscher's contention that the Right "decided not to fight Stalin because they were afraid of Stalin striking a bargain with the Left" assumed correctly the existence of these kinds of fears but incorrectly stated that the Right "decided not to fight" (*ibid.*). Bukharin, Rykov, and Tomsky resisted for over a year and became discouraged only after having been defeated.

[26] *Ibid.*, p. 447.

"Notes of an Economist" and other texts. The insight and correct anticipation of events was now Bukharin's.

In February 1930 Trotsky, evaluating Russia's new collectivization and industrialization course, emphasized that the Left opposition never demanded nor expected the liquidation of classes in five years but viewed the disappearance of classes as a long-term process within the framework of a victorious world revolution. Also, the Left did not want to slash any more of the kulak's income than was necessary for industrialization. An administrative liquidation, as undertaken by Stalin, was never their intention.[27]

The accusations ascribing sinister designs to the Left were unwarranted. But curiously enough, Trotsky's ever-growing criticism of Stalin's version of the "Left line" made him and other critics from his camp, such as Rakovsky, feel uneasy: were they not now opposing Stalin from the right?[28]

During 1930 Trotsky's proposals for both internal and international policies became entirely indistinguishable from the Bukharin line. On international affairs, especially on Comintern's attitude toward German fascism, Trotsky pressed hard, with great lucidity, for a revision of the fatal "third period" with its ultraleftist course, and demanded a united front with the Social Democrats against the Nazis—a "Bukharinist heresy" of long standing, very much vilified by official spokesmen.[29] Since the early 1930s, Trotsky's criticisms of internal policies had grown more "Bukharinist" every month: the "tempos" of industrial growth, he claimed,

[27] *Biulleten' Oppozitsii*, no. 9 (1930), p. 6. This is a periodical Trotsky edited after having been exiled from the Soviet Union.

[28] Deutscher described this embarrassment of Trotsky when he criticized Stalin's ultra-Leftist "third period," *The Prophet Outcast*, p. 42. But the same would apply to a growing body of Trotsky's criticism and counterproposals on other aspects of Soviet policies.

[29] Molotov accused Bukharin in wanting a united front with the Social Democrats. See Molotov's speech to the Central Committee in December 1930, *Bol'shevik*, no. 3 (1931), p. 20. He was talking there about an old Bukharinist sin.

were too quick, the collectivization drive was folly, the standard of living of both workers and peasants had to be improved, and so on. Soon he demanded that "dekulakization" and the whole adventurous offensive be stopped, forced collectivization discontinued, and the whole program of industrialization reformulated. His prescriptions recommended caution, realistic targets, refusal of orientation on full autarchy, the need to appeal to workers for collaboration and participation—instead of stifling their initiative by heavy pressures.[30] The leadership's panic, leading to the liquidation of the NEP rather than just retouching it where necessary, was strongly criticized. A text written in 1932 is even more explicit. In that year, the readmission of *kolkhoz* markets and other signs of retreat by the government were proof for Trotsky that "the correct, economically sound collectivization should have led not to the jettisoning of the NEP, but rather to a gradual transformation of its methods."[31] In the same article Trotsky strongly endorsed the market mechanisms as being indispensable during the transition period. This was probably the first time since his exile that he recommended this method in such a categorical form. His overall formulation of policies to be applied during the transition period (he would not listen to official claims that the Soviet Union was already in a directly socialist stage of its development) primarily included state planning, market mechanisms, and Soviet democracy.[32] In addition the refusal to accept mass coercion as a method of building socialism (especially as a method of driving peasants into *kolkhozy*), the critique of "supertempos," advice to "retreat" coupled with appeals for caution and rationality, and the categorical demand to cooperate with social democracy against nazism—constitute the complete "restatement" of Bukharin's "rightist platform" of 1928–1929.

If Trotsky adopted ideas from "Bukharinism," Bukharin

[30] These can be found in *Biulleten' Oppozitsii*, no. 9 (1930), pp. 1–8, no. 10 (1930), pp. 2–7, and no. 20 (1931), pp. 13–15.

[31] *Ibid.*, no. 3 (1932), p. 9.   [32] *Ibid.*

borrowed concepts from "Trotskyism." In April 1929, in a secret resolution against Bukharin (published many years later and therefore unknown to Trotsky), the Central Committee officially argued: "Bukharin's declaration claiming that we do not have intraparty democracy, that the party becomes bureaucratized, that party secretaries are not elected . . . that the current party regime became unbearable, is completely untrue and utterly false."

This critique of Bukharin, which sounds today so much like a self-indictment by the party's leadership, was followed by the characteristic statement: "It is worth noticing that Bukharin slid here into Trotsky's positions, as expressed in the latter's notorious '8 October 1923' letter to the Central Committee—and Bukharin in fact means what Trotsky meant then—the freedom of groups and factions in the party."[33] The party's solemn denials were in fact confessions, and this was why they remained unpublished at that time. But the accusation of sliding over to Trotsky's position on this point was correct. Stalin's general assumption, which he proclaimed with growing obstinacy, that Left and Right were basically the same proved a better judgment than the two had of themselves. He therefore found it necessary to destroy them as a common "criminal conspiracy."

[33] *KPSS v Rezoliutsiiakh i Resheniiakh S'ezdov* (7th ed., Moscow, 1957), p. 561.

CHAPTER FOUR

Models in Soviet History: "War Communism" and the NEP

In order to gain a better insight into the historical record with a view of its significance for our general theme, it is important to review the main stages of Soviet history in a more systematic way, with the more personal aspects receding somewhat into the background and the impersonal ones coming to the fore.

Although relatively short, Soviet history displays considerable variety, not only because of the intensity of drama and flow of events but also because of its basic traits, which form a sequence of distinct socio-political models. The party monopoly of political power, its declared aim of the reconstruction, socialization, and nationalization of some key sectors in national economy were, to be sure, constant throughout the existence of the Soviet state. Otherwise, such essential features of socio-economic systems as the scope of the state sector, the relations between it and private sectors or those between the state and social classes, the scope for admitted or tolerated market and monetary mechanisms, the character of economic and noneconomic incentives and their interrelation, and finally, the degree of cultural plurality as well as scholarly and even political debate outside and inside the party were variables which combined into different patterns or "models."

Before the revolution the Bolsheviks, with their elaborate ideology, might not have been aware of how crude and underdeveloped their notions were about the kind of society and economy they were going to build once in power. But they soon discovered this deficiency. Lenin even frankly acknowledged it. At the same time, some of their preconceived ideas, inspired by Marx and other socialist writers, influenced them so deeply that the smaller their experience in and the scantier their ideas about practical affairs, the more stubborn their devotion to basic precepts, which seemed to them self-evident. Keeping this in mind, it is fascinating to observe the constant clash of illusion and fact, of the sense of reality and commitment to ideology that shaped Bolshevik policies in quickly changing circumstances.

Except for the first, the changing models were never preceded by any theory or insight into the character of the next phase. Nevertheless they astonishingly display a certain repetitiveness of basic traits, a kind of circularity.

The period that Maurice Dobb treated as "the first eight months"[1] is too short to allow any extensive conclusions about the theory and practice involved in the policies of Lenin's government at that stage. The theory was quite rudimentary. Lenin vaguely formulated it in an article written in September 1917 and referred to it in the spring of 1918 to justify his current policies against the criticisms of the Left, then headed by Bukharin.[2] The Left pressed for immediate measures of large-scale nationalization and thus, in the perspective, for a direct and swift transition to socialism.

Lenin reacted strongly in tone, although not too vigorously in argument; characteristically, he admitted that the failure to follow large-scale nationalization was "a retreat" from current party expectations (later, in 1921, he reacted similarly); still, he argued in 1918, this was not just a retreat but rather a return to previous conceptions, formu-

[1] M. Dobb, *Soviet Economic Development Since 1917* (rev. ed., New York, 1966).

[2] Lenin, *Sochineniia*, vol. 34, pp. 151–159, and vol. 36, pp. 283–314. For these two articles in English, entitled, respectively, "The Impending Catastrophe and How to Combat It" and "Left-Wing's Childishness and the Petty Bourgeois Mentality," see *Collected Works*, vol. 27 (4th ed., Moscow, 1960–1969), 1965.

lated in the September 1917 article. Lenin already used the term "state capitalism" to describe the strategies for achieving socialism under a Soviet government and the transition system it intended to create.

Many party members were bewildered by the use of such a term to designate the system that they would be building, but Lenin was stubborn enough to stick to this term for some time and to return to it later at the introduction of the NEP.

In Lenin's view during the first months of his government, a full transition to socialism was a matter of at least a generation, if not longer; the main difficulty—the main enemy of socialism—was the chaotic, elemental petit bourgeois forces of this backward country. He repeated this diagnosis about the "main enemy" often enough, although it did not seem to accord very well with the parallel slogans about the alliance he wanted to strike with the poor peasantry, itself a segment of the forces of chaos. But another argument was even less reconcilable with the alliance—indeed, it was a contradiction. The only progressive forces in Russia—so ran the argument—were those who possessed "organization capacity on the scale of millions" and habits and knowledge of accounting and distributing goods on a scale of a national economy. Obviously, only capitalists and their organizers were such people; it was therefore necessary to stop nationalizing, to stop persecuting capitalists, and to begin collaborating with them. Big capital could be a progressive ally. Therefore "workers control" in factories should stop short of becoming actual worker management and even, one would surmise, from declaring formal ownership of the enterprises.

At the factory level, "workers control" meant close scrutiny, and at the national level this would be magnified by the workers state, but such an arrangement, although under a socialist government, could not be called otherwise than "state capitalism." He taunted the too impetuous leftists such as Bukharin and Osinsky, promoters of the counter-

75

idea of "state socialism," that such "state capitalism," if it could be achieved, would constitute enormous progress for Soviet Russia.

It is not difficult to understand Lenin's motives in launching this concept. Socialism by shortcuts was not his idea then—not yet—and revolutions abroad seemed at arms reach. Capitalists therefore might be willing, he hoped, to collaborate with the Soviet government, and this collaboration would not only help Russia to progress but also would preserve the general Marxist scheme according to which socialism could only follow a developed capitalist economy. Lenin was therefore ready to limit socialist vistas, provided control rested firmly in the hands of a socialist government, capable of securing the next stage, once conditions matured for it. But otherwise he felt that both the doctrine and control of the historical process would be synchronized more if something like capitalism did in fact develop first—with capitalist help, to be sure—to be followed by socialism later in the most "regular" way.[3] However, the capitalists did not cooperate, and the whole scheme failed. It is generally accepted among researchers that the great wave of nationalization did not begin until the outbreak of the civil war in June 1918, and that this course was not intended. A. Nove writes that: "the evidence, though mixed, is still consistent with the intention to maintain a mixed economy for a considerable period."[4]

The character of the state organization and of the economic life under "state capitalism" remains a rather obscure problem. For example, the role of the market forces was not even debated and did not interest Lenin, as he later testified, although there was clearly no intention to eliminate either money or markets.

[3] See R. Lorenz, *Anfänge des bolschevistischen Industrie Politik* (Cologne, 1965).

[4] A. Nove, *An Economic History of the USSR* (London, 1969), p. 54; and see E. H. Carr, *The Bolshevik Revolution, 1917–1923*, 2 (London, 1952), 272.

But in the strains and agonies of the civil war, "state capitalism" soon withered away, and the majority of the party was led to believe that the war economy measures applied during this period offered the shortcut to socialism that had been dubbed a childish "leftist" dream a short while before. The conceptions that evolved during the war were no less astonishing than "state capitalism," and from them a short leap led straight into "war communism."

This new formula had no specific theoretical antecedent in Bolshevik programs that could be quoted to buttress it. It evolved because of the interplay of action imposed by the contingencies of war and the combination of psychological needs of leaders and followers alike engaged in the battle for survival, which only the hope for "utopia" can provide, with a set of vague notions about communism—which had never been thought out seriously and which Marx deliberately left obscure because its establishment was too far in the future.

Nevertheless, "war communism" had far-reaching consequences for the subsequent development of the Soviet system. It was characterized by its concentration on a central task—winning the civil war. The methods used were successful and included the centralization of both production and distribution by the bureaucratic central offices (*glavki*) and the military or militarized administration. In fact, it was a harsh rationing system, characterized by the widespread coercive mobilization of labor into "labor armies," the coercive requisitioning of peasants' produce by armed squads, and the elimination of regular markets (only the black market remained). Additional use of terror both inside and outside the economy paralleled these "administrative" methods.

Although grain commerce, foreign trade, natural resources, and food supplies had been previously monopolized, by the end of 1920 even tiny enterprises were nationalized, especially during the last wave of such drives in that year.

Since economic mechanisms and incentives had been destroyed, the whole system was activated by a combination of coercion and an appeal to enthusiasm and moral commitment, an appeal that had an affinity with the proletarian sense of justice embodied in a few basic principles: equality in the distribution of the food ration to worker and political boss; the *partmaximum* principle—the stipulation that a salary of a ranking party official could not surpass the average salary of a skilled worker; and the actual elimination of money from dealings between the state and its employees, most of the salary being paid in kind and in free services. Thus communications, rents, and so on were declared free. In 1920 preparations were made to abolish money transactions entirely, and decrees were prepared to discontinue the levying of taxes in money, and to scrap the central bank.

Undoubtedly in the "red" camp, many people lived in an atmosphere of heroism and enthusiasm, which could be sustained only by their genuine belief in the already attained higher social system, and the egalitarian spirit which was prevalent in the party and among many of its supporters undeniably boosted morale.

This egalitarian spirit was dampened to some extent by the introduction of a system of single managers in factories to replace the committee system, by a general trend toward increased administrative power, and by a simultaneous weakening in the position of trade unions. Moreover, Moscow dominated local party organizations and supplanted elections with appointments.

But these deviations could be easily explained by arguing that the war had necessitated such measures and that local party organizations, badly undermanned, had urged Moscow to appoint leaders for them, instead of electing them in a democratic way. There was even a stronger sedative for whoever might have had qualms about this or other harsh practices: the belief that something more than the war economy justified them. The term "war communism" implied that the most progressive system on earth was just installed *deus ex machina* by the most expedient, unexpected, but irreversible leap to freedom.

It is puzzling how readers of *State and Revolution* could interpret a centralized, bureaucratic requisition system, based upon *razvërstka* (apportionment), as "communism." Important and maybe obvious psychological strains can be invoked. Additionally Marxist conceptions of market categories should be considered as an important cause for inducing leaders to mistake a war inflation for a genuine harbinger of disappearance of money and monetary incentives in the economic and ethical behavior of people. Soviet writers just after war communism, and indeed Lenin himself at the introduction of the NEP, saw that these beliefs were erroneous. The greatly hailed *razvërstka* seen in 1918–1920 as a method of building socialism caused, as Lenin stated, a defeat more crushing than any that the kulaks, Pilsudski, or other enemies could have inflicted because it precipitated the country into a menacing political and economic crisis.[5]

A short time after the civil war, L. Kritsman, a Bolshevik party organizer and economist, analyzed the methods used during this period in a frank and impassioned critique. For him, centralization and the elimination of money constituted the advent of socialism. But the economy lacked an-

[5] Lenin, *Sochineniia*, vol. 44, pp. 158–159, and compare with a text from 1919, *Sochineniia*, vol. 39, pp. 167, 274, where the same *razvërstka* is presented as the very essence of socialism. This term means: allocation of quotas for distribution and delivery, here quotas of foodstuffs to be requisitioned from peasants. *Razvërstka* became the most hated symbol of communist civil war policies in the eyes of the peasants; curiously, it acquired also a very pejorative meaning in party circles during the NEP, denoting coercive policies. Note also the pejorative term *razvërstochnyi azart*, "lust for requisitioning," for the same kind of policies. For a very good, short description of the "war communism" practice and philosophy including data on the abolition of taxes in cash and the state bank, see A. Aikhenvald, *Sovetskaia Ekonomika* (Moscow, 1927), pp. 216–219.

other attribute of socialism: planning.[6] Whereas in capitalism pricing was the regulator of the economy, in the proletarian economy during that period the regulator amounted to shock methods (*udarnost'*), which he described in the following way: a dearth of products in one sector of the economy prompted the leadership to declare them shock targets (*udarnye*) and to give them top priority.[7] While production of the deficient goods increased, other branches of the economy were neglected. "Consequently the shock economy of 1920," which might have seemed rational then, brought about "the most accomplished form of the proletarian natural-anarchistic economy."[8] Thus according to Kristman, a noncapitalist, proletarian economy could be anarchical as a result of a lack of planning, even though the two other elements of a socialist economy—centralization and supplanting of money —were already present.

The student of the Soviet Union in the 1930s will be struck by the similarity of the story of "shock" and "nonmonetary" methods leading to anarchy, to the situation prevailing under the first Five-Year Plan, which will be discussed in the next chapter.

Centralization, abolition of the monetary system, and planning were largely accepted by all Bolsheviks as *sine qua non* principles of socialist economic organization. These concepts, it should be remembered, were derived from "dialectic" rather than from empirical data, and the model consisted of *a priori* traits so as to constitute an antithesis of a capitalist economy. In capitalism the law of value, in its different forms, regulated the economy through an interplay of spontaneous forces in the market, but the socialist economy would eliminate money, prices, wages, profits, and the other capitalist market paraphernalia. Socialism and socialist planning were conceived uniquely in terms of a distribu-

[6] L. Kritsman, *Geroicheskii Period Russkoi Revoliutsii* (Moscow, 1926), pp. 114–121.
[7] On *udarnost'*, *ibid.*, p. 121.   [8] *Ibid.*, p. 122.

tive function in kind, where economic activity was no longer concerned with market categories such as merchandise, value, and cost but with human needs served by products created to satisfy them. Elimination of private property was an indispensable precondition for the elimination of private producers, and the disappearance of private producers exchanging commodities would lead to the elimination of both the markets and the category of "commodities." This logic was responsible for the following conception, if not illusion: the more nationalization, the narrower the market, the nearer the advent of socialism, or the larger the socialist sector. For Lenin as well as for Bukharin, who expressed such ideas in works written during the civil war and endorsed by Lenin, only direct exchanges between the state and the peasant were "socialist"; exchanges based on buying and selling, with money as intermediary, were capitalist.[9] In 1918 Lenin thought that market categories and monetary devices were unavoidable during a long period of transition, but the length of that transition period would depend on how long private sectors, especially the small-holding peasantry, would continue to exist; these categories alien to socialism were tolerated for reasons of expediency and were bound to disappear, as Stalin still maintained in his writings of 1952.

But when Lenin suddenly found himself in a situation in which all the allegedly "capitalist" mechanisms began to disintegrate under the strains of war, the party leaders fell prey to the illusion that the dream was becoming real. They began to speed up the dismantling of those mechanisms and to replace them with more direct controls and distributive administrative techniques, apparently as a deliberate implementation of a suddenly rediscovered theory.

This conception of a socialist economy explains why the illusion could spread, why with undue obstinacy it was adhered to for far longer than the economy could bear, and

[9] See one example among many, in Lenin, *Sochineniia*, vol. 40, p. 304, where he says: "commodity exchanges, viz. capitalism."

why it was disastrous. It will also explain some of the vicissitudes during the next stages of development.

It should be remembered that the doctrine of market relations in socialism, best expressed in the Bolshevik theoretical literature by Bukharin's *Economics of Transition
Period,* was an old socialist doctrine, clearly stated by Marx
and Engels and later accepted by the entire Marxist movement.[10] But another conception, also helpful in explaining
the "war communism" utopia, consisted of identifying the
spread of socialism with etatism. In a sense, this concept
grew logically from the economic premise: if markets disappeared and centralized planning took over, with its
distributing and disposing of matériel and men in direct
"physical" terms, then by implication administrations were
to replace the market mechanism. But it was never stated
nor intended by socialist thought that the process of expanding socialism would become tantamount to the growth
of the state machinery. On the contrary, it was understood
that administrations would be needed; but the state, as the
coercive machinery in service of the class enjoying the
greatest economic power, would soon begin to dwindle.

The imprecision of these conceptions added greatly to
the self-deception of presenting a growing oppressive
machinery as the very symptom of expanding "communism." It was the withering-away doctrine, as it was tri-
umphantly restated by Lenin on the very eve of the revolution, that helped view expanding nationalization as a token
of the disappearance of classes, which, in turn, heralded the
beginning of the melting away of the state. This was a deep
fallacy. The withering away thesis, conceived in such terms,
though so deeply and obviously libertarian, served as a
sedative that anesthetized the revolutionary Bolsheviks and
made them build a Leviathan when they thought they were
entering the free world of their dreams. This applied to
the civil war, and even more so, later. However, it should be

[10] This is well shown in W. Brus, *Ogólne Problemy Funkcjonowania Gospodarki Socjalistycznej* (Warsaw, 1964), pp. 29–52.

remembered that while some of them soon began to scrutinize critically the growing state apparatus, its estrangement from the masses, and the deviation from original ideologies, they rarely revised any basic concepts. When some undertook such a revision, it was far too late. Under the heading of "socialization" a centralized apparatus grew to massive proportions and enhanced the power of the state on an unprecedented scale. As the spread of socialism was identified with the spread of state power, statism became a synonym for socialism, and any autonomous factor came to be considered antisocialist anarchism. Such identification became the central ideological formula of Soviet socialism up to the present, although the other part of the "war communism" fallacy, the attitude toward market mechanisms, would be revised and dispelled altogether.

But, to sum up the "war communism model: a few features in the policies adopted during the civil war eventually hardened into a distinct system of directing society and managing the economy, and was correctly perceived as such by contemporaries, although their epithet to describe it, "war communism," is less convincing. The general traits of this system included a full-fledged "command economy" with a rigid centralization of decisions and allocations of producers' and consumers' necessities through an expanded rationing system; elimination of markets and money incentives, to be replaced by a combination of coercion with devoted, enthusiastic commitment; "shock methods" or "priority methods" as a guiding principle for solving problems; mobilization as one form of coercion-cum-exhortation coupled with the pure coercion embodied in mass terror.

But the application of such methods in the economy meant, *ipso facto*, an overall "administrative system" with centralized bureaucracies dictating and prescribing in detail ways of acting also in noneconomic sectors; in terms of relations between state and society, it meant an overpowering superiority of the state apparatus over society and over

83

the rights of individuals. It is not superfluous to repeat that in the Soviet context such a militarized state and bureaucratized economy could plausibly become ideologically consecrated as "communism," and that certain concepts in Marxism made such a misconception possible and perfectly sincere.

Although the central features of the model that had arisen during the civil war had ended in disaster, the crisis was easily attributed to the appalling realities of war rather than to the systemic traits. Until the situation reached emergency proportions and was acknowledged, such traits plausibly could be singled out as the tools that made it possible to achieve an unprecedented victory of undoubted historical dimensions.

NEP

The New Economic Policy was a surprising negation and complete reversal of the "war communism" policies.[11] At the moment of its introduction, it was certainly not intended to be such a comprehensive turnabout. The first steps, the cessation of food requisitions from peasants and its replacement by a regular tax in kind, were intended to avoid a fatal break with the peasants and to prevent an incipient jacquerie. But this first move triggered the rest and led to a remarkable *volte-face*, which astonished the world as well as the Bolsheviks.

The antimarket practices and theories of "war communism" still strongly influenced these initial moves. First, Lenin thought that the peasant, unhappy about the requisitions, would settle for an organized and predictable direct barter (*tovaroobmen*) between state industries and peasants, without trade, markets, and intermediaries.[12] In such

[11] Cf. Carr, *The Bolshevik Revolution*, vol. 2, and his *Interregnum* (London, 1954), pp. 4–5.

[12] For Lenin's initial intention to avoid a market economy and to introduce rather "a socialist goods-barter" and then the admission that it was necessary to operate a deeper retreat, see *Sochineniia*, vol. 44, p. 206.

a way, Lenin hoped to appease the peasants and preserve socialist practices as he defined them. Since direct exchange failed, Lenin retreated to markets, money, and capitalists. Only six months after the introduction of the tax in kind, he declared that the regime had retreated not only to "state capitalism" (a term resurrected after a three-year abeyance) but also to "state regulation of trade,"[13] by which he ment private trade, the *bête noire* of the previous system.

Lenin realized quickly that the first measures were swiftly leading the regime in a direction that unavoidably transformed the whole framework. It was not easy to explain the whole turn to bewildered party members. Even the top leaders were confused and sought theoretical rationalization to analyze the situation and to forecast its results. Lenin tried to provide such a theory. He declared frankly that the NEP was a retreat "in an orderly fashion" to "positions prepared in advance" from previous ones which hitherto enjoyed full ideological consecration. Here Lenin discontinued the military metaphor and tried to justify the turn by proving that it was not as new to Bolsheviks as they now painfully perceived it, but was merely a resumption of previously accepted positions. He used his pre-civil war "state capitalist" conceptions to prove that cooperation with capitalist forces and a turn to capitalist practices by a Bolshevik government were not betrayals but good strategy with theoretical antecedents.

The search for such antecedents were not just maneuvers for mass consumption, but genuine and very hectic attempts to understand reality and to find new theoretical conceptions for policy formulations. Unfortunately, the concept of "state capitalism," rejected by Preobrazhensky and Trotsky, proved unworkable once more. Lenin sought to collaborate with "progressive" big capitalists, he hoped that they might help him fight "the main enemy," the petite-bourgeoisie. But finally he was forced to reorient his whole strategy and to make concessions and an alliance with precisely "the main

[13] *Ibid.*, pp. 229, 215.

enemy" of the previous scheme.[14] Foreign and domestic big capitalists were not forthcoming to participate seriously in Lenin's plans and invest in "concessions" or "partnerships" with the Soviet government; instead, hundreds of thousands of small manufacturers, merchants, and small traders emerged, ready to conduct private business with or without state help. This was what the country, especially the peasants, needed in order to make the crippled economy move again.

Lenin had difficulties in explaining to the party and to himself the overall strategy, and for this he was deeply embarrassed.[15] Once he admitted retreat, he was asked, "For how long?" His answers were contradictory. In October 1921 he expected that "the retreat [would] soon end" with the resumption of "the offensive," and in March 1922 he, in fact, announced that "the retreat ended." This was followed by tortuous explanations of the means and reasons for its end and the character of the new stage: it was now time for a "regrouping of forces." Then, in the same speech, he argued that there was no other way to socialism but the NEP. But in November 1922 he confessed: "we are retreating once more for a new regrouping," but candidly acknowledged: "we do not know yet how to regroup." In the same speech he declared that the NEP would be followed for a long time but reassured his audience that "no one of

[14] The concept of "state capitalism" involved, at the beginning, only cooperation with capitalists, mainly from abroad, as it was hoped for in 1921–1922. As this hope did not materialize, Lenin began to use the same term to cover collaboration with small local capital and trade. Somewhat later the term came to mean the actual practice of concessions to small private sectors and especially to peasants. By this token the concept lost its meaning and Lenin, in fact, abandoned it in his article "On Cooperation," *Sochineniia*, 45 (Moscow, 1964), 73–75 (in English in *Collected Works*, vol. 33 [Moscow, 1966], 467–472).

[15] See Carr, *The Bolshevik Revolution*, pp. 273–279, for Lenin's hesitations in explaining "war communism" and NEP; but Carr did not specifically mention the attitude toward "market categories" as one possible factor behind the conundrum.

our previous slogans were forgotten." Finally, he countered his own slogan, "NEP for good," with "for good but not forever."

Parallel to the confusing ("we attack, we retreat . . .") vacillations, other threads of thought appeared, and a more positive and more serious rethinking began. One question was creating trouble and had to be answered: if the NEP was only a temporary retreat from "war communism" policies, it was necessary to reassert these latter policies as party objectives for the long run and to explain the failure to implement them by circumstances or by the premature character of the steps taken. But if, on the other hand, the pre-civil war line made sense, what then was "war communism"? Lenin said it was an error. But he did not explain in what sense the NEP was a "retreat" if "war communism" was not an advance.

Bolsheviks sought the answer and also searched for an ideological reappraisal of the NEP. Lenin himself, as we just saw, explained that "war communism" was a complete error and that war stringencies erroneously had been mistaken for a shortcut to socialism. He leaned toward the concept of a prolonged transition period of a generation or more; and he increasingly became convinced that NEP policies provided a valid method for reaching socialism not only in Russia but also in other countries, including the developed ones—provided they still had an important petit bourgeois sector.[16] Finally, the NEP became for him a "long series of gradual transformations into a large-scale socialized economy."[17]

This process of adapting theory to the new reality was understandable. As Lenin concentrated the efforts of his government to make the NEP work, naturally enough, at the first signs of success, he found collaboration with the peasants more meaningful than just a bare, tactical neces-

[16] The texts are in Lenin, *Sochineniia*, vol. 43, p. 340, and vol. 44, p. 6.
[17] *Ibid.*, vol. 44, p. 6.

sity. Commerce now became his big slogan, and he began to taunt his fellow civil war heroes for their inability quickly to acquire the skills of business and to learn market techniques. "Learn to trade" became the great commandment, and the central lever that, if mastered by the government and the state industry, would help in inducing the country, especially the small peasants, to engage in the process of the now much-vaunted "gradual transformations" of the Leninist strategies themselves and even, partly, of their objectives.

Such revisions in the NEP could not go on without affecting the attitude toward market mechanisms in the long run. It is true that the adoption of market relations and the re-admission of merchants and private entrepreneurs were a result of a compromise with the peasants. Everybody in the party saw such a compromise as the very basis of the NEP. Opinions differed widely as to the dangers involved in the operation and to the scope and prospects of these concessions. The debates that threatened to tear the party asunder after Lenin's death are well known and covered by a wide literature.[18] The competing schools tried to analyze the nature of the NEP and its relationship to the prospects of building socialism. A particularly dramatic debate raged over the great issue of whether the NEP was a congenial environment for, and compatible with, the industrialization of the country.

But even before these great debates broke out, Lenin's ideas at the end of his career clearly pointed to the conclusion that he favored both the NEP and markets over the long term. Bukharin continued this line of thought after Lenin. The Left, especially in Preobrazhensky's trenchant formulations, although they did not hide their belief in the very transitional character of the NEP, they firmly denied

[18] For the debates, see chapter "The Great Debate" in Nove, *An Economic History*, and Carr's volumes, especially *Socialism in One Country*. A. Erlich's *The Soviet Industrialization Debate* (Cambridge, Mass., 1960), is the most authoritative treatment by an economist.

the accusations of their retractors that they were aiming at its violent elimination. At that time, Stalin made different pronouncements in favor of the NEP, but finally, as we know, substituted his Five-Year Plan for it.

At this stage, it is important to emphasize that in many quarters there was a growing and deeper realization that some of the basic traits and mechanisms of the NEP were of a more lasting value than just transitory concessions. Reality itself taught its lessons: the NEP quite successfully made coexist two principles—state action and market forces —which the more orthodox approach considered to be irreconcilable. The realities of the civil war seemed to bear out this attitude, and Marxist theory concurred that the socialist state and market anarchy (identified with capitalism), cannot coexist. When the NEP was introduced, Bolshevik leaders still continued to view the situation in terms, as Lenin once said, of "who beats whom" (*kto-kogo*). But soon Lenin himself began changing his opinion about "whom to beat," in other words, "who the enemies were." In his initial concept of "state capitalism," which he would abandon shortly before his death,[19] big capitalists were expected to become allies and the small holders, the bearers of petit bourgeois anarchy, were the main enemy. The NEP made him change his mind diametrically.

Trotsky, too, in a brochure written in August 1925, developed positive expectations about long-term prospects of the NEP and defined it as "cooperation and competition" between socialism and capitalism.[20] In narrower terms of economic policies, this meant cooperation and competition between the "plan" and the "market" and in social terms between the state and the private sectors, terms that were vaguely identified in Bolshevik thinking as "socialism" and "capitalism." In the same vein, Preobrazhensky, in defining

[19] In his article "On Cooperation."
[20] L. Trotsky, *K Kapitalizmu ili k Sotsializmu* (Moscow, 1925), p. 6.

89

the NEP, defied Lenin's "state capitalism" by avoiding the use of that term altogether and by describing the NEP as a "mixed," socialist economy.[21] He implied, however, as Trotsky had, that the elements of the "mix" were competing, but that one of them would eventually disappear. From his definition Preobrazhensky deduced further conclusions about the then-current mechanisms of the Soviet economy and its driving forces. According to him two "regulators" or "laws" operated in the economy and explained its main tendencies. In the private sectors "the law of value" was the regulator, similar to the one operating in a capitalist society. Some forms of this law still influenced the state, or socialist, sector, but they were no more than subsidiary there. The state sector had its own regulator, "the law of primitive socialist accumulation," and the two regulators, each valid in its own sphere, were simultaneously competing and reflected the long-run incompatibility of the state and private sectors.

There was certainly good insight in Preobrazhensky's version of the "two regulators." Even in the West today situations created by market forces displaying their own momentum force governments to step in to "correct" unacceptable phenomena. Obviously, the principles guiding state action are different from those inherent in market forces; two different regulators certainly appear and even clash.

But Preobrazhensky, as we saw, also maintained the traditional fallacy concerning market mechanisms, which, he claimed, are inherent only in the private sectors but are imposed on the state sector "from outside." He therefore predicted that as socialist accumulation increased, and private sectors were eliminated, the "law of value" and its market mechanisms would also disappear.

Bukharin met Preobrazhensky's "two regulators" headlong. His position was somewhat awkward on this point, as he himself spoke about two distinctly different sectors, state

[21] In his lecture given to the Socialist Academy, *Vestnik Sotsialisticheskoi Akademii*, October-December 1923, p. 304.

and private, and could not deny that their internal principles were different. But he worried about the strongly expressed antagonistic character of the two regulators in Preobrazhensky's formulation. Politically, such an assertion
undermined the viability of the NEP and contradicted Bukharin's own belief in the existence of a firm basis for an
alliance of the state with the peasantry. This is why he
emphasized that the state's plans and the peasant markets
should not be seen as mutually exclusive, not even in the
long run, but should be seen as "a correlation," as complementary principles. Socialism would be built "on the basis
of market relations," and it seemed odd to assume that the
very foundation of socialism was antithetical to such
relations.

The difficulty that plagued all the participants in this in-
tra-party debate was that the "law of value" had become
confused with "market mechanisms," which in turn had
tended to become identified with "private sectors," especially the peasantry. Nevertheless, without a direct revision,
Bukharin proposed a far-reaching solution to the whole im-
broglio: his own "law of labor outlays" (or "proportional
labor outlays").[22]

In brief, he maintained, on the basis of extensive quotations from Marx, that behind the "law of value" there exists
"a material content" that is valid for every society: the need
to distribute the existing labor force proportionately between different areas and branches of the economy. Such
a proportion is assured in different socio-economic forma-
tions through different mechanisms, the "law of value" being one of them. As socialism develops, the "law of value"
would fade into the basic, underlying law that would become the foundation for a conscious regulation of the economy through the plan. In the transition period, therefore,

[22] For Bukharin's "law" see "K Voprosu o Zakonomernostiakh
Perekhodnogo Perioda," *Pravda*, 21, 23, and 26 July, 1926. More
on "two regulators" from Preobrazhenskii, *Novaia Ekonomika* (Moscow, 1926), pp. 36–39, 118–124, 231.

there is not a clash of incompatible principles but a correlation between different mechanisms of the same basic law. In this view, the NEP exhibits not just two but more such mechanisms. "The law of value" functions in the simple commodity areas (peasantry); "production price" is the mechanism that applies to the private entrepreneurs, and "productivity of labor" is the guiding principle of the state sector. But the general law in operation behind all of these is the same (and is the one that already functions in the state sector, which is seeking the best economic results with a maximum economy of resources), thus offering the basis for viewing the NEP as a unity, a system to be studied and seen as such.

The theoretical evaluation of the validity of Bukharin's and Preobrazhensky's views is not easy, but they represent a valid effort to find and formulate principles of economic life to serve as a groundwork for a theory of the Soviet economy and as a guide for planners.

Whatever the theory, the practices of the NEP included both planning and markets though interspersed with tensions and clashes, which could be interpreted as either a collision of irreconcilable principles or as transitory difficulties resulting from insufficient coordination between them. The fact remains that the planning theory and practice during the NEP were influenced originally and naturally by the general socio-economic and political framework, which "plan and market" epitomized. First, it was "not a command economy," as A. Nove asserted.[23] The plan was then a guide and a forecast, not an order, although it moved slowly toward such a pattern at the end of the 1920s. The state did not manage the economy with such tightly centralized machinery as it did during the first Five-Year Plan. Industrial plants—or rather the intermediary administrative units, the so-called trusts or syndicates—had some degree of autonomy (more in the consumer goods sectors and less or none in heavy industry sectors). Also, profitability

[23] *An Economic History*, p. 100.

92

achieved in operations on the market, in competition with
the private sector, and with other state enterprises was actively sought and served as a criterion of economic viability
for the state-owned outfits.

Trotsky, who adopted wholeheartedly the NEP at its inception,[24] perceived clearly the importance of this aspect
for state industry. In a brilliant brochure, written in 1922,
which was warmly endorsed by Lenin, he saw at this early
stage this facet of the NEP environment that transcended
its strictly peasant-oriented interpretations. Obviously, this
environment had something to commend itself as a strategy
to help state industry to reassert itself. Trotsky explained:
"In order for every enterprise to become a component of a
unified socialist organism, functioning in a planned manner,
a transition period of acting in market conditions is necessary which will take many years. In the course of these
years, every enterprise and group of enterprises should, to
an appropriate degree, adapt itself to the market and control itself through the market." He stated that the "control
through the market" was the core of the NEP. Thus industry needed NEP methods, too. Supervision of industries by
the state administration from above had to be implemented
"from below" by market controls. "Politically its [the
NEP's] importance consisted mainly in a concession to the
peasantry, but its significance is *by no means smaller* as an
unavoidable stage for developing the state industry during
the transition from a capitalist to a socialist economy."[25]

[24] Trotsky could afford to endorse the NEP wholeheartedly because he too had some previous positions to fall back on. He was,
in fact, the first to have advocated NEP-like changes as early as February 1920, but his proposals were then rejected by the Central Committee. Trotsky then turned to his plan of etatization of the trade
unions, but this too was rejected by Lenin, who was soon to adopt
the NEP (on this both leaders agreed). For Trotsky's proposals of a
new policy toward peasants, see Carr, *The Bolshevik Revolution*, vol.
2, p. 280, and Trotsky, *Novyi Kurs* (Moscow, 1924), pp. 57–58.

[25] Trotsky, *Nep Sovetskoi Vlasti* (Moscow, 1922). Lenin expressed
his approval of this brochure in *Sochineniia*, vol. 54, p. 314.

Trotsky shared with other Bolsheviks the prognosis that a nonmonetary planned economy would develop, but it is revealing that he could view the market economy and its methods as "healthy" and "unavoidable" for socialist industry during this important historical period. Trotsky also underscored the significance, for both the peasant and the fully nationalized state sectors, of economic incentives as indispensable levers for the running of the economy. The market mechanism best served this purpose. Appropriate stimuli were crucial, and market incentives provided them to both peasants and factories. Trotsky also saw the importance of granting enough autonomy to factory crews and their management as a powerful incentive for deploying initiative on the job.[26] This was obvious to many authors and leaders. The negative results of the rigidly bureaucratic methods of the civil war period, including the suppression of autonomy and individuality of enterprises, organizations, and administrative regions were largely acknowledged and discussed during the NEP. The abolition of bureaucratic management of state industry, to which the pejorative term *glavkizm* was applied, was seen as one of the central merits of the NEP reversal. Thus the dangers of bureaucratic, mainly administrative coercive methods of management in the state sector were generally acknowledged and the NEP could boast of having dismantled such a pattern.

Another important principle central to the NEP was "co-operation." It was the last, and the most comprehensive of the revisions undertaken by Lenin before his death. Later, it was heavily distorted by party propaganda, but the propagandists were right in underlining "Lenin's cooperative plan" and had good reasons for blurring its meaning.

In fact, there was no such plan, only an article—"On Co-

[26] Trotsky, *ibid.*, p. 119, and he repeated this theme in *K Kapitalizmu ili k Sotsializmu* (Moscow, 1925), p. 5, but here only with regard to peasants and with a strong emphasis on the dangers of stratification that the market economy was going to produce.

operation," one of the last five Lenin wrote.[27] In it he revised his conception of peasant cooperatives, which he had previously considered a bourgeois institution. He contended that such a voluntary cooperative movement, which catered to the peasant, should be seen in Soviet conditions as the road to socialism *par excellence* and as essentially a socialist factor. The road would be long. A "cultural revolution" bringing, to begin with, simple literacy to the country was its necessary prerequisite, but this would be the safest road.

This new approach seemed so crucial to Lenin that he now felt, as he often did at a crossroad, that the central objective of the revolution—socialism—had to be reformulated. Consequently, he stated that socialism was nothing else and nothing more than "a regime of civilized cooperators."

How serious and how definitive was such a formula? Socialism was still far away, and Lenin all too often felt that he could use the term as an appeal to mobilize the citizenry to undertake some urgent tasks. When he felt that electrification was the goal, communism became "Soviet power plus electrification"; was not he now using a similar procedure with the rediscovery of peasant cooperation? (It should be remembered that Lenin primarily used cooperation to mean the grouping of peasants for the commercialization of their produce; common production, rather realistically, was not even mentioned in this article.) Were these reversals tactics, strategy, or principle?

The answer is not easy; but the fact remains that the realities and policies of the NEP inspired Lenin to promulgate a doctrine that allowed a concept of "socialism" which could be disassociated from the exclusive statism that prevailed both earlier and later and that still remains at the core of the Soviet conception of socialism. During the NEP period, such "nonstatism" was encouraged by the following features of the NEP "model": coexistence of a centrally

[27] Lenin, *Sochineniia*, vol. 45, pp. 73–75.

planned sector with several cooperative and private ones, a "mixed economy" with *market categories* accepted as tools in economic life; significant decentralization inside the state sector itself and the nonimperative character of economic planning; a relatively free interplay of social factors and interests, collaboration of the party with different groups of intelligentsia and experts, without the imposition of a too rigid ideology; cultural and relative political pluralism (Marxists and non-Marxists could still debate, and opposition within the party still existed); curtailment of the terror apparatus, exclusion of mass terror as a normal method, and the creation of a stable legal system with "due process"; an evolutionary approach to the process of industrializing society and to restructuring it, and a moderate use of censorship in a culturally and socially pluralist setting.

Briefly, it is possible to say that the NEP model was a "liberal dictatorship." Some of its tasks were seen as temporary, while others, as we have shown, began to acquire in certain party quarters more legitimacy and validity than that dictated by the expedient need to placate the peasants. For about eight years a system was created and functioned with a style, or rather pattern, of relations between state and society that, through several revisions of different dogmas (the reevaluation of cooperation, the redefinition of socialism, a rethinking of market mechanisms, and a reassessment of the class character of the peasantry), began to develop into a well-defined principle. This was the system that Bukharin tried to preserve and for which he became the chief advocate in the party.

CHAPTER FIVE

Swing of the Pendulum:
Stalin's Model

THE inauguration of the first Five-Year Plan and the collectivization drive dramatically reversed the NEP model. During this "revolution from above," a definitive "anticapitalist" drive was undertaken to eliminate private peasant agriculture, to destroy the more wealthy farmers, and to abolish private trade, industry, and domestic crafts. Together with the private sectors, as old theories seemed to warrant, markets and market categories were now supposed either to be eliminated or maintained just as formal, dying, temporary auxiliary devices. Nothing was to remain as an obstacle to a nonmonetary, rationally and "directly" planned economy, and hence to the advent of the purest socialism.

Thus, the plan was supposed to replace fully the market-and-plan approach and the mixed economy. Full etatization of the economy terminated the coexistence between public and private sectors. Rigidity, on an unprecedented scale, eradicated cultural pluralism. Bureaucratic rule, with its multiple and ubiquitous controls, eliminated social autonomy and imposed itself on society. Finally, the ruling party, which still functioned during the NEP—although in ever-diminishing scope—as a political organization with debate and opposition, now lost its political rights and was remolded into a very different body dominated by a hierarchical structure similar to the military one and it submitted to police control and to murderous purges. Whereas the NEP had erected an elaborate legal edifice and seriously strived to achieve "socialist legality," during the Five-Year Plan this framework was utterly destroyed and re-

97

placed by a system of extralegal, crude coercion and mass terror. Society and the party itself were forced to accept the new course of ruthless and relentless pressure. The drive culminated in a political autocracy, one of the most despotic and whimsical in modern history, and in a state-run "command economy." Eventually, after a quarter of a century marked with outbursts of feverish and bold improvisations, the new regime was created and developed its routine patterns. In this process any traces of the NEP seemed irretrievably buried, and a deep affinity with the civil war period, unmistakably reappeared; both the *glavkokratia* and the *razvërstka* systems, the nonmonetary economy and overall rationing, and many more of the attributes of "war communism" were revived, although the point should not be overstated. Predictably, some new and different traits appeared. After the initial and particularly acute period, in the middle of the second Five-Year Plan, rationing of common goods was abolished, although it remained for producer's goods; and *kolkhozy* markets were reopened even earlier, though other forms of private trade were forever banned.

Other differences that distinguished the civil war period from this one should be mentioned. During the former, pro-regime forces were strongly egalitarian, whereas in the new phase, the regime quickly became antiegalitarian and created new elites enjoying considerable privileges. In the earlier period, the leadership at the top and at the second echelon preserved enough independence in the political system to allow them both participation in policy making and scope for initiative. In the latter the rule became autocratic, with strong quasireligious and nationalistic overtones. During the civil war, the party membership, although unified and disciplined, still had access to the leadership and the right to dissent, appeal, and influence, whereas under the Five-Year Plan this right was lost.

Furthermore, unlike the civil war period, Stalin's Russia undertook a feverish industrial expansion. This industrial

STALIN'S MODEL

dynamism involved a vast effort in schooling the population
but was coupled with an obsessive destruction of much culture and science. While even the natural sciences suffered
heavily, art, literature, and the social sciences were muzzled
and stifled. The population, the party, and the leaders
themselves were denied the right to analysis and self-analy-
sis. In the midst of a feverish activity all behaved as if blind-
folded, unaware of the direction they were taking and ignorant of the emerging socio-political mechanism in their
own society.

Under these conditions, the industrialization drive, especially during the very first plans that shaped Russia's economic system, was accompanied by an astonishingly inadequate development of theory. Selected ideas, from the
heated debates of the previous period on industrialization
and planning, somewhat influenced the policy makers. Preobrazhensky's "law of primitive socialist accumulation"
might have inspired Stalin; so did, eventually, the thinking
of the planners and economists who opted for an extreme
teleological conception and declared, as Strumilin once did,
that objective laws in Soviet economy probably did not exist
at all and that the leap to "the kingdom of freedom," which
Engels had predicted, was already occurring. The plan itself, Strumilin maintained, would be the law, but planning
was and would remain more of an art, creating its own
norms rather than yielding to external restraints other than
technical and natural norms and laws.[1] At the same time
another economist, S. Turetsky, enthusiastically painted the
picture of the emerging socialist industry as taking the form
of "a gigantic combine of successive production phases" in
which the prices of capital goods were no more than accounting units with a purely conventional significance. The
young and ardent planner, N. Voznesensky, attacked the
"opportunists" who wanted to combine the plan with spon-

[1] S. Strumilin, *Problemy Planirovania v SSSR* (Moscow, 1932), pp.
14–16, quoted by W. Brus, *Ogólne Problemy Funkcjonowania Ekonomii Socjalistycznej* (Warsaw, 1964), p. 142.

99

taneous forces. Market anarchy, he maintained, "with the laws of value which regulates the movement of the capitalist market society," would be defeated soon.[2]

Turetsky and Strumilin, both prominent economists, continue today to reevaluate their ideas of 1929; but at that time they clearly favored giving the political leadership full freedom of action according to its will without any guidance or restraint, and this was in fact occurring. Economics was stifled, as were the planners. The political leadership seized complete control over the process and brushed aside strictures, "regulators," sophisticated work on a "balance of national economy," mathematical models of growth, studies on investment allocations and effectiveness, models of accumulation and consumption, research on management methods, studies on scientific organization of labor, and many other endeavors, which were discontinued during the 1930s and abandoned until at least the mid-1950s. But these studies were the very tools of planning. Among them the "balance of the national economy" which, as a modern Soviet writer has stated, was "a tool of utmost importance for fixing rates of growth and proportions in developing the national economy," and its rejection could not but end in "negative results for practical activity."[3]

Scholars, some of them Soviet, have characterized the furious industrialization of the 1930s as thoughtless haste. This was not without precedent in Russian history; another impetuous industrializer, Peter the Great, two hundred years earlier acted similarly, according to an eminent historian, on the precept: "first rush—think later,"[4] which could well serve as the motto for the initial stages of the "big drive." Considering the subordinate role of planners

[2] S. Turetskii, *Planovoe Khoziaistvo*, no. 10 (1929), quoted by Brus, *ibid.*; N. Voznesenskii, *Pravda*, 8 October 1931.

[3] A. Efimov, *Ekonomicheskoe Planirovanie v SSSR* (Moscow, 1967), pp. 132, 213–214; and A. Efimov, *Sovetskaia Industriia* (Moscow, 1967), pp. 242–243.

[4] V. Kliuchevskii, *Sochineniia*, 4 (Moscow, 1958), 166–167.

and economists and the domineering role of political leaders in the whole process, the personal traits and idiosyncrasies of a few personalities marked deeply the Soviet system during the crucial formative years. For example, the refusal of expert advice and the adoption of "pure practicism" in shaping institutions and determining the allocation of resources and the fate of men expressed the personal predilections of Stalin.

While the influence of individuals on historical phenomena should not be overstated, it cannot be ignored that in the pyramidal power structure the men or man at the top is more than an individual: he is an institution, a powerful one. Although he is part of a larger system that imposes restraints on him, his actions can have lasting influence on the history of the country, provided he is powerful enough. Stalin was such an individual; his power was immense, and the industrialization process magnified it.

Stalin did not say much about the theory of planning, and his last writings do not disclose any coherent body of concepts relevant to building and running a complex industrial society, except a reliance on the continuation of the methods already in use. There is no doubt that the whole process was an immense improvisation, guided by the rule of thumb, hunch, and all too often by despotic whims. Nonetheless, a few simple and important practical rules are discernible that guided his policy making, especially in the way of fixing targets and achieving them. In a letter written to Lenin in 1921, Stalin gives a rather unique insight into his approach to planning, which still clearly guided him in later years. Lenin, at that time, sought experts to staff the newly established Gosplan. Stalin, manifesting a characteristic mistrust of "professors" who lacked indispensable "healthy pragmatism," urged Lenin to appoint to the Gosplan "men of live politics, ready to act on the principle of 'report fulfillment.' "[5]

[5] Quoted in Iu. Flaxerman, *G. M. Krzhizhanovskii* (Moscow, 1964), p. 172.

101

Stalin used the language of a civil war commander, and he clearly mistook the procedures of deploying men in combat with the infinitely more complex concept and activity of planning the development of a national economy. But the civil war influenced him deeply. The launching of the industrialization drive in the late 1920s gave vent to his and his faction's reliance on the "report fulfillment" style. When a socialist economist, almost a quarter of a century later, assessed the Soviet economic system and those of the Eastern bloc as "a *sui generis* war economy,"[6] he was just recording the final outcome of what officially was called "an offensive."

Undoubtedly this style and approach were unavoidable when the core of the economic policy consisted of tempos. "Tempos decide the whole thing!" This dramatic slogan was intended by Stalin to mobilize energies and imagination. But the leadership used terror in order to make sure that these tempos would not be scrutinized nor derived from any principle other than the need to rush. To ask the crucial question "how much, and why so much?" was treated as treason. The same obtained with the parallel problem of rate of accumulation, which rapidly increased at the expense of consumption and remained at a very high level. This practice constituted one of the main traits of Soviet industrialization. The "primitive accumulation" thesis was adopted wholeheartedly and frantically. Its original author, as we know, had carefully set out a host of qualifications, limitations, and conditions, which showed that he understood the question "how much?" He attempted to answer it in terms appropriate to long-term interests of the country; but the Stalinist leadership's answer was extremely crude. Analysis and questioning were equated with treason. Stalin understood plans as temporary sets of targets that, however high, had to be surpassed. During the proceedings

[6] O. Lange, "The Role of Planning in Socialist Economics," in M. Bornstein, ed., *Comparative Economic Systems* (Homewood, Ill., 1965), p. 200.

of the Seventeenth Party conference in February 1932, he spontaneously interjected: "The five year program is in our eyes a minimum. We will have additional annual control figures which will be enlarging the five year plan from year to year. And we will, beside it, have 'counter plans' which will lead to further expansion of the five year plan."[7]

Hence, the core of Stalin's program, as E. Zalesky saw it, was the building of as many factories as possible. This approach contradicted the one taken by even the staunchest "teleologists" in the Gosplan who labored on the draft of the first Five-Year Plan. They were worried about some internal coherence of the plan and still saw growth in the framework of correlated targets and subject to certain constraints. But theories of economic growth were rejected. "Stalin derided openly theories of growth which he had formally condemned as 'bourgeois deviations.'"[8] In an unpublished speech given in 1929, Kalinin best explained the rationale behind the policy. Although he was speaking about building *sovkhozy*, the principle clearly applied to investment policies at large. "Is it more rational," he asked his audience, "to invest 500 millions in new sovkhozy, or in the intensification of the old ones?" Whereas the capitalist approach, he contended, would choose the latter, "from the point of view of the Soviet state it is profitable to invest in new *sovkhozy*. And why so? Because we unleash new productive forces."[9]

Thus, the "unleashing" of productive forces became the guideline and was understood as a prescription for the maximum outpouring of investment into giant enterprises with-

[7] *17-taia Konferentsiia VKP(b), Stenotchet* (Moscow, 1932), p. 233. The "counterplans" were supposed to have come from factories that undertook to do more than the plan envisaged. But such planning "from below" was a party campaign.

[8] E. Zalesky, *Planification de la Croissance et Fluctuations Economiques en URSS, 1918–1932,* 1 (Paris, 1962), 68, 70.

[9] E. Turchaninova, *Podgotovka i Provedenie Sploshnoi Kollektivizatsii Sel'skogo Khoziaistva v Stavropol'e* (Dushanbe, 1963), p. 101, quoted from archives.

103

out any regard to coordination, correlation, proportion, and long-term considerations, which were now considered treasonable measures intended to curtail the salutary "unleashing."

Salient features of the "unleashed" process included haste, orientation on quantity, and "priority method." Haste, a curious constant of economic policy making, deeply influenced the whole process and the resulting system. The "tautness" of planning was a predictable consequence of the rush. Quantity became an obsession applicable not only to material output but also to such "unquantifiable" values as literature, arts, and education. Quotas had to be fulfilled and, even more important, surpassed.

"Priority method" meant concentrating efforts on the most important economic sectors—usually metal, machinery, and fuel—fixing high quantitative targets for them, and then giving them a favorable treatment in the allocation of resources and finance, with the relative neglect of the rest of the economy.[10]

"Priority methods" in fixing targets also bred "shock methods." They certainly were useful as a way out of the economic chaos that was created during the first Five-Year Plan. There was no other way to overcome this chaos and to save key sectors but to prepare a list of "shock sites" for preferential treatment. This was similar to the "shock method" of "war communism," which became, in a new form, one of the tools of economic policy. The leadership felt that common sense and the fixing of a simple set of priority targets, if correctly chosen, would provide the impetus to the growth of the whole economy. But it seemed lost on Kalinin that a growth strategy that neglected too

[10] Cf. A. Notkin, ed., *Struktura Narodnogo Khoziaistva SSSR* (Moscow, 1967), p. 55, and I. Malyshev, who ridicules the whole idea in *Ekonomicheskie Zakony Sotsializma i Planirovanie* (Moscow, 1966), pp. 26–27. Also see Zalesky, *Planification de la Croissance*, pp. 158–169, on the return of civil war policies and the priorities approach shown to be the counterpart of tautness and haste.

numerous "nonpriority" sectors in order to serve favored projects fettered economic development in many ways and had other incalculable effects not only on the economy but also on the evolution of society and the state.

Indeed it was bizarre that in this "planned economy" the very idea of planning was sacrificed. The concentration on a few priority targets, the refusal to apply more sophisticated methods in selecting them, the unwillingness to think in terms of a national economy as a whole, and the insistence on surpassing quotas, harassed the planners and forced them and their subordinates to yield to constant pressures, to delay the submission of plans, and to marvel at the capricious reversal of targets announced by telephone from the Politbureau, with which they either acquiesced or were threatened with jail for the slightest attempt at dissent.[11]

Administrative methods and routines, obviously, began to take root and gather experience but the main planning effort did not advance much beyond the development of techniques for a short-run, tenuous matching of ends and needs. The targets that were forced upon planners were too often unattainable. The whole process proceeded by jerks and leaps, constantly plagued by inadequacy of resources and lack of reserves; and, in any case, the only blueprints for planners and managers were the short-term targets. Long-term prospects, the main idea behind planning, remained neglected for a generation at least.[12]

[11] Strumilin, then still one of the leaders of Gosplan, already had told the story in 1929. His planners, he said, prefer to "stand" for higher tempos, rather than "sit" (in prison) for lower ones. See *Planovoe Khoziaistvo*, no. 1 (1929), p. 109. In later years "sitting" would mean eventually perishing.

[12] On Soviet planning being rather a short-term exercise, see G. Grossman, "Notes for a Theory of the Communist Economy" in Bornstein, *Comparative Economic Systems*, p. 142. For larger studies, see N. Jasny, *Soviet Industrialization* (Chicago, 1961); S. Wellisz, *The Economics of the Soviet Bloc* (New York, 1966); Zalesky, *Planification de la Croissance.*

105

However, some methods evolved to help run, if not actually plan, the growing industrial establishment, and these are indispensable for an understanding of the whole model. The concentration of decision making at the top of the administrative machinery, the preference for "physical planning," i.e., in tons and meters rather than in values and the emergence of a tangle of bureaucracies and their proliferation were interrelated and mutually reinforcing factors that shaped the system. The heavy involvement with microeconomic activity, unavoidable in conditions of priority targets in physical units, and the equally inevitable exclusion of pricing and cost accounts as important criteria, contributed to "the hierarchical character of the plans and the vertical character of the interlinks among the different segments of the economic apparatus."[13]

The same factors account for the imperative character of the plan. It became a state law and an order to act. Each order, however, was composed of so many detailed targets that they often contradicted themselves and tended to confuse rather than guide. The reliance on "priority targets" led to the prevalence of "physical units" or "crypto-physical units"[14] as the methods of accounting and calculating. Expediency was no less a factor than ideological conviction in the emerging model. Expediency and necessity of the "physical planning" accounted for the adoption of the "material balances," an indispensable but extremely unwieldy method for securing a measure of internal consistency in

[13] Brus, *Ogólne Problemy Funkcjonowania Gospodarki Socjalistycznej*, pp. 120–121. Chapter 3 contains an illuminating outline of the administrative model. For more descriptions of this model, see R. Davies, "Planning a Mature Economy in the USSR," *Economics of Planning*, vol. 5, nos. 1–2 (Oslo, 1965), and vol. 6, nos. 1–2 (1966); A. Erlich, "Development Strategy and Planning: The Soviet Experience," *National Economic Planning* (New York, 1967). For a good Soviet text, see Malyshev, *Ekonomicheskie Zakony Sotsializma*.

[14] Grossman, "Notes for a Theory," p. 143. By "cryptophysical" he meant computations in terms of constant prices.

terms of demands and supplies.[15] From this emerged another, powerful mechanism in the Soviet planning and managing of the economy: the administrative distribution of inputs, mainly capital goods, to producing units, "a rationing system of production means."

The system of centralized material allocations (*mattekhsnab*) became "the most powerful weapon at the disposal of the central authorities . . . not the police or the party apparatus."[16] This assessment is correct insofar as the movement of supplies to producers is concerned. But while neither the police nor the party carried supplies, they were very necessary in order to counterbalance some problems that kept arising in the functioning of supply flows.

The *mattekhsnab* became the Soviet substitute for the market mechanism in the sphere of capital goods, a mechanism eventually more powerful than planning itself. Here was an institution, still very much viable today, that was an original creation of Soviet economic practice, and it accounts for many aspects of the whole model. Its domination of plants through control over inputs was so strong that autonomy for the local producing units was virtually ruled out. It contributed heavily to imparting to the economic body the notorious rigidity that fettered manueverability so essential in economic systems.

At the same time, planning and material supplies, as they evolved, were very time- and personnel-consuming. In fact, they caused the rapid growth of numerous bureaucracies,

[15] Description and explanation of "material balances" will be found in Wellisz, *The Economies of the Soviet Bloc*, pp. 145 ff; H. Levine, "The Centralized Planning of Supply in Soviet Industry," in Bornstein, ed., *Comparative Economic Systems*, which also explains the material technical supply system, the *mattekhsnab*. On "Industrial Materials Supply," see also A. Bergson, *The Economics of Soviet Planning* (New Haven, Conn., 1964), chap. 7.

[16] Grossman, "Notes for a Theory," p. 152. Mattekhsnab is abbreviated from *material'no-tekhnicheskoe snabzhenie*—material-technical supply.

with their self-propelling need for more controls, more officials, and more detailed targets, in order to counteract the equally growing tendency to evade the detailed targets, partly at the grass roots and partly by the officials themselves.

The steep downturn of 1929, and the drive for overall industrialization at a moment when experience was scant, conceptual elaboration was quite insufficient, and cadres were unavailable, account for the impact the very first years of the drive had not only on the methods of planning but also on the institutional setting, indeed the political system itself. The years of the first Five-Year Plan left an indelible mark on the ways of running the economy and on many other institutions as well.

The self-propelling forces inherent in planning and *mattekhsnab* dynamically interacted with other factors inside the system to trigger a powerful propensity to expand totalitarian controls. The spillover from the devices used in running the economy into the system at large did not escape the attention of researchers in the West and in Russia itself. The political context of the command economy, Gregory Grossman remarked, "is almost certainly authoritarian."[17] Detailed administrative controls were a legitimate outcome of the "physical" planning. A Soviet source confirmed: "Planning in physical units presupposes a system of administrative controls functionally interwoven into a hierarchical economic structure," whereas "planning in financial indicators does not require, presumably, such an extended structure of the planning system."[18] Nevertheless, this scholar, in fact, did not favor the "financial indicators" and seemed to prefer the ones the other authors unsympathetically called "administrative methods."[19]

[17] Grossman, *ibid.*, p. 14.
[18] R. Tsvylev, in B. Gnedenko, ed., *Problemy Funktsionirovania Bol'shikh Ekonomicheskikh Sistem* (Moscow, 1969), p. 160.
[19] See, for example, M. Fedorenko, *Diskussiia ob Optimal'nom Planirovanii* (Moscow, 1968), p. 16.

The outcome was an ever-growing concentration of centralized power and an ever-expanding network of controls. For example, agrarian policy reflected this. By destroying almost at a stroke the old agrarian system and installing a new one by administrative fiat, nothing in this field worked any longer by its own momentum. The party saddled itself with an exacting and unexpected task. If the *kolkhoz* system was to function, the party had no choice, as Stalin explained in 1933, but "to immerse itself into all the details of *kolkhoz* life and *kolkhoz* management."[20]

In the countryside more than elsewhere, the whole process of economic development assumed an increasingly administrative coercive character. The state apparatus has completely dominated economic life, and this fact marked the polity very deeply. The monopoly in both the economy and the polity, which now became welded more solidly than ever further enhanced the already strong propensity in the system to glorify its practices, whatever they were, and to present them as the *summum* of wisdom.

As propaganda and dogmatization were pushing out scholarship and theory, a planning system that had adopted practices largely prevalent under "war communism," when planning was practically nonexistent, could become sanctified as dogma. In fact, it was no more than a significant throwback to emergency and rationing practices, the ultimate success of which, during war communism, left a deep impression on the participants of the civil war. Now this inspiration helped to justify the Soviet concept of planning which once more became intimately concatenated with coercion, unbridled activism, and a high centralization of power. All these features, as said, were already present in the civil war. But they were "administration," not "planning." As Bobrowski stated, "it can be said in this sense that at the cradle of Soviet planning one finds a tendency favorable to centralization, to unlimited enlargement of the scope and the imperative character of planning. [And that] con-

[20] Quoted by A. Geister, *Pravda*, 15 July 1933.

109

cepts of administration and planning, which began to be distinguished during the NEP, came closer anew."[21]

Another attribute reminiscent of the civil war was the *glavkokratia*, the tendency to erect huge central bureaucracies in Moscow that shuffled men and resources all over Russia. There reappeared also the familiar predilection for the "direct socialist products barter," which Lenin cherished in 1919 but later rejected without however explicitly revising the theory in question. When the post-Leninist leaders finally repudiated the NEP, Stalin once more returned to familiar themes; he rehabilitated the "physical" indicators and hinted at the Sixteenth Congress in 1930 that although the circulation of commodities (*tovarooborot*) and the money economy still existed, they would automatically disappear with the end of propertied classes, especially peasant small holdings, and that this would happen in a few years. Ten years later he was more cautious.

At the beginning of 1941, in comments on the draft of a textbook on political economy, Stalin admitted the existence of laws in the economy, especially the "law of value." This caused a sensation among the experts who heard about this "novel" discovery. But World War II, which interrupted the preoccupation with these concepts, strengthened the belief in state power rather than in economic laws, and, in 1952, when Stalin resumed the same debate (about the same textbook), he still maintained that market categories, though unavoidable for a time, still soiled the purity of Soviet socialism only because the still incompletely socialist *kolkhoz* property survived. One day when the *kolkhozy* will become transformed into state enterprises (*sovkhozy*), the country will finally accede to the much-coveted system of "direct barter."[22]

---

[21] Cz. Bobrowski, *U Zródeł Planowania Socjalistycznego* (Warsaw, 1967), pp. 52–54, 146.

[22] *16-tyi S'ezd VKP(b), Stenotchet* (Moscow, 1930), p. 37; and Stalin, *Ekonomicheskie Problemy Sotsializma v SSSR* (Moscow, 1952), pp. 51–52, 54–55, 67–68. For Stalin's sudden admission of the

Such obsession could not be explained mainly by Stalin's fidelity to the classics of Marx or Engels. He had no qualms when he brushed aside Engels' propeasant liberalism. Rather, it resulted from a deeply felt need to perpetuate a mirage, not unlike the "war communism" illusions. This time, too, there was a war to be won, though of a different kind.

Certainly, an industrializing strategy that gave priority to the rapid development of heavy industry with such implacable onesidedness could not have succeeded without the capacity of the political system to force society to yield to the pressures, hardships, and irrationalities that such a plan imposed. However, once the "tempopathology" was unleashed, all institutions, including the party, had to be transformed. Amidst the strains of industrialization and because of it a singular process of state-building was taking place. By eliminating markets, private traders, and private peasants, the regime claimed that it was expanding socialism. Stalin insisted that markets and peasants bred capitalism, therefore their transformation or abolition meant that the realm of freedom had expanded. In fact, it was the Leviathan state which was expanded, partially by using the methods of "war communism" on a large scale because the overriding task was to control the "bearers of capitalism." But they happened to be the bulk of Russia's popular masses.

Success in control was as essential to Soviet industrialization as were purely economic strategies. Just as economics and politics reinforced each other in this process, so did use of coercion and the refusal of economic thought. The weaker the sophistication and theoretical maturity of the concepts behind the economic practice, the stronger the reliance on the crude coercive capacity of the state. Hence,

---

"law of value" (and laws in general in the economy), in January 1941, see A. Pashkov, "Obshchie Voprosy Ekonomicheskoi Teorii Planirovania" in M. Fedorenko, ed., *Problemy Ekonomicheskoi Nauki i Praktiki* (Moscow, 1972), pp. 25–26.

the "command economy," as it historically evolved in the Soviet Union, inherently included state coercion on a mass scale. The secret police and the procurator seemed more to hinder than to help economic life. Nevertheless, they were ubiquitous in factories and *kolkhozy*, not only to prevent pilfering but also, so they claimed, to ensure proper economic accounting (*khozraschët*).

Once coercion and control became the general practice of appropriate machineries, the emerging vested interests had to generate an appropriate ideology. Precedents, when available, were welcome, so "spontaneity" now became the main enemy, as it had been in the civil war; anarchy and markets became synonymous with it. Right-wingers supposedly were the political agents of this spontaneity (*samotëk*), which led right back to capitalism through the intermediary of foreign intelligence.

Planning in "physical units," direct allocation of resources, and direct procurements from peasants (a quasi-tax in kind) in the 1930s, became the prevailing practices, and theories of "socialist barter" became the ideology sanctifying the interests of the administration. "Socialist barter" was extolled by jobholders because it seemed to offer a better device for controlling processes and men than "indirect" techniques, such as market mechanisms. Thus, direct and centralized control over resources and men, with its orders and red tape (all *nariady, zaiavki, zagotovki*, and *glavki*) was a product of Russian and Soviet history not less than of Marxism.

In his last writing Stalin clearly stated why he wished the market to disappear and barter to prevail. This would enable the center to better master production processes for the general interest. *Kolkhozy* and the exchange of commodities were the last obstacles on this road.[23]

Thus, a "war economy" served as the basis for an administrative superstructure of overlapping bureaucracies, which became a unified politico-economic apparatus on the

[23] Cf. Stalin, *Ekonomicheskie Problemy*, pp. 67–68.

top and bifurcated into separate political and economic state bureaucracies on the lower echelons. The experiences and improvisations of the early 1930s enriched the borrowings from the civil war, and these features of the system in planning and other state functions remained substantially unchanged for a generation,[24] if not longer.

The state building process under Stalin had the astonishing feature of replicating methods of organization within different areas of activity. In creating its new model of the economy, the party, the main political agency of the system, was itself entirely transformed. Just as the state, the party became dominated by a centralized, hierarchical structure, a counterpart in many ways to the "command economy," avid to control both factories and writers. Factors that prompted the system to view market categories and other expressions of spontaneity in economic life as pernicious contributed also to the opinion that any autonomy was a possible source of opposition and heterogeneity in politics.

The imperative and detailed plan for the economy had its counterpart in a monolithic ideology for the control of social diversity.

To sum up, the model that emerged in the 1930s on the ruins of the NEP was a "command economy" which exhibited the following traits: (1) a high degree of centralization of economic decision making and planning; (2) comprehensive character of planning; (3) preference for physical units as instruments in accounting; (4) the use of "material balances" for obtaining internal consistency of the plans; (5) a centralized administration for material supplies, which operated as a rationing system; (6) the imper-

[24] This was stated by the academician Dorodnitsyn, *Izvestiia*, 15 May 1963, quoted by E. Zalesky, *Planning Reforms in the Soviet Union, 1962–1966* (Chapel Hill, N.C., 1967), p. 53. Cf. Bobrowski: "Towards the end of the first five-year plan the constitution of the Soviet planning system almost in all its aspects can be considered as finished," *U Zródeł*, p. 151.

113

ative and detailed character of plans; (7) a hierarchically organized administration within factories; (8) the relegation of market categories and mechanisms to a secondary role, mainly to the sphere, albeit important, of personal consumption and to labor; and (9) coercion by the state, as direct organizer of the economy with its ubiquitous controls and etatization not only of the economy but of the other spheres of life as well.

This system proved to be immensely dynamic and contributed to the economic development of Russia; the regime erected in this process, known as "Stalinist," propelled Russia into the modern age. The system certainly had its internal logic; otherwise it would not have been able to function. The devices in economic management—"physical units," material-technical supply system, "material balances," detailed character of planning, priority approach—were not in themselves bureaucratic whims. These methods are appropriate, to some extent, in any economic planning, but here they became the main ones,[25] and they certainly account for the system's successes. Similarly, although the economic process was not planned to the extent that propaganda claimed, it was strictly managed and organized, on an unprecedented scale and exclusively by the state. While the state plays an important role in economic development in other countries, private initiative and different social factors also had a role, sometimes the leading one. Not so in the Soviet Union. As etatization expanded to all sectors of the economy, the concentration of decision making at the highest level became unprecedented. Political and economic power merged into one, and totalitarian controls spread to create an "ideal type" of a state economy, the traits of which became stretched to their limits. If controls, concentration of power, coercion, and priority were necessary, they tended to become pervasive, overall, autocratic!

As feverish industrial activity unfolded, the system soon

[25] Cf. A. Nove, *The Soviet Economy* (3d ed., London, 1968), chap. 12, esp. pp. 325–332.

began to show its shadows. The factors accountable for dynamism were followed by growing dysfunctional phenomena, which developed a whole set of crippling tendencies. The central factors which bred these phenomena were state interference and controls and the unrealistic, overambitious economic growth rate. Together they contributed to the emergence of countervailing forces that hampered economic development and the "purity" of the model.

In these two important areas, the state clearly "took too much upon itself," as a critic clamored. The drive against small commerce, artisans, and entrepreneurs, particularly against the peasant smallholders, conducted under the slogan of an anticapitalist offensive, resulted in "commercial deserts," huge black markets, mass pilferings, sprawling bureaucracies, and, more important, a severely oppressive course in Soviet history that the opposition desperately tried to prevent.

The imposing of impossible "tempos," at a time when commerce declined and agriculture was utterly disorganized, contributed to a situation of acute social and economic crisis that only mass terror could control. Crackdowns on small-scale production coupled with an exclusive orientation on huge projects heightened the crisis, helped create a drop in the standard of living—quite unprecedented in peacetime—and heavily distorted the whole economic development, which led to a considerable slowdown in the growth rate. From 1929 to 1932, targets for industrial growth were, respectively, 21.7, 32, 45, and 36 percent, but the official figures of actual growth for those years were 20, 21.8, 22, and 15 percent. In 1933, when the more moderate target of 16.5 percent was adopted, only a 5 percent rate was achieved. These figures, it should be remembered, were certainly exaggerated.

But the picture for the whole period of five-year plans (*piatiletki*), up to the war, was not less telling in this respect. Revised official figures published in the 1960s claimed an average annual rate of industrial growth of 19.2 percent for the first Five-Year Plan, 17.8 percent for the second, and 13.2 percent for the (unfinished) third plan.[26] This constituted the "leveling off curve" that critics, who were later punished for having been right, had expected. There were strictly economic and political limits to what could be attained. But there was neither an economic nor a political science that could predict those limits. Economic decision, based only on political criteria devoid of any consideration of cost, created new problems, and forced on the state tasks which it was ill prepared to handle.

A few powerful leaders, undisturbed by any formal checks or countervailing powers, viewed the national economy almost as a simple, privately run "factory," which could be regulated down to the smallest detail and was expected to perform whatever was ordered. Ignorance of economic realities inherent in such an approach was enhanced by the brushing aside of economics. For twenty years there was not even a textbook of political economy, and this discipline was temporarily dropped from the curricula. The disdain toward statistics was manifested by the renaming of the statistical agency as the "national accounting" agency. This was a direct result of central authorities trying to run an enormous and growing economy as a simple tribal one that would be perfectly manageable within the framework of "healthy pragmatism."

Thus, the drive was curiously marred by contradictory and damaging countertendencies. The gain resulting from the expansion of investment was partly lost by the slowness of construction and prolonged trouble in the new industries during their gestation. Benefits derived from the introduction of the newest technology were offset to a large degree in the long run by the tendency to neglect the already developed industries and the failure to induce them to inno-

[26] The figures are from *Narodnoe Khoziaistvo SSSR v 1970 Godu* (Moscow, 1971), p. 131.

vate. Particularly pernicious was the appearance of a set of counterincentives to growth that amounted to a "phobia of innovation" (Grossman's term). Similarly, in agriculture, where collectivization allowed for the squeezing out of procurements, stagnation resulted with dire consequences for the standard of living and the productivity of labor.

Taut planning that tended to squeeze growth soon manifested all the weaknesses of an economic organization put into high gear without appropriate reserves in resources, materials, and capacities and developed many of the troubles of an anarchic system: inflationary pressures, depression, and misuse of resources, with a shortage of materials and technical supplies in one sector and surpluses or frozen capital goods in others. Production in factories was uneven, proceeding in jerks and spasms, because of faulty supply or other factors inherent in a system of numerous and unattainable targets; this situation existed within the economy at large. In fact, an overcentralized economy caused a situation in which "planning becomes fictitious. What actually is obtained is an elemental development." Not unsurprisingly, "in all the socialist countries in the period of highly centralized planning and management, there were many elemental processes of this type."[27]

As internal coherence was sacrificed, the investment plans were not secured with the necessary resources, big installations were erected without the necessary or complementary services, and branches developed without a modicum of coordination between them. In short, the essential benefit expected from planning, namely "a sound general structure" corresponding to social needs,[28] was lacking in the economy. Planning became bogged down in detail, and paradoxically the overall economic structure, its propor-

[27] O. Lange, "The Role of Planning," p. 207.
[28] J. Kornai, *Overcentralization in Economic Administration* (Oxford, 1959), pp. 181–204. Janos Kornai is a distinguished Hungarian economist.

117

tions, and interrelations evolved spontaneously and sporadically without any planning. In particular, the emerging mechanism had no innate incentives for growth but tended to waste, low quality, and conservative routines.

The whole model evidently suffered from a deeply imbalanced growth pattern and an inherent mechanism that generated a staggering amount of waste in resources and an unbelievable maze of irrationalities in their allocation and other fields of economic activity. Among the stupendous and baffling traits of the Stalinist period were the mass schooling of the population coupled with the murderous destruction of the educated cadres and the imposition of so many sacrifices for the sake of defense together with the annihilation of the best officers.

The cost of the whole process kept growing, and the reserves for "building without bricks" obviously were bound to reach their limits eventually. Even in such a rich country the sources of extensive growth—labor surplus, easily found and extracted raw materials, an important railroad network —were not unlimited. The method of increasing present growth at the expense of future growth was too irrational and self-defeating in the long run, and its price was heavy. Throughout the system imbalances and maladjustments produced signs of stagnation. Too much prodding from above and lack of initiative, or inertia, from below contributed to the internal weakening of the Stalinist system. The model was continually beset by the contradiction between the spurts devised to make people act in accordance with the state's wishes and the counterincentives bred by contradictions inherent in the control-and-target system, which oriented people to act according to their own motivations, values, and impulses—often quite different from the official line or against it. Many people continued to use existing loopholes in order to defend their interests and did not exert their best efforts in pursuing the officially imposed plans and aims.

118

Thus, widening gaps appeared between the interests of producers and those of the state apparatus.

Stalin, then, bequeathed to his heirs both a great industrial power and an inefficient economy.

As a result of the very dysfunctions of the "command system," and in spite of the powerful levers at its disposal, the system was unable to develop itself fully in its textbook purity. As differences developed, they contributed toward making the system more "mixed" than was ever to be admitted. In short, a kind of elusive but real, distorted but indestructible, countermodel subsisted and developed informally inside the main pattern.

While market mechanisms were only secondary in the theoretical model, and money played but a "passive character" in planning, they were of prime importance to citizens and to their perception of the economy in which they lived.

First, even the official model allowed the labor force and consumer goods some degree of market-type bargaining, behavior, and pricing. People were paid in money with which they purchased goods. This created an important breach in the prevailing administrative "physical" pattern. Another apparent anomaly emerged when the planners found that they had to price capital goods, although in theory these rarely left the closed circuit of the state economy and thus were supposed to be distributed rather than marketed. The cost to the economy for these misconceptions was considerable. As counterpart to the deficiencies of the material-technical supply system and the failures of pricing, the factories were hard pressed to fulfill targets, inadequately supplied with the necessary resources to do so, and developed ways of their own to meet the quotas. An important network of middlemen, "pushers" (*tolkachi*), and "suppliers" (*snabzhentsy*) emerged, which helped the harassed director of a factory, *kolkhoz*, or *sovkhoz* to obtain the necessary supplies that, although officially allocated to them,

119

would never reach them through official channels. They also bartered, exchanged services, and employed less orthodox means to acquire necessary but unallocated resources. Thus, a kind of market even for capital goods evolved and was tolerated by the government. Impossible to eradicate, it helped the economy to work better.[29]

Such networks soon became rather important and employed thousands of people, although the legality of such action was questionable. Probably no factory and no agricultural farm could have afforded to avoid having and using such intermediaries. Otherwise they risked the failure of their plans and the loss of their bonuses and jobs. At least such practices were well intentioned; they helped to achieve aims that were officially promoted. But, as in any market, some were more skillful than others, and the methods employed to obtain goods and semifinished products could be used for nonapproved and illegal aims, too. In fact, the semitolerated practices of the so-called gray markets often merged with entirely illegal black markets, with their numerous categories of speculators, always ready and able to obtain any article available somewhere in the governmental warehouses but in short supply in the shops. The speculators of different types acquired merchandise, with the help of factory managers, or from the official commercial stores (where stealing and pilfering were constant) and also from another officially organized but rarely acknowledged special network of supply for the privileged, which one observer even called "the third economy" (the first being the officially acknowledged one; the second, the illegal black market).[30] Such phenomena were characteris-

[29] The informal practices that Soviet managers developed, including the *tolkachi*, are well described in J. Berliner, *Factory and Manager in the USSR* (Cambridge, Mass., 1957), chap. 12. See also chap. 2 for the informal arrangements through connections and favoritism called *blat*.

[30] The journalist K. S. Karol wrote about his impressions as a result of a trip to the USSR in "Conversations in Russia," *New Statesman*, 1 January 1971, pp. 8–10.

tic of the command economy after the liquidation of the NEP, and they have thrived ever since.

Thus, in a sense, the NEP was never entirely eliminated. Many former merchants, traders, and kulaks disappeared, but they were soon replaced by numerous black marketeers, and by new categories of intermediaries emerging from the nationalized industries and serving them in the best mercantile spirit. A Western scholar, in discussing unofficial trade in capital goods, concluded that besides the "fundamental model" of the command economy a market model, secondary in importance but influential, coexisted with the first, and that "the models taken together apply to Soviet industry over the entire period since the early 1930s."[31]

Both trade in capital goods and the illegal circulation of consumer goods to those who could afford to buy them clearly indicate that markets and market phenomena acquired an important role in Soviet economy, and a particular importance in the daily life of the citizenry.

In addition, *kolkhoz* members, *sovkhoz* workers, and numerous city dwellers kept private plots, which generated agricultural production and commerce. They produced a staggeringly large share of the gross agricultural output of the country—one-third or more by some estimates—and were responsible for much of the diet of the city dwellers and for the livelihood of the peasant family. Survival of the peasant family and that of the *kolkhoz* system depended upon this production. It was nevertheless no more than a tolerated activity with frequent restrictions and interference that had dire consequences for the country's food production each time this happened. These were allegedly non-Soviet, transitory sectors, bound to disappear "in the next stage."

The existence of the different parallel economies and networks during Stalin's regime, which continue today, exer-

[31] D. Granick, *The Soviet Metal-Fabricating and Economic Development* (Madison, Wisc., 1967), pp. 214, 227–230.

cised a deeply disturbing and corrupting influence on many Soviet citizens. The widespread "commercial spirit" among many of them is widely known. Self-interest, not that of the community, is popular wisdom, and heroic figures of propaganda clichés are not the prevailing model. "Socialist man" has not yet become a reality. Self-seekers, utilitarians, pilferers against which the press constantly fights, proliferate and penetrate party ranks. Russian terms for these categories—*rvachi, khapuny, deliagi, raskhititeli*—offer additional testimony to the numerous varieties of such characters.

Also, from the official point of view, the phenomenon of "labor turnover," when masses of workers since the early 1930s wandered from factory to factory in search of better working conditions, belonged to the "non-Soviet" ways of behavior. These quite natural movements were condemned by officials as an expression of materialistic impulses, as "chasing after the longer ruble."

But such preaching was not only counterproductive but also contributed to the emergence among the lower-paid and underprivileged popular classes of their own class consciousness, which no amount of control or terror could extirpate. Their own perception of privilege and power in the system could not be altered by propaganda. Daily life taught them about the power and self-seeking of the bosses (*nachal'stvo*). The "us" and "them" dichotomy, particularly disagreeable to the propagandist, leads people's perception of class reality far from the official idyll with its supposedly nonantagonistic and friendly classes—workers and peasants—and the layer of the intelligentsia placed between the two. This shallow cliché is irrelevant, as are also the exhortations of the *nachal'stvo*, when the working man knows that people on important jobs have not only power but also special supply networks. "The laboring man" (*nash brat, rabochii narod*) gets the orders and the hardships, while others give the orders and enjoy privileges. These are the terms in which reality is perceived, although not necessarily rebelled against.

Class differences and the development and existence of different countercultures, unofficial or inimical to the official ones, highlight the complex social pattern that developed inside, outside, and against the officially accepted model. In economic and social behavior, such countermodels became permanent inside the rigid formal framework and contributed heavily to distortions, counterincentives, and cleavages in Soviet society, at the same time accumulating multifarious tendencies and contradictions that eroded and corrupted the tightly controlled system of the *piatiletkas*. This model could not cope with such a nexus of social and economic realities. When the cork came off in 1953, an overhaul of the system was already long overdue.

The descriptions pertaining to the Stalinist model contain many traits that are still valid for the post-Stalinist period and will be discussed in Part II. Until 1953, a sequence of changing patterns with rather abrupt and unexpected transitions emerged following emergency situations. Each new stage always lasted longer than the previous one: eight months of revolution, almost three years of civil war, eight to nine years for the NEP, and at least twenty-five years for the command economy, if it is conditionally agreed that this stage actually ended with Stalin's death.

Obviously, these different historical stages display not only variety but also some common traits, which allow us to group the four periods into two alternating blueprints: a "mixed economy" displaced by a "command economy," replaced once more by a "mixed economy," which was finally ousted by another type of a "command economy." In both species, important features in the whole system, including the political sphere, were intimately linked to and often reflected the appropriate correlations obtaining in the economic sphere.

Common to each of the two patterns were the relationships between market and plan or, on a larger scale, between state and social classes. The changing patterns were thus repeating some basic aspects, making the Soviet historical drama a two-act play replayed several times with different sets and casts. Was it that Soviet history had only two prototypes from which to choose? Or has it today reached a stage where the narrow choice is enlarged by historical development and old dilemmas can be forgotten? As this inquiry into the pertinent problems of the post-Stalinist system continues, tentative answers may yet be found to such questions.

PART TWO

ECONOMICS AND THE STATE

CHAPTER SIX

The "Command Economy" under Scrutiny

UNDER Stalin's dictatorship, Soviet Russia industrialized and developed, and at his death she emerged as a superpower, second only to the United States. His successors, although they knew they had much to mend in the system left by Stalin, nevertheless claimed that Russia would soon surpass the United States as the leading power. With a low standard of living, substandard agricultural production, and still very large rural population, such a boast about the Soviet Union's economic prowess seemed ludicrous and was scorned and dismissed as propaganda by many Westerners.

But the Soviets had based their prediction on the evidence of the rates of their economic growth, although these also encountered, especially during the cold war, Western incredulity. But the rates of growth were impressive and they primarily contributed to Russia's spectacular rise, in a very brief period, to the rank of a superpower. And if such rates remained constant, the simplest calculation was sufficient to show that the Russians had a basis for their self-assurance. Russia's GNP in the 1950s had increased at a rate of some 7.1 percent, whereas that of the United States grew at a rate of 2.9 percent. If this continued, every five-year plan would narrow the gap between the two, and Russia would overtake and win the economic competition in a matter of time. Some Western economists reached this conclusion in the 1950s and believed that the language of such figures was inexorable. They thus accepted in fact the Russian prognosis—though with different qualifications. The data on Soviet growth up to the late 1950s supported such a view.

Suddenly and unexpectedly for the Soviet leadership and even for some Western economists, the Soviet growth rates declined. According to Soviet and Western economists, the turning point occurred in 1958. "Through the decade of the 1950s," an American economist noted, "the Soviet economy was the leader in growth performance among the principal industrialized nations. Since 1958 Soviet growth has slipped markedly from an average annual 7.1 percent for the eight preceding years to a rate of 5.3 percent for the six succeeding years."[1]

The dwindling rates of growth might have been seen as rather predictable, but an additional set of phenomena occurring simultaneously in the Soviet and in the capitalist economies complicated the picture.

First, calculations by Soviet economists showed that the declining rates of growth were accompanied and partly explained by a diminishing rate of growth of labor productivity, disquieting if not ominous in itself. But further data disclosed more: the productivity of capital, the other crucial factor in an economy's performance, was falling as well. Table 1 shows the dwindling "dynamics of the efficiency of industrial production," to use the term employed by Soviet researchers.

These figures indicate the trends in the industrial performance, which worried the Soviet researcher and leader alike. During the three quinquennia described above, capital formation remained on a very high level, but the results of the accumulation did not match the effort. Rates of industrial output were dwindling considerably, and therefore the productivity of capital in industry, measured here as ratio of output per 1 percent of fixed assets, was showing a steep downward trend. Simultaneously, productivity of

[1] For the vicissitudes in anticipating Soviet economic growth, see, for example, A. Gerschenkron, *Economic Backwardness in Historical Perspective* (New York, 1965), pp. 264–269. The quote is from U.S. Congress, Joint Economic Committee, Subcommittee on Foreign Policy, *New Directions of the Soviet Economy*, 89th Cong., 2d sess. (Washington, D.C., 1966), p. 6.

TABLE 1

Dynamics of Efficiency of Industrial Production
(rate of average annual growth in percent)

Year	Fixed Capital Assets	Industrial Output	Increase in Industrial Output per 1 Percent of Increase on Fixed Assets	Growth of Productivity per Worker
1951–1955	11.4	11.3	1.16	7.6
1956–1960	11.5	10.4	0.91	6.3
1961–1965	11.1	8.6	0.77	4.8

Source: A. Notkin (ed.), *Struktura narodnogo khoziaistva SSSR* (Moscow, 1967), pp. 270 and 272.

labor was rapidly slowing down. The coincidence of the downward trends of factor productivity was particularly disquieting during the period 1951–1958.

When figures for transportation, construction, and agriculture—all, on the whole, less efficient areas than industry, especially agriculture—were added to the data on efficiency in industry, they revealed a trend toward growing inefficiency.

More recent figures quoted by Khachaturov, corresponding member of the Academy of Sciences, confirm that these trends in industry applied to the whole sphere of material production. His criterion for economic efficiency is the ratio of the physical volume of the national income to the sum of fixed and circulating assets in the national economy (in fixed prices). This index shows that a ratio of 62 kopeks of national income to every ruble of assets in 1959 fell steadily to 53.2 kopeks in 1965 and to 50.6 in 1968. The author knows that this trend can partly be explained by the efforts to effect structural changes in the economy, but he nevertheless considers the trend as pernicious, whereas

129

his own data for the United States for the period 1957–1963 show an improvement of the similar indicator.

One of the underlying causes of these unfortunate phenomena is disclosed by a related ratio measuring the efficiency of the investment effort. Here the increment of the national income is related to the increment of the combined fixed and circulating assets, and for the period 1964–1968 the ratio—43 kopeks per ruble—is much lower than the one quoted earlier.[2]

Although this chapter deals primarily with data for the 1960s as they became available to Soviet researchers or emerged through their studies, the official figures for the period 1968–1972 are worth mentioning. They claim some improvement in growth of GNP and labor productivity, probably arresting the downward trend. But productivity of capital and of investments kept dwindling, and a further worsening of efficiency, notably in industry, is predicted and deplored by the authors of the current ninth Five-Year Plan.[3]

[2] G. Khachaturov, in A. Rumiantsev, and P. Bunich, eds., *Ekonomicheskaia Reforma: Ee Osushchestvlenie i Problemy* (Moscow, 1969), chap. 7, pp. 195–197. For a Western study on efficiency of the Soviet economy, see A. Bergson, *Planning and Productivity Under Soviet Socialism* (New York, 1968), pp. 64–65. The author studies Soviet static and dynamic efficiency, in comparison with other countries, and concludes that the Soviet performance fares quite well—when compared with the worst of the capitalist performances. For an additional Soviet study of the same problem, see Ia. Kvasha in A. Notkin, ed., *Faktory Ekonomicheskogo Razvitiia SSSR* (Moscow, 1970), chap. 6, pp. 150–153.

[3] Results of the first two years of the current five-year plan—1971 and 1972, particularly the latter—show that the planned targets for productivity and overall growth were not reached. For sources, see note 11, Chapter 13. But the efficiency indicators actually show a further worsening and this is officially acknowledged in *Gosudarstvennyi Piatiletnii Plan Razvitiia Narodnogo Khoziaistva SSSR na 1971–1975 Gody* (Moscow, 1972), p. 235. The phenomenon is explained in this text by the efforts to correct disproportions and maladjustments before an improvement of these indicators can be achieved.

All in all, such data, now made available to the Soviet public, show the real culprit behind the slowdown: inefficiency. Some computations indicated more clearly just what was the price of inefficiency. The national income grew by 54.5 billion rubles (in 1958 prices) from 1961 to 1965, but at the same time the productivity of investment fell by some 15 percent. Had this not been the case, the national income during those years would have soared by an additional 217 billion, not 57 billion rubles.[4]

The economy was still growing, to be sure, even respectably so by contemporary standards, but the Soviet rates stopped being exceptional, and some capitalist countries, and other socialist ones, began to do as well or better. The same applied to the crucial labor productivity indicator. Every Soviet citizen could read the quotation from Lenin asserting that "labor productivity is, in the last analysis, the main, the most important factor for the victory of the new social system." This would normally have been quoted with a sense of pride, but now it might point to a very different prospect. For if the negative trends were to continue, several capitalist countries, including the United States, would definitively beat the Soviet Union at its own game.

Thus, the late 1950s and the 1960s presented an entirely new situation than the troublesome 1930s. Capitalist countries learned to better master their economic performance at a time when the Soviet economy was losing much of its dynamism. Obviously, in the long run, Russia's position as a superpower was at stake, not to mention an ideological setback. Growth figures could no longer back the claim of the "superiority of Soviet socialism."

That the country found itself in this situation could be explained in part by such factors as the unwarranted claims of propaganda and the blind destruction of critical thought. Studies in history and modern economics, which could eventually enlighten the public and the leaders, were not

[4] A. Notkin, ed., *Struktura Narodnogo Khoziaistva SSSR* (Moscow, 1967), p. 59.

permitted at a time when a growing, complex organization could no longer be run by the prevailing conventional wisdom of the numerous bureaucracies. A thick veil of pompous, empty, untested assumptions presented as "laws of socialist economy" was imposed on the universities and institutes of research; but self-deceiving claims to superior "scientific policies" could not be effective against the real processes of history, which presented the nation with surprising twists, unwanted and unexpected fluctuations, and spontaneous outcomes and did not honor the commitment to planning or the claim of its "superiority."

Unnoticed for some time were those self-defeating features in the economic mechanism that had appeared in the early 1960s. Growing means devoted to accumulation and investment ironically led to falling returns on investment and a dwindling growth rate.[5] Data on national income revealed this. In fact, the Soviet Union was investing in physical inputs at a much quicker rate than the United States, if not at the same volume as it officially claimed in 1970,[6] and the results of this growth were quite disappointing. Research showed that the growing cost of the operation slowed down the whole process, and that the strategies employed had become blatantly counterproductive and urgently needed revision. The unilateral devotion to priority of investment in heavy industry, which was supposed to be the main secret of success,[7] together with huge injections of labor force and coercive political pressure, appeared as factors in this slowdown. Yet dogmas and the practices behind them were tenacious. Heavy industry still continued to be lavishly pampered, at the expense of consumption, with relatively more products serving heavy industry rather than

[5] Cf. S. Pervushin, V. Venzher, A. Kvasha, et al., *Proizvodstvo, Nakoplenie, Potreblenie* (Moscow, 1965), pp. 25–27, 82.

[6] *Narodnoe Khoziaistvo SSSR v 1970 Godu* (Moscow, 1971), p. 82.

[7] Cf. Pervushin, Venzher, Kvasha et al., *Proizvodstvo, Nakoplenie*, pp. 72, 109, 177–178.

benefiting consumption. "Production for production's sake" certainly expressed the position of the Soviet economy, and neither the standard of living nor the national income adequately benefited from it.

Thus, the old strategy of growth began to turn sour. Its unilateral application turned the intrepid industrializers into mediocre or bad *khoziaeva*—a peasant term for husbandry and thrift. The orientation on squeezing resources, which had worked as long as resources were available for extensive use, had deleterious effects on the system. While the state could exert heavy pressure to obtain the necessary resources, it did not use them either sparingly or efficiently. Thus, for some time, proper management of resources, in itself a source of growth, was lost on the system. Russian peasants and many workers called this mismanagement "bad *khoziaïn*," because, despite the building and industrializing, waste and poverty remained. The fine points of economic management and planning, such as quality, productivity, spirit of innovation, and optimization—a term in fact officially banned for quite a time—were beyond the capacity of Soviet institutions. For a time, there was more squandering than budgeting of resources, and internal mechanisms inimical to innovation and efficiency became deeply embedded in the whole pattern. But shadowy counterincentives and disabilities inherited from the years of the "big drive" continued to take root. They finally began to block the wheels. Factors of low efficiency began to assert themselves, and no amount of pressure or exhortation could stop the ominously coinciding downward trends of the productivity of both labor and capital.

It was time, quite clearly, to awaken and act. Old strategies and methods had become inadequate; new ones were needed. The United States, powerful and innovative, continued to grow economically; Germany, Japan, and France had recovered from the war and had expanding growth rates, as did China, which had adopted new methods for achieving industrialization after abandoning Soviet models.

133

The Soviet Union had to confront this reality in a competitive and complex world. In the midst of a new technological revolution, to leave intact a conservatively biased economic planning and managing system with its inbuilt "phobia of innovation" was a sure way toward, as a French saying goes, *manquer le rendez-vous avec l'histoire*.

The Renaissance of Economics

The first task consisted of repairing the damage that had been inflicted on the nation by the stifling of scholarship for some twenty to thirty years. The lag of at least twenty years in economics, according to one Russian economist, was part of the incalculable "cost" of the years of industrialization. Scholarship had not developed, its achievements were not introduced into the economy, and this, in turn, further contributed to the retardation of economic science. "But in our days twenty years mean so much in science. Weren't some two-thirds of all the knowledge accumulated by mankind obtained in the last twenty years. . . ?"[s]

Some time after Stalin's death the leadership was forced to encourage its economists. With official blessing, a start was made in 1957–1958. The inspiration came from older scholars who had already been prominent in the field in the 1920s, some of whom returned from camps and exile to chairs and institutes.

At the forefront of the movement were V. S. Nemchinov, a statistician of the old school, and another economist of stature, V. V. Novozhilov—who later earned a Lenin Prize for his work.

The economists, on the whole, responded in a remarkable manner. Talent was available. Very soon many bright young people began to flock to the new branch, thirsty not only for knowledge but also for new languages on social

[s] V. Novozhilov, *Problemy Izmereniia Zatrat i Rezul'tatov pri Optimal'nom Planirovanii* (Moscow, 1967), p. 25; *Problems of Cost-Benefit Analysis in Optimal Planning*, trans H. McQuiston (White Plains, N.Y., 1970).

realities, and in those years their optimism was boundless. They felt that they were needed and that they had both support and freedom.

In the revival of Soviet economics, the branch of mathematical economics emerged. Although the Soviet mathematician Kantorovich first formulated the principles of linear programming in 1939, his work remained unnoticed. He argued that mathematics could be used to find optimal solutions for economic problems provided prices were closely linked with the optimal plan (the concept of shadow prices) and expressed scarcity and utility, not just average cost.

It was Novozhilov who was the first to understand the potential for economics of Kantorovich's mathematical apparatus, and somewhat later Nemchinov stepped in to lend the talented mathematician his support. Soon laboratories, faculties, and institutes began to mushroom, and a vigorous school of mathematical economics appeared. In addition, Lur'e, Vainshtein, Volkonsky, Belkin, and many others eagerly worked on optimal plans for the whole economy or its separate sectors. This development is still in upswing today.[9]

Mathematics, however, was not enough; economic theory was lacking. It had to be created first. Significantly, in 1959 the Academy of Sciences appointed a committee of leading economists—representatives of different schools of thought, several of which had emerged once debate was allowed— to work out recommendations for "ways of computing values," or rather for fixing correct prices (the real "bottleneck in Soviet economy," according to Novozhilov). The

[9] For a history of Soviet mathematical economics, see M. Ellman, *Soviet Planning Today* (Cambridge, Mass., 1971). Details are from I. Birman's lively book, *Metodologiia Optimal'nogo Planirovania* (Moscow, 1971), pp. 3–28. See also G. Hardt, et al., *Mathematics and Computers in Soviet Economic Planning* (New Haven, Conn., 1967); and A. Zauberman, *Aspects of Planometrics* (New Haven, Conn., 1967).

committee worked for a year, instead of the initially al-
lotted three months, and was unable to make any recommendations. Every member of the committee defended a
different opinion.[10] The previous, meaningless uniformity
was dead, but no theory of prices was available. A big nation was reaping the fruits of dogma—economic science
had to be built from scratch (and from borrowings), but
at least the awareness of *scio ut nescio* was certainly
salutary.

Parallel to the developments in economics were those in
planning and management, where proposals were made to
change traditional practices and to undertake experiments
in these fields: Professor E. Liberman, in "Plan, Profit, Pre-
mium" (*Pravda*, 9 September 1962), proposed that more
autonomy be granted to enterprises: that the planned indicators that were imposed from above be changed, and that
the incentive system be reshaped. He was a harbinger of
the reforms to be launched three years later. Simultaneously, institutes and managers offered numerous plans, and
the press opened its columns to other proposals and debate.

But the new would not be realized without fierce battles
—in part in scholarly terms, but at first mainly of an ideological and political character—against the old. The new attitude toward economics and its main task—now seen as
efficiency and optimality—was to fight for the acceptance
and awareness of the scarcity of resources (no need to be
that thrifty if resources are abundant by definition) and the
concepts of utility and marginal analysis. Such ideas were
bourgeois heresy according to the adherents of the formerly predominant and officially backed "political economy."
Without overcoming the opposition of entrenched dogmas
and the powers behind them, there was no leeway for new
ideas.

[10] On the academy's committees on prices and the different theories
that emerged there, see V. Nemchinov, *Obshchestvennaia Stoimost' i
Planovaia Tsena* (Moscow, 1970), pp. 3, 381–403.

The better minds among the older economists, knowing this time that they had appropriate political cover, opened fire against the existing system of economic management and the ideological constructions that had justified the current methods. A host of other men, scholars, and officials, seconded by some factory managers and technicians, joined in giving vent to the accumulated grudges and dissatisfaction with the performance of the system and with the conditions under which they had to work.

At the same time institutes and economic agencies, such as Gosplan and some of the economic ministries, engaged in serious studies of the country's economy and, in many cases, resumed work on problems or tools that had been conceived in the 1920s but dropped in the 1930s. New methods and concepts, especially by mathematical economists, econometricians, and planimetricians, began to appear, attracting enthusiastic youth who contributed to the assessment of the national economy and, probably, did not much relish the fact that certain planning techniques were more sophisticated, more advanced, and more effectively used in the West than in the fatherland of planning.

From the late 1950s and mainly during the 1960s, the debate in the field of economics turned into a real, sometimes bitterly fought, battle.[11] In the struggles many cherished dogmas of the past were attacked, and some of them, though still well entrenched, were totally discredited or considerably weakened. The superiority of "sector A over sector B"—the thesis that demanded the priority in means and rates of growth for heavy industry over other sectors as a *sine qua non* of socialist development—was now either recognized by some as having had only relative and tem-

[11] Examples of such vivid debates are in *Ekonomisty i Matematiki za Kruglym Stolom* (Moscow, 1965), which contains minutes of a conference that took place in 1964; M. Fedorenko, ed., *Diskussiia ob Optimal'nom Planirovanii* (Moscow, 1968), reports on a debate that took place in 1966.

porary validity in the early stages of industrialization or as having been theoretically unsound; in any case, this "sacred cow" was now openly attacked as having become counter-productive.

A similar treatment was reserved for several other dogmas or myths. The supposedly socialist essence of the "physical units" (as against the "capitalist" essence and the transitory character of market categories and of pricing) was now categorically rejected. Most notably, the scholarly validity of the whole "political economy"—the textbook clichés officially endorsed by party *imprimatur*—was now attacked as backward, dogmatic, and irrelevant to the problems of the economy.[12] Obviously, such attacks heightened the debates and aroused vigilant counterattacks by fundamentalists of all kinds. But they were on the defensive. Reformers keenly aware of the need to develop new approaches to pricing, management, planning, and economics in general had to clear away many obstacles. First, they fought simple ignorance. For example, Sobolev, a reputed mathematician, patiently explained to an audience partly composed of old-fashioned stalwarts of orthodoxy that the term "margin" was not at all some deadly bourgeois sin but simply an elementary and indispensable notion in mathematics.[13]

The authority behind the dogma was also assailed virulently. "Stalin's faulty treatment of the subject of political economy and particularly of the political economy of socialism," wrote the late academician Arzumanian in 1964, "as well as his false conception of the role of this science, led to

[12] For attacks on the official "political economy" see "introduction" to Fedorenko, ed. *Diskussiia* and *passim*; R. Judy, "The Economists," in G. Skilling and F. Griffith, eds., *Interest Groups in Soviet Politics* (Princeton, N.J., 1971), is highly informative on many aspects that have been discussed here.

[13] See academician S. Sobolev's speech in *Ekonomisty i Matematiki*, p. 64. Mathematicians played an important role in the revival of Soviet economics.

138

the impoverishment of its content and to the emasculation of its revolutionary-practical significance."[14]

The problem, however, was not in Stalin's ideas but rather in the strong presence of his numerous followers—politicians, economists and administrators—who exhibited a deeply ingrained preference for "direct methods" in counting and controlling. Nemchinov attacked "barter" (*priamoi produktoobmen*) as "contrary to the contemporary conditions of the complex and deep division of social labor which characterizes all the spheres of the socialist national economy." This was "an unfounded and erroneous idea,"[15] but one that encouraged viewing a national economy as "one factory" run from one center—the basis of the whole set of "administrative methods" of the system. Malyshev, deputy head of the Central Statistical Office and a staunch reformer, made these ideas and methods the main target of his scornful sorties. With such attitudes and approaches, he charged, "socialist production is being equated with some primeval economy of an archaic tribe or with a peasant family of the ancient times." According to him the partisans of such practices were totally ignorant of economic realities and kept dreaming of "programming to the smallest details the whole national economy in physical indicators."[16]

Such opinions already pointed to the formation of camps and schools, not only of an economic but also of a political character. The more strictly economic problems, concerning value, pricing, planning, and proposals for change in the model, gave birth, as one would expect, to numerous

---

[14] The late academician Arzumanian spoke to a meeting of the Presidium of the Academy of Sciences, *Vestnik Akademii Nauk*, no. 9 (Moscow, 1964), pp. 4–5. Quoted in Judy, "The Economists," p. 223.

[15] Nemchinov, *Obshchestvennaia Stoimost'*, p. 249.

[16] I. Malyshev, *Ekonomicheskie Zakony Sotsializma i Planirovanie* (Moscow, 1966), p. 25. He was deputy head of the Central Statistical Office and obtained his doctorate by presenting a thesis on planning before his premature death in 1966.

schools and subschools among the economists and officials fighting their opponents and trying to form indispensable alliances in scholarly, administrative, and party circles. In particular, schools of thought emerged, even in mathematical economics, which differed in their approach to such Marxist concepts as the "law of value" and the "substance" behind prices; the validity of market categories in a socialist economy; the reliability of "optimal planning" and its search for an "objective function" of the national economy, with the related fascinating problems concerning the very aims of economic activity—questions for social philosophy no less than for economics; finally, the formation and role of pricing in planning.

The debate resulted in the widespread acceptance of two ideas: first, market categories are not alien to socialism but inherent to it, and second, some new relation must be found between the central plan and the market mechanisms. Beyond the wide acceptance of these two theses in their most general form, the schools differed on just about everything else. For example, opinions on pricing and value ranged from orthodox Marxism, through revised Marxism, to non-Marxist and anti-Marxist views. Naturally, many ways also were offered to shape the new model. The new economics, in order to assert its validity, undertook a study of the national economy, its mechanisms, and trends. Of course, relevant institutions were also submitted to the most critical scrutiny. Without such an investigation the causes of the alarming slowdown of the performance could not be discovered.

Gradually, as a picture of the Soviet economy emerged, its management invited harsh criticism. Inertia, routine, vested interests, cabals, dogmas, faulty practices, dysfunctions, and disabilities were some of the shadows of the system that the "new look" disclosed to the Soviet public, which knew of them from everyday experience but had previously had no chance to view the overall situation or to see valid figures showing the range and scope of the problems.

Thus, the first and obvious step was criticism and exposure of the failures. Disappointment over the results rather than self-complacency became the tone of many writers.

The obvious theme for the most minute scrutiny became the most important governmental function in the Soviet state: central planning and the managing of the economy. Proudly proclaimed as the foundation of all achievement, it also had to bear the brunt as mainspring of all the dysfunctions. It was this lynchpin of the Soviet model that was found wanting and weakness-ridden. Obviously, every side of the planners' work—the techniques involved in doing the job, fixing the targets, and getting results from subordinates —were studied, as was the whole institutional setting, including the structure of management from the central government to the lowest echelons of the producing units, the supply system, the external and internal relations of bureaucracies, and the general links between administrations and producers.

For the first time since the NEP, centralization ceased to be an absolute ideological virtue. Its excessive character, damaging results, and theoretical limits were considered. "The very possibility of centralized management of the economy is always limited by the real level of socialization reached by the productive forces." Therefore, centralized management "may be used only in certain limits." In other words, the degree to which decision making is concentrated in the higher echelons is to be determined by some objective criteria and cannot be left to the whim of a bureaucratic hierarchy. Inversely, how much independence is to be granted to enterprises must be decided after consideration of factors such as the level of organization and available technology, the amount of concentration of production forces, and the relative objective degree of independence or "separatedness" of enterprises in turning out their output.[17]

Both to impose plans from above without considering the

[17] S. Dzarasov, "O Metodakh Upravleniia Sotsialisticheskim Khoziastvom," *Voprosy Ekonomiki*, no. 10 (1968), pp. 33, 38.

objective limits to mastery that centralization actually can achieve over the multitude of plants and to ignore at the same time the indispensable degree of freedom to be granted to grass-roots producing units condemn planning to sterility. Much of such planning "will remain suspended in the air," and enough good arguments from the past to sustain their thesis were mustered. Centralization is necessary and beneficial only when it is properly adapted to the character of the productive forces[18] or, in other words, when it fits the technological and economic level of the branch in question, or of the national economy at large.

To be sure, most of the debaters never questioned either the very idea of planning or the indispensable degree of centralization on which planning had to be based. But their findings implied that the degree to which decisions are concentrated or dispersed within the hierarchy and among economic agents should not be entrusted to the purely political will of a central authority. Authors stressed the existence of objective criteria and constraints, which revealed their concern for the role of science and probably of public opinion in interpreting them. Such limits should not be brushed aside by impetuous and despotic powerholders, with the dire results well known from Soviet history.

The performance of the existing planning system, not the principle of central planning, attracted all the criticism. Writers promptly singled out phenomena damaging to the very image that the planning myths tried to entertain. For example, inflationary pressures and their results could not be avoided and sometimes were quite badly controlled, with the resulting characteristic consequences of dwindling productivity and lack of incentives.[19] It was the one-sided-

[18] V. Kashin, et al., in O. Kozlova, ed., *Upravlenie Sotsialisticheskim Proizvodstvom* (Moscow, 1968), p. 88; Vereshchagin and Denisov, *ibid.*, p. 23; Dzarasov, *Voprosy Ekonomiki*, p. 73.

[19] Notkin, *Struktura*, p. 42, stated that inflationary pressures occurred "even" in a socialist economy and had similar consequences.

ness in the application of the criteria of central planning that contributed to disproportions and malfunctions.

Thus, instead of a steady and regular economic development that was supposedly inherent in the planning, the new look discovered the existence of wide fluctuations, ups and downs, starts and jolts, which made the economic organism shiver—with its factories unable to set for themselves a regular rhythmical work pace, resting lazily for some time after they "stormed" frenetically toward the deadline of the fulfillment report.[20] Largely deplored by Soviet economists and the authorities alike, under the pejorative terms "campaigning" and "storming," the reasons for such jerkiness were easily traced to the lack of self-regulating and self-correcting mechanisms in the system, to the ways the planners fixed—and so often changed—their targets, and to the structural deficiencies of the supply system. The same factors accounted for the fact that the economy could not avoid the creation of large amounts of idle, unused capacities, as well as unsold and unsalable surpluses of some commodities, overproduced and refused by consumers.[21]

There was a propensity for the Soviet economy under the planning system to behave as unpredictably as a market economy, as Oscar Large deplored, and to impose on pro-

[20] In *Obshchestvennaia Stoimost'*, p. 249, Nemchinov said that some 60 percent of the output in Soviet factories is being produced during the "storming" of the last decade of every month.

[21] Kashin, et al., *Upravlenie*, pp. 74–77, contains some figures about unsold goods. From 1950 to 1965 stocks of unsold goods grew by 3.5 times and reached the impressive sum of 34.97 billion rubles. During eight months of 1966, commercial organizations failed to acquire from producers food products worth 1.5 billion (mainly butter, for 657 millions). As the authors demonstrated, the population had enough money to buy, they just refused to buy goods of bad quality. At the same time producers' goods also remained unmarketed, or kept accumulating in some parts of the economy when they were badly needed in some other. The surplus of equipment that remained unused grew very significantly during 1965–1967 and reached the 4 billion mark.

143

ducers and consumers uncertainties that were incongruous with planning.[22] The plans were capable of inflicting heavy damages on the economy—as numerous Soviet writers state —and of engendering trends as chaotic and anarchic as those experienced by their capitalist competitors. "Subjectivism," and "voluntarism," which ruled supreme in Soviet planning and managing—another common charge against the planners[23]—were damaging to the concept of planning not only because of the anarchy they caused but also because all too often they transformed planning into a sterile exercise that was unable to reach its targets—especially the central one: a continuous, comprehensive, and well-balanced development of the economy.

The reasons for such deplorable phenomena lay in the main features of the Soviet planning system: a set of commands, each of which was conceived as law for the participants in the process, and the heavy concentration of decision at the hungry and power-greedy center, which was flooded with information that it could not properly digest and so tended to lose touch with reality. As the planners were unable to ensure enough consistency in planning and as their indicators devised from above to guide the producers never were and could not be coordinated among themselves, the interventions of the center in the economy could only be highly arbitrary.

Local managers could extricate themselves from such contradictory demands only by manipulating the numerous loopholes—a constant factor in any overcontrolled bureaucratic system—and by still giving the planners either the prescribed quantities or, all too often, just the impression of having attained them. Consequently, the uncontrollable and "voluntaristic" high-level planner faced a heavily fettered, punctiliously supervised producer. The whole sys-

[22] Cf. A. Kahan, "Agriculture," in A. Kassof, ed., *Prospects for Soviet Society* (London, 1968), p. 273.

[23] See Chapter 8 on "subjectivism" and "voluntarism" in the action of the state.

tem, thus extremely rigid at all levels, became, in Nemchinov's words, "a straitjacketed, highly fettered system (*zalimitirovannaia . . . sistema*)."[24]

More had to be said to explain how and why the system managed to ensure a high rate of resources for accumulation and why it lacked the ability to use them efficiently. It could direct growing sums to investment but it lacked criteria for allocating them with the best profit to the economy; it was efficient in making factories follow prescribed targets but destroyed incentives, so that the reported fulfillments were hiding too much that remained neglected. Paradoxically too, a system so heavily planned from above left the factory unplanned, unable to prepare itself correctly for future tasks because of "lack of perspective on the plant level."[25] It was emphasized that "hurling on the factories literally tens of thousands of orders, instructions, and other legislative acts, which regulated its every step,"[26] would not help the factories, which lacked the freedom to act in spheres where they had the expertise. Factories remained the weakest, most vulnerable link in the planning system—its "Achilles heel," as yet another Soviet author stated.[27]

In a system thus overplanned from above and underplanned from below, a dichotomy developed between the propensity of the center to fix and enforce its directives according to its logic and the absence of adequate incentives throughout the productive organization to identify fully with these directives and to respond with enthusiasm. Much was done to fulfill the quantitative target—not always achieved, to be sure—but this simultaneously engendered

[24] See V. Nemchinov, "Sotsialisticheskoe Khoziaistvovanie i Planirovanie Proizvodstva," *Kommunist*, no. 5 (1964), p. 76, which is reproduced in the brochure *O Dal'neishem Sovershenstvovanii Planirovaniia i Upravleniia Khoziaistvom* (Moscow, 1965).

[25] Efimov and Kirichenko, in A. Efimov, ed., *Ekonomicheskoe Planirovanie v SSSR* (Moscow, 1967), pp. 274–275.

[26] Kashin, et al., *Upravlenie*, p. 93.

[27] Iu. Iakovets, ed., "Tsena i Predpriiatie," *Reforma Stavit Problemy* (Moscow, 1968), p. 64.

145

a sort of work-to-rule behavior, which meant that quality was neglected, innovation was stifled, and much ingenuity was employed to hide resources, in order to defend oneself from meeting the quota of the rigid plans. The energy deployed by factory managers to reach targets was matched only by the inventiveness used to outmaneuver the higher agencies in order to obtain the smallest plan with the highest gain for themselves. Little attention was left for the economic development of the factory in terms of growing efficiency, productivity, and profitability. The objectives of the plan and the actual progress of the system in economic terms diverged. Making their enterprise a booming economic entity would not interest either the workers or the managers. Even when a well-done job led to profits, these were appropriated by the state. For the producers to have profits or to have constant losses meant the same; the managers knew that the government would finish by covering such losses. One source illustrates this phenomenon: during the years 1958–1964 most of the profits were taken from enterprises and only some one-fifteenth to one-nineteenth of those profits were used for premiums and incentives for distribution to crews. Additionally, the depreciation funds were taken out by the state and used for its investments, mainly in new plants, leaving the factories already in existence without sufficient funds and without rights to improve and renew.[28]

These problems undermined the existing model and its ideological assumptions. The emergence and persistence of such a rift between the plan and the objectives of the factory crews, between their ways of doing things and the economic development of the country, required a more insightful analysis and remedial proposals. In itself, such a phenomenon would be a sufficiently eloquent diagnosis of the situation—and a serious disability. Strumilin explained that the lack of interest shown by producers, in particular

[28] *Ibid.*, pp. 64–66. See also S. Strumilin, "Khoziaistvennyi, Raschet i Problema Tsenoobrazovaniia," *ibid.*, pp. 5–25.

by workers, in the results of the operation of their factory was the result of their receiving only a negligible part of the factory's stimulation funds. "They are asked to deploy considerable additional energy, and are rewarded by a few dimes. In that way interests of workers are disregarded, because the fruit of their labor is being confiscated by the state."[29]

The incentives and motivations for people in a large system are not easily invented in planning offices. A discordance between targets proposed by the state and the incentives (or lack thereof) that guide the actual behavior of the social groups in question cannot be mended by propaganda. But before this question was explored in the literature, it became clear that the existing planning-and-managing pattern did itself lead producers into performing tasks that were seemingly good for the plan, but in fact were very harmful for the economy. According to Novozhilov, the incorrect planning practices, the indicators, and in particular the improper ways of measuring cost and results of production "spur economic activity to superfluous expenses, to a pursuit of illusory results, engender contradictions between economic accountability (*khozraschet*) and the plan, between the interests of the enterprise and the interests of the national economy. . . ."[30] This gap had to be closed if the downward trend of the economic performance were to be stopped and the technological revolution successfully deployed, so that Russia would remain securely at the top.

Two Critics

In a popular book, the well-known airplane designer, O. I. Antonov, discussed the damaging rift between the indicators of the plan and the stimuli and incentives inducing factory crews to perform tasks differently from what was officially expected from them.[31] His scathing indictment of

[29] S. Strumilin, *ibid.*, p. 22.
[30] Novozhilov, *Problemy Izmerenia*, p. 3.
[31] O. Antonov, *Dlia Vsekh i Dlia Sebia* (Moscow, 1965).

147

the indicators—as they were applied before the 1965 reform—and indeed of the planning system of which the indicators were the outstanding product, led him to the conclusion that "the damages inflicted on the national economy because of the insensible indicators of the plan are so big and unbearable" that its overhaul must begin immediately.[32] For those who did not yet know enough about it from the press, his book, written in a lively and colorful language, supplied dozens of instances of the irrational behavior of managers and of workers who were forced to wreck plans and destroy goods because of the contradictions in the system.

For example, two workers who were employed to unload bricks quickly from trucks did so by throwing them on the ground, usually breaking some 30 percent of them. They knew that their actions were both against the interests of the country and against simple common sense, but their work was assessed and paid on the basis of a time indicator. Therefore, they would be penalized—indeed would not be able to make their living—if they were to arrange the bricks carefully on the ground. Their way of doing the job was bad for the country, but, on the face of it, good for the plan! So they acted against their consciences and intelligence, but with a deep feeling of bitterness against the planners: "You don't want it done in a way good husbandry would have it, you keep pressing only for quicker and quicker! Well then, get your bricks! Bang! Bang!"[33] Thus, all over the country, decent and responsible citizens, perfectly rational beings, acted in wasteful, almost criminal ways.

On the scale of the national economy the above example and many others indicated the planning system's failure to induce people to work with care and to introduce healthy management. Antonov notes some important consequences of this system, besides its incalculable degree of waste. The clear-cut national objective of raising the technological level of the economy and the standard of living of the population

[32] *Ibid.*, p. 190.　　　　　　　　　[33] *Ibid.*, p. 125.

was surreptitiously replaced by a host of objectives of separate enterprises, ostensibly coordinated by the plan, but actually pulling in different, if not opposite, directions. Another important flaw was the unavoidable distrust among the grass roots, lower echelons, and higher-ups. As Antonov explicitly states, the higher echelons assume that the lower ones will not behave in a way that best serves the national interest; and they therefore contribute to further limiting the freedom of enterprises to action. But there is a pernicious logic in this distrust that spares no one. The higher-ups cannot be trusted either, and must be thoroughly and meticulously supervised by those at the very top. Thus, the central bodies are so busy with details that they have no time for problems of principle and long-term policy. As every important competence and power are concentrated above, elements of self-regulation of the production process on the lower echelons are impeded or excluded. Those echelons, especially the factories, lack sufficient autonomy to act with flexibility and efficiency; the higher administrations, on the other hand, glutted by a flow of information they cannot master, lack the capacity "to propose thoughtful measures for the improvement of work." Antonov vividly illustrated the "sergeant major" style of the administrative machinery: "The percentage of defective goods and wastage are big? Lower it! The growth of labor productivity is too slow? Raise it! Overemployment of labor force? Curtail it! The quantitative production target is not fulfilled? *Davai, davai!*"[34]

The old call of "*davai, davai!*," still so much present in Soviet life, permeated industrial relations in the country. Bosses of all ranks were used and instructed to press for more and more from the unreliable and sluggish producers, while at the same time clichés about the working class "ruling the country" were constantly heard. From the story of the two workers unloading and breaking bricks, Antonov concluded: "No, at this moment they did not feel they were

[34] *Ibid.*, pp. 35–36, 134–135, 172–173.

fully empowered bosses of their country. A blind soulless force of *stereotyped* planning reduced them to the role of shaky little screws in a huge, mysterious machine, not geared to thrifty handling of national wealth and disrespectful of sometimes hard and sweaty but inspiring and beautiful labor."[35]

Antonov was probably inspired by Nemchinov, who also expressed concern about the "abnormal relations" between the planning organs and the factories.[36] The notoriously uncoordinated indicators were a common theme of the two authors, as was the cybernetic terminology they used to deplore the lack of feedback in the system. But the academician, naturally, tried to diagnose the system and to theorize about it. He thought that the central economic leadership had a "primitive understanding of the interrelationship between big and small economic systems,"[37] and this seemed to be a big source of trouble. On the one hand, the mechanism of planning was such that "every line and column of the plan have their boss," but the plan as a complex entity was not sufficiently cared for and not adequately insured.

Coordination of the different parts of the plan was the most vulnerable part of this mechanism and its central weakness. Nemchinov listed the inadequately correlated functions and sectors, one of the most deplored being that the "system of planned pricing is not organically welded into the general pattern." There was a plan for production and for material supplies, but prices were detached from both. The supply system in itself was full of inconsistencies. Of the many malfunctions in the economy, one was a damaging dispersal of resources and the subsequent loss of control over their use to "numerous fund-receivers and to countless natural funds." Planning had its own inadequacies. "There exists a constant rift between the plan's targets for output and those for material supplies, between the

[35] *Ibid.*, p. 125.
[36] Nemchinov, "Sotsialisticheskoe Khoziaistvovanie," p. 7.
[37] *Ibid.*, p. 53.

volume targets of the plan and the effectiveness indicators (rentability), between the use of production capacities and the introduction of new technology. Plans for production, labor resources, financing, and supplies are far from being interconnected satisfactorily."[38]

So much for Nemchinov at this stage. He was one of the intellectual driving forces behind the renaissance in Soviet economics, and his role consisted not only of opening the floodgates for a critical review but also of offering proposals for reform. Before discussing them in the next chapter, it is necessary to complete the economists' critique of the state of affairs. Lack of coordination between the different parts of the plan, which Nemchinov exposed, led to an improperly balanced economic structure and to its corollary—low efficiency of the whole economy.

A less inhibited look and a better knowledge of Western economies, especially the American one, and their investment strategies and uses of GNP provided the Soviet researchers with criteria to understand better the deficiencies of their own economic structure. Inadequate correlations and proportions between the different areas of the economy, and the interrelationships inside these branches—as economists explained to the policy makers—were the results of past investment strategies. Some of the signals pointing to misdirection of resources and to an unfavorable structure included the neglect of agriculture; the emphasis given to construction materials and mining at the expense of machine building; the mining of coal at the expense of petroleum extraction; the building of huge hydroelectrical stations at the expense of thermal stations; the relative weakness of the light industries (which absorb less capital); and the small share of investment in chemistry and electronics. The most costly and less effective capital-absorbing branches played an exaggerated role and dragged down the performance of the economy, whereas the modern, innova-

[38] *Ibid.*, p. 6.

tion-inducing, and material-economizing branches were underdeveloped and still awaited their turn.

The picture gets even more expressive when compared to that in the United States. Soviet agriculture absorbs about five times more labor and has a productivity that is (according to official Soviet estimates) five times lower. Timber cutting, mining, and building industries swallow a much bigger share of resources than their relative contribution to the GNP. On the other hand, transportation, communications, electricity, machine building, industrial servicing, chemistry, electronics, computers, and light industry, as well as commerce, occupy a much more important place in the American economy than in the Soviet one and account largely for the heavy downward trend of the Soviet productivity of capital and labor.[39]

[39] This is a very brief and approximate sketch of the problem, just in order to draw attention to the whole issue. For a Western source on the comparative composition of capital and ways of using the GNP in the United States and the Soviet Union, see S. Cohn, "Soviet Growth Retardation: Trends in Resource Availability and Efficiency" in U.S. Congress, Joint Economic Committee, Subcommittee on Foreign Policy, *New Directions of the Soviet Economy*, 89th Cong., 2d sess. (Washington, D.C., 1966), pp. 107, 118. For Soviet studies dealing mainly with problems of economic structure, see Notkin, *Struktura*, pp. 18–19, 277–280; also the contribution by S. Kheinman, "Sovershenstvovanie Struktury i Intensifikatsiia Promyshlennogo Proizvodstva" in Pervushin, Venzher, Kvasha, et al., *Proizvodstvo, Nakoplenie*, pp. 187–188, Premier Kosygin in his September 1965 speech announcing the reforms, *Pravda*, 28 September 1965 (translated as "On Improving Management of Industry, Perfecting Planning, and Economic Stimulation of Industrial Production" in *New Directions*, pp. 1033–1093) dealt with the problem at length and appealed to economists to study the problem and to help with solutions. S. Kheinman in *Kommunist*, no. 14 (September 1969), pp. 72–73, and confirmed the worries that the structural weaknesses of the economy are causing. Obviously, many years will be needed to correct this kind of deficiency. Kheinman showed how agriculture, extracting industries, and timber procurement absorb labor and capital beyond proportion to what they contribute to the national income (27 percent of all investments, 31 percent of all fixed capital); and such a heavy load on national resources "limits the possibilities of developing the

One major area of economic activity, in fact the main strategic factor of economic development, the investment policy, was now also very seriously reconsidered and continued to be an important topic of research. The practices of capital construction, for a generation the main thrust of economic policy, were conducted without appropriate criteria and resulted in creating perennial problems. The issues of depreciation and renovation policies concurred in accentuating structural weaknesses and low efficiency, if not sheer inefficiency. Long delays in completing industrial construction and a very long gestation period are notorious weaknesses in the Soviet economy, which looks even worse today, according to one source, than it did in the 1930s. "Overinvestment" (*perekapitalizatsiia*) is the name of the dysfunctional phenomenon, and its result is the constant tying up and immobilization of enormous resources in the protracted process of planning, constructing, and putting into operation new enterprises or renovating old ones. It takes two or three times longer to build a factory in Russia than it does in capitalist countries, and the slowness of this process is a crucial factor "in slowing down technical progress, increasing capital absorption, deteriorating the technological structure of capital investment, creating unfavorable changes in interbranch proportions, causing growing losses and the freezing of resources."[40]

transforming industries and the sphere of services." This structural infirmity also "raises substantially the labor and capital absorption" and contributes to low productivity of capital.

[40] V. Krasovskii, "Perspektivnye Problemy Kapital'nykh Vlozhenii" in M. Fedorenko, ed., *Problemy Ekonomicheskoi Nauki i Praktiki* (Moscow, 1972), pp. 202–203; and V. Krasovskii in Notkin, ed., *Faktory*, chap. 3, p. 93. For a comparative length of construction, see also P. Kuznetsov, "Informatsia i Upravlenie v Sisteme Material'no-technicheskogo Snabzheniia" in B. Gnedenko, ed., *Problemy Funktsionirovaniia Bol'shikh Ekonomicheskihk Sistem* (Moscow, 1969), p. 264. He stated: "The time it takes to construct industrial objects of comparable complexity [in the USSR] is three to five times longer

Such practices explain how so many new and sometimes quite modern plants could barely compensate for the neglect and growing obsolescence of equipment in the already functioning older factories. The depreciation policy, which did not leave the managers enough funds for renovation (most of the proceeds were taken out to be invested in new plants), contributed to a quick aging of the Soviet machine park.[41] In any case, this, as well as other factors, made it unprofitable for producers to engage in innovation. Sticking to old methods and old products was safe; innovation was penalized. Such was the background for the "phobia of innovation" that still plagues the system.[42] The price to be paid for it was incalculable.

The faulty intersectorial structures and specialization (or inadequate cooperation) of different services was revealed by the deplorably heavy load of resources engulfed by the inefficient and enormous "capital repair services." The depreciating and all-too-slowly replaced installations needed constant repairs, for which there were no specialized and modern facilities. Every plant tried to mend its deteriorating machinery as best it could by its own means—this activity engulfed 27 percent of the gross capital investments in material production and a good deal of the labor force; for example, one-third of all the metal cutting machine tools in industry were in the repair shops of factories.[43]

Furthermore, "the utterly inflexible (*sui generis* rationing) system of material supplies"—Nemchinov's *bête noire* and the mainstay of the "direct physical indicators"—was

than in the USA or in England." He charges the material-technical supply system for being a prime hindrance to improving such deplorable performance.

[41] Efimov, ed., *Ekonomicheskoe Planirovanie*, pp. 308–309, offers details about the excessive aging of the Soviet machine park. See also his *Sovetskaia Industriia* (Moscow, 1967), p. 297.

[42] See G. Grossman, "Innovation and Information in Soviet Economy," *American Economic Review*, 16, 2 (May 1966), 121–122. "Phobia of innovation" is his term.

[43] Krasovskii, "Perspektivnye Problemy," p. 206.

forced to distribute means of production through endless funds and subfunds in detailed physical denominations, so that the economy experienced perennial supply shortages and production suffered from delays and haste with 60 percent of the output being produced in the last decade of every month. A quarter of the total working time was lost because of the supply deficiencies in factories.[44]

The Soviet reading public, which could not have known that much from personal experience, was by now enlightened by these staggering facts. In particular, it became much better informed about the real situation in regard to competition with the United States. The triumphant announcements that the United States had been outstripped in the output of steel could not make people any less skeptical. At the same time, they could read in the official statistical handbook for 1970 that Soviet productivity of labor was in industry only half of the American; that in agriculture it was no more than one-fifth; that the Soviet national income was only 65 percent of the American (Western sources would probably say this is exaggerated); that the volume of Soviet investment equaled that of the United States.[45]

That the comparison was much less favorable in 1913 is historically important, but today the competition with the United States is very different because of the arms race and space effort. No one knows exactly how heavily armaments and space drain the economic resources of the country, but available estimates indicate that the Soviet effort in defense is probably not smaller than the American in terms of the physical volume of resources involved—but this is at the expense of a much weaker economy.[46] This weaker economy

[44] Quoted from a Soviet source in Ellman, *Soviet Planning Today*, p. 89.

[45] *Narodnoe Khoziaistvo SSSR v. 1970 Godu*, p. 82.

[46] For an evaluation of Soviet military expenditure see M. Boretsky, "Comparative Progress in Technology, Productivity and Economic Efficiency: USSR versus USA," *New Directions*, pp. 154, 231–233,

spends one-third of its GNP on investment—twice the American share—and renovates its installations twice as slowly; 46 percent of its industrial workers are unskilled or barely skilled and perform manual labor in auxiliary, entirely unmechanized occupations. Again, a comparison with the United States standard is probably quite discouraging. For example, in the relatively efficient machine-building industry, every third worker either loads or unloads goods or is employed in internal transportation, whereas in the United States one transport worker serves twenty-five to twenty-six basic production men.[47]

There is an acute shortage of qualified laborers in Soviet industry, and a plethora of unskilled ones. There is also a surplus of engineers according to the official handbook and propaganda (2,486,000 in the USSR compared to only 905,000 in the United States in 1970).[48]

Presented as a victory, the figures on engineers are perhaps an indication of enormous possibilities still ahead if organization, productivity, efficiency, and modernization are successfully applied. Certainly, for the moment, it is just a statement of serious inferiority, without any guarantee that the gap is narrowing. Khrushchev's promise to catch up with the United States in 1970 is now realistically delayed by the current Five-Year Plan to 1975, which has as its goal the industrial and agricultural output of the United States in 1970.[49]

Improvements and some progress have been undeniable,

---

and S. Cohn, "Soviet Growth Retardation," p. 122. Khachaturov, in Rumiantsev and Bunich, eds., *Ekonomicheskaia Reforma*, chap. 7, p. 202, without quoting figures, offered more than a hint at the magnitude of the Soviet security effort.

[47] These data are from Zhamin, in Notkin, ed., *Faktory*, chap. 5, pp. 125–126; and A. Efimov, in Rumiantsev and Bunich, eds., *Ekonomicheskaia Reforma*, chap. 4, p. 131.

[48] *Narodnoe Khoziaistvo*, pp. 119–120.

[49] *Gosudarstvennyi Piatiletnii Plan*, p. 337, but the terms of the promise are not excessively buoyant. In 1975 it is hoped to reach the U.S. level of 1970, in absolute, but not per capita, terms.

and further advances will occur during the current Five-Year Plan. Nevertheless the promise of overtaking is as unreal in the early 1970s as they were ludicrous to critics in the early 1960s.

The wave of criticism of the 1960s which was the object of our study in this chapter culminated in a verdict best expressed by Nemchinov who castigated "an ossified, mechanical system in which all the directing parameters were given in advance and the whole system was fettered from top to bottom, in any given moment, and at any given point." It was no longer a question of some passing symptoms or even a mild disease. The whole planning and managing pattern was drastically infected.

A tocsin was sounded: "An economic system so fettered from top to bottom will put a brake on the social and technological progress, and will break down, sooner or later, under the pressure of the real processes of economic life."[50]

[50] Nemchinov, *O Dal'neishem*, p. 53.

CHAPTER SEVEN

In Quest of Remedies

THE critique of the economic performance and of the economic mechanism helped planners to realize that tinkering with details and the notoriously numerous organizational shake-ups would not do. It became appropriate to discuss the need to replace the whole "administrative system."

Obviously, many powerful officials and scholars did not agree. They preferred to preserve what the reformers tried to scrap and to invigorate it by using better technology and engineering, as well as by improving methods and the quality of management. These opinions often influenced the top leaders.

But the more critical reformers saw in the inability—or the weak ability—of the existing arrangements to generate or assimilate more diligently advanced technology symptoms of problems the solution to which lay beyond the reach of engineers. The trouble was more basic, and became clear as in-depth analysis and diagnosis proceeded.

In fact, some general lines of thought became largely accepted and beyond controversy. In the face of the growing shortage of labor and the diminishing returns on capital, further advance became conceivable mainly on the basis of improving efficiency and intensifying the use of resources. Not unnaturally, this new situation helped to reintroduce into scholarship and the thinking of planners the notion of "scarcity" of resources and the need to consider "utility" of goods as economic categories of great importance. These concepts were openings for a new way of thinking, which was indispensable for the new turn toward intensification and higher productivity. Another postulate that became largely accepted as a precondition for a higher degree of efficiency was the need to restructure the economy so as to correct its major imbalances and strengthen the most dynamic and innovation-oriented sectors and branches.

These three postulates became official slogans, although critics also proposed other remedies. According to them, many tensions, contradictions, and dysfunctions arose from the clash, inherent in the whole pattern, between "interests of social groups" or of "society," as they saw it, and state policy and its plans. This was a very complicated problem, and it was not easy for the leadership to admit it openly without loss of face. But this was implied when economists and some leaders agreed that the old way of stepping up investments in order to overcome the numerous obstacles to growth would only further exacerbate the malaise. "The exaction of saving at the expense of consumption" could no longer work in a situation of a growing deficit in labor resources.[1] The standard of living had to be improved in order to create incentives for productivity, for which an entirely new strategy of economic growth was needed, not a minor change in priorities and emphasis.

Quite properly, the first institution to be completely overhauled was the planning network and its methods. As the head of Gosplan's Research Institute stated, intensification of the national economy, including efficiency of investments, could not be achieved without eliminating the taut plans that caused a chronic deficit of raw materials, metal, electricity, and equipment. Reserves were indispensable all over the system, including excess capacities.[2]

Nemchinov formulated expansively what had to be improved in planning. He stated in his seminal article in *Kom-*

[1] A. Bergson, *Planning and Productivity Under Soviet Socialism* (New York, 1968), p. 18.

[2] A. Efimov, in A. Rumiantsev and P. Bunich, eds., *Ekonomicheskaia Reforma: Ee Osushchestvlenie i Problemy* (Moscow, 1969), chap. 4, pp. 132–133.

munist: "The basic and main task consists in having the mechanism of planning tied up with the system of economic accounting and with the system of social funds of the enterprises."[3] This meant that planning had to make use of market categories and to offer the necessary autonomy and material incentives to crews of direct producers, a huge task when the question "how?" is posed. Viewing the problems of planning and centralized management in modern cybernetical terms, Nemchinov saw that the flexibility of a self-regulating system provided with the indispensable feedback loopholes was lacking. Other cyberneticists and systems analysts seconded Nemchinov. A dangerous information glut deprived the avid centralizers of the possibility of planning and managing effectively because the overburdening of the managing organs created a situation where these organs lost the sense of correct direction; and, finding themselves unable to process the floods of information, they were forced to make decisions that were voluntaristic and far from being the best possible.[4] One of the results of the glutted communication system and inability to master information flows was the constant lagging of the center's orders. The trouble was that the revolution "together with the dirty waters of exploitation splashed out the child of feedback relations" but "the need of self-regulation and feedback relations grows, to use a figurative language, in proportion to the square of the system's complexity, and now, when our industrial apparatus became a highly complex system, it is impossible to run it effectively without introducing into it a big measure of self-regulation and, consequently, without organizing feedback loopholes."[5]

[3] V. Nemchinov, *O Dal'neishem Sovershenstvovanii Planirovaniia i Upravleniia Khoziaistvom* (Moscow, 1965), p. 53.

[4] V. Ul'ianov, V. Garkavi, and Iu. Borisov, "Nekotorye Voprosy Sozdaniia Otraslevoi Avtomatizirovannoi Sistemy Upravleniia v Khimicheskoi Promyshlennosti s Primeneniem Vychislitel'noi Tekhniki," in B. Gnedenko, ed., *Problemy Funktsionirovaniia Bol'shikh Ekonomicheskikh Sistem* (Moscow, 1969), p. 277.

[5] O. Antonov, *Dlia Vsekh i Dlia Sebia* (Moscow, 1965), p. 145.

In addition to these already quite exacting demands on the planning system, the mathematical economists added another, formidable one: they wanted planning to become "optimal." Just to balance the plan to make targets for output meet the necessary resources was insufficient in the era of efficiency. A more exact balance was now needed in order to achieve not just any proportions in the economy, but "a precisely computed system of optimal proportions"[6] that could be attained through the techniques of linear programming and other devices of mathematical economics.

All these demands were seen as preconditions for reinvigorating the economy; they pointed to a need to redesign the whole management pattern all the way up the hierarchy. If at the top the planning institution had to learn an entirely new job, the one at the bottom, the producing unit (the enterprise, or firms grouping several of them), also had to acquire quite a new function in the system. Without granting both considerable autonomy, there was no way, many economists maintained, to make the whole system flexible and to introduce the desirable feedback mechanism. Improving the operating conditions for the enterprises was the crucial link in the therapy. Seen from below, changes to be introduced in the system implied a more complete revision than the one envisioned from above. At the top, hopes could be entertained that improved flows of information and better communications could be achieved with the help of computers and systems analysis so as to enable them to maintain the prevailing highly centralized management without basic alterations in the position of the lower echelons. Thus, better performance by the enterprises could be eventually realized with the help of the enhanced control capacity of the center and its agencies.

However, many of the prominent mathematical economists not only opposed the idea of intensifying the economy mainly through reinvigorating the controlling capacity of

[6] L. Vaag, *Problemy Sovershenstvovaniia Planirovaniia* (Moscow, 1967), p. 72.

161

the center, they also rejected the very possibility of succeeding by this method. They favored a complete redesign and reform,[7] and claimed that the existing degree of centralization was in itself dysfunctional and untenable. If planners wanted to strengthen their grip on basic economic trends, they had to concentrate on the essentials of the national economy as a whole, whereas the bulk of current affairs had to be tackled where it arose—in the enterprise. For this purpose, new relations between the plan, the central authorities, and the production units (plants or firms) had to be found. The fettering of the plants, the suppression of their capacity to operate freely enough, was the most serious defect of the existing arrangement. It seemed crucial to find ways of inducing and stimulating the thousands of factories, rather than the thousands of bureaucrats in planning offices, to fight for innovation, productivity, and efficiency. Under the existing system of planned indicators, all these economic virtues left factory crews rather indifferent.

Obviously, if the producers were to gain substantial leeway for initiative in operations, they could no longer remain mute subordinates of their superiors. The situation in which the enterprise bore the entire burden and the full responsibility for losses, and in which the administrative agencies—ministries, *glavki*, planners—were not at all blamed however damaging and irrational their demands, had to be changed. The essence of the new approach was expressed in the demand "to put the administrations on *khozraschët*." The trouble was, as a scholar in juridical science explained, that in the existing administrative system

[7] The late A. Vainshtein argued that solving Soviet problems by recentralizing is possible in abstract theory, but in practice tools are not yet available and will not become quickly available for such solution. Yet the problems still press; therefore there is no way but to decentralize. See his speech in *Ekonomisty i Matematiki za Kruglym Stolom* (Moscow, 1966), p. 155.

162

the governmental organ superordinated to the factory "decides by himself what are the means it requires, and fixes the percentages to be levied from subordinated plants, for its own maintenance. The experience of recent years shows that in cases when an administrative apparatus is maintained at the expense of subordinated organizations, it tends to grow quickly, and, in search of activity, tends to exercise an increasingly detailed petty tutelage over the enterprises."[8]

The logic of this position was far-reaching. If the system wanted the factories to become profitable and to respect cost-accounting criteria, this principle had to be applicable throughout the pyramid. There was no way of curing the apparatuses of their inept meddling and unfeasible plans, so often changed in the course of the year, except by making them pay for their errors as well as by interesting them directly in performance and profitability; in other words, the higher administrative organs, ministries included, were to become "cost-accounting organizations," directly responsible for losses incurred in their branch as a result of their management.[9]

This was one facet of the approach, so strongly expressed by the staunch reformer Malyshev, among others; the economy had to be managed by economic methods as opposed to predominantly administrative ones. The larger aspect of the search for an efficient and dynamic enterprise—there could be no dynamic system without a dynamic grass roots organization—implied that the relations among "the plan," the central economic administration, and the factories and producers' associations had to be based on "economic levers" rather than on direct orders and imperative prescrip-

---

[8] R. Khalfina, in M. Fedorenko, ed., *Diskussiia ob Optimal'nom Planirovanii* (Moscow, 1968), p. 178.

[9] See A. Birman, "Sut' Reformy," *Novyi Mir*, no. 12 (December 1968), p. 203, and M. Fedorenko, *O Razrabotke Sistemy Optimal'nogo Funktsionirovaniia* (Moscow, 1968), p. 26.

tions. "Indirect links" were to become the mainspring. This meant that the central planner would achieve his objectives by acting through "economic incentives."

Such incentives would replace "direct" methods—orders and sanctions—which was the main method and weakness of the prevailing administrative and highly centralized system. For neither the sanction nor the administrative order offered sufficient information, nor did they provide the necessary incentive to solve economic problems. When such orders, as it often happened, were countered by other types of information—notably prices, local conditions, and different human proclivities—the centralist approach would normally use sanctions in order to secure the application of its instructions. But an administrative sanction "as the economic experience of many centuries has amply demonstrated, is a less effective stimulus to production than the economic or moral interest."[10]

Thus, predominantly administrative planning and over-centralized management used stimuli, which were—in the long run—inherently inferior to "economic levers" and "indirect methods" and which failed to stimulate mass initiative and creativity throughout the system—another important condition for the solution of the impending problems. The dreams of the impetuous centralizers to maintain control were directly contradicted by those of the democratizers.

Democratization, then, was a new theme, which grew out of the discussion of the use of "economic levers" versus the "administrative" ones, and which became a source of major controversies in the 1960s and 1970s. Before turning to this issue in the next chapter, it is necessary to consider the narrower economic terms even though they constantly overlap with other aspects. At this juncture, a further reproach to the strictly centralized pattern was made: such a system organized all relations down the ladder on hierarchically

[10] V. Novozhilov, *Problemy Izmereniia Zatrat i Rezul'tatov pri Optimal'nom Planirovanii* (Moscow, 1967), p. 34.

vertical command lines, with orders flowing down and information up and with the almost total exclusion of direct horizontal contacts among enterprises. Some economists now argued that horizontal contacts were indispensable for an optimally functioning economy. "The rigid subordination of automata" did not suit the needs of the economy.[11] Freedom for horizontal contacts and exchange of information and goods, and a degree of autonomy without which such contacts cannot be established, had to be introduced, although in this view no autonomy of this kind could be absolute. This would annihilate planning. On the other hand, planning could not abuse its (now discredited) coercive commands, although some degree of administrative interference was unavoidable.

Different blends of prerogatives and a new division of functions and rights in a framework of a different conception of regulating the economy had to be discovered. In Novozhilov's terms, "the most important tasks should be regulated in a dual way—directly and indirectly—all the rest, only indirectly through norms for costs and profits."[12]

There were, quite naturally, different ways of achieving this goal, but the consensus among the reformers seemed to be that central planning should concentrate on long-term macroeconomic objectives—the overall proportions in the economy, main lines of investment policy, and technological progress. However, the microeconomic level should use "parametric" methods, secure an appropriate legislative framework defining long-term conditions and norms, and use taxation and levers such as credit, rates of interest, and, particularly, pricing.

The enterprise would in such a way be working in an environment that would be powerfully influenced by the parameters imposed by the government and its central

[11] A. Katsenelinboigen, I. Lakhman, and Iu. Ovsienko, *Optimal'-nost' i Tovarno-Denezhnye Otnosheniia* (Moscow, 1969), p. 63, and see pp. 60–63, for the general argument.

[12] Novozhilov, *Problemy Izmereniia*, p. 41.

plan, but in its everyday activity it would be left free to work for consumers rather than for the plan, and for this purpose, some economists thought, it did not need any other plan but its own.

This applied in the first place to well-established mass production lines. In due course, the whole "planning through orders" could be shed. Some argued that detailed plans were unavoidably bureaucratic and induced unnecessary meddling in everyday affairs of enterprises, but what was necessary was "a plan providing just a frame, a kind of a crystalline grille for the national economy which should offer enough space for the deployment of free initiative by enterprises, workmen, collectives, and localities, [such initiative] flowing freely between the main economic partitions which remain centrally planned." Basically, the central plan should take care of new products and new breakthroughs.[13]

Such an attitude looked extreme, and it certainly had far-reaching implications. But it was not isolated. It was only one of the versions in the search for accommodating "vertical links" with "horizontal" ones, or combining planning with the market. Although the search for an opposite solution—fixing all output targets and modalities of producing them from the center—also continued quite assiduously, the prevailing opinion among the reformers was that the "centralizers" were mistaken in assuming that a national economy was basically a huge enterprise and that relations among its parts were mainly of a technological character. Instead, the national economy was an enormously complex

[13] V. Kashin, et al., in O. Kozlova, ed., *Upravlenie Sotsialisticheskim Proizvodstvom* (Moscow, 1968), p. 95. There are different schools among the reformers, including those quoted here, but most of them are far from any utopian demand of abolishing all administrative measures in a planned, indeed in any, modern economy. Their main problem, it will be argued, is to change the relations between the imperative-administrative and the economic-autonomous ingredients in the new model.

set of aggregates and enterprises, and their relations were not only technological in character but also economic—and these in fact were the predominant ones.

The discovery of "economics" and of the relations between parts of the national economy confirmed the need to reformulate appropriately the links between state plans and the maze of economic agents. Plans, seen from this angle, could and should not try to do more than fix the aims of economic action; this could consist of a target for profit or efficiency, not necessarily for output. The ways of doing and achieving this aim were best left to the producers themselves. A slightly different version of the role of planning held that the plan should not "manage" but only "regulate" the economy.[14]

Some mathematical economists, using mathematical algorithms worked out by Western scholars, presented the organization of the national economy as a hierarchically ordered set of "blocks," each of which was a relatively independent model with its own optimality criterion. The lower blocks would not get targets from the higher, but a price (a price, rather than a multitude of prices) which would guide the lower echelons in working out their own plans in such a way that these plans would be profitable for the economy at large. This meant that they would conform, in the final analysis, to the national plan but through a different mechanism for economic regulation and stimulation.

Enterprises in such a scheme would enjoy a high degree of autonomy and at the same time would remain closely linked with the higher "blocks," through primarily an iteration process: the upper level listens to the demands in resources and responds by adapting flexibly prices that it hands out downward, but it also imposes some constraints concerning resources.

[14] This is based on I. Birman, *Metodologiia Optimal'nogo Planirovaniia* (Moscow, 1971), pp. 30, 33.

167

This was one of the ways of solving the "plan and market" riddle. The same source[15] reported another way of solving the same problem by a different mathematical technique, using game theory instead of the algorithms of linear programming.

These and many other versions and proposals did not claim to offer complete and proven ways, but they expressed a growing consensus that the way of intensifying the use of resources in the Soviet economy, as well as achieving correct proportions of the economic structure and of harmonizing social and local interests, necessitated the combining of planning and the market. This idea had different formulations. Novozhilov stated the sought-after aim: planning should move from its character as "directive" (administrative order) toward one that is actually "an economic imperative." Mathematical tools and computers would help in finding the combination of "optimizing the national plans and optimizing price formation." This would impart to the plan a new strength and relieve the planners from trying to reach "an unfeasible task": "to solve in a centralized way a multitude of local planning equations and to secure their fulfillment through administrative methods." The degree of coordinating "the plan and the *khozraschët* —another formulation for "plan and market"—was such a central task that it became an explicit condition for proving "certain important advantages" of the socialist economy. The measure of such a coordination would be "the criterion for evaluating the perfection of economic management."[16]

Such was the bequest of the recently deceased professor. In order to coordinate or combine the plan and market into a harmonious system of a managed national economy, an economic theory had first to be created, and this could not be done without tackling the formidable problems of "the law of value" and of pricing.

[15] *Ibid.*, pp. 33–34.
[16] Novozhilov, *Problemy Izmereniia*, pp. 19, 32, 33, 364.

Prices, Markets, Value

Economists—whether of a mathematical or more traditional bent, those interested more in national planning or in the functioning of the factory, those looking at past trends and distortions or dwelling mainly on present difficulties and irrationalities—all agreed that the pricing system must be rethought and reworked. The methods of fixing prices that were established in the 1930s followed the same pattern until the mid-1960s.[17] They were more or less arbitrarily fixed, since no clear theoretical insight guided the planners on this score. The tendency during those years was to look at pricing as of secondary and dwindling importance; and the *khozraschët* principle, or profitability criterion that was applicable during the NEP, was eroded during the 1930s and finally was replaced by the administrative regulation not only of the gross output but also of labor inputs, salary funds, supplies, and most of the other essential conditions of functioning of factories.[18] Prices and other cost-accounting categories lost their importance in influencing the behavior of both administrations and factories. Similarly, the manager of a plant no longer considered profitability. Capital, too, became an allocated resource, with no price charged for its use.

Although seen as unimportant during the prolonged reign of "physical planning," pricing, naturally, could not be eliminated; products continued to be priced, and arbitrary methods of fixing them inexorably exercised their influence. Without correct prices, interest on capital, rent on land, or on other resources, planners were deprived of criteria for an efficient allocation of resources and investment

[17] A. Efimov, ed., *Ekonomicheskoe Planirovanie v SSSR* (Moscow, 1967), p. 239.

[18] L. Bliakhman, "K Polnomu Khozrashchëtu" in Iu. Iakovets, ed., *Reforma Stavit Problemy* (Moscow, 1968), pp. 45–46. This article offers a brief history of the "accounting principle" (*khozraschët*) in Soviet economy. See also p. 66.

policies. They had no idea of relative scarcities, nor did they know or care for the careful assessment of the cost of products. They inflicted upon the central administration the enormous task of fixing some 7 or 8 million prices, which were obsolete almost as soon as they were promulgated. One obvious result of such practice was a sprawling official-dom, for this exacting activity alone required a lot of man-power. Other functions of control and distribution had a similar effect, breeding inefficient bureaucracies that en-gulfed energies and resources much needed elsewhere.[19]

The distortions caused in the national economy by faulty pricing were deep; and numerous malfunctions, as well as the problem of inefficient use of resources from which the system much suffered, stemmed directly from the neglect of this apparently secondary factor.[20]

The larger theoretical issue behind pricing was the "law of value" in socialism and the character of the product in this economy. S. Strumilin—who during his leadership in Gosplan (until 1930) became a prominent spokesman for the teleological school in planning which doubted the very existence of any objective laws in economic life—after some thirty years of experience, bitterly attacked the believers in "direct exchange of products" and the practices that pre-vailed under their rule. The widely accepted opinion (probably rather following Stalin's, as Strumilin himself ex-plained) denied the existence of the "law of value," let

[19] D. Kondrashev, *Tsena i Stoimost' v Sotsialisticheskom Khoziai-stve* (Moscow, 1963), pp. 219–220. Referring to both prewar and the immediate postwar practice of subsidies to heavy industry, the author said "that the whole economic apparatus of the country was busy with computing the accounts with the budget for the losses incurred [by the enterprises], whereas serious economic work was neglected." Ia. Kvasha, in A. Notkin, ed., *Faktory Ekonomicheskogo Razvitiia SSSR* (Moscow, 1970), p. 138, has shown the growth of numbers of econ-omists and planners from a total of 879,000 in 1941 to 1,196,000 in 1968.

[20] A. Notkin, ed., *Struktura Narodnogo Khoziaistva SSSR* (Moscow, 1967), p. 86; and Nemchinov, *O Dal'neishem*, p. 29.

alone any regulating role, and maintained that the products of state factories—especially the producer goods, which circulated between state-owned units and did not reach nonstate users—were not commodities at all but just "products"; in this view, socialist production could not be seen as "commodity production" at all.[21]

This approach served as a theoretical justification for "administrative planning" in general and for the mishandling of pricing in particular. But eventually, enough proof accumulated to show that value categories still existed. Against the still very vigorous "antimarketeers," the majority of Soviet economists yielded to evidence and accepted that, in all its sectors, the Soviet economy was and is a commodity producer. This meant that on the whole the products were exchanged and not just directly appropriated and distributed. Producers could not appropriate products without selling their own in exchange. Pricing and money were indispensable economic categories, and the existence of the market, albeit a "socialist market," could no longer be denied. Rather, all the necessary consequences of this compelling reality should be drawn and practices based on negating such realities of Soviet economics should stop.

Evidently, the whole problem is one of enormous theoretical and ideological complexity. It involves rethinking Marx, economic theory, and Western economic theory and practice, reappraising theories of socialism, reviewing the principles and prospects of Soviet socialism—an enormous task, for which Soviet social and economic thought is still ill-equipped. In fact, no theory, Western or any other, has commanded the necessary grasp of the complexities of modern social and economic systems to offer the Soviets authoritative advice on the whole range of problems they face.

Soviet economists, and no doubt politicians as well, split problems of value, markets, and the commodity character into several groups, or schools, in their approach to the of the economy. For the staunch antimarketeers, as they

[21] S. Strumilin, in Iu. Iakovets, *Reforma*, pp. 5–6.

dubbed themselves, such categories were no more than "a foreign body" in the socialist system, to be eliminated as soon as possible.[22]

Another opinion would admit that commodity-money relations existed in the Soviet economy but, paradoxically, would not accept that the products of state sectors are commodities, thus joining the previous school, though with a concession to reality.

In the wake of the reformist effervescence, another group developed the view that commodity production and money-commodity relations (commerce, money, profit, credit, etc.) belonged to the core of the socialist economic structure, although they would underline that a difference of principle remained between such relations when based on private property, as in capitalism, and commodity production based on socialist property.[23]

Inside this last group of rather ardent "promarket" reformers, a line of theoretical thought developed which maintained that the objective relations of socialist production were of a dual character. The big part, probably the bulk of products, were commodities and thus circulated through a market exchange process. There were, however, sectors and circumstances where products entered social circuits not as exchange values, but through acts of direct appropriation and allocation. Such "directly social relations" might become widespread only on a very high level of economic development when differences and divergent material interests between groups of people would have disappeared. As this was far from being the case, such "directly social relations are not as yet generalized." The So-

[22] For the opinion, which still had enough followers in the 1960s and 1970s, that socialist production relations are basically nonmarket relations and that the market categories play but a subsidiary role, see N. Tsagolov, ed., *Kurs Politicheskoi Ekonomii* (Moscow, 1963), pp. 205–207, 289.

[23] Cf. L. Leont'ev, "Glazami Vdumchivogo Ekonomista," *Novyi Mir*, no. 1 (1969), pp. 251–252.

viet socialist economy should not therefore be seen in "either-or" terms, socialist production being both of a commodity (*tovarnyi*) and noncommodity type. The historical stage reached by the economy dictated which forms should prevail and in what proportion, and as long as analysis showed sectors where commodity relations prevailed, in this sphere, "a free, unfettered economic activity of enterprises, freedom of independent decision on all the questions concerning production and marketing" should obtain.[24]

Relations pertaining to the "directly social" sphere necessitated decisions by a unified center to guide and to coordinate where appropriate. Hence the appearance of relations of subordination and superordination, and clashes between private (or group) and general interests; such clashes and their outcome decided how these contradictory relations finally became integrated.[25]

In addition, it was necessary to find out why "money-commodity relations" (a euphemism that some authors preferred to "market relations") did not disappear, as the classical theory had anticipated, but rather proved to be a vitally important mechanism of the socialist economy; and what happened to Marx's "law of value" or the labor theory of value, which was supposed to be the substance behind the prices of commodities.

Answers given to these two big questions differed significantly.[26] The fact that Soviet enterprises turned out not just "products" but "commodities" that had to be exchanged through the mediation of prices could not be accommodated within the previously predominant conception of the economy as an essentially huge "one factory, one office," as Lenin had dreamed in one of his more utopian moods.

[24] For this school, see V. Shkredov, *Ekonomika i Pravo* (Moscow, 1967), pp. 61–62.

[25] *Ibid.*, p. 62.

[26] Katsenelinboigen, Lakhman, and Ovsienko, *Optimal'nost'*, pp. 88–93, survey the debate and the different answers to questions on value and price. For the causes of the persistence of market relations in socialism, see pp. 94–109.

The complexity of the economic organization had to be accepted and understood quite differently in order to account for the persistence of the market phenomenon. Writers pointed out that the economy was composed of thousands of producing units, enterprises, and factories that were relatively independent, quite distinctly separated from others; and such "separateness" of the producing units does account, for some authors, for the fact that the relations between such producers take on the form of money-commodity relations.[27] The same factor, incidentally, as many would emphasize, made it impossible for a central plan and a centralized management to do the job without relying to a high degree on the same market mechanism.

Other conceptions explained the persistence of market categories and the need for a market mechanism as a result of the division of labor, or by the impossibility to organize economic life on "vertical command lines" only, without allowing for a degree of freedom for "horizontal" links between enterprises, without the interference and even bypassing of administrative superior agencies. In any case, it was characteristic that whatever the explanation given to the roots of market phenomena, most of them were used as theoretical justification for the very practical need to grant more autonomy to producers. If what they produced were commodities, not just products that superior agencies could appropriate and distribute, then the production and circulation of their output demanded a "free, unfettered activity of enterprises, independently solving all the problems connected with production and marketing of commodities."[28]

The same theoretical basis was used to press for yet another important change in the way of introducing and perfecting "money-commodity relations"—the dismantling of

[27] Lenin spoke of a national economy as "one factory," in *Sochineniia*, vol. 33, p. 101. For "separateness" as cause for the subsistence of money-commodity relations, see V. Lopatkin, *Tovarnye Otnosheniia i Zakon Stoimosti pri Sotsializme* (Moscow, 1963), p. 18.

[28] Shkredov, *Ekonomika*, p. 62.

the administrative supply mechanism for producers' goods (the material-technical supply system) and its replacement by a wholesale trade network. This demand was first made by A. Birman, soon taken up by Nemchinov, and finally incorporated as official objective in the decisions of the Twenty-Third Congress in 1966. But it was never implemented.

Second, the mainstay of accepted dogma held that a "substance" consisting of "socially necessary labor outlays" finally decided the level of prices of commodities. This approach claimed the full authority of Marx and prompted many orthodox Soviet economists to look for ways of fixing prices by computing the quantities of labor invested in production.

Such computations proved an impossible dream, and the fallacy contributed to the fact that the Soviet economy was deprived of a valid price theory and of appropriate pricing methods. But overcoming accepted dogma was extremely difficult, not only because of the sheer weight of orthodoxy but also because of the intellectual challenge involved in creating a new economic theory to replace the old one. But the "facts of life," as Soviet authors like to say, helped to erode and challenge this untenable position, a sacred ideological tenet; and competing schools appeared that offered their own approaches in the matter. Some, like Novozhilov, proposed a modernized version of Marx's theory but with the indispensable injection of marginal analysis and the introduction into the theory of pricing of concepts of utility and scarcity.[29] Others claimed that no "substance" existed behind the prices and that they could not be explained by labor alone, isolated from other factors such as capital assets, raw material, and natural resources. Only by including

[29] In *Problemy Izmereniia*, pp. 355–362, where he also polemicized with R. Campbell who contended that Novozhilov's theory was not Marxist anymore; see also R. Campbell, "Marx, Kantorovich, and Novozhilov: *Stoimost'* Versus Reality," *Slavic Review*, 40 (October, 1961), 402–418.

labor as one of the factors involved in production could prices be computed rigorously. This thesis was defended by mathematical economists who accepted and highly recommended market relations but did not acknowledge any link between the function of the market mechanisms and the "law of value."[30] It is probable that a minority among the mathematical economists do not believe in market mechanisms at all, although most of them do subscribe to the theory of "shadow prices" formulated by Kantorovich, for whom such prices have not much to do with labor value but consist of mathematical evaluations of resources involved in the optimal plan, which are computed as part of the process of elaborating such a plan.[31]

Differing schools of reformist economists in the Soviet Union and Eastern Europe agreed that optimal planning could not be achieved without rationalizing the pricing methods and without integrating them organically into the plan; that the coveted self-regulating mechanisms and feedback could not be created without turning to basically economic methods; that if the enterprises should gain the indispensable autonomy, initiative, and creative drive, they would have to work for consumers, not for bureaucratically fixed targets; that they should care for profits, and that they should be guided from above mainly by general parameters, with prices as the leading guide posts.

Briefly, such theorists said: the economy should reorganize as a socialist market, in which most of the outputs and inputs, including capital goods, should circulate freely.

[30] Katsenelinboigen, Lakhman, and Ovsienko, *Optimal'nost'*, p. 101, and see pp. 104–109. A systematic exposé of the Soviet "economic laws," including the "law of value" and debates on pricing, is in A. Nove, *The Soviet Economy* (3d ed., London, 1968), chaps. 8 and 11.

[31] L. Kantorovich explained his theory of pricing to an audience of mathematicians and economists in *Matematiki i Ekonomisty*, pp. 63–106. His main work is *Ekonomicheskii Raschët Nailuchshego Ispol'zovaniia Resursov* (Moscow, 1959); *The Best Use of Economic Resources*, trans. P. F. Knightsfield (London, 1965).

Nemchinov's Blueprint

How should a socialist economy function? The projects and
outlines are numerous, and are beyond the scope of this
study. But it is apparent that the influence of Lange's pre-
war model, as well as his postwar writings, and that of
Yugoslav practice, whether acknowledged or not, remain
strong. The search for other or similar solutions will continue for some time. Nemchinov, who probably summarized
a large body of opinion from scholars and managers, offered the most comprehensive critique of the system and a
functioning model as an alternative.

He aimed at an entirely new economic system, which he
called "a cost account planning system,"[32] through which he
hoped to achieve, as Novozhilov later approvingly com-
mented, "an optimal combination of centralization with democratization of economic management." In order to reach
it, Nemchinov bluntly declared that the existing "*razreshitel'naia i razverstochnaia sistema*," another picturesque,
untranslatable Russian-Soviet term that indicates "a licens-
ing-distributive system," should be replaced by a different
system of economic regulation in which the very notion of
planning should be revised. From Lenin he secured the
definition of the planning principle as "proportionality consciously sustained," from which he further concluded that
the achievement of the desired proportionality would be
secured by different and more efficient ways than the detailed target system of the familiar annual plans; that current planning must regain "the role most proper to it as general frame of reference of economical activity of enterprises
and their associations"; that the central plan had to create
powerful funds that would help the planner to intervene
efficiently and carry out the necessary corrections; that such
funds were not available in a system that relied on orders;

[32] Nemchinov, *O Dal'neishem*, pp. 12–17, 39–48. He was strongly
supported by Novozhilov, for example in his short statement "Novaia
Faza Sotsialisticheskogo Khoziaistvovaniia," in Iakovets, ed., *Reforma*,
pp. 31–35.

177

instead of such orders planning regulation should rely on legislation to provide long-term norms legally binding on all economic agents, such as ratios for deductions from profits in favor of incentive funds, branch norms for investment effectiveness, minimum salaries for *kolkhozniki*, etc.; very few indicators should remain in the central plan; a new and better information and regulation network, based on the banking and financial system, would also help to improve long-term and current planning; such channels were superior to bureaucratic supervision and banking could provide a better service of national accounting and regulation and would perform these tasks in a more efficient way.

In the framework defined by the long-term norms, or by economic legislation, the enterprises and their associations must be free to conduct their economic activity, such as marketing, acquisition of capital goods, disposal of depreciation funds, and to decide about increasing production for which there is a strong demand.

The criterion of rentability had to guide enterprises, and it would become important for planning by helping to combine the aims of the central plan with profitability at the enterprise level, as well as central with local interest.

In line with this new look on economic levers and material incentives, the main tool for operative guidance and management of the economy should become the legally binding contract. The enterprises would be free to enter contractual, bilateral, and multilateral agreements with suppliers of their choice, marketing their products through the firm's own stores or other networks, and acquiring them directly from suppliers or through governmental wholesale trade. Within the limits of the existing laws (*normativy*), the contractants would agree upon quantity, quality, prices, and so on. Knowing the conditions of their contracts and the state's control figures as contained in the governmental annual plan, the enterprises could compose their own output and financial plans; and there would be no need for the sum of those plans, the overall figures of economic activity, to conform strictly to the annual governmental control figures, which would serve for accounting and orientation purposes only.

From this model, it is possible to recognize the source of the *plan-karkass* idea of some younger economists. In the new pattern of relations between the state and the economic units, the factory's own plans would not need any formal approval by the state, although an indirect approval nevertheless would have to be earned from the state in its capacity as a powerful customer. Enterprises and economic agencies would submit their plans every year to territorial planning organs, in several variants, stipulating their program of production, variants of possible assortment and scope of output, the cost of their plans and the structure of their capital funds. Guided by their own criteria of optimality and mindful of national plans, the planning and managing organs would choose the bidders who made the best offers. Orders would be placed by the state, and signed contracts would become binding on everybody.

Such a model implied the introduction of an element of competition; a high degree of planning from below as a factor in economic life; and the introduction of a full-fledged market mechanism whereby both the state and the enterprises would operate under binding legal agreements and norms, and where both sides could abstain, to a large degree, from this or another deal if the conditions were not suitable to them. Nemchinov died in 1964, before he could elaborate the details of his plan or answer the numerous queries arising from it. But the general direction of the changes he sought was clear. It is not difficult to see how much an Ota Šik owed to Nemchinov, who probably was one of the main, if not the main, source of inspiration and encouragement for Czechoslovak and other reformers.

"Social Interests"

With this or similar projects and blueprints, studies and debates sprang up in the Soviet Union and ever new questions and problems were raised. The rethinking of economic doc-

179

trine became pervasive, and a whole range of issues never previously allowed to be raised at all were submitted to scrutiny. The fermentation of ideas in this process was without doubt remarkable. Revisions, reversals, rejection of previous dogmas, open-minded questioning of practices, and an uninhibited look at the West amounted to a real renaissance, even a revolution, in Soviet economic thinking. They represented a major break with the previous ways of viewing the economy and much else.

Economists discovered the forgotten person, the consumer; they began to press hard for the reformulation of the objectives of production, recalling that they were basically oriented to the satisfaction of societal needs and should not be seen as ends in themselves. In general, they urged production and economic activity to serve consumers and to adapt to their orders. By old standards such an approach meant yielding to "consumption moods," a supposedly clear capitalist goal. But economists retorted: "The order of the consumer, his demands, are not whims, not a fashion, but the very necessity of progress. Being economic by their very essence needs influence production through economic levers better than any administrative norms. . . ."[33]

The attention to consumer needs led to the larger concept of "social needs" and to the previously unused concept of "interests." The orthodox ideological framework imposed a view of a more or less harmonious or increasingly harmonious social structure composed of supposedly "two friendly classes," workers and peasants, and one "allied layer," the intelligentsia, in which global social interest was easily perceived and represented by the party. Such arguments were among the central tenets of the ideological framework used to justify the party's policies and monopoly of power, and they were characteristically among the central assumptions of the textbook "political economy."

Critics now charged that neglecting consumption and consumers amounted to neglecting social needs; the failure

[33] Kashin, et al., in Kozlova, ed., *Upravlenie*, p. 94.

180

to understand basic social realities and the incapacity to operate by relying on social interests led the system to prefer the seemingly easier way of administrative pressures. But by crushing interests of social groups and of individuals, by treating them as simple cogs in a machine, the system forced people to look after themselves in different ways, with damaging results for both economics and morals.[34]

The debate on market mechanisms and the "commodity" producing capacity of Soviet enterprises already implied the possibility of such a turn toward the discovery of the concept of "interests," not only as a theoretical construction but also as an operational concept and a postulate for programs of change. The more conservative among the "marketeers" (*tovarniki*) stopped short of heresy, but others overstepped the line and purported "the existence inside the framework of socialist property relations of distinct interests proper to different links of which the social division of labor is composed."[35] To this the more dogmatic spokesmen predictably retorted: "The socialist enterprise does not and cannot have any distinct interests of its own, analogous to the interests of a private entrepreneur."[36]

Behind this clash was the reappraisal of the role and place of socialized or state property. The party's own school for social studies defended the view that state ownership was the mainstay of the new social system and the basic source of a new class solidarity and social unity. However, the economic debate revealed that the presence of a powerful owner did not at all preclude the appearance of either group interests or a deep discordance between the interests of the owner (the state) and the producers. There was no

[34] Cf., for example, Birman, "Sut' Reformy," pp. 109, 202, where he writes against viewing working people as just cogs in the economic mechanism.

[35] V. Batyrev, *Problemy Politicheskoi Ekonomii Sotsializma* (Moscow, 1963), p. 215.

[36] Lopatkin, *Tovarnye Otnoshenia*, pp. 26–27.

automatic identity between the state as proprietor and the factory crews whom the ideology and the very principle of nationalization presented assiduously as the real bosses (*khoziaeva*).

Conservatives could not easily stomach the different picture that emerged from the study of economic (and social) realities. The feeling of being the actual boss of the factory was supposed to become a powerful incentive for labor and management. Such deep involvement of the masses in decision making would ensure the success of their factories and offices. But the crews never accepted the view that they were "owners." Rather, they saw an owner—the state—that exercised its ownership rights jealously and despotically. This became a source of estrangement and begot counter-incentives that no amount of propaganda and party surveillance could suppress or correct.

One way in which the system creates estrangement is to foster apathy among the producers, and Strumilin attributed this to the denial of workers' and administrations' "direct participation in the profits created by their labor."[37] The official dogma and practice overlooked the basic truth that the source of revolutionary enthusiasm of the masses lay in their hope of satisfying everyday needs, no less than some long-range historical aspirations. These everyday interests could not be delayed with impunity for too long a period. Quotations from Lenin were easily found to prove, if proof was needed, that ideas must be fused with the material interests of those who are involved in the production process and in the economic struggles. Plans that do not consider or that damage economic interests of the producers, the critics categorically asserted, would not be implemented. Overzealous administrators, whatever the office they occupied, were reminded, on Marx's authority, that an idea "which becomes detached from interests is utterly compromised. . . ."[38]

Thus, the rebirth of economics generated a need for the

[37] Strumilin, in Iakovets, *Reforma*, p. 22.
[38] Kozlova, ed., *Upravlenie*, p. 116 (quoting Marx).

allied branch of sociology. The economists knew that their field did coincide with other disciplines. The notion of "social interests" that emerged in economic writings was an illustration of such an overlapping, and it belonged legitimately to the sphere of sociology. And sociology did in fact make its appearance almost simultaneously with economics, although this newcomer was too dangerously competing with the traditional brand of "historical materialism" and was much closer supervised by party watchdogs than economics.[39] Nevertheless, sociology, whatever the controls, engaged in the same kind of confrontation with the older dogmas as economics did; it was just done more evasively.

Eventually, pressures arose in scholarly circles for the official admission of yet another branch of social inquiry—political science—but after some stirrings and debates, the "license" was refused. But the official flight from the realities of intellectual and political life could not prevent the discussion of concepts either in a "gray" or "black market" of ideas, of which *samizdat* is one of the well-known instances.

Reforms and Conservative Backlash

The economic reforms—a very complex and far from finished set of measures—were launched at the end of 1965, as a legitimate child of the ideas that had been broached by the reformist economists and that continued to be debated in subsequent years. It is quite remarkable that an alliance of politicians, managers, and scholars could be formed to embark upon the complicated venture. Premier Kosygin, probably the main political force behind the whole enterprise, launched the reforms in September 1965, and the ac-

[39] Sociology was accepted and existed in the 1920s. (Bukharin's work on historical materialism was subtitled: *A Textbook of Marxist Sociology*), but was later banned as "bourgeois." On Soviet sociology, see Z. Katz, "Sociology in the Soviet Union," *Problems of Communism*, May–June 1971, pp. 22–40. A Simirenko, ed., *Soviet Sociology* (London, 1967); D. Lane, "Ideology and Sociology in the USSR," *British Journal of Sociology*, 21 (1970), 43–51.

tual changes adopted were, unsurprisingly, extremely cautious. Nevertheless, the measures announced then were directed toward "economic methods and levers" desired by reformist economists and managers. A. Birman, one of the most enthusiastic promoters of the economic reforms, hailed the September measures as a turn as important as the two major previous turns in Soviet history: the proclamation of the NEP in 1921 and the introduction of Stalin's centralized administrative system in 1929–1930.[10]

The officially endorsed reforms fully accepted the importance of the money-commodity relations and proceeded to revise the theory and practice of the pricing method. The importance of the profit indicator was recognized and it became, together with the volume of sales, an important planning criterion, replacing the previous target of global output and a host of other detailed indicators, many of which were dropped. The enterprises got more autonomy and some leeway for direct relations with each other, and at the same time firms (associations of enterprises) were fostered and their role steadily increased at the expense of certain prerogatives of the previously all-powerful ministries. These ministries, incidentally, were reintroduced by the reforms to replace the decentralized system of regional councils of the national economy (sovnarkhozy) with which Khrushchev had experimented without success.

In addition, more realistic pricing methods, charges for capital, and the computation of profits as a ratio of capital

[10] For an official outline of the economic reforms, see A. Kosygin's speech, "On Improving Management of Industry," *Pravda*, 28 September 1965, and A. Birman's comments in "Thoughts After the Plenum," both translated in U.S. Congress, Joint Economic Committee, Subcommittee on Foreign Policy, *New Directions of the Soviet Economy*, 89th Cong., 2d sess. (Washington, D.C., 1966), pp. 1067–1093. See also E. Zalesky, *Planning Reforms in the Soviet Union 1962–1966* (Chapel Hill, N.C., 1967); M. Ellman, *Economic Reform in the Soviet Union* (London, 1969); A. Balinky, et al., *Planning and the Market in the USSR: The 1960's* (New Brunswick, N.J., 1967); numerous articles on different aspects of the reforms can be found in the files of *Soviet Studies*.

assets, to promote a more rational attitude toward the basic economic resources, were started. At the same time, enterprises were granted the right to use a larger share of their profits to finance some of their investments, or to create different stimulation funds to be distributed as premiums for good performance to workers and managers.

Such reforms, with their emphasis on markets, incentives, and indirect levers, ran into difficulties in subsequent years. As the reforms were, albeit cautiously, implemented, the opposition to them kept gathering force. The flurry of ideas and the beginnings of their implementation seemed to have opened dangerous floodgates, which more conservative forces thought should be closed before it was too late.

From their point of view, the new ideas, even those apparently apolitical, extolled a more flexible economic system, with its "economic levers" and hence indirect (instead of the customary and tested direct) controls, which appeared to be cracks in a powerful dam. Further demands for a large diffusion of prerogatives, autonomy, and rights over the entire system and a redefinition of relations between central authorities and localities prefigured a new division of influence, privilege, and power, the emergence of new institutions, a different leadership, a new political mentality, and a new climate of social relations. Many in positions of power correctly felt that continuing on such a road would be suicidal for at least important parts of the ruling apparatus and for whole sectors of officialdom. The events in Czechoslovakia served as evidence for the arguments against market methods, decentralization, and new models. Prague was an example of how undue reformist zeal could undermine the party's rule and its grip.

Predictably, the opposition to reforms grew fierce and venomous. Opponents arose from the ranks of professors of political economy, who had built their careers on dogmas entirely divorced from economic realities, and using heavily the bogey of capitalism they sniffed out "deviations," "revisionism," and other "mortal sins" in every new idea.

But more important were the other people supporting

them in the party apparatus and in the ministries, whom the reformers named "supporters of administrative methods," or more pejoratively, "primitive centralizers." Such individuals would accept changes to improve coordination and efficiency but only to strengthen at the same time the controlling power of the centralized machinery.

A different way of grouping the fighting camps is to divide them into "supporters of economic methods" versus different schools of "statists" (my term). The "statists" fight against "economic methods" because "they diminish the role of the state in the management of the economy, weaken the planning principle in the economic development, lead to a contradiction between private interests and social ones."[41] Some "statists" would also argue that the reformers tried to create a system in which engineers, technicians, and economic leaders would gain the upper hand in the system at the expense of the party.[42]

In the course of actual reforms since 1965, the efforts to sabotage them were aided by forces of inertia, routine, and habit. The vested interests that thrive on the maintenance of familiar methods and, finally, ignorance and lack of appropriate cadres both in the higher echelons and among factory managers created many additional obstacles.

Conservatism and inertia can be expected, of course, to inhibit major changes in any system. In the Soviet situation, an additional factor is operating: the monopolistic ideology, steeped in glorifying and justifying any existing policy or practice of the government and especially of the party, tends to enhance the conservative forces. As the system was created by the party, it was duly consecrated ideologically in the process. The resultant stifling of initiative and an atmosphere highly uncongenial for debate plays into the hands of *status quo* forces and denies the system the creativity of free opinion, information, and criticism. The party's role as a specific politico-administrative monopoly

[41] A. Birman, "Sut' Reformy," p. 188.
[42] Cf. Zalesky, *Planning Methods*, p. 120.

186

was and is the underlying issue. The party is literally everywhere, including factory shop floors, with the local, territorial, and the cell's secretariat keeping watch, not to mention the controlling agencies of the state apparatus, the secret police, and the procurator's office. For such a structure even to contemplate the disappearance of most cherished methods was a threatening prospect. For those used to identifying "socialism" with "direct controls" everywhere, the economist-reformers appeared to be dangerous antisocialists, at least potentially.

Against this background, it is easy to understand that the suppression of Dubček's and Ota Šik's reforms in Czechoslovakia was aimed at internal critics no less than at the "irresponsible" Czechs. Šik's criticism and proposal immediately recalled Nemchinov's recommendations.[43]

The new conservative coalition, which seemed to have gained the upper hand before the events in Prague and which received a considerable boost after the suppression of the Czech "revisionists," turned to the more traditional ways of appeals and pressures for more discipline, sense of duty, and ideological fervor. At the same time, with numerous problems pressing for solutions, this trend banked on the help of technology and science, computerized management, and improved information flow, in order to modernize the administrations and improve economic performance without endangering the *status quo*.

This was the apparent rationale behind the latest wave of reform announced in March 1973, at the moment this text was undergoing final revision before publication.[44] Al-

[43] On this point, compare the observations by F. Fejto, *Histoire des Democraties Populaires. Après Staline* (Paris, 1969), p. 425.

[44] This time the reform is no more than a reorganization of the industrial enterprises into strong "associations" (*ob'edineniia*) or firms, patterned after the "trusts" of the 1920s and the modern U.S. corporations. To this bodies, each of which will comprise a number of enterprises throughout the country, will be delegated many functions and prerogatives hitherto granted exclusively to the ministerial level; at the same time, the prerogatives that were granted to the enter-

though not unreasonable in themselves, such reforms were undertaken exclusively in management and administration, in quest of pure efficiency but with little mention of "indirect levers," "democratization," and so on. This time the operation is in the sole hands of "reasonable and responsible" people who certainly have learned that big industrial corporations elsewhere are hierarchically organized and very efficient, innovation-oriented producers; they have no reason to think that something similar in the strictly managerial-technical sense could endanger any of the existing political institutions. On the contrary, a big boost in production along these lines could prop up the image of the rulers and the pattern of power to which they are committed.

Whatever the current fate of the reforms and the less optimistic atmosphere of the early 1970s on Russia's internal front, the ferment of the 1960s, with its critical ardor and creative thrust in the field of economic thought, opened a new chapter in Soviet scholarship and, in many ways, some irreversible trends in the economic life of the country. The debate offered to the Soviet reading public a new picture of the past and present problems of the economic model, a wealth of information, particularly a more truthful image of Western realities and of the comparative performance of the competing systems—and all this became part of the arsenal of the Soviet intelligentsia. It supplied citizens interested in the problems of their country with indispensable material for better insight into these problems and a propensity to explore more deeply the mechanisms governing their polity.

---

prises in the earlier stage of the reform (and embodied in the "status of the enterprise") will be conferred upon the management of the multifactory firm. For details of this reorganization see official announcement in *Ekonomicheskaia Gazeta*, no. 14 (April 1973), pp. 3–4.

CHAPTER EIGHT

Critique of the State

ECONOMIC debates and some reforms, as the previous chapter showed, frightened conservatives because of their eventually political repercussions. Many in the West, too, thought that the introduction of market mechanisms and more autonomy granted to enterprises would necessarily spill over into the political sphere and begin a chain of events leading to the introduction of political plurality into the system. At least there would be a weakening of the ministerial state bureaucracy and a reshaping of power patterns.[1]

Such was certainly the logic of the situation, although there was more than one such "logic." Experience in many countries shows that market mechanisms can function in authoritarian political systems without harming them; they often are quite neutral in cases where democratic institutions deteriorate; furthermore, democratic institutions are not an indispensable prerequisite for high productivity and technological innovation.

But it remained a fact that one of the possible outcomes of the reformist drive might be a significant change in the political institutions; and this was immediately obvious in the very configuration of the camps that emerged in the debates and in the reforms. Many economists quite clearly expressed their distaste for primitive administrative methods, or even for less crude ones, as the predominant way of running the economy, and they saw themselves as a party to a

[1] Cf. A. Shonfield, in *The World Today*, no. 3 (March 1970), pp. 96–97.

dispute with a camp of supporters of such methods. Reformers wanted to make the planners more efficient by divesting them of unmanageable functions and to reinvigorate the economy by decentralizing and even democratizing the whole system by lending more power to lower rungs in the administration and to grass roots units and their crews. Even giving workers a say in running the affairs of the enterprises was broached, whatever the "Yugoslav" overtones of such demands.

Against such demands and programs rallied the "centralizers," those who preferred the strengthening of the center and its powers by streamlining the managerial machinery and by the use of electronics, and who hoped to achieve in this way a better mastery of information flows and a better grip on the producers. "Democratization" was not important to them and, rather, was to be avoided.

Thus, the emerging camps were at the outset political in the sense that they clearly wanted the reforms to lead to quite different institutional arrangements with a different configuration of power.

The spillover from "economics" to "politics" was even more direct and unavoidable, more straightforward in the realm of ideas and theories than in the eventual chain of future events. In fact, researchers followed the logic of their critiques and demands to grant autonomy to enterprises, into larger aspects of political and social problems. They pointed out that such autonomy was not conceivable without developing market mechanisms, and some of them— examining "social interests"—reappraised the character of social ownership of the state and the very meaning and essence of socialism.

Such ideas gradually unfolded, moved from the more strictly economic to the larger socio-political aspects, and en route triggered many ideological principles.

One important question unavoidably haunted the debaters as they studied the faults of economic organization, trouble with productivity, and lack of incentives: why did

190

methods employed in the past harden into "a whole system of disproportions" without being mended in due time?

Before entering this risky field of exploration, economists first hinted cautiously and indirectly at where the trouble lay. The planners, numerous texts maintained, had been placed above the producers and above "the economy" and had become detached from it. They were not supervised except by their immediate superiors, and they bore no material or other responsibility for the irrational, faulty, disproportion-breeding decisions, which weighed heavily on producers and the national economy. They alone decided the criteria, the ways, means, and the price that had to be paid by others. It was time, Nemchinov, Venzher, and a host of other critics maintained, to make the planners bear the responsibility, and pay, if necessary, in hard cash from their pockets for the faults of their planning.

In the Soviet context, the meaning of the term "planner" was ambiguous. In its "innocent" use it meant the planning agencies. But these agencies had bosses. The "planner" could easily become a euphemism for "government" or even "the state." The accusation of arbitrariness launched against planners and against their decisions could not bypass the government of the country, the system's central leadership —which was the real "planner" and which actually did not submit to any constraint, any supervision, or any legal or political responsibility. This was why statements delivered in an economic language about the planner standing above the producers, not accountable to anybody, and imposing damaging decisions on factory managers, could at any moment become dangerously close to being critical political statements about the character of the Soviet state and the position of its rulers.

In fact, there was no way out without passing such a threshold. Some reached the conclusion, at least for the state of affairs that obtained before the 1965 reforms, that the slackening of the economic performance had its deep causes in the socio-economic organization, in the institutions

191

running the economy that showed signs of self-closure impeding their ability to respond adequately to the growing complexities of economic life. Senior economists charged that the system did not have the capacity to "readapt" (*perestroit'sia*), to reorganize planning and management institutions so that they would match the new conditions.[2] The outspoken Antonov, using his trenchant metaphors, poked fun at the traditional party methods of solving almost any problem. The panacea was to find "the appropriate people," to fire the indolent, and to give everyone orders. In practice, however, managers and party members were fired, but the drawbacks remained and new ones even appeared to replace them. "Cut off one head of the dragon, and two new ones appear. Once again society raises its sword to strike out, and the next head bites the dust; but new ugly heads grow which poke out their tongues to taunt us and to devour the nation's wealth."[3]

To a mind trained in Marxist texts, a classical formula was self-evident in such conditions. This accumulation of phenomena pointed to a discrepancy between "production forces" and "production relations," and the conclusion had to follow that the inadequate "production relations" hampering economic development must be adapted to the "production forces," otherwise crises developed. (This was another way of repeating the charge of the system's incapacity to overhaul institutions [*perestroit'sia*].) Unfortunately, some time during the early stages of Soviet development—so the modern argument ran—this classical truth was "underestimated."[4]

[2] See S. Pervushin, V. Venzher, A. Kvasha, et al., *Proizvodstvo, Nakoplenie, Potreblenie* (Moscow, 1965), pp. 17, 242; *Production, Accumulation, Consumption*, trans. S. P. Pervashin (White Plains, N.Y., 1967).

[3] O. Antonov, *Dlia Vsekh i Dlia Sebia* (Moscow, 1965), p. 12.

[4] V. Kashin, et al., in O. Kozlova, ed., *Upravlenie Sotsialisticheskim Proizvodstvom* (Moscow, 1968). The same was stated by Egorychev, Moscow party secretary, at the Twenty-Third Party Congress, in *23-ii S'ezd KPSS, Stenotchet* (Moscow, 1966), p. 125. In fact, they have

Officially, this was said about the period under Stalin. But modern economists observed and were worried by phenomena that had occurred later, in the 1960s, and they continued to use the same formula and to find others to tell the leaders that they had not yet stopped "underestimating" the basic postulate.

A further idea in Soviet social and political thought was redeemed by the economic debate: "social interests" and their contradictions. The controversies on autonomy to be granted to enterprises brought about a sharp clash of opinions on the larger issue of separate interests of factory crews. Dzharasóv, e.g., the author quoted earlier, knew and accepted the concept of "separateness" of enterprises as a source of market categories, then retreated into the safe "statist" dogmas that specific separate interests of enterprises just did not exist. Was it not a fact that the director of the enterprises was a state nominee who had to work according to the state's orders and, as a subordinate to the state, did he not thereby serve general social interests? The same argument, in a different version further maintained that the enterprise belonged to society. Society "created it and it is free to liquidate it, not to speak about preempting resources from it."[5]

The new outlook explicitly and systematically challenged this still powerful official dogma. The factories, not "the state," were the real producers, and enterprises had interests of their own, which not only differed, but were sometimes contradictory and conflicting to each other and to the state; conflicting interests might also exist inside the factories between the administration and the workers.[6]

The unrealistic negation of diversity of interests made the

---

followed the party secretary word for word, but they have drawn conclusions that are more far-reaching than those of the party secretary.

[5] V. Lopatkin, *Tovarnye Otnosheniia i Zakon Stoimosti pri Sotsializme* (Moscow, 1963), pp. 26, 27.

[6] Cf. L. Loginov, in Kozlova, ed., *Upravlenie*, pp. 114–115.

leadership blind to the fact that it was the very existence of different social interests and conflicts that did "not allow the economy to operate only through direct command planning." The reasonable way out consisted of supplementing such planning with material stimulation, making possible the satisfaction of the numerous, independent, specific interests of factories, factory departments, and individual workers.[7] The official textbooks on economics, instead of immersing themselves in details of economic life and social reality, presented the standard ideological formulas and preferred to use such obscure, high-sounding phrases as "social property on production-means unites people, secures genuine community of interests, and comradely collaboration." But if the phraseology were true, whence did all the numerous fights and sometimes sharp contradictions in Soviet society arise? Economists avoided talking about sharp conflicts of interest and mistook wishes and hopes for reality. The problems did not result from insufficient consciousness, subjective reasons, or "not understanding the tasks," but from deeper objective factors. Although social property did in fact create a certain amount of community of interest and eliminated the contradictions inherent in the institution of private property, the introduction of social property did "not at all eliminate contradictions which the social forms of property on production means [brought] forward."[8] This was, once more, Antonov.

Such critics challenged many cherished dogmas. The party was told in fact that *its* economic theory did not match social reality. And its conception of "socialism," which disregarded social interests, also became quite a problematic one. Thus the new theme of "interests" in Soviet conditions became an important, as well as a politically and ideologically explosive, term. Planning could not become effective and unifying as long as this simple concept

[7] *Ibid.*, p. 115.
[8] Antonov, *Dlia Vsekh*, pp. 16–19.

was drowned in generalities and misconceived in practice. The very idea of socialism was gravely compromised in this case. A Soviet author could not always frankly state this, but he implied it. For too long a time, interests of people were replaced by "tons and cubic meters," maintained the economist Birman. For him the "interests of the working people" should have been the focus, but clearly they were not so. Their satisfaction "should constitute the basis of the whole economic policy of the victorious proletariat, and it is appealing to and working through these interests that should form the basis of the mechanisms for the construction of socialism and communism."[9]

More Seeds for a Political Theory

Whatever problem was approached by the student of the economic system—be it planning, the maze of the *matsnab* organization, pricing, the status of factories, material incentives, microeconomic phenomena and tensions, or macroeconomic disproportions—each eventually came to the problem of the power of administrations. If an administration were free to decide how much it would extract from subordinated producers for its own upkeep, it would tend to grow in size, as would its appetite for control. Khalfina had pointed it out adding that arbitrariness was invited and fostered in such a way; if management were overcentralized, the initiative of the grass roots units would be fettered and the whole production process pathologically deformed; if the plan were declared all-powerful, as Malyshev said in one of his texts, then the economic relations of human beings would be seen as of secondary importance, or just of a subsidiary character, turning this into an approach "which acquired the solidity of a prejudice."[10] The next step would then be for top echelons to declare themselves in

[9] A. Birman, "Sut' Reformy," *Novyi Mir*, no. 12 (December 1968), p. 190.

[10] I. Malyshev, *Ekonomicheskie Zakony Sotsializma i Planirovanie* (Moscow, 1966), p. 25.

possession of the formula of "the general interest" and to claim that this formula was superior, morally and otherwise; the complex web of social relations with their groups, interests, points of view, and conflicts—in brief, the "civil society"—could then be safely disregarded. The Soviet peasantry, *kolkhozy*, and agriculture in general illustrate the results of such procedures, but numerous other examples show initiatives fettered, interests crushed, bureaucracies flourishing, market categories misunderstood and misused, and unwarranted dogmas imposed forcibly from above. The common denominator in these situations was now seen as "politics" getting detached "from the economy" in one formula, "from interests" in another; and one central phenomenon followed although it was described in different terms: "unwarranted extra-economic administrative pressures," "bureaucratic distortions," "economic voluntarism," and finally just "subjectivism" and "arbitrariness."

Thus, arbitrary action of an enormously powerful agency —only a powerful one could afford to be arbitrary throughout a historical period—was the common thread of the different analyses. The state—or rather the institution that ran the state machinery and provided the lynchpin for the whole regime—was naturally the one factor at which all the criticism was aimed and which seemed to be the source of many, if not most, of the problems.

What other agency could engage in "unjustified extra-economic coercion" in Soviet conditions, or impose concepts for which there was no basis in reality, or disregard social interests on a large scale?

If it were true, as Malyshev formulated it, that the essence of the economic reform consisted in condemning this "extra-economic administrative pressure,"[11] then it also would be true that the very central point of those reforms was the problem of the structure of power in the state. If economic thinking and search for remedies were to have any meaning, they had to investigate "the state," not just

[11] *Ibid.*, p. 57.

"the economy," and to engage in developing a full-fledged political theory.

Whatever the difficulties of such a tendency, economic thought began to venture on this road with the discussion of the immense power of the state administration, its abuse, and the sources of such arbitrary abuse.

Enough had been said about the harm done; authors began to consider very seriously the strictly political problems. In general terms, rather timidly at first, one author admitted that "the administrative method of management [contained] the danger of abusing the power with which the administrator [was] endowed."[12] He did not define the conditions favoring such behavior. But some others, following the lessons they had learned from economic realities, said more: "Administrative methods of management are directly dependent not on human economic interests, but on the authority of the government in power, and it is precisely in this fact that the possibility of voluntarism lurks hidden, like a butterfly in a chrysalis."[13] The same applied to centralization, which was not wrong in itself, even indispensable, but if laws of economy were disregarded such centralization became "a brake on economic development."[14]

This statement implies the need to submit the state to checks, in order to tame its proclivities for subjectivity and damaging arbitrariness. Reformers were able to suggest some solutions to this crucial problem; at this junction, Engels' authority could be used to emphasize the urgency to supervise the state closely and to understand better its essence. The well-known formula that the state represented interests of the ruling class, an important Marxist tenet, was an insufficient solution to Soviet dilemmas. A larger problem than the relation between the state and the class it rep-

[12] S. Dzarasov, "O Metodakh Upravleniia Sotsialisticheskim Khoziaistvom," *Voprosy Ekonomiki*, no. 10 (1968), p. 37.

[13] Kashin, et al., in Kozlova, ed., *Upravlenie*, p. 81.

[14] Vereshchagin and Denisov, *ibid.*, p. 23.

resented had to be studied, namely the relation between the state and "the economy" in more general terms. And here Engels had the following to offer: the action of the state in the economic field, he explained, might have three possible results; it might suit the general trend in the development of the economy, and then such an activity of the state was helpful; it might act against the trend or laws of economic development, and in this case the state was condemned to suffer, as the history of all important states proved; and there could be a third, intermediate course, when the state partly hampered and partly favored economic develop-ment. "It is clear," said Engels, "that in the second and third cases political power may cause enormous harm to eco-nomic development and may result in a massive squander-ing of energies and materials."[15]

This quotation, as far as I know, never appeared in Soviet literature until it was unearthed and used by supporters of economic reforms. The authority of Engels and the topical-ity of what he had said in this quotation or elsewhere could be embarrassing, and one of the best ways to silence such a founding father was to worship him but not to study him. As soon as serious study became possible, some texts be-came thunderous. Marxist theory was a powerful weapon to study change in social systems, an appeal both to under-take such studies and to engage in promoting such change. In particular, the Marxist approach to the study of the state may not be less suitable for today's Russia. Basically, in the Marxist view the state served as a tool for expressing inter-ests of ruling classes; but at the same time, as part of the superstructure, it was bound to follow and to adapt itself to the needs and changes in the socio-economic basis, or to cause damaging results if this was not done. Such concepts seemed to throw much light on the situation in which the

[15] Kashin, et al., *ibid.*, p. 72, and, quoting K. Marx and F. Engels, *Polnoe Sobranie Sochinenii*, 37 (2d ed., Moscow, 1965), 417. This is from a famous letter written by F. Engels to C. Schmidt from London on 27 October 1890.

Soviet state found itself. Thus, some economists were fond of the above-quoted passage. But Engels' approach was particularly distasteful to the *status quo* holder, because it was his state that got caught committing two sins, which, Engels thought, would be mortal for a state: lack of capacity to adapt its institutions to needs of the "basis" and, in consequence, the creating of obstacles to economic development.

Shkredov's Treatise

The politically relevant ideas studied above were more or less dispersed over pages of texts, basically concerned with other problems and venturing rather sporadically into the more explosive considerations of a theoretical political character. But no effort to present a comprehensive theoretical framework was known in Soviet literature until the publication in 1967 of V. P. Shkredov's *Economy and Law* (*Ekonomika i Pravo*)—a rather short but extremely dense theoretical study conducted on a high level of abstraction. It was the first and, for the time being, unique theoretical treatise dealing with the complex interrelationships among economics, politics, society, and law in which the hitherto dispersed remarks, ideas, and feelings of numerous econom-ists were reunited into a coherent whole, presented on a higher level of reasoning and argument, and in which the deeper causes of phenomena and trends were sought. Although his formulas seem dry and apparently remote from current problems, the book is a condensed formulation of the basic problems facing the Soviet system in the throes of economic reforms. This was strongly underlined by the enthusiastic review of *Ekonomika i Pravo* published in *Novyi Mir* before Tvardovsky was purged from the editorial board. The reviewer suggested that the reader would no doubt be able to "recognize in the abstractions the reflection of phenomena present in real life."[16]

[16] V. Georgiev, "Ekonomika i Pravo," *Novyi Mir*, no. 10 (October 1968), p. 278.

The main topic of the book was political theory. The author formulated his principal theme as "the correlation of objective production relations with the subjective-volitional, human economic activity."[17] He also stated clearly that the solution of this particular problem, although seemingly a theoretical one, was nevertheless urgent, because one of the imperatives of Soviet economic life was "to fully overcome voluntarism in the management of the national economy." In fact, Shkredov analyzed the Soviet state and a set of traits in the whole system that became known as Stalinism in both the East and the West. But he avoided this term, and for good reason. First, it would have made publication more difficult. Second, a quarter of a century of a country's history could not be explained solely in terms of the actions of a personality. Thus, neither Stalin's name or the term "cult of personality" were even mentioned, but an interesting hint was nevertheless dropped.

The author accepted the general Marxist premise that the state expressed economic interests of the ruling class, and "politics," in general, was an expression of "economics." Lenin had even said that "politics is but concentrated economics." Shkredov added to this formula some important qualifications. Lenin's statement should be corrected by the rejoinder that politics does not overlap with economics entirely, because it depends on many additional factors.[18] For example, the state must take care of the interests, not only of the ruling class but also of those of professional state administrators—and significantly, of the interest of another specific group, state leaders.[19]

In the Soviet literature studying the Soviet state, this was the first time the existence of such a group was mentioned and the fact acknowledged that it might have some specific

[17] V. Shkredov, *Ekonomika i Pravo* (Moscow, 1967), pp. 21–25, from Marx and Engels, *Polnoe Sobranie Sochinenii*, 13 (Moscow, 1960), 315.

[18] *Ibid.*, p. 94.   [19] *Ibid.*

interests of its own. An extremely promising realization indeed for the furthering of political sociology!

Other factors that influence political decisions were put forward: international relations, ideology, and the influence and personal qualities of leaders. The author concluded that the state enjoyed a considerable autonomy in its relation to economic (and social) forces.

This autonomy, or relative freedom, was a source of voluntary actions with regard to economics, which of course were not automatically arbitrary. But a further condition that made arbitrariness and estrangement from economic reality even more possible arose when material interests of a person or a group (administrations) were asserted independently of the situation and performance of the economic units subordinate to those groups. Here "larger possibilities [were] created for arbitrary voluntaristic action."[20] In such cases the administrations were not only not stimulated to actions objectively indispensable to production, but also might even be pushed to do just the opposite and so damage the development of the economy.

Further enlargement of the scope for acting arbitrarily arose in a planned economy. Subjectively, leaders might have the best intentions, but because they did not substantially take reality into account—and in a planned economy they might do so more easily than elsewhere—not only would damage be done, but also these leaders finally would discover that their free action was not as free as it seemed to them.

Shkredov clarified this slightly confusing argument in the following way: in the sphere of production relations arbitrary action, strictly speaking, could change practically nothing; but it was different in the sphere of appropriation and the distribution of output. Here voluntaristic action had much more leeway than in the sphere of direct production.[21]

[20] *Ibid.*, p. 14.   [21] *Ibid.*, p. 12.

201

Shkredov shows that the formula employed to define the scope and limits to arbitrariness of a leader was parallel to the formula applied to the state in general. In other words, the freedom of action that leaders could enjoy was conditional upon the freedom of action possessed by the state they ruled. The personality of the leader did not create the very possibility for large-scale arbitrariness, it was created by the circumstances and conditions in which such leaders lived and operated.[22] Shkredov preferred, therefore, to concentrate on the study of those conditions that allowed the state to acquire so much detachment from economic and social realities and to offer to its leaders the possibility of unleashed and unbridled fantasies or phobias. The author here concurred with Marx. According to Marx, the personality could not be credited with having created the very conditions of which he himself was a product; speaking about Louis Bonaparte, Marx polemicized against Victor Hugo, who "did not notice that he [made] this individual great instead of small by ascribing to him a personal power of initiative such as would be without parallel in world history." Marx then explained his own method, which he applied in studying Louis Bonaparte. This consisted of showing how the real class warfare created conditions permitting "a grotesque mediocrity to play a hero's part."[23]

Did Shkredov use such quotations from Marx to hint at what he really thought about Stalin? The answer is not known, but the author has a clear preference for the Marxian tradition in explaining Soviet history. One might wonder how the Soviet equivalent of *18 Brumaire*, written about Stalin, would look once the Soviet state stopped dictating what could and could not be studied. One might guess that Shkredov would probably show how the state, and the particular leaders engaged in voluntaristic action, would finally come up against very tangible limits, espe-

[22] *Ibid.*, pp. 14–15.
[23] *Ibid.*, p. 15. Shkredov is quoting from K. Marx and F. Engels, *The 18th Brumaire of Louis Bonaparte*.

cially where economics was concerned. The existing level of technology, division of labor, prevailing economic values, and the system of needs created by historical development were the constraining factors that Shkredov actually explored. Production relations were not simply relations between people; they were material relations and therefore a seemingly unbridled élan would finally, "find itself in the world of natural inevitability."[24] The sooner this is understood, the better for everybody.

More on Shkredov's conception of the state and the character of its actions can be gathered from his treatment of property relations and the role of law. This issue helped him to discover one more source for the state's freedom of action and, on this occasion, to revise an important "sacred" principle of Soviet ideology. Shkredov's particular blend of economic determinism, coupled with a realistic understanding for the state's degree of autonomy, inspired his views on this and on many other points.

For Shkredov, law is an expression of volitional and conscious action of the state in the sphere, among others, of the national economy. As an expression of the state's will, law is especially powerful in defining property relations or changing them because property—the power of men over things—is basically a volitional relation. But this was an important challenge to accepted dogma: property relations should not be mistaken for production relations. Robbery, or expropriation, especially if undertaken on a mass scale —such as the kind rampant during revolutions—might change the subjects of property (including both production and consumer means) and might therefore influence the continuation of the production process. This would create an "illusion that possession precede[d] production and determine[d] production."[25] But the illusion was dispelled as soon as the reproduction process began. Production relations would go their way and would finally influence property relations. The latter, which are juridical in character,

[24] *Ibid.*, p. 17.   [25] *Ibid.*, p. 25.

possess a considerable autonomy and durability. They might as well not undergo any changes for long historical periods, whereas during the same time the economy might move several stages ahead and change considerably. Shkredov therefore affirmed that the real social forms of the actually functioning production forces were production relations and not property relations.

Property relations, state property as unique or the highest form of socialist property, became a canon of Soviet ideology and a cornerstone of the "political economy." For Shkredov, the orthodox approach indulged in a deplorable "confusion of economic and juridical relations," which became widespread in the Soviet Union "as a result of a whole series of reasons."[26] For this approach, which he flatly accused of "Proudhonism,"[27] socialist property remains constant whether production involves hand tools or automatic lines. Hence, the real relations within the social structures of socialism stopped being seen as historically developing. Economic conceptions were made dependent on voluntaristic juridical ones, with the implication that economic categories would develop only when changes occurred in the juridical form of property. But if such changes did not take place as they should, "then economic categories [would] become ossified."[28] Making economic categories reflect juridical ones instead of reflecting material and historically dynamic relations of the socialist economy was a betrayal of a basic Marxist tenet. Shkredov appealed for a return to Marx in order "finally [to] overcome the juridical conception in political economy" and to study economic relations properly. For him the erroneous conceptions had to be dismantled because "objectively they serve[d] as theoretical reproduction of the practice of economic voluntarism."[29]

Such critical ideas opened the way for a new realistic view of the role of nationalization of industry in Soviet his-

[26] *Ibid.*, p. 3.
[28] *Ibid.*, p. 188.
[27] *Ibid.*, pp. 160–163.
[29] *Ibid.*

tory and socialism, where Shkredov also offered fresh insights.

For him, law, an extraeconomic factor, played an important role in economic life so far as it was backed by state compulsion. Thus, law functioned as a factor of extraeconomic coercion. It influenced men's will and their volitional relations in the production process; it might change and regulate property relations, but law or compulsion in general could "neither establish nor change nor regulate production relations."[30] Law could not save production relations that became obsolete nor destroy new relations that were developing in conformity with the technological changes.[31] It cannot augment the existing amount of capital goods or accumulation means. In itself legal compulsion is not a creative act and, whatever the power used, new production relations cannot be created by force.[32] The state can help and promote new relations, especially by aiding in the destruction of obsolete forms; but if the state is unreasonable enough and strong enough, it can, in fact, accomplish "any destructive work" and may create obstacles for development as well as destroy existing material wealth, production means, and consumption goods.[33] State compulsion might therefore easily turn into a massive destruction of production forces, especially when the state uses extralegal methods (rather illegal methods, when it broke its own laws); compulsion employing legal forms have at least the advantage of introducing some form of order and thus allowing economic activity to continue.

Having stated that production relations, the "real" economic life, suggested something different from what official property laws included, the author inevitably asked: Who is the real holder of property in Soviet conditions? Formally the state is the only owner and realizes its ownership right through the institutions that directly contact the enterprises. But the formula that the state is the only proprietor

[30] *Ibid.*, p. 48.   [31] *Ibid.*, p. 49.
[32] *Ibid.*, p. 46.   [33] *Ibid.*, pp. 45–46.

was insufficient for Shkredov. The problem was further complicated by the fact that the Soviet state not only wielded political power but also managed directly the national economy. The state discharged certain functions of a proprietor, but also was above the producers and the proprietors. If it were the sole proprietor, then the state regulation of property relations would become a question of self-regulation.[34]

He did not deny that the state legitimately exercised the right of ownership of production means and of goods "in the aggregate," as an abstract entity, but ownership was not production. Production was conducted in enterprises, and they were therefore, whatever the laws, the real possessors (*rasporiaditeli*) of things without which the state was incapable of appropriating anything. Objective study showed the economic separateness of enterprises; consequently this situation also determined their separateness as proprietors.

He explained that the state of the economy was such that two different types of relations coexisted within it. One consisted of direct links among strongly interdependent, highly concentrated, and technologically advanced units, which were mature enough for direct unified management, with central controls and direct disposal from above. But this was not the whole picture of the economy. Many of the producing units were economically separate, independent, and the relations among them—and throughout the national economy at large—were still of a money-commodity type. As long as this was the case, Shkredov inferred, resources and products should become objects of property of the separate producing units. As the two relations, the direct-natural and the market type, coexisted in the economy, so should two property relations coexist.

On this basis the author sharply criticized those for whom the juridical concept of socialist property was tantamount to exclusive property of an abstract, personified society. They were unable to explain how the existence of

[34] *Ibid.*, pp. 99–100.

commodity relations within the state sector could be squared with the denial of property rights to enterprises on their production means and produce.[35] For the holders of such views, state property appears to have been a heap of different things submitted to some mythical will. But in reality, the state's will as proprietor could not exist at all "beyond the separate and the specific."[36]

Ownership, Plans, and Law

From the critique of the prevailing conception of state property and the role of enterprise in the economy, which was a patent novelty in Soviet theory, three distinct ramifications, departing from official concepts, developed: the interpretation of historical events and dilemmas of the past, especially of Soviet nationalization and its role in the development of the state system; new ideas on planning; and, finally, new general propositions concerning the definition of socialism.

Shkredov knew well that he attacked the very heart of official dogma when he crossed swords with the view that "property [could] be socialist only when it [amounted] to all-national appropriation and disposal at least of the decisive means of production."[37] For Professor Kronrod, who defended this latter conception, to grant the enterprise rights of appropriation and disposal would mean the loss of its socialist character, because another socialist principle, economic equality of all the units participating in the economic process, would thereby be violated. For this school, which still dominates official Soviet thinking, an enterprise had no property rights. Its underlying concept held that the enterprise did not, and could not, have any special interest different from the interests of the state as a whole.

To this conception, which according to critics contributed so heavily to the difficulties now being debated, the new look, here represented by Shkredov, proposed an al-

[35] *Ibid.*, pp. 178–179.   [36] *Ibid.*, p. 107.
[37] *Ibid.*, p. 186.

ternative. Returning once more, although from another angle, to the familiar idea of "interests," Shkredov maintained that unique property was multifaceted simply because the underlying social reality was not some abstract uniformity; property could be separated into parts, because society is a totality in which, on any level, especially that of appropriation and disposal, special separate interests must emerge. These interests, naturally enough, were not identical with the state's interests; if the former were suppressed or disregarded, the production process would be impaired because producers would have difficulty putting into practice their volitional domination over objects, and social contradictions would grow sharper and more exacerbated.[38] To avoid this, the previous state-enterprise relations had to be revised. The state's rights as universal proprietor should still hold, but the monopoly of such property rights had to be denied to it. The state's rights as proprietor "should not swallow the rights of specific and particular proprietors," and the right of the state cannot be fully independent of the rights of the enterprises.[39]

In the wake of these ideas, Skhredov made another clarification: in Soviet thinking private, personal property was erroneously regarded as a second-rate derivative, whereas the truth was that social and personal property were both derivatives of socialist production relations. Property rights resulted from the work of individuals in socialist enterprises, and therefore it was an error "to reduce socialist property only to the social, leaving aside the personal property."[40]

Historical events in the Soviet Union caused socialism to be identified with the exclusivity of state property and with an overpowering monopoly of the state, which gave birth to the specifically Soviet "state socialism." This was not Shkredov's term—but it was clearly the target of his criticism and the object of his study. Overall but premature

[38] *Ibid.*, pp. 102–103.   [39] *Ibid.*, p. 158.
[40] *Ibid.*, pp. 118–119.

nationalization of the main sources of economic activity and of much else besides seemed to have been the source of trouble. In line with his concepts on the scope and limits for volitional coercive action, Shkredov explained the problem: the state's action, including such juridical steps as nationalization, could help or hinder production forces but could not overstep material limits inherent in any given historical stage.[11] Nationalization took place in Russia at a period when the economy was not yet ready for such a step; therefore the process of reproducing the capital goods *qua* state property encountered great difficulties. Shkredov's formula for the source of difficulties is already familiar to us from the previous exposé: formal, juridical socialization was not backed by an adequate degree of socialization in the production process itself.[12] The two, on the contrary, clashed. Capitalists could be expropriated and eliminated but not market factors, which depended on the state of the economy and not on juridical formulas.

The state was not entirely devoid of some possibility of action of its own choosing. The monopolistic proprietor could and did manage to concentrate resources on key branches; he organized education and developed science. But so long as the economy continued in a state of relative immaturity (judged by the separateness of factories, their insufficient specialization, weak concentration, poor equipment), the economy was torn asunder by a basic contradiction between the regulatory function of the proprietor-state and the laws of the market economy. This contradiction was expressed essentially through the tense relations between the state and the enterprises. In the situation prevailing at the beginning of Soviet history and for decades thereafter, letting the enterprises enjoy full property rights over their production would in fact have meant the domination of market forces over the enterprises and, indeed, could wash away the whole regime. At the same time, the obstacles encountered by the enterprises in the way of their

[11] *Ibid.*, pp. 124–125.   [12] *Ibid.*, p. 125.

efficient functioning as producers of commodities created difficulties in economic development. Therefore the reproduction process and the whole of economic life could continue only as a result of the application of a certain degree of extraeconomic coercion.[13] As a result, centralized management clashed with cost accounting;[14] the real socialization of industry, which could take place only through a deeper integration, specialization, and a higher technical level, was hampered and the separateness of enterprises was perpetuated. On the other hand, centralized management, and its central planning, suffered from inefficiency and exhibited an insufficient mastery over economic life and development.

Planning, the pride of the economic system, was based in official theory on the juridical fact of state ownership of all means of production according to an accepted canon: state ownership offered not only a possibility to plan but also made it imperative and all-embracing. The new theoretical approach, in trying to illuminate the contradictions and tensions from which planning and the economy had suffered for decades, maintained that the claims were exaggerated and that the scope of planning was excessive because the juridical socialization of the means and products did not coincide with economic socialization.[15] This is the author's key notion for the explanation of the limits to both central-

[13] *Ibid.*, p. 131.

[14] A similar idea is in V. Novozhilov, *Problemy Izmereniia Zatrat i Rezul'tatov pri Optimal'nom Planirovanii* (Moscow, 1967), pp. 29–30, 32–33; in the 1930s "plan" and "market" (*khozraschët*) clashed and "plan," that is, centralization and administrative measures, had the upper hand—and this was unavoidable in the strains of reconstruction and the unfavorable international circumstances. This implies a degree of justification of some policies in the 1930s and explicitly the need for more centralization and a lesser scope for market categories —but, as we already argued, it does not imply a justification of more than just that.

[15] Shkredov, *Ekonomika*, p. 64.

ization of economic power and to the scope of central planning and for his distinction between "formal" and fully effective planning. In the Soviet situation, its property right drove the state to control and to plan the full range of economic activities, but such functions became in part an empty shell. The monopoly on property, the main justification for a highly centralized management, did not, in itself, assure centralized direction and effective control over production, exchange, and distribution.[46] Real mastery of economic life—economic freedom, as it were—could be achieved only if objective limitations, dictated by the stage of economic development reached by the country, were fully understood and accepted. Otherwise, a plan that tried to overreach itself, in an economy composed of a multitude of enterprises badly specialized and poorly equipped, could only be compulsory, rigid, and detailed and would force the enterprises to act in opposition to the plan. When such became the behavior of thousands of factories, the contradiction between plans and what is planned, between plan and the market, between general and particular interests, made serious planned development impossible.[47] The transformation of formal into real planning was a long process, and juridical formulas and constant organization and reorganization of apparatuses would not help very much. The overcoming of the disproportions depended, first, upon building up the reserve capabilities and products and, second, upon planning that was well coordinated with the needs of the separate production and consumption cells.[48]

A plan had to be flexible, capable of reacting quickly and of adapting itself to the flow of economic life. Otherwise, the plan would be "transformed into an aim in itself, into an object of blind worship."[49]

Planned management, if it were to be worthy of its name, had to consider and react to changing circumstances, and

[46] *Ibid.*, p. 65. [47] *Ibid.*, p. 69.
[48] *Ibid.*, p. 73. [49] *Ibid.*, p. 75.

therefore its norms should be flexible to the demands of life.

But the erection of such a planning system was made impossible by the existing state conception that identified "plans" and "law." Contrary to the planning norm, which is flexible so that it can fit action in flux, the legal one is a common uniform measure for men, relations, and situations of the same type, thus unavoidably rigid and inflexible. The influence of law on economic life is limited.[50] Therefore, to confer upon the plan the form of law and upon planning targets the status of legal norms—to proclaim that "the plan is law (juridical)—is a theoretical error."[51]

The juxtaposition of "law" with "plan" was a result of strictly Soviet conceptions of state property. On this ground the state usurped the right to be an economic administrator and planner. But these functions were not, properly speaking, political (they were not a state form); state property did not determine the essence of centralized management, it determined only its form.[52] It was thus the juridical formula that made planned management take on the form of an administrative legal management.[53]

Shkredov saw in this situation the basis for numerous malpractices. It was urgent to defend economic life from "legal" and "illegal" interference, from the flow of administrative acts, countless amounts of instructions, decisions, and all kinds of prescriptions.[54] The economy had to be defended "from any arbitrariness, whatever its source."[55] Because of the legal status given those floods of regulations, the planning system became a source of irresponsible activity with the planners and state managers themselves free from any legal regulation. Planned management, so important an activity, fell outside the sphere of genuine juridical regulation.[56] An economic activity such as planning had to be placed in a clear legal framework, instead of being, as

[50] *Ibid.*, pp. 84–86.
[52] *Ibid.*, p. 80.
[54] *Ibid.*, p. 88.
[56] *Ibid.*, p. 86.

[51] *Ibid.*, pp. 82, 86.
[53] *Ibid.*, p. 81.
[55] *Ibid.*, pp. 90–91.

it was, a legal norm in itself.[57] Legality in economic life was a condition for healthy economic activity.[58]

Shkredov made bold pronouncements. He made it clear that inept interference in the economy by the state and its arbitrariness had to be eliminated. His sharp formulas brought into the open the hints, implications, or hidden thoughts of the whole clan of reformers, all of them suggesting that changes in the management of the economy implied the redefinition of the role of the state. The reforms in the economic system had to reform the system. To do this, the functions of the state, its sins and limitations, its role in economics, its relation to society, had to be analyzed; in fact, the very foundations of the socio-political system had to be scrutinized.

Thus, criticism once unleashed bred further debate. In the same vein, critical thought also had to propose remedies and alternatives, otherwise it could become a sterile exercise. The question arises: did any contours of some different models of a political character emerge from the existing thought, other than Nemchinov's blueprint for the economy? In other words, did any programs for political change emerge from the debate?

[57] But the chairman of the Gosplan, N. Baibakov, is not ready to accept such an approach. "The plan is law," he stated vigorously, "and nobody is allowed to violate it," in *Kommunist*, no. 5 (March 1970), p. 34. This statement was well in line with the tightening up of screws following the December 1969 Central Committee Plenum, which appealed for more discipline and controls and foreshadowed the scaling down of the economic reforms by the Twenty-Fourth Party Congress in March 1971.

[58] Shkredov, *Ekonomika*, p. 91.

CHAPTER NINE

What Next? Programs
for Change

THE preceding chapters have shown how the clearing of
the ground began and how astonishingly numerous taboos,
fetishes, and consecrated practices, central to the functioning or to the beliefs of the system, were exposed or proposed to be scrapped. Not that the notions or actions attacked were actually overcome—far from this, especially
since Russia at the moment of writing this book is going
through another swing of the pendulum, though milder
than previous such swings, toward enhanced controls and
conservative backlash; but the inroad was made and seems
irreversible, at least in the intellectual life of the politically
aware groups. The existing planning methods were exposed
with all their deficiencies and limitations; state monopoly
on property, the pillar of the ideology backing up the state's
system, was shown to result from a confusion of juridical
with economic concepts, which was theoretically non-Marxist, if not anti-Marxist, and, in any case, a source of abuses.
This concept, claimed to be pivotal to socialist society, was
declared by the new wave to have been pivotal to a system
that became obsolete. The state itself, its self-image of infal-
libility, and its monopoly to praise itself limitlessly were
heavily questioned; and the state's claim to be the quasi-
automatic and sole representative of social interest
appeared as capable of destroying as of building, of overriding willfully social interests as of representing them. Although political science as such was not allowed to develop,
it was symptomatic that it did appear. "Politics" in the Soviet Union, by the very character of the system itself, is
everywhere. It is no small wonder that it broke through in

works of economists, even when authors did not intend to be "political" at all. Logical categories followed their compelling internal sequences. Censorship can censor only official publications; it cannot censor situations and it cannot prevent concepts from emerging and circulating.

But what was to be done? Not surprisingly, only elements of programs for change and of alternative models were available, scattered through various writings, mainly of economists. Proposals for the functioning of the economic model were numerous, but it was more difficult in the Soviet Union to present outlines of what could be called "political programs." Nevertheless, bricks for such programs to reshape the social and political system emerged, albeit most often in fragments and in the form of mild suggestions that nevertheless should not be overlooked.

The study of politico-economical and social interrelationships is seen by the best minds as an urgent affair; the very eagerness to study such problems is, in the existing party-ideological framework, almost tantamount to a political postulate. It has been shown how persistently the theme of arbitrariness of administrations and of the state appeared in the writings of economists. Although posing the problem did not yet mean solving it, it did imply a demand for a solution. To say that the state may run amok, become detached from social interests, or do "unlimited" damage was already a beginning of at least a request for some sort of constitutional reform. To say that administrations and leaders not only represent "general interests" but develop some of their own implied a right to investigate such interests and to exercise social control over them. Curbing the state, redefining its role in the sphere of economics, and finding ways to make it refrain from undue interference emerged as the main problems for the students of the system and the urgent task for its politically minded public. To replace or reshape the bureaucratic centralized agencies, now obviously inadequate for their tasks, to unleash more initiative of producers and of social forces in general were the big

215

aims. Obviously, such goals could be reached only through a redefinition of roles and relations between state and society, limiting and reorganizing the former, diminishing its prerogatives and immense power, and redistributing it in new ways over different social groups. The craving for more autonomy for producers and social groups and the thirst for enough independence to do their jobs adequately complemented the demand for rights to defend particular interests, as well as for a say in formulating what the "general interest" should be. Such was the general orientation of much of the reformist thinking.

Practical proposals for eliminating abuses and for curbing the power of established agencies in economic life were numerous. The basic demands for autonomy and rights for enterprises aimed directly at taming the power of central economic administrations, as did the introduction of market methods and market criteria, without which enterprise autonomy was meaningless. The idea of "putting the administrations on *khozraschët*" tried to remedy a situation in which the economic state apparatus hovered over the producers, and tended to follow its own logic rather than serve the economy. Incorporating higher administrations into the economic system instead of letting them dominate it became a reformist slogan. The administrations should stop being political apparatuses whose criteria all too often contradicted the interests of producers (their own group interests contradicted too many other interests) and thus remedy the chasm between administrations and producers. The administrations had to work on the same principles of profitability and accountability to consumers as the factories subordinate to them. They should lose salaries, premiums, and compensations and should pay fines to factories for incorrect and damaging decisions. This should apply to ministries, *glavki*, and planning agencies. If previous numerous reorganizations had been fiascos, it was because the main problem was misunderstood, which consisted in finding

216

ways to include the apparatuses into the economic system and to teach them to use "economic methods."[1]

It was bluntly stated (in relation to agriculture) that the situation in which the planner gives orders that wreck the economy, leaving the whole mess to be cleaned up by the producer, had to come to an end, and that the planner should bear responsibility for his miscalculations and defects.[2] In a similar vein, even more radically, there had been an appeal for a reversal of relations between administrations and producers: "state apparatuses should be at the disposal of the producer (not the other way round as it used to happen)."[3] In this case, regional administrations were asked to serve *kolkhozy* and not to give commands to them. Other sources, especially many plant managers and top-level economists, wanted this spirit of service to be imposed on all administrations, at least up to the level of ministries. Did they want accountability on a higher level too? In any case, the central planners and the central plan were under critical pressure to revise and reshape. Here, too, turning to "economic methods" meant a deep change in the character of the whole activity; all the proposals of a Nemchinov, repeated by many others, aimed at an extensive overhaul of the whole planning-supplying system.

These demands had an impact on the entire economic sphere. A remolding of the planning-supplying system in line with such demands could only mean that a substantial part of the state machinery—a source of governmental controls, red tape, wasteful and inefficient procedures, and arbitrary, detailed supervision and chicanery—would have

[1] See, for example, A. Birman, "Sut' Reformy," *Novyi Mir*, no. 12 (December 1968), p. 303, but the theme is to be found in numerous other sources—which have asked for exercising pressures "through the ruble" (*udarit' rublem*), against bureaucratic nonchalance and irresponsibility.

[2] V. Venzher in V. Venzher, et al., eds., *Proizvodstvo, Nakoplenie, Potreblenie* (Moscow, 1965), pp. 273–274.

[3] G. Lisichkin, "Smelye resheniia," *Novyi Mir*, no. 9 (1968), p. 155.

to disappear. The demand to scrap this despotic machinery, an important component of the existing state, could be interpreted as a quest for far-reaching changes in the outlook of the state.

Next, the critique of the previously predominant concept of the "political economy" preaching "primacy of production" over consumption, and the parallel primacy of the plan over social needs, suggested a sharp turn in the opposite direction: toward equal rights, if not supremacy, of consumption; the affirmation of the primacy of "social needs" over "production"; and the predominance of producers over bureaucrats. The inferior status of factory crews, managers, and workers emphasized the complete subordination to the will of state agencies. On the one hand, planners and supervisors hurled floods of orders at their subordinates. On the other, the entire producing apparatus was actually deprived of legal means to defend itself and had no rights that were stated clearly enough and actively enforced.

Therefore, besides putting these despotic agencies with enormous powers of control on the highly constraining *khozraschët* regimen, clear legal regulation was demanded, as was automatic intervention of the procurator, when the planner-manager *qua* planner or manager was caught displaying an excessive administrative ardor.[4]

The same problem and the same urge to curtail the state's power, as has been seen, was formulated in terms of implications more far-reaching than the strictly economic. Nat-

[4] E. Liberman and Z. Zhitnitskii, "Ekonomicheskie i Administrativnye Metody Khoziaistvennogo Rukovodstva," *Planovoe Khoziaistvo*, no. 1 (1968), p. 24. "Many state agencies are internally opposed to legal limitations on their administrative rights. They consider their main task to be the establishment of a strict labor discipline, and therefore any limitations on their rights are, from their point of view, inappropriate at present." The authors retorted that discipline should be asked from administrators too since their obligation is to respect the rights and interests of the enterprise, which has to be guaranteed and enforced by law.

218

urally enough, "producers" used in the context of economy meant in sociological terms "classes" and "social groups." The new key terms popular among scholars, such as "social interests" and "group interests," were anathema for the exponents of the existing state ideology.

The decisive divorce from the official arguments on these themes could have a deeply liberating effect on social sciences, as well as a deep impact on politics. The demand to ensure enterprises with means to defend themselves against encroachments from above, if met, might spill over into other spheres of social life. It would serve as a first step toward wrenching rights for social group activity and initiative, and toward forcing the state to safeguard rather than violate these rights. It is legitimate, I believe, to interpret in this way a pronouncement such as "the state should act through group interests, however divergent or contradictory, the alternative being the use of crude force."[5] The rediscovery by some authors in state theory of the term "civil society," with a few hints about the possible swallowing of the "civil society" by the state,[6] was extremely significant, too, and exhibited the same type of urge to reassert society against the state and gain or regain freedoms lost to the state in the process of forced industrialization with its terror, purges, rigid controls, and arrogation of powers almost unprecedented even in Russian history.

Equal Rights for Peasants (Venzher)

An illuminating example of an almost fully fledged program conceived to safeguard the interests of a social group is provided by the fight conducted by some circles for a new

[5] Opinions parallel to those expressed by Shkredov and other Soviet authors on society as "complex and heterogeneous," with group interests and their clashes, are widespread in other East European countries. For some information on such opinions see H. Skilling and F. Griffiths, eds., *Interest Groups in Soviet Politics* (Princeton, N.J., 1971), pp. 12–16, 17–18.

[6] V. Kopeichikov, *Mekhanizm Sovetskogo Gosudarstva* (Moscow, 1968), pp. 39–40.

219

place in the system for the peasantry. The interest in this case is enhanced by the fact that it did not concern a strategic elite, such as scientists or managers, but a whole social class, hitherto the lowest on the scale of prestige and influence in the system—if not the most discriminated against and most distrusted. After the Twentieth Party Congress, a lively and candid literature began to develop, describing the miseries of rural life, its total submission to an incompetent, capricious, and often self-seeking bureaucracy—not to mention the vicissitudes that resulted from the policies and methods used by the central government.[7] A school of "peasantists," including novelists, journalists, and scholars, with some backing in the top party spheres developed and demanded an end to the inferior status of the peasantry both on grounds of economic expediency and in larger terms of social justice. Concurrently, a group of historians who had, during the early 1960s, engaged in a remarkably vigorous study of the Soviet peasantry and the collectivization process attacked many features of this policy, especially "the violation of Lenin's principle of voluntary choice (to join or not to join *kolkhoz*)" and the crippling effects of Stalin's policy with its "unjustly downgraded procurement prices,"[8] which amounted to a ruthless exploitation of peasants for a whole historical period. This was the strongest and most open criticism in Soviet writings of the policies of the 1930s, although other specialists did the same in other

---

[7] Novelists such as Zalygin, Iashin, Abramov, Stadniuk, Dorosh and Ovechkin could be grouped under the heading "peasantists" because of their interest in peasants and peasant life under the Soviet regime. Solzhenitsyn's novel *The House of Matrena* contributed to this trend.

[8] M. Vyltsan, N. Ivnitskii, and Iu. Poliakov, "Nekotorye Problemy Istorii Kollektivizatsii SSR," *Voprosy Istorii*, no. 3 (1965), p. 25; also M. Vyltsan, "Material'noe Polozhenie Kolkhoznogo Kretst'ianstva v Povoennye Gody," *Voprosy Istorii*, no. 9 (1963), p. 116. Among other titles let us mention V. Danilov, ed., *Ocherki Istorii Kollektivizatsii Soiuznykh Respublik* (Moscow, 1963), and Iu. Moshkov, *Zernovaia Problema v Gody Sploshnoi Kollektivizatsii* (Moscow, 1966).

ways. While the party leadership put an end to this trend after the Twenty-Third Party Congress, it could not prevent the same ideas from reaching the public from a very different source—a beautifully written biography on Lenin's last years in power, showing Lenin busily noting (and later circulating to the Politbureau) what he heard from peasants about their situation in the Soviet state. "Agriculture cannot be run under a stick . . . it will not work in such a way," they complained. Significantly, the problem of the peasants in Soviet society was stated in this text in strikingly positive, programmatic terms. The author quoted Lunacharsky whose opinion Lenin allegedly shared, viewing the peasants as the "dearest part of the Russian revolution,"[9] a new and unusual formula for the reader of Soviet political literature. It might be taken as a motto to inspire those who press for equal rights for peasants and for the democratization of the Soviet polity at large.

The most convincing and articulate spokesman for these ideas, the economist V. G. Venzher, was attacked by Stalin in his last book for having advocated the remittal of the means of production to the *kolkhozy* and the liquidation of the state's Machine Tractor Stations (MTS), in whose hands these basic means were concentrated. In a series of articles and two books,[10] Venzher developed a set of theses of an ideological and political character that were entirely akin in spirit to those of other reformers.

The official line, when talking about the situation of agriculture and of the peasants, was ready to accept some criticisms of the previous policies—the devastating results of these policies were too obvious, and everybody knew them.

[9] E. Drabkina, "Zimnii Pereval," *Novyi Mir*, no. 10 (1968), pp. 30, 72. One may surmise that these opinions are quoted for their actual connotations. Whether Lenin did in fact see peasants as the "dearest part" can be debated.

[10] See "Osobennosti Kolkhoznoi Ekonomiki i Problemy Razvitiia," in *Proizvodstvo, Nakoplenie, Potreblenie; Kolkhoznoe Proizvodstvo i Zakon Stoimosti* (Moscow, 1965), pp. 255–303, and Venzher, *Kolkhoznyi Stroi na Sovremennom Etape* (Moscow, 1966).

221

The state was ready to do much to improve the situation. Even the slogan of "reinforcing *kolkhoz* democracy" was advanced by the state, but such good intentions were always followed, almost obsessively, by the rejoinder: "*kolkhoz* democracy develops in conjunction with governmental leadership. The *kolkhozy* cannot develop in a spontaneous *laissez-aller* manner. . . ."[11] But was not this so much cherished state guidance the very source of so many diseases?

This was the gist of the argument of the embattled pro-*kolkhoz* writer Venzher. It seemed astonishing to discover in the Soviet Union people who had to fight *for kolkhozy*. But the wretched situation of Russian agriculture and official ideological predilections contributed to a high degree of neglect and disdain for the *kolkhozy*. Officially, it was always the *sovkhoz* that, being a state enterprise, was supposedly the superior socialist model and the example to which the *kolkhoz* had to lift itself up in order to become "fully socialist." In the meantime, a *kolkhoz* was considered an inferior form and even a source of "alien" tendencies, not only because of the attachment of the *kolkhozniki* to their private plots but also because the *kolkhoz* was not state property but cooperative group property, allegedly the last entrenchment for and mainspring of market phenomena still lingering in the Soviet system.

For Venzher, official predilections notwithstanding, the *kolkhoz* was a viable organization, and its weaknesses had to be put entirely at the door of the "external links" that hampered its development.[12] The main culprit was the state, its unthoughtful decisions and policies. The *kolkhoz*, Venzher explained, had two important characteristics—it was a producer of goods and a cooperative organization. Both features were misunderstood, and the very principles that would have allowed the *kolkhoz* to prosper were

[11] V. Tshikvadze, ed., *Politicheskaia Organizatsiia Sovetskogo Obshchestva* (Moscow, 1967), p. 277.

[12] Venzher, *Proizvodstvo, Nakoplenie*, p. 257.

flouted. It was inhibited and fettered as producer (like everybody else) by detailed prescriptions from above, including how, what, and where to sow; and it was the *kolkhoz* that was forced to bear the losses for inept decisions. But if nobody was ready to pay for the *kolkhoz's* debts, nobody should have been allowed to interfere with the affairs that the *kolkhoz* alone knew best how to tackle. The planners inflicted on the *kolkhozy* such damage that it was many years before they recovered. But it was unjustified to impose planning targets from above on the *kolkhozy* (Venzher was categorical on this score).[13] Since the *kolkhoz* was a producer of goods for the market, the principle of equivalent exchange had to govern its relations with the customers, including the state. The slogan, therefore, that characterized his approach was "equal rights in the deal," and with the state in the first place.

The author does not hesitate to draw far-reaching conclusions from this position concerning past and future policies. Past policies were based on state-imposed and ruthlessly enforced procurement quotas, which took the best part of the *kolkhozy's* produce for a price that, for a quarter of a century at least, did not even cover production costs.[14] Venzher categorically condemned such policies. All those imposed quotas *in natura* "were not economically justified. Consequently, compulsory deliveries and sales, as they existed in the recent past when they were fixed by administrative fiat, instead of being based on contracts advantageous to both sides—*did not and do not correspond to the cooperative character of the kolkhoz production* [emphasis added]."[15]

---

[13] *Ibid.*, p. 273.

[14] Cf. Venzher, *Kolkhoznyi Stroi*, p. 241. V. Lopatkin, *Tovarnye Otnosheniia i Zakon Stoimosti pri Sotsializme* (Moscow, 1963), pp. 235–240. He shows that in 1953 the prices paid to producers for the main agricultural products covered only one-fourth to two-fifths of the cost of production.

[15] Venzher, et al., eds., *Proizvodstvo, Nakoplenie*, p. 275.

The whole previous method of central planning and bureaucratic dominance when, as he saw it, "the planners [bore] no responsibility whereas the respondant [had] no bearing on the planning" generated in him a feeling of outrage. "This is an inadmissible violation of the rights of the *kolkhozy*," he exclaimed, "from which nothing good can emerge."[16] The heavy weight of material losses crushed the *kolkhozy*, "whereas the affairs were not run by the collectives themselves, but by all sorts of governmental organs and committees."[17]

Obviously, the picture that he painted did not show "state guidance," allegedly the very condition for "*kolkhoz* democracy," in a very favorable light. Autonomy and freedom from this kind of guidance were preconditions for a thriving agriculture. Venzher maintained that the *kolkhoz* was socialist *par excellence*, not because it was working on nationalized land, or was following orders from the state's central plans, but for a very different reason. Nationalization of the land was not at all indispensable, as the experience of the "people's democracies" had shown; it was no more than a product of specifically Russian historical conditions. The *kolkhoz*'s group property was a legitimate, full-blooded socialist form in its own right in no way inferior to any state form.

Thus, the reformist wing exploded another favorite fetish —the superiority of the *sovkhoz*. Venzher and others claimed that although the *sovkhozy* were placed in a privileged position compared to *kolkhozy*, with their deficits covered by the state and their technological equipment twice as large as that put at the disposal of *kolkhozy*, it was

[16] *Ibid.*, p. 274.

[17] Venzher, *Kolkhoznyi Stroi*, p. 274. It is fair to underline that recent years saw considerable improvements in Soviet agriculture resulting from more investment, better prices paid to producers, and introduction of guaranteed salaries to *kolkhozniki*; but not much has changed in terms of autonomy for *kolkhozy*, and no spectacular change occurred in productivity, efficiency, or incentives to innovate.

the *kolkhoz* that had proved to be a more reliable agricultural producer.[18] Thus, while the state pampered the *sovkhoz* with more and superior equipment, it was the *kolkhoz* that did better, notwithstanding the discrimination.

For Venzher it was the *kolkhoz* that was superior; this followed clearly from his contention that the *sovkhoz* was not a form indispensable for the construction of socialism; it was, not unlike the nationalization of the land, a product of the circumstances and emergencies of the dramatic Soviet history. There was another reason too, an even more important one, that made the *kolkhoz* rather than the *sovkhoz* the model for future development. The internal organization of the *kolkhoz* was more akin to the character of a socialist order than a bureaucratically run state enterprise. Because of its cooperative character, it already prefigured the type of social self-management with its democratic principles that the socialist organization would adopt and expand. The *sovkhoz*, if it was to rise to a higher stage of development, had better learn this principle from the *kolkhoz*.[19]

The challenge to "sacred" dogmas, promulgated by official propaganda, was here striking. Underlying such assertions were obviously different conceptions concerning some essential principles of the social order. Already in the late 1950s some theoreticians, with considerable support from important leaders, publicly proposed measures for the effective receipt and enforcement of the rights of the *kolkhoz*

[18] Venzher, *ibid.*, pp. 41, 264–266; G. Lisichkin, "Chelovek, Kooperatsiia, Obshchestvo," *Novyi Mir*, no. 5 (1969), pp. 169–173. Similar contentions are made by F. Mun and O. Trubitsyn, *Opyt Sotsiologicheskogo Izucheniia Sela v SSSR* (Moscow, 1968), pp. 84, 53–54; figures quoted in A. Emel'ianov, ed., *Ekonomicheskie i Sotsial'nye Problemy Industrializatsii Sel'skogo Khoziaistva* (Moscow, 1971), pp. 33, 40, 57, show higher yields for most of the important crops, as well as higher rentability, in *kolkhozy*—though in the *sovkhoz* there is more machinery and a slightly more professional labor force (better paid, too).

[19] Venzher, *Kolkhoznyi Stroi*, p. 41.

225

peasantry. Similarly, Venzher sought a new form for the interrelationship between the state and the *kolkhozy*, in order to make it conform to the hitherto disregarded essence of the *kolkhoz* organization—its cooperative character. It was this principle that, Venzher charged, was utterly misunderstood by Stalin. The *kolkhozy* had to be allowed not only a flourishing internal democracy but also local voluntary inter-*kolkhoz* cooperative organizations, coalescing gradually into an inter-*kolkhoz* representation on a national scale. These organizations were to be autonomous and nongovernmental, with a democratically elected leadership, in order to provide an agency precisely to represent and, one surmises, to defend the interests of the peasantry in its dealings with the state. Such an organization was seen as having a potential for considerable economic power: it would found and run factories, deal with supplies for its members, negotiate procurements and sales to customers and government agencies. The state would deal with such an autonomous and rather powerful organization. The main problems to be solved by this type of relation were, on the one hand, to give the peasantry genuine representation with spokesmen from its own ranks and, on the other, to help in creating new institutions in the countryside. The aim was to reach a situation, said Venzher, in which the countryside, "instead of administrative management organs," would have a cooperative system acting on the basis of community principles (*obshchestvennye nachala*).[20]

Apparently these formulations were well covered by texts found in the party's 1961 official program, which is clearly

[20] Venzher, *Proizvodstvo, Nakoplenie*, pp. 298, 303. Venzher returned to these ideas in subsequent books, but they were already launched earlier in the 1950s by another writer Vinnichenko who allegedly had Khrushchev's backing for this project. D. Poliansky, a Politbureau member, was also advancing similar ideas, though one can doubt whether they gave to it the broad justification and meaning that Venzher put into it. On Vinnichenko and Poliansky see S. Ploss, *Conflict and Decision Making in the Soviet Union* (Princeton, N.J., 1965), pp. 158, 174–175.

not too popular with the ruling coalition of the early 1970s. Venzher greatly differed with the vague generalities of the program. He clearly intended to put teeth into the *obshchestvennye nachala* by actually building an organization capable of offering the peasants not only the status of an "interest group" but also the means to act legitimately as "a pressure group." In this way, side by side with the state sector, an autonomous organization representing a whole class was supposed to appear, enjoying both equal rights and a fully acknowledged place in the socio-political system; it would also become an important check on the state and, in fact, bring to an end the state's total sway over the peasants. More significantly, according to Venzher, the cooperative principle was superior to the one prevailing in the state sector; *kolkhoz* cooperative associations would include the *sovkhozy*. The hierarchical bureaucratic forms prevailing there, as in any state factory, would have to give way to new forms of social democracy. Ownership would evolve into a third form, different from the one in the state sector but clearly more akin to the one they hoped to see flourish in the *kolkhoz* cooperative sector. As Venzher saw it, ownership would be permeated with cooperative forms and the cooperative principle.[21] Before this happened, as a result of a long process, he envisaged the coexistence of different forms of property with different forms of internal organization: state property, property of different social bodies (like the inter-*kolkhoz* unions), and mixed forms and partnerships of all kinds. The central tendency in all of them would consist in strengthening the democratic principles and the *obshchestvennye nachala*.

Thus, for the seasoned propagandists, seemingly similar formulas meant, at most, some relaxation of controls, while for Venzher they meant something more substantial. Both sides apparently took their words from the same breviary. Venzher stipulated: "The development of communist relations is unthinkable without a gradual transition of the

[21] Venzher, *Kolkhoznyi Stroi*, pp. 162–163.

whole of social life to the self-management principle which would exclude the need to have a state machinery."[22] He did not believe, one can surmise, in the liquidation of the state at one stroke, and probably not even in its full disappearance at any time. He did not advocate the withering away of administration, or of the running of the state "by every cook," but favored strong economic organizations, especially for the peasants. He wanted such institutions to be democratic and specifically opposed any further extension of state power. It could be inferred that the state should immediately grant real autonomy to social groups and classes, without waiting for the ideologically promised withering away of the state and the establishment of a fullfledged communist society, as the party program asserted. Venzher's theses recalled Lenin's *State and Revolution* and his last pronouncements, in which he defined socialism as "a system of civilized cooperators," a very novel idea for Lenin himself at that time, and one, Venzher said, that Stalin had failed to understand.[23]

Ownership, Democracy, and Socialism

But the problem lay no longer in Stalin but rather in conceptions of the essence of the Soviet present and future, expressed partly in safe formulas taken from official documents, but also partly in bold new ones that thoroughly revised the accepted doctrines of Soviet state socialism. Venzher's ideas were analogous to those expressed by Shkredov. Both reformulated the conception of socialism according to "cooperative-democratic principles" for managing society, and to "social ownership," which under Soviet conditions serve as a theoretical legitimization and underpinning for the rights to democratic self-management.

Venzher's conceptions about the *kolkhoz* cooperative unions, aiming at new politico-institutional arrangements, merged with the concept of "interests" in social realities.

[22] Venzher, *Proizvodstvo, Nakoplenie*, p. 302.
[23] Venzher, *Kolkhoznyi Stroi*, pp. 142–143.

The same applied to his vision of the cooperative essence of socialism, which challenged the theories on state ownership and joined the critics of Soviet state socialism. Similarly, Shkredov's refusal to accept the "monopoly of the abstract personified society," the mythical construct used to back up the state's supervision of every aspect of society, backed Venzher's socialist program. In Shkredov's polemics against an orthodox view, he rejected the prevailing idea that "the owner cannot but be a monopolist who . . . personally appropriate[d] and dispose[d] of everything."[24] In this new view, the monopoly of the state on property and on production means, coupled as it was with omnipresent and all-devouring state bureaucracies, mutilated a checkered, complex, and composite society. The reformers thus implied that a living socialist structure could be built only on the basis of access by social groups to social responsibilities and on that of freedom to run affairs democratically.

Shkredov's idea of state ownership might be interpreted as follows: in the context of the Soviet state, the state-ownership concept assumed the role of an ideological bloc that had to be removed in order to smooth the process of change. This was the meaning of the proposition that producers and other groups had to be recognized as co-owners of the production forces and that the state monopoly of ownership had to be ended. A whole program of democratization was contained in such reasoning. Nationalization had to give way to socialization, and the enormous sources of power represented by the means of production had to be put at the disposal of a cooperative democratic organization.

But the previous passage was my own interpretation; let us now express it in Shkredov's own words. Rejecting state monopoly as the supposedly sole basis for true socialism, Shkredov stated: "Making large masses of working people participate in the monopoly of disposal (including the private appropriation of the surplus product in the interest of groups and individuals) does not eliminate the socialist na-

[24] V. Shkredov, *Ekonomika i Pravo* (Moscow, 1967), p. 186.

229

ture of property; on the contrary [such participation] is an indispensable attribute of socialism."[25]

The novelty of this formula in the Soviet context is self-evident. It was a new ideological concept for the critique of official socialism and for the formulation of programs for change all over Eastern Europe.

Who would bring about all these changes? What social forces could be relied upon to press for a new model of socialism? Who could convince or force the party to enter on such a road and would it be willing to do so? On these questions, involving direct proposals for political action, the sources do not provide an answer. Nevertheless, the proposals tending to extricate social forces from the grip of the supercontroller, the appeal to unleash the initiative not only of the intelligentsia, but also of large popular masses of peasants and workers, pointed in the direction of a version of democratic socialism.

Such proposals of a socialist democratic character simultaneously constitute a program for the reinvigoration of the economy. Democratization of economic management, extricating the producers from bureaucratic fetters, was an insistent demand of Novozhilov. He wanted to make state plans effective and powerful, but he explained that the economy was too complicated to be run from the center and provided with detailed tasks by a central plan conceived as a "plan-as-command." Sanctions and other administrative pressures became the main method to enforce the plans, but such "enforcing" was an inferior incentive to economic activity that eventuated a labor productivity lower than economic and moral incentives could produce. The way for plans to become a real economic imperative was through adequate combination of the plan with the *khozraschët*. Conceived in a distinctly anticentralistic spirit, this was a central theme of economic reformers. As long as this combination was not achieved, the rule of coercive but inefficient "administrative methods" could not be avoided, and

[25] *Ibid.*, p. 187.

democratization of economic life was impossible. Now this postulate, in Novozhilov's texts, is presented as the only way to make plans real and the economy boom. "Democratization of management is necessary . . . for the development of creative activity of popular masses. The larger the creative participation of [the] masses in developing the economy and culture, the quicker the rate of economic growth."

It is highly significant to find this kind of democratic manifesto hidden among complicated mathematical symbols. Mathematics and democracy is, today, an interesting new alliance in Soviet intellectual and political critical thinking. Novozhilov presented his postulate not merely as a device for improving productivity of labor, but as a "cultural" demand: such extensive participation of the masses in economy and culture "is one of the most important historical laws."[26] At this juncture, Novozhilov joined Venzher and others. The economic reforms, in the vein of "plan and market," is seen as an indispensable precondition for larger socio-political vistas: "to transform . . . organs of planning and of accounting into organs of social self-rule."[27]

Such is not, for the time being, the direction in which events in the Soviet Union are moving. Already the difficulties encountered by the economic reforms make it clear to many that a bureaucratically conceived and operated reform, without the collaboration and active participation of the masses, could easily be blocked by bureaucratic sabotage. A. Birman, one of the outstanding intellectual driving forces behind the movement for economic reform, in an article published at the end of 1969,[28] criticized what seemed to him to be a too narrow approach that concentrated excessively on problems of management, with the exclusion of some other, more important aspects. But those neglected

[26] V. Novozhilov, *Problemy Izmereniia Zatrat i Rezul'tatov pri Optimal'nom Planirovanii* (Moscow, 1967), p. 39.

[27] *Ibid.*, p. 32.

[28] A. Birman, "Samaia Blagorodnaia Zadacha," *Novyi Mir*, no. 12 (1969), esp. pp. 177–182.

aspects regarding some essential features of the social system happened to be the crucial ones. Improvements in economic performance could not be achieved by predominantly administrative-technical measures, as the current approach had it, nor did the solutions lie mainly in material incentives. These incentives, however important, ceased to be effective once a certain threshold was reached—after which deeper and more noble human behavior would come to the fore and would have to be satisfied. Even from the countryside, Birman maintained, signs were forthcoming that the peasant did not want to see any more ready solutions and formal answers to complex questions imposed on him by somebody outside. What the peasant wanted was both a more pleasant life and the possibility of thinking for himself.

Birman forecasted that this problem, not yet very urgent in the countryside and elsewhere, would soon become widespread. Economic progress could not be achieved merely by more technology, better professional training, and higher earnings. Higher productivity of labor imperatively demanded something that was ostensibly "an irrelevant matter": the participation of the workers in management. For Birman this was indispensable both on empirical and doctrinal grounds. He offered enough data to prove that the reforms had not brought about the new style that was hoped for, had not aroused enough creativity, and often were met with skepticism, opposition, and indifference. Often workers simply did not know what it all was about and did not think it concerned them very much. The same seemed to apply to many other categories besides the manual workers, although this was only implied in Birman's text. The gist of his argument lay in the contention that he shared with Novozhilov: without a wave of creativity of the masses, no sizable progress could be achieved. A real new upsurge could be hoped for only by eliciting the participation of large groups of workers and technicians, "of the collectives," in dealing with problems of production and management. It is interesting to learn that for him the fate of a social formation was decided finally by the capacity to elicit such mass involvement. He said that capitalism was unable to achieve it, but he did not hide the fact that the Soviet system had not done much to promote such principles either. This was a grave deficiency, and a violation of some basic principles. According to Lenin, socialism did not mean only a higher standard of living, nor mere participation; as Birman emphasized, it meant "putting into practice ways of management by the working people themselves," and he developed a more general formula of a doctrinal-theoretical character, derived from Lenin's work: "Socialism is a society of working people which is managing itself through the state."

Because a Soviet author cannot state directly that such a formula has not yet been realized, he would use more careful wording: "Isn't our economy incurring losses because of our failure, as it goes, to implement more fully this Leninist behest?"[29]

The problems of democratization of economic life, which

[29] *Ibid.*, p. 176. Soviet factories have workers' "production meetings" and different voluntary workers' committees, but they do not count for much in practice. At least one sociological study confirmed this impression by quoting results of a survey carried out in enterprises of Sverdlovsk, on the functioning of one type of such voluntary workers' bureaus—the bureau for technology. The survey showed that these committees and circles are rather anemic institutions, without serious prerogatives and influence. The administration and the party have taken very little interest in them, and many participants in these committees flatly stated that they did not understand the objectives of such bodies. Others declared that there was "no way to make administrations consider seriously proposals of such voluntary workers' bodies, not even of the general workers' production assemblies." See G. Vasil'ev "Nekotorye Problemy Sovershenstvovaniia Raboty Dobrovol'nykh Obshchestvennykh Organizatsii," in M. Rutkevich, ed., *Processy Izmeneniia Sotsial'noi Struktury Sovetskogo Obshchestva* (Sverdlovsk, 1967), pp. 204–207.

233

many reformers had enunciated, were no longer simple propaganda slogans. The reformers meant what they said. Birman warned against pinning too much hope on panaceas such as computers, better information networks, and streamlining the administrative ladders. Machines could not replace men, neither could they replace what Birman considered to be the main problem of the system: mass creativity. Democratization should be introduced slowly, but the process should be begun immediately. Unfortunately, this has not taken place as yet. Instead, once more, "the new approach to economy which," Birman claims, "the party is asking for, is being replaced by new *indicators* of planning and stimulation."

Birman believed that economic reforms failed to provide a substantial cure for Soviet economic ailments because of their inability to create substantial enough changes in the ways the social system was functioning. In fact, the very ways in which the existing order works and is doing things serve as obstacles to the reinvigoration of the economic performance. Birman, who sought deeper changes, reformulated the very concept of socialism and challenged important ideological assumptions. In terms of directly political demands, this should lead to programs for democratization of political institutions. But economists cannot ask openly for more than economic democracy. To demand some forms of political democracy openly would be unpublishable, and eventually harshly punishable. "An allied socialist country" was invaded for having tried to do just that.

Nevertheless, one document, presented to the party leadership, contains a detailed program for democratization of Soviet political life. The document was not officially published in the USSR and was not written by economists, even though economic problems were accounted for and served as a point of departure for their analysis.

At the beginning of 1970, the document in question was presented to the Politbureau by the scholars A. D. Sakharov, V. F. Turchin, and R. A. Medvedev.[30] It is very closely related to the ideas in the new literature that sprang up during the economic debate, but it explicitly enunciated political demands that did not normally appear in economists' works. The document's merit consisted in that the authors felt less inhibited and much freer to bring boldly the different arguments of the debate—elsewhere often only hinted at, sketched, or put forward timidly and partially—to a logical conclusion, to dot the "i's" and cross the "t's," and to call phenomena and demands by their full names. Different economists, especially those who engaged in the study of the state, had pointed to what in the Sakharov document became a central thesis: economic reforms were not the full answer and could not succeed without far-reaching reforms in the political system.

According to the document, the prospects for development were gloomy. The Soviet Union had stopped narrowing the gap with the United States, the lag had begun to grow anew, and all the signs pointed to the incapacity of the Soviet system to master successfully and, at least at the same pace as the United States, the modern technological revolution. If urgent measures were not taken, the numerous signs of stagnation in economy and society would transform the Soviet Union "into a second-class provincial power."

Socialism was not guilty of this misfortune. On the contrary, it was the accumulation of antisocialist phenomena in Soviet life that bore the responsibility for hindering the development of the Soviet polity. The numerous problems to be solved, especially in the field of economics, needed the collaboration and extensive application of science and a profound change in the methods of administration and

[30] The full and apparently reliable text signed by the three authors was translated and published in *Le Monde*, 11 (April 1970), 2, and 12–13 (April 1970), 4. An English version is available in *Survey*, Summer 1970, pp. 160–170.

management. But the traditions and antidemocratic norms that appeared in public life during the Stalinist period, and which were not yet eliminated from the system, thwarted the necessary reforms. Science and modern management could not develop without public debate, extensive publicity, freedom of creation, and free circulation of information, and it was precisely these demands, and the people behind them, that were suspect if not persecuted by the authorities, whereas mediocrities, careerists, disciplinarians, and conformists were encouraged in all walks of public life. Hence, amplifying the demand and the analysis made in more measured terms by Birman and in more abstract and theoretical and less directly political terms by Shkredov, the three concluded: "The problems facing the country cannot be solved by one or several individuals who hold power and know everything. What is needed is the creative participation of millions of people all over the ladder of the economic system. What is needed is a vast exchange of information and ideas. In this lies the distinction between contemporary economy, and, for instance, the Ancient East"; without reforms in administrations, without freedom of information, a spirit of competition, and, especially, "without far-reaching democratization our society will not be able to enjoy a normal and healthy development."

Thus, in terms that were politically trenchant and understandable to every literate person, the three authors stated that economic difficulties resulted mainly from noneconomic factors. It is in the polity that the difficulties reside. "Measures which do not eliminate this obstacle are doomed to inefficiency." Novozhilov's and Birman's points finally were expressed in directly political terms.

The current policies did just the opposite of what was needed: the denial of information, freedom of debate, and creativity; the empty and oppressive formulas of a dogmatic ideology that killed ideological debate; and, finally, persecution of writers, political critics, and even people sincerely proposing partial improvements—all fed and

236

dangerously deepened the reciprocal distrust and misunderstanding between the state and the intelligentsia. The authors claimed that a full-fledged break had occurred between the state and the intelligentsia, and such a break, in a period when the role of the intelligentsia was growing, "is nothing less than suicidal."

According to the authors of the program, healing this breach was the most urgent task, and once done it would allow many others to be tackled. This was why they proposed their program of reforms, to be instituted during the next quinquennium with more to come later. As patriots and "responsible" citizens, the authors did not appeal directly to the masses to press for such changes. They had written a memorandum primarily for the Politbureau and appealed to its members to launch democratization, in the very Russian way, from above.

What did they expect from the same leaders who were responsible for the current stifling atmosphere and oppressive measures? One could surmise that they were informed enough to know that some influential leaders were sympathetic to their theses. Or they might have decided that an initial step had to be taken by offering a program and opening a debate; if their assertion were true that many members of the intelligentsia and students, as well as managers and some administrators, shared their views, then the memorandum might make some political sense in the long run. On the other hand, one could assume that the writers were seriously afraid of many forces in their country that could exploit any uncontrolled and nonsupervised democratization. Such dangers could come, as they themselves stated, from individualistic, antisocialist forces, and also from some forces that the three called "demagogues of fascist type." Besides these dangers from the Right, in another context, some inexplicit danger from the extreme Left was mentioned, and it was plausible that the authors, in order to avoid all menacing prospects, would sincerely prefer their program to be adopted by the party and enacted gradually from above. In fact they seemed to warn the party that failure to introduce changes would help those antisocialist elements in Soviet society raise their heads, because they would be able to exploit the growing economic difficulties, the tensions and mistrust between the party and the intelligentsia, as well as the existence in Soviet society of widespread petit bourgeois mentality and nationalist tendencies. The country thus faced the danger of "sliding to Right and Left," although the peril from the Left was not explicitly defined, and the authors worried more about right-wing tendencies. The "vestiges of Stalinism," still very strong in the Soviet Union, made such dangers more palpable, not only because they would delay the solutions of economic problems but also because they would have pernicious long-term effects on the general intellectual and moral outlook of society, causing "a general deterioration of the creative potential among representatives of all the professions."

Freedom of information and of debate, and revival of a creative ideological and political life, were indispensable remedies to save the country from gloomy prospects. The defrosting of ideological life was a demand especially underlined in the memorandum. Ideology must be debated publicly and examined competitively. Democratization was urgent, and, "with its plentiful information and inherent atmosphere of competition, would render its dynamism and the indispensable creativity to our ideological life—to social sciences, art, and propaganda—by eliminating the ritualistic and dogmatic style and official bureaucratic hypocrisy which plays such a major role today in this domain."

Therefore, whether the authors expected Brezhnev to eliminate precisely these negative phenomena is of secondary importance here. But they painted a critical picture of the situation in terms that constituted a very sharp and outspoken indictment of the party's policies. They even criticized some of the aspects of Soviet foreign policy, notably for overextension and overambitiousness—a field that is untouchable, even more than others, in the activity of the top leadership.

The document concluded with a fifteen-point program for change. The central theme was democratization, and the proposals followed directly from the central principle: freedom of information, including publicity on governmental affairs; free contacts with foreign countries, including tourism, free flow of press, books, and radio broadcasting; a new law on the press, especially the abolition of censorship, and freedom for groups of citizens to launch publications; liberation of political prisoners; better public control of prisons and asylums; independence of the judiciary, publication of transcripts of political trials; the abolition of mention of nationality in passports, and of their registration in police stations for authorization for residence in big cities; reform of the educational system, including freedom for teachers to think and to experiment, the same freedom being asked for cadres in other fields of activity; strengthening of the role of the soviets, including the Supreme Soviet; and introduction of multiple candidates for elections both to soviet and party positions.

Hints for a Critique of the Party

In both the criticisms and the proposals for new arrangements, the most sensitive and explosive theme—the role of the party—was surprisingly almost totally absent; but there is no doubt that the issue is a major one for any reformist thinker because of the central position the party holds in the Soviet system. The critics of economic performance— whether they mentioned "the planners" or "administrative methods" or arbitrariness of the state—meant "the party." The party—the mainspring and self-proclaimed agency of power, the sovereign decision maker in all spheres of life— must take all the arrows, although it does not like it and does everything possible to deflect them to some other target.

239

But the growing social and economic problems and the search for solutions created the need to rethink and revise the role of the party in the system. Shkredov suggested something on this account. The key conception here is the relative autonomy of the (interdependent) spheres of "economics" and "politics."[31] He posited the possibility of clashes between the two spheres, or rather between economy and state[32] and, in fact, such clashes have never stopped at any time in Soviet history. But the reasons and rationale for such clashes changed, according to the changing circumstances during the stages of development through which the Soviet Union passed. In emergencies, wars, and especially during the initial revolutionary period, when a new social system had to be established against great odds, the primacy of "politics" over "economics" was obvious and unavoidable. The imperatives of survival in revolution and civil war dictated measures that were economically unsound but politically unavoidable. Shkredov cited, as examples of such measures, the egalitarian division of land among the peasants and the economically unfounded nationalizations extending to medium and small enterprises.[33] But he and other economists showed also how such supremacy of the state can lead to economically harmful and politically indefensible decisions. Since the damaging aspects in the action of the state did not stop manifesting themselves, Shkredov felt that the famous formula of Lenin, who stated that politics has primacy over economics, had to be revised. The formula arose during the troublesome first years of the precarious existence of the regime;

[31] Shkredov, *Ekonomika i Pravo*, p. 14, has as its subtitle: *On Principles of Studying Production Relations in Connection with the Juridical Form of Their Expression*; and it underlines both the connection between the "relations" and their "forms" and the independence of the forms once they were created. Engels' letter to C. Schmidt is here probably the main source and influence; see K. Marx and F. Engels, *Selected Works*, 2 vols. (Moscow, 1962), 2: 490–496.

[32] Shkredov, *Ekonomika i Pravo*, p. 93.

[33] *Ibid.*, pp. 93–94.

but now it would be an error, in Shkredov's terms, "to make an absolute out of Lenin's conclusion about the primacy of politics over economics, to transform it into a truth equally valid for any conditions of space and time."[34]

All the reformers, Shkredov included, are aware that a new stage has been reached, in which the social system and the Soviet state no longer face external dangers (the borders being more secure than at any previous time in the history of Russia); there are no more internal class enemies eager to overthrow the Soviet system and to enhance the previous order; there are no excuses therefore for delaying the indispensable rethinking and reorganizing of the system; there are no longer any reasons for procrastination in rendering to economic and social factors the autonomy they need and without which the system gets jammed. In the situation where no classes hostile to the regime exist inside and no serious direct threats come from outside, the essence of politics is changing, or should be changing. As Shkredov stated, the contents of politics should now consist in co-ordination and combination of individual and collective interests of groups and social classes and in securing conditions for economic progress.[35] But in order to create this type of new politics, the party is asked to change its methods and style, in light of the emerging new principles. Shkredov's enthusiastic reviewer in *Novyi Mir* summarized his approach as follows: it is indispensable to distinguish three relatively independent spheres: the sphere of economic management and planning, the juridico-political (or state juridical), and the party political sphere.[36]

In terms of actual functioning of the whole system, such distinctions presuppose very different mechanisms and a new distribution of functions and prerogatives among the institutions of the three big spheres. The economic activity had to be performed, run, and coordinated basically by the

[34] *Ibid.*, p. 94.   [35] *Ibid.*, p. 95.
[36] V. Georgiev, "Ekonomika i Pravo," *Novyi Mir*, no. 10 (1968), p. 278.

241

producers through their appropriate agencies. The state was implicitly asked to stop running the economy directly, this being a specific, nonpolitical activity. The slogan "economy to producers, not to political functionaries" would summarize this approach. But the role of the state, which was asked not to manage the economy directly, was still very important, since it had to ensure the legality, the regularity, and legitimacy (*pravomernost'*) of the activity of the economic agencies. Thus, the state was to play a role in the economy, but only as the "political leadership of the economy" operated mainly through laws.[37] The state should define general rules and a general framework but leave the implementation of plans to economic agencies, which have the specific expertise.

The third sphere, the "party political" one, had to apply itself to instill unity of purpose and coordination among state and economic organizations as well as to mediate and coordinate the different social interests. How this was to be accomplished was not explained, at least in explicit terms. But something can be gleaned from the negative argument, stating how the party should not act. Shkredov's reviewer stated that the party would relinquish "administration and regimentation" over economic life. (Sakharov added that it had to stop this in many other fields, including ideology, and many intellectuals no doubt agreed.) On the one hand, reformers, who clearly wished to eliminate the constant petty and inept interference by the state in everyday economic activity, invited the party to stop meddling in both the economic sphere and in the everyday activity of the state machinery. Considering that the party was still a very specific supergovernment, a controlling network and decision maker (which reserved for itself such decisions as it wanted to make), the proposals of the reformers, based on the growing shortcomings of such methods, are aiming at a deep change in the character of this agency. Shkredov,

[37] Shkredov, *Ekonomika i Pravo*, p. 96.

among them, admits that the party should play the role of guide and general unifying factor, but added that the party should use "methods as prescribed by its statutes, and according to legislative guidelines."[38]

Besides the appeal to limit "administration and regimentation," two important, although rather tactfully expressed, prescriptions are implied. The first reminds the party of a promise it had made in 1919, never repeated, and never fulfilled: that it was bound to act within the framework of the Soviet constitution and of Soviet legal principles. However, considering that the party, an extraconstitutional factor and unfettered by any such limitations, made and broke constitutions, Shkredov's demand that the party act "in accordance with legislative guidelines" meant nothing less than a demand that the party become a political institution within the framework of the Soviet constitution. The exact meaning of this can be interpreted in different ways, one of which is as follows: the party obtained its power from a congress of Soviets—here is where real sovereignty lay and here is where it has to be returned.

The second prescription said that the party as *avant-garde* acted according to the principles declared in its statute. This statute proclaimed that the party was a political factor and *avant-garde*, acting through education, persuasion, and so on. According to such texts, the party should not be what it actually became: a state administration *sui generis*. Thus, by returning the party to its statute and by trying to bind it to constitutional principles, Shkredov and others imply that the party has to stop meddling with the economy, end its rule of the state administration, and concentrate on formulating general political principles for reconciliation, coordination, and political leadership.

How this should operate in practice is anybody's guess. Such modalities of functioning cannot be predicted by pure theoretical thinking anyway, and many proposals and

[38] *Ibid.*, p. 97.

243

models could be envisaged. Some reformers may have clear ideas about this, but do not feel free to express them; many others simply do not know yet. In any case, in political life, the shape of institutions is rarely planned; they are hammered out in political struggle and through experience. But the demand for very essential changes is unmistakable. And, it seems that the reformists and their spokesmen are not daydreamers. They analyzed real problems, the urgency, scope, and depth of which they correctly and objectively depicted in their texts, even though their analyses and remedies were different.

Some of the propositions expressed situations and moods already a reality, albeit not yet officially acknowledged. The emerging new social structures are even more of a reality, breeding new forces, ideologies, and pressures. If economic difficulties continue, they will contribute to tensions, which in turn will induce different social groups to develop their own approaches and outlook which not only will constantly differ from the ones preached by the party but also will penetrate the party apparatus itself. Much of this is already happening. If this analysis is correct, it is possible that much of what has been quoted here is far from being an opinion of isolated individuals. Even such themes as the perniciousness of ideological rigidity, the weakness of party guidance, the unsuitability of its administrative methods and functions, and the obsolescence of existing cultural and political controls are already widespread, and for many circles self-evident. If this is true—we would refrain from any categorical assertions on this score—then the outlines for progress presented in this chapter represent trends that have already taken root, are accepted in ever-wider circles of the intelligentsia and are penetrating as well some layers of administrators, managers, and party *apparatchiki*. It is therefore probable that Sakharov et al. are not alone in asking for freedom of ideological debate, information, and political thought. R. Medvedev's *The Book on Socialist De-*

mocracy suggests a whole program that is even broader in scope than the *Common Manifesto*.[39]

Such action by individuals takes courage. The risks involved are great, but what unofficial manifestoes say often just dots the "i's" on what is largely expressed in published books. It may well be that courageous authors know that some groups in the party hierarchy understand them and would offer some support when circumstances allow.

Most of the authors quoted, including the unpublished text, expressed evidently, first and foremost, the interests of the growing Soviet intelligentsia or of important parts of it; they did not often talk specifically about the working class, for instance, and it is not inconceivable that for some of them the working class is an inert, if not politically conservative, class, not interested in democracy in any case. Democratic arrangements, freedom of information and creation, besides the beneficial results they might have on the state of affairs in Russia, would first serve the intelligentsia, consecrating the already important role, prestige, and privileges of some parts of it; thus, such programs did not engage in proper social criticism but mainly directed it against the flaws of the political system, aiming first at a very serious overhaul of the polity.[40] But whatever the silences of the program writers, if some of their reforms were achieved, an important step forward would be accomplished toward a further clarification of Soviet political life,

---

[39] *Kniga o Sotsialisticheskoi Demokratii* (Amsterdam, 1972); *De la democratie socialiste*, trans. S. Geoffroy (Paris, 1972).

[40] It is fair to add that it is very difficult in the Soviet system to come out openly with social criticism and defense of the interests of the working class, similar to Venzher's defense of peasants. "The working class," "the ruler of the country" is the regime's pet myth. Who else but the party should defend "the ruling class?" The leadership would not tolerate any intermediaries between themselves and the working class; but sociological writings, in a piecemeal way, already have begun to contribute to a more realistic image of what the working class is, thinks and feels about its position in society.

and many tendencies, social or other, temporarily latent, or confined to a subterranean existence, would come to the open and enter the political arena. Without political democratization such results would be impossible—unless there is an unpredictable social upheaval.

For the moment, the dialogue between the spokesmen of the intelligentsia and the current leadership is a *dialogue des sourds*. This leadership well understands the role of science for the solution of the numerous problems assailing the regime; it is science and technology that is being seen by them as the decisive medicine, rather than political or even economic reforms, with all their unpredictable bottle-imps. Therefore, in its way, the leadership is trying to court some key groups of the intelligentsia, offering them, as Brezhnev expressed it, "an alliance of the working class with science," a slogan rather new in Soviet political life. Sakharov, too, proposed to the party an alliance of the same kind; but whereas the current leadership is ready to offer social privileges, material rewards, some sectorial freedoms, and a limited influence in certain spheres of political decision making, the Sakharov document tried to prove that a narrow elitist solution would not be a remedy for a further modernization of Russia. They demanded a full-fledged democratization of the system, real power to larger social groups, to the intelligentsia first and foremost, and political franchise for everybody.

A look at broader social phenomena, which shaped and kept influencing the polity, especially the ruling party, may provide a better background for understanding the roots of the different trends within the Soviet political arena. The next part will try, cursorily, to cast a glance at the party as it faces a new society.

PART THREE

SOCIETY AND PARTY

CHAPTER TEN

"Civil Society" Recovering

BEFORE resuming and concluding the main theme of this study—the political aspects and ideas of economic debates over the last four decades—there will be a slight digression in the next two chapters from the main theme into some areas that are important as background to understand current and future debates. In this way some more of the links that are missing in the debate because of the political constraints to which Soviet scholars are submitted will be supplied. It is the task of this work not only to introduce the historical dimension of the discussion so long as it cannot be broached in Soviet conditions, but also to supply some data on trends that can be discerned inside the party insofar as the study of this apparatus in the Soviet political system is neglected and inaccessible for open debate to Soviet scholars.

Our brief investigation will emphasize aspects that have not yet been sufficiently studied in Western literature either.

The industrialization years during the period of the pre-war five-year plans can serve as a suitable departure point for an outline of factors that shaped the Soviet political system. These years were indeed crucial in forming the party-state institutions. The strictly economic tasks over which the party presided during those years were a basic factor. Economists who emphasize that economic growth and its methods entail far-reaching institutional changes in the whole system can find in Soviet history a perfect illustration for such a thesis. Once a policy of speedy and forced industrialization was adopted, the whole institutional set-

249

ting was reshaped to serve the central task and to help the center to control the process. The economic activities as well as the institutional changes were imposed from above. It was "a revolution from above," and this is a second crucial factor for the understanding of the character of the Soviet polity.

Once initiated, such a revolution from above imparted enormous pressure from the center on a reluctant, mainly peasant country. Although it was hoped that in this process the country would soon mature, the initiative from above tended to remain there. Instead of being a transitory measure, "the dictatorship of the proletariat"—the whole process of enforcing from the center plans, targets, indicators, rewards, and penalties, controls and constraints—exhibited rather naturally a capacity for self-perpetuation. The institutional network was reorganized so as to allow a powerful center to impose on the country and on all the executive bodies the conduct and the norms it wanted.

This was true not only of institutions engaged in economic planning and management but also of the political system at large. Shaped in such a way, crystallized into a highly centralized dictatorial setup, the system acted through a peculiarly twinned set of hierarchical bureaucracies, well-fused at the top: the state machinery, supervised by a second hierarchy—the party. In both apparatuses, a common pattern of power and prerogatives prevailed. Power was concentrated at the apex, and the lower echelons of bureaucrats, as well as the party rank and file, were asked to obey and to execute "with enthusiasm" the tasks prescribed in detail. The nationalization of economy, which resulted in a sort of disenfranchisement of the rights of direct producers for the benefit of the higher state machinery, had as its counterpart in the political field the phenomenon of "nationalization" of political life, with citizens being deprived of political rights for the benefit of the top leadership.

250

That the functions of executive decision making, in economics and in politics, are fused at the top are momentous facts that got their final shape during the Soviet industrial revolution. To preserve their vision of the aims of this revolution and their capacity to continue to guide society and mold it, the leaders felt forced to expand their monopoly to all the important spheres of social life and to exercise tight controls over all of them. At the same time, the state machinery and the party organization had to be shaped to become agencies capable of exercising such controls. Consequently, not only the state machinery but also the party, especially the latter, were forced to become more than anything else a machinery geared to controlling society and administrations, a function that naturally tended to absorb most of its energies.

Thus, what characterized best the relations between the party and society was the relation between controlled subjects and controlling agents. The concept of a guide became misleading. A guide shows the road and is followed; if not, he does not very much care to force his customer to be guided. A dictatorial party can guide, but only if it teaches people to participate and creates conditions in which they can do it, including an increased voice in shaping the guide himself. Otherwise, the guide becomes a power nexus interested first in preserving his power whatever the price.

This is what happened to the Soviet party. Imposing on the country both economic plans and political programs, as well as one *weltanschauung* and even aesthetic views, without giving citizens the right to contest (participation does not have much meaning without the right to contest), the party had to devote itself to building controlling networks and devices to impose its will. The results for the very character of the system were far-reaching: a disciplinarian bent on the whole activity; powerful bosses facing rather inert masses; fidelity to bosses and hierarchies rather than to values and programs; fictions and myths such as "Soviet

251

democracy—highest form of democracy," "participation of the masses," and other exercises in rhetoric; the impoverishment and unilateral development of culture.[1]

Such were the processes that shaped the party and the Soviet system at large during the years of industrialization. But the industrialization, at the same time, brought about enormous changes in the country. It developed a powerful, complex economy and gave birth to an entirely new social structure. Politics reigned supreme during the quarter century of hectic industrial and state building. A few decades later, the institutions that had originally been created in haste for the purpose of coercing a peasant nation into the industrial mold were now facing a different reality: the economy could no longer be run by primeval methods, and a variegated and complex society could no longer be pressed into obedience by crude disciplinarian devices.

A factor that facilitated the task of the party was the indisputable historical achievements of the country under the existing system; many of the party values and much of the new system became accepted and internalized by the public. But past achievements, whatever their legitimizing role, could not replace adequacy of institutions or cover up their inadequacy in a new situation for too long a period. The new economy and society began to impose changes on the party. The reign of "politics" and its freedom of initiative and breakthrough, as in the 1930s, had gone. The relatively easy formulation of simple central goals, using simple, crude methods to achieve them, became a thing of the past. The historical situations that had created the party and the whole system that had given the party its glory and its internal organization had also passed. The economy became a source of problems to be solved, and the social forces, some of them entirely new in Russian history, began asserting themselves. Capacity to formulate complex strategies to achieve multiple goals, ability to reorganize in order to

[1] Cf. S. Ossowski, "Spoleczne Warunki i Konsekwencje Planowania Spolecznego," *Dzieła* 5 (Warsaw, 1968), 293.

match new realities, finding new ways of controlling or getting acceptance, mobilizing support from social groups, which sprang up during those years and which turned out to be both indispensable and self-assertive, presented the party with formidable new tasks and problems. In order not to lose control, it slowly began to change under the pressure of realities to the creation of which it had contributed, but which in many respects it was unprepared to face.

In the past the party had faced a relatively backward social system, which it managed to restructure thoroughly and ruthlessly by a set of methods; but these methods shaped the party itself in the process of accomplishing this radical transformation, and the result of the interaction of these three factors was momentous. The party became an organization of an unprecedented type: a bureaucratic-political administration, highly centralized and geared to mobilization, regimentation, and control, entirely different from what it had been under Lenin. The same can be said about the leadership and its relations with their party comrades.

The organization exhibited the capacity to cut through the class loyalties of its membership and to mold them in the light of its values. Those especially who entered the ranks of the party apparatus, which dominated the party entirely, developed new loyalties and new interests as a ruling machinery, acquired values different from the ones they may have shared as young revolutionaries in a revolutionary party, and became a self-centered ruling group. Position, privileges, power—and ways of exercising and enjoying them—became a nexus of factors that strongly encouraged identification with the *status quo*, and the *status quo* with general social interests. Actually the party developed elaborate mechanisms for preserving its power and its supremacy, and was helped in this by social groups who enjoyed and shared a privileged position. Naturally, it became a vested interest, more powerful than others, which, although in a position to express many general interests, was also strongly influenced by the inherent propensity to pro-

253

tect its own power first. Such a posture of a professionally ruling organization encouraged tendencies to self-closure, and the appearance of rifts between the party and the multiple and complex interests of society, presents the much less dynamic, and more *status quo* and self-preservation-oriented party, with a more stringent set of challenges and pressures.

The pressures from the economy, largely discussed in previous chapters, were generated by weak productivity, sluggish innovation, indifferent or self-seeking behavior of producers, and obsolete planning and managing methods, all exercising a heavy downward pressure on the economic performance. These problems accounted for the sense of urgency in different circles to rethink the main principles on which the economic system was built. The reforms and reformist thought pointed to the need to restructure the relations of the enterprises with consumers and administrations, to change the ones between state and economy and the state and the producers.

From the new social texture came a parallel pressure on the system to evolve and to adapt. The country, still in a hectic process of urbanization, has had the majority of its population in cities since the early 1960s. The peasantry is still an important sector, but its ratio of the population has dwindled from 83.19 percent according to the 1926 census, when only 12.74 percent declared that their livelihood came from outside agriculture to some 20 percent today (excluding the population in the *sovkhozy*). Today agriculture employs about 27 percent of the active population, in both the *kolkhozy* and the *sovkhozy*.

There were about 5 million industrial workers then, 3.8 million officials, and only about 137,000 classed as professionals. Today the industrial working class is the biggest single class in society—about 62 million people in industry, building, and transportation, with over 20 million in industry alone—another big change and a new factor in Soviet history, although the political significance of this fact is not yet clear to anyone.

Another important development is the quickly growing nonmanual, white-collar sectors, which Soviet statistics terms "intelligentsia" because of the nonphysical content of their work. Here is a real maze of social groups and subgroups, including a huge scientific establishment, a technical intelligentsia, and several so-called strategic elites in and outside the state administrations. In contrast to the earlier figure of 137,000 professionals, 16 million people are engaged in science, health, education, and art, and this sector is growing more quickly than the working class. The latter grew 2.7 times from 1940 to 1970, whereas the former grew 3.3 times. During the same period, the number of scholars increased 8.9 times and reached the impressive figure of 900,000 researchers and university teachers, whereas in 1913 there had been only 12,000 of them.

To complete the picture, there are 2.5 million engineers and 4.5 million technicians although there were only 190,000 in both categories in 1913; and there are 4.5 million university students as opposed to 127,000 in Tsarist Russia.[2]

Thus, Russia was transformed, in a relatively short period, from a basically agricultural country of *muzhiki* to a modern, urbanized, industrial-agrarian structure.

From such a new social structure with its new classes and numerous groups of strategical importance to the state comes pressure for different concessions, positions of privilege and influence, and the right to participate.

A new society, then, better educated than ever before, capable of creating—and in fact constantly creating—dif-

[2] The figures are from *Statisticheskoe Obozrenie*, no. 5 (1928), pp. 88–90, and *Narodnoe Khoziaistvo SSSR v 1970 Godu* (Moscow, 1970), pp. 522–523 and the whole section on "Labor" (*Trud*) in this publication. See also data on the social structure and professional composition, based on the 1959 population census, in G. Osipov, ed., *Industry and Labor in the USSR* (London, 1966), pp. 27–28, 40.

ferent group values and finding ways for asserting and defending their views and interests, is continually presenting the party with demands that amount to a bill of rights, including recognition of interests and the right to defend them, freedom for autonomous activities, and, to sum up, an entirely new relationship with the state.

The new social reality is marked to an important degree by social differentiation. As a result social inequality and class tensions have become an increasingly influential and troublesome factor. Under conditions in which the state's mobilizing capabilities in a new, more relaxed economic setting are weakened and cannot be used so easily as a brake on social tensions and class warfare, class and group cleavages and the concomitant social tensions progressively may find their way into the open and profoundly mark Soviet political life, particularly if the standard of living does not rise quickly enough. The very existence of the new Soviet sociology is a result of the acknowledgment by the leadership of the complexity of the new society and of the social tensions inherent in it, which cannot be managed without being understood. But first this sociology had to admit, more or less candidly, the facts of social inequality in Soviet society and try to analyze it. Sociologists studying different classes, social groups, and youth have described reality more accurately than propaganda has acknowledged. Timidly, but with some obstinacy, sociologists have tried to explain the disturbing phenomena (efforts to whitewash have also been present). First, they have posed the ideological question: "Was not socialization of property supposed to eliminate the basic sources of inequality?" Some sociologists have concluded that ownership of production means might well be common and, in regard to production means *in toto*, everybody might be equal.[3] How-

---

[3] For some facts and debates on social inequality by sociologists, see, for example, M. Rutkevich, ed., *Processy Izmeneniia Sotsial'noi Struktury Sovetskogo Obshchestva* (Sverdlovsk, 1967), esp. contributions by G. Mokronosov, "O Kriteriakh Vnutri-klassovykh Razlichii

ever, use and management of these means have not been less important, and it has become a source of social inequality. This has happened because different groups of working people have actually been using and mastering unequal amounts of production means as a result of their roles in the division of labor, based on their skills, education, and so on. Thus, abstract property rights do not determine a person's or a group's social position, but his role in the production process and his control over nationalized wealth do.

Some other sociologists even began to probe into the delicate matter of the specific reciprocal positions of those who give orders and those who take them. The problem of inequality led them to discuss the problem of power, however veiled the terms.

Others studied and disclosed the rather low standards of instruction and professional preparation of most Soviet youth and the whole working class; the majority of Soviet workers are engaged in crude physical labor, working with only a few machines or with their hands. Not more than 15 percent of the workers enjoy a higher standard of living because of their higher qualification; the numerous lower

---

v Sotsialisticheskom Obshchestve," pp. 5–13, V. Radionov, "Ob istochnikakh Vnutri-klassovogo Deleniia," pp. 14–20, and F. Filippov, "Sotsial'nye Peremeshcheniia kak Faktor Stanovleniia Sotsial'noi Odnorodnosti," pp. 93–101; Iu. Arutunian, *Opyt Sotsiologicheskogo Izucheniia Sela* (Moscow, 1968), pp. 39–40. V. Shkredov, *Ekonomika i Pravo* (Moscow, 1967), p. 63, said "Insofar as the managerial work is confined to the specialized sphere of activity of a definite layer in society, the specific material interests of this layer are also being preserved." In general, on the different scales of the administrative ladder in a bureaucracy the interests are different and hence "in a socialist society substantial social and economic differences still exist between people as bearers of production relations—not to mention the class differences between workers and peasants."

State ownership does not eliminate this inequality, nor does it eliminate objective contradictions between those interests. "State ownership is the form in which these contradictions exist, one of them being the contradiction between the concentration of administrative power and the objectively existing relative independence of the enterprises."

257

officialdom is equally poor.[4] Alienation must unavoidably arise, because it is undeniably present in any system where people work not for pleasure or from a sense of civic duty, but only in order to make a living. It may even become sharper when educated youth morally and academically prepared for highly qualified jobs become simple workers in low-skilled jobs, because economic development is slower than the production of high school graduates. This, too, is a big problem in the Soviet Union today,[5] a source of frustration and a waste of economic potential.

Against these facts and realities, some writers have challenged the official fiction of a working class presumably inspired by a feeling of mastery over its working place (*chuvstvo khoziaina*).[6] In fact, official sermons castigating the widespread sluggishness, absenteeism, and tendency to change jobs in search of higher pay also contradicts this ideological fiction.

The explosive potentialities of these facts have forced the party to engage in complex social strategies that have contributed even further to its hardening into a shrewd manipulator fighting for the preservation of itself rather than for the ideals of the founding fathers. It urgently needed and

[4] On the labor force and its professional and educational standards see chaps. 5–8 in A. Notkin, ed., *Struktura Narodnogo Khoziaistva SSSR* (Moscow, 1967), and V. Zhamin, in A. Notkin, ed., *Faktory Ekonomicheskogo Razvitiia SSSR* (Moscow, 1970), chap. 5, pp. 125–126.

[5] Zhamin, *ibid.*, pp. 116–117.

[6] An article by a *kolkhoz* chairman, N. Sotnikov, in *Pravda*, 6 January 1968, complains against the big limitation on the development of agriculture, which is "the insufficiently developed sense of *khoziain*." He is quoted in A. Emel'ianov, ed., *Ekonomicheskie i Sotsial'nye Problemy Industrializatsii Sel'skogo Khoziaistva* (Moscow, 1971), p. 138. The authors of this book confirm that this is a general worry, because the existing ways of organization and remuneration cause in peasants an absence of interest in their work and an indifference to the soil. Antonov made a similar assertion about city workers (see above, Chapter 5, pp. 148–150. For more sources see Z. Katz, "Sociology in the Soviet Union," *Problems of Communism*, May-June 1971, p. 34.

received a social cushion between the power summit and the underpaid and alienated base, between the leadership with its privileged entourage and the working masses. The growing intelligentsia actually has played such a role, and some of its groups have reaped substantial bonuses for their willingness to help. These groups formed a part of the privileged apex, which has been very much interested in the preservation of the existing order or, at best, in the minimal rationalizing touches to make things run better.

But a politically and socially powerful summit facing large underprivileged masses with a growing intelligentsia in between re-created the possibility of a fateful junction of forces of which the leadership was well aware. It was such a junction that made the Tsarist empire explode. As long as large masses are poor but press for more, and groups of intelligentsia, even if socially privileged, are deprived of political rights, a re-creation of radical politics, with *intelligenty* joining workers and offering them leadership, is certainly a theoretical possibility. The party, or some of its leaders, has often applied methods that proved how well aware they were of such dangers and appealed to nationalist feelings and to the anti-intellectual leanings of workers, trying to set them against critical intellectuals, those "parasites" who live well but keep pestering and complaining— a theme largely employed, for example, at the proceedings of the Twenty-Third Party Congress in speeches by Sholokhov, Epishev, and Solomentsev.

The party also has controlled Marxism. This has been done by adopting, nationalizing and freezing it into a boring and ineffectual catechism. This move is clever. The vocation of Marxism is the analysis of class realities, of class forces hiding behind various facades, of the social realities in political power structures, and of discovering human alienation resulting from industrial organizations and political helplessness. The Soviet system cannot pass unscathed through criticisms that apply such categories.

An obvious step for a political system operating in such

259

complex circumstances was the need to appeal for help to the social sciences. This was an urgent one because such sciences were previously banned, and therefore the feeling of ignorance of realities with which the party was dealing had to be rather acute, at least among the more modern and educated Soviet leaders. Cybernetics and systems analysis, which serve as a basis for computer and management sciences, mathematical economics, and sociology, sprang up and mushroomed, enjoying an immense popularity among the young generation.

Although all of those fields are capable of being used "technically" in the service of any government seeking remedies and recipes, they all have under Soviet conditions the same politically embarrassing potentialities. If the original Marxist categories should prove unbearable for the system, the categories of cybernetics would not be charitable either. In terms such as the system's "learning capacity," "feedback," and "self-steering," and especially in terms of "communications" and their "channels," the shortcomings of the Soviet political system and of the organization and methods used by the party have been staggering, as specialists including Nemchinov, Glushkov, Trapeznikov, and Sakharov have told the leadership. Of course, the political conclusions of such specialists and the character of the changes they have recommended are different. Some have pressed for the emancipation of societal forces and initiatives; others have been ready to help out the leaders by offering them better methods of control. Still others have tried to work out clever compromises.

The new sociology can be a double-edged sword. The very act of studying and disclosing realities of society can become embarrassing. But this has been a minimum price to pay, if the regime wants to harness this discipline to the task of improving its performance, vitality, and legitimacy. In fact, the new Soviet sociology has the capacity and interest in helping the system to achieve a workable internal equilibrium and in smoothing social contradictions, not unlike the role played, according to some analysts, by functionalism in America. Indeed, concepts akin to functionalism began to permeate Soviet sociology, just as Marxist concepts have combined with structural functionalist concepts in the West.[7]

Unfortunately, or rather fortunately, the social sciences, even when controlled from above, often tend to break through the narrow limits imposed on them by their official or unofficial sponsors and users. Not only sponsors but also the general state of society, the character of its tensions, and the relations among its classes and political forces influence the role, direction, and use made of the social and other sciences.

Among the results of the emergence of a new social structure in the Soviet Union, the very appearance of new social sciences there, and the critical potential they possess, as the debates of the economists amply illustrated, is in itself an event of great importance. One further consequence follows inescapably: all these sciences use languages that have almost nothing in common with the official "dialectical materialism" still adhered to (known as *diamat*), the mainstay of the official ideology.

It is a fact that the admission of the new disciplines had to be wrested in fierce fights with conservatives, as the victory of these new languages epitomizes the erosion and decline of orthodox ideology. Once more, not only has the development of the new social sciences tolled the knell of many old dogmas but also the very societal variety, differentiation, stratification, and complexity constituted a fertile breeding ground for values, beliefs, and ideologies that it has been impossible to suppress. When social interests diverge and clash, when the political system shows some slack in its capacity to master the multifaceted and pluralist social reality, these interests will find their expression in di-

[7] This is A. Gouldner's thesis in "Notes on the Crisis of Marxism and the Emergence of Academic Sociology in the Soviet Union," *The Coming Crisis of Western Sociology* (London, 1971), pp. 447–477.

rect or roundabout ways; they will reject, challenge, or simply ignore official concepts or values, and will create or adopt many different ones.

Attentive observers have no difficulty in discerning in the Soviet public a whole gamut of different beliefs, political, religious, nationalist, authoritarian, democratic, liberal, and fascist, not to mention various ethical and philosophical conceptions. The official version of ideology is adhered to by some, but more often than not it only offers clichés to be used for lip service or on solemn occasions, but often without much relevance to reality.

It is thus not implausible to surmise that under the officially claimed political homogeneity, Russian society has a subterranean political reality, presenting *in potentia*, and even at the present time, a large spectrum of opinion. Were these allowed to express themselves, the picture would be clearer; and everybody, including the rulers, would have known the real political physiognomy of their society. Since these trends have existed either in a clandestine or more often in a diffused semiconscious state, rarely presented in public speeches but very widespread in life, the capacity of the party to control such political varieties has been minimal.

In fact, the capacity of all kinds of politically "alien" conceptions to penetrate the party itself is probably very high. Of course, this is no more than a supposition that will eventually be amply borne out by research on the party or by the appearance in the open of intraparty cleavages. The whole political gamut, other than the strict orthodoxy preached by the leadership and the propaganda networks, exists latently in the party as well as in society; and the very possibility of this being so will become clearer after an examination of the role of the rank and file in the party. The fact that the party in its official positions or in largely accepted unofficial practices has often yielded to public moods and deeply seated beliefs not always of the most progressive variety can be illustrated by the growing role of nationalism, sometimes of a virulent brand, in Communist parties all over Eastern Europe.[8]

If this general assumption is true, it would mean that much of the official language and creed is not only unconvincing but too weak to protect the party from external influences; it is forced slowly to adapt to and assimilate older creeds that remained impervious to the onslaught of superficial ideologies—a high price to pay for a fake monolith and shallow propaganda. The more the ex-revolutionary party hardens into a vested interest oriented toward the preservation of what exists, and toward stability rather than toward change—a phenomenon that arises naturally in any organization or among individuals who manage to accumulate wealth and are then unwilling to risk losing it[9]—the more it will lose its initial ideological vigor and tend to yield to the taste and beliefs of influential groups. Not infrequently, such shedding of old feathers, in fact, has been accompanied by vociferous propaganda and declarations of faith to the old catechism, testifying more to the death of the old creed than to any real fervor.

Such a loss of ideological vitality explains why some com-

[8] F. Fejto, *Histoire des Democraties Populaires. Après Staline* (Paris, 1969), shows such processes of "growing nationalism penetrating the ruling parties in Eastern Europe which take on different forms." A debate in "Discussion," *Slavic Review* 32 (March 1973), 1–44, offers a rich material on the awakening of national feelings in Russia, taking on complicated shades and trends, running from a legitimate scholarly or amateur interest in the Russian past and its culture, through searches of a mystical "national soul," and to manifestations of a virulent chauvinism. The participants of this exchange, J. Haney, T. Bird, and G. Kline, also document the serious debate and even sharp clashes between partisans of different interpretations of nationalism, chauvinism, internationalism, and humanism going on in the Soviet Union today. The position of the party is ambiguous, no doubt because of the fact that similar trends exist and compete inside the party itself and do not allow it to come up with a clear-cut stand on these sensitive issues.

[9] This tendency in ruling Communist parties is analyzed by R. Tucker, *The Marxist Revolutionary Idea* (London, 1969).

munist parties have been sucked into social milieus and ideologies they previously fought and have been content with preserving only the shell.

When the capacity of the party to instill its values has been impaired, its efficacy has been weakened. Some communist parties have found vigor and capacity to engage in new ways, others have not. Tito, Mao, Kadar, Dubček, Ceausescu, and Gomulka are different cases ranging from radical turns in policies and a deliberate destruction of the party in order to build a new one to an impotent drift and loss of influence.

Changes in the Party

The new economic and social structure unavoidably imposed changes on the party. The process of substantial change began in the party and the polity with Stalin's death.

At the top of the party's hierarchy, group leadership replaced personal rule. A decision of the Central Committee had sanctioned this change when in 1964 it forbade any one leader to be both premier of the government and general secretary of the party.

The phenomenon of "collective leadership" was not just a temporary arrangement resulting from some fragile equilibrium among competing leaders. Rather, it was an expression of deeper structural changes influencing the patterns of political power. The complexities of the tasks facing Soviet leaders today and a new equilibrium of forces inside the party apparatus imposed this new method of leadership, as they had determined much of the new style in politics. The enlargement of the apex of the power structure is the important phenomenon behind the new style with its more sophisticated businesslike management methods, use of experts and preliminary studies in decision making, and the elimination of the glaring inadequacies of an oppressive-punitive approach to subordinates within the hierarchy. The broadening of the apex of power first meant the

264

inclusion of larger groups of the apparatus in a more meaningful participation or influence in decision making and the
creation of suitable conditions in which these groups would
work and enjoy their position. The higher echelons in the
apparatus now gained for themselves the formal conditions
they needed for their political and professional activities,
including job security. These groups checked the leadership's capricious and unpredictable autocracy, where
an efficient bureaucracy could not function. Therefore,
prompted by common interests, it regularized much of the
policy-making process and introduced some rules into the
power play. The enhanced role for the Central Committee,
at least when the central leadership has been involved in a
deep conflict, and its capacity to serve as mediator or as a
kind of supreme umpire have reflected the new role that
high-level bureaucrats managed to secure for themselves.

At the same time, upper layers became an arena of politics. They are cracked by cleavages and form alliances in
order to press for positions or for policies. Since Stalin this
game is no longer dangerous and does not imply much
more than the normal and predictable political risks: frustrated promotion or demotion without ouster from the circles of the privileged and often with a chance for a comeback.

Also, it can be assumed that the place and role of intermediary echelons of the party and government bureaucracies are enhanced, and that they even enjoy some possibility of participation in shaping policies. Apparently, this
has not been openly acknowledged and institutionalized
but, rather, grudgingly conceded because of the greater
capacity of the middle and lower echelons to engage in the
sabotage of decisions from above if these are not to their
liking. Thus, the opinions of such intermediaries have to be
considered in policy decisions, in order to secure their support in executing "the line."

An additional phenomenon now attracting much research

in the West—and frankly acknowledged by some East European sources—has been the enhanced access to political influence of groups, personalities, experts, and lobbies external to the apparatus and bureaucracy, but capable of exercising pressures and gaining a hearing.[10] As a result of this pressure-group reality, the Soviet *pays politique* has become much larger than the one in the previous stage of dictatorship; the political process has become more complicated, offering more scope for influence with more channels of pressure by more social forces.

Regularity of procedures, due process in many spheres of life, and an enhanced role for juridical forms of litigation have expressed the trend of rationalization and modernization in the system, resulting from the complexity of problems, pressures of the social milieu, better education, as well as a wide acceptance of the basic traits of the system by large sectors of the population. The rule of terror on a mass scale has gone. Only the persecution of dissidents has disclosed an arbitrary behavior on the part of the security agencies. But even in this sphere, a certain restraint and some forms of process have been imposed as a result of the party's better control of these agencies and of the existence of external and internal pressures to which the leadership has to some extent responded.

These changes were the inevitable result of the deep structural transformation of the whole social setting with its growing differentiation and new educational standards of the population and of the elites. The social composition of the party and the character of the cadres followed suit. It is now a party with a clear predominance of the nonmanual classes, a predominance not only in influence but also in numbers. They form probably one-half of the party membership, although a minority of about one-third in the pop-

[10] For the most recent Western collective work on Soviet pressure groups and their new role in Soviet politics, see H. Skilling and F. Griffiths, eds., *Interest Groups in Soviet Politics* (Princeton, N.J., 1971).

ulation.[11] The party does not even try any more to have working class majorities in its ranks; it declared itself officially as the party of the whole people in a state of the whole people, which now supposedly espoused "proletarian values," and almost frankly acknowledged its orientation and dependence on the growing professional classes. But it also, appropriately, acquired a more consultative style, became more than before a bargaining-and-brokerage type of organization, applying "concrete-sociological" surveys before taking some decisions, using computers, and taking much more cognizance of communications and information.

Such new features in style, which expressed deeper structural changes, meant a change in the party's internal spirit and in its real role in society. As the party became oriented toward the establishment and preservation of existing patterns and their perpetuation into "the next communist stage," it assumed a new basic position in the country. With the loss of the previous dynamism, however strong its power remained, the party acquired a defensive attitude; its ambitions turned rather more outward, beyond the frontiers, to relatively easy external successes and spectaculars appealing to the patriotic feelings of the population. But inside ambition was diminished, and the main effort has been spent on operating and improving the routine functions of running an apparatus by using safe remedies and without taking risks. Bold new perspectives and great breakthroughs have gone with the current leadership. The Twenty-Fourth Party Congress, held in the spring of 1971, was an excellent illustration of this state of affairs—a smoothly running, boring ceremony, long "businesslike" speeches by

[11] T. Rigby offered a detailed study of the changing social composition of the party throughout its history in his *Communist Party Membership in the USSR, 1917–1967* (Princeton, N.J., 1968). Official data on the social composition of the party, given by L. Brezhnev in *23-ii S'ezd KPSS, Stenotchet* (Moscow, 1966), p. 96, show that 37.8 percent are workers, 16.2 percent are *kolkhozniki*, and 46 percent are officials and others.

267

leaders, no new ideas or vistas, some proposals for the re-distribution of resources and tasks, mere routine.

The execution of mainly day-to-day tasks made many observers wonder whether the party was not dragging its feet, whether it lagged behind the needs of society, whether it yielded to processes rather than mastered them, or whether it drifted into changes rather than initiated them. An examination of current policies confirmed such an impression. Sometimes the party tried more to obstruct the innovations than to implement new policies.

All these structural and institutional changes have indicated both to Western and some Soviet observers that the Soviet state and society has undergone a deep metamorphosis; that it has left one stage of development and has entered a new one, the transition into which has been difficult to define because the terminology of the cold war and of Stalinism proved inadequate for the task; that new forms of political life more complex than those of the previous twenty years developed and have continued to appear. It is apparent, too, that the party has undergone a transformation "from a mobilizing to an adaptive type," according to M. Fainsod; from an imposed hierarchical structure to "an established one," in the terms of S. Huntington; from a monolith to an agglomeration of interests, as V. Aspaturian maintains; or that the basic structure, according to G. Skilling, did not change but exhibited "an incipient pluralism"—a phenomenon that M. Duverger anticipated when he spoke of "a virtual pluralism" as a possibility in monoparty systems. G. Skilling thinks that Soviet politics has recently been operating "in a group conflict situation"; according to C. Johnson, the party has become "an arena of politics"; and J. Hough elaborates by saying that the party machinery has changed from a disciplined one-voice machine to one with "a broad and shifting variety of alliances."[12]

[12] For Skilling, see his "Groups in Soviet Politics, Some Hypotheses" in Skilling and Griffith, eds., *Interest Groups*, p. 44; V. Aspaturian is

Thus, numerous changes have revealed an ongoing transformation from one type of dictatorship to some other pattern; correspondingly, the party too has undergone change and has continued to evolve into some other type of organization. But the whole process is far from finished, and its future direction is far from clear. Some in-between stage, a transitory hybrid form, currently exists; simultaneously, the party's capacity to respond to challenges facing it by devising viable responses has been deficient in many respects.

Current Policies: Monolithism Again

An examination of current policies and of the internal organization of the party can help in obtaining a better insight and in formulating a better diagnosis.

The study of the responses of the leadership to some of the challenges and problems can be illuminating, and the period between the invasion of Prague and the Twenty-Fourth Party Congress which will be examined offers enough material. In fact, the conservative hardening and counteroffensive had already manifested itself during the Twenty-Third Party Congress, and culminated in the invasion of Czechoslovakia and in the Twenty-Fourth Party Congress, which conspicuously retreated or froze reformist endeavors and supported the *status quo* on all problems.

The predominant themes in official pronouncements on internal and bloc relations during the period revealed a return of an old-fashioned, orthodox line—or at least the rhet-

quoted by Skilling, "An Introduction," *ibid.*, p. 16; J. Hough, "The Party Apparatchik," *ibid.*, p. 49; for Johnson, see his "Comparing Communist Nations," in C. Johnson, ed., *Change in Communist Systems* (Stanford, Calif., 1970), p. 26; for Huntington, his "Social and Institutional Dynamics," in S. Huntington and C. Moore, eds., *Authoritarian Politics in Modern Society* (New York, 1970), pp. 40–44; M. Duverger, *Political Parties* (London, 1955), p. 279; M. Fainsod is quoted from "Transformation of the Communist Party of the Soviet Union" in D. Treadgold, ed., *Soviet and Chinese Communism* (Seattle, 1967), p. 68.

oric, unearthed from what seemed to some to be prehistory, did. Many openings and new assumptions concerning the Eastern bloc as well as internal programs and perspectives, which had held some promise in the previous period, were now either silently dropped or openly repudiated.[13]

In relations with world communism, the previous Khrushchevian thesis on "different roads to communism" was now repudiated, although without a frank divorce. Heavily underlined was the thesis that building socialism was subordinated to "general laws," equally valid everywhere. This was a clear counterthesis to the "different roads," a term that has now almost disappeared from Soviet propaganda and has been replaced by the acknowledgment of the existence of only secondary "local conditions."

Not surprisingly, the not-too-hidden intention of such statements has asserted itself with growing obstinacy: Moscow is the unique spot where the formulas embracing the planet can be conceived. There can be no varieties in Marxism-Leninism! These slogans have become the war cries of the renewed orthodoxy with its unmistakable Moscovite flavor. Marxism-Leninism is a unitary theory equally applicable everywhere.[14] This is the lesson that propaganda tries to hammer into heads interested too much in novelties. All this amounts to a tug of war against polycentrism and a return to the Stalinist thesis of the priority of the Soviet model and the primacy of Moscow. In its efforts to reimpose control and uniformity on the bloc countries, Russia has prodded them into a "military consolidation" as a "sacred

[13] The reader will find all these ideological and political theses presented to the country by L. Brezhnev on the occasion of the Lenin centenary in *Partiinaia Zhizn'*, no. 9 (1970); for considerable detail about the theses of the Central Committee, prepared earlier for the same centenary and intended to serve as basis for the party's propaganda work, see *ibid.*, no. 1 (1970). These were still valid policies four years later.

[14] *Partiinaia Zhizn'*, no. 1 (1970), p. 4. This is a bimonthly publication for party cadres.

270

duty," asserting that to follow any other course amounts to treason.[15]

The unmistakably Soviet, if not Great Russian nationalist flavor, is evident in an explanation to the public, published in *Pravda*, of the criteria the party used in formulating its foreign policy. The party "is guided in the first place by the interests of our country, the interest of the socialist international system, and the entire communist movement."[16] Priority, quite frankly, is given to the interests of Russia as a criterion for formulating policies, and those of the bloc and world communism are secondary. The obvious and "natural" realism of such an approach and its unintended sincerity seems unaware of the big question whether the "interests of our country" are a sufficient basis for a unique variety of Marxism-Leninism.

Although presented as a tool against "imperialist threats," the pressure on the bloc countries for "military consolidation" had nothing to do with such threats. Russia has adopted coexistence policies in its foreign relations and has engaged in the ordinary kind of competition for influence with the United States and China, and it is neither seeking adventure nor expecting troubles from the West. The pressure on the bloc countries has been intended to reimpose Soviet controls on them, and "military consolidation" seemed to be the best way to achieve this aim. All the same, the larger perspectives have been strictly peaceful and inward-oriented. The party activists have been told clearly: "Now the main influence on international relations is being exercised by us through our economic activity."[17] This was both an appeal to concentrate on domestic affairs and a reassurance to those who feared too many initiatives and adventures abroad and to those who did not favor wasting resources on foreign aid.

In this perspective "world communism" has to fend for

[15] *Ibid.*, no. 9 (1970), p. 32.   [16] *Pravda*, 13 January 1970.
[17] *Partiinaia Zhizn'*, no. 10 (1970), p. 8.

itself, although Moscow still asserted that its version of Marxism-Leninism was the only legitimate one.

The apparent contradiction is partially explained by the Chinese problem. But many themes of Soviet propaganda as well as their policies, although apparently intended for export to bloc countries, have been reflections of internal processes and worries. In popular and theoretical journals, ideological conservatives have preached for some time now the themes of party *monopoly* and party *monolithism* as central and universal tenets of this unique Marxism-Leninism. Adherence to these principles has become the main criterion for distinguishing the faithful from the revisionists; advocacy of the "slightest diminution" of the party's traditional role has been considered treason and counterrevolution.

The argument was even presented by some Soviet specialists in a more sophisticated form: while different social groups may need political expression of their own and a monoparty system may not have been an original principle of Leninism, the behavior of the Mensheviks and the Socialist-Revolutionaries (S.R.'s) made collaboration with them impossible, and forced the party to rule alone; furthermore, the growing homogeneity of society in the course of socialist development eliminated the basis of multiparty systems. Multiparty systems as a temporary device are tolerated in some popular democracies, but opposition is not, and cannot be allowed.[18]

Renewed assertions about homogeneity and the "growing" monolithism of the party as the "highest commandment," about the rule "of the working class," and about the Soviet system "the highest type of democracy" in existence, followed.

[18] See theoretical pronouncements on the party by M. Lebedev, "Partiia v Politicheskoi Sisteme Sotsializma," *Sovetskoe Gosudarstvo i Pravo*, no. 2 (1970), p. 9 and *passim*; also by A. Slepov and I. Iudin, "Partiia v Politicheskoi Sisteme Obshchestva," *Kommunist*, no. 14 (1969), pp. 49–51.

It is amusing to find among the flood of old orthodox themes this last one: that Soviet democracy is "the highest type" (somehow "the most democratic" Stalinist constitution was not mentioned). But it has persisted because this claim tries to answer the growing demands from inside and the acrimonious criticisms from outside, especially from the Czechoslovaks during their "spring"—against the bureaucratic and disciplinarian, hierarchical and authoritarian internal regime of the Communist Party.

Thus, the Soviet press was full of articles trying to deride and cast opprobrium on such concepts as "socialism with a human face" and "socialist humanism"—all in quotation marks, as if these were dirty words; the same punctuation was applied to demands such as "freedom of press," "freedom of political opposition," "freedom of artistic creation," and other presumably antiproletarian and antisocialist slogans.

That the quotation marks were intended for internal consumption no less than for the use of would-be reformers abroad is beyond doubt. Czechoslovaks, Poles, and Rumanians do not read the numerous articles in *Kommunist* and *Partiinaia Zhizn'*. Many in the Soviet Union itself think that the principles of party organization and much of the government's policy making have become obsolete and inadequate at this stage in the country's development. Some do not understand—and even dare to write letters to *Pravda*—why, in the mighty country that broke the enemy encirclement, eliminated hostile classes, and built a socialist society, the party still must behave like an army, or a disciplined bureaucratic hierarchy.[19] The demands for all kinds of freedom have been growing inside the Soviet

[19] *Pravda*, 11 February 1970, in its section on "Partiinaia Zhizn'" ("Party Life"), mentions, for example (with understandable disapproval), a letter by a Soviet engineer, a party member, questioning the need, in the new conditions, to stick to the existing version of "iron discipline" in the conduct of party affairs.

273

Union,[20] and it is against these demands that frantic reassertions have proliferated about the existence of only one correct Marxism-Leninism and the legitimacy of only one party that can formulate it. Obviously, such a party has to be disciplined, its policies made at the top, without any participation by the membership in important decisions. In fact, the scope of controls it claims for itself presupposes really superhuman abilities in leadership and a superhistorical quality in such a party: "The CPSU formulates the political line, provides leadership to the masses, guides the economic, socio-political and spiritual life of society, unites, coordinates, and leads the activities of all the sections of the management system," both directly and indirectly through administrations and soviets.[21] How has Soviet democracy fared under these conditions? How could popular sovereignty be reconciled with the existence of such a dominant agency, which has not allowed any opposition?

Nevertheless, the tightening of the official line has not resulted in more self-assurance. Otherwise the party would not need to reassure itself and to repeat endlessly that "the workers of our country have convinced themselves from countless examples that the Communist Party has never pursued any interests other than the interests of the people."[22]

It does not seem that the masses have accepted this doctrine; and the archconservative Tolstikov, former secretary of the party in Leningrad, in his speech to the Twenty-Third Party Congress almost openly admitted as much, when he appealed for a "further strengthening of faith in the party's

[20] A "civil right movement" has existed for some time and still exists in the Soviet Union, illegally, although it seems at the moment of writing weakened by a police clamp-down. For some sources on the whole dissenting and civil rights movement see A. Brumberg, *Protest and Dissent in the Soviet Union Today* (New York, 1970); P. Reddaway, comp., *Uncensored Russia; Protest and Dissent in the Soviet Union* (New York, 1972).

[21] *Partiinaia Zhizn'*, no. 1 (1970), p. 13.

[22] *Kommunist*, no. 14 (1969), p. 6.

word," the faith that the party would solve all the pending problems.[23]

The party has retained its control, and the masses have not shown any inclination to rebel. Yet there has not been automatic "faith in the party's word." Mass skepticism, indifference, apathy, and minding one's own business as well as the growing criticism among different groups of the intelligentsia might be a better assessment of the situation. The party has tried to reassert its position and to tighten its grip on the whole bloc, but particularly on the internal front. In order to combat the "lack of values" among Soviet youth and to thwart further erosion of party ideals, highest party officials imposed new restrictions and appealed for a more comprehensive "patriotic military education" of the young. Such a proposal, made by important officials at the Twenty-Third Party Congress—in peacetime—has been often repeated and partially implemented. Some of the leaders in the ex-Leninist party clearly ran out of values to offer its youth. It is characteristic and pathetic that such a reversal to the slogan on party monolithism and discipline became not only the main strategy for the quelling of polycentrism but also the main answer to economic problems as well. One logic and one strategy permeates the whole current line.

The new "tough" line proposed as a remedy for the growing economic difficulties appeared dramatically in December 1969 after the Central Committee Plenum, which was devoted to economic problems. This session scrapped important aspects of the economic reforms, if not its very soul, and presented instead a renewed demand for discipline, strengthened party interference and controls, and a renewed reliance on party-mobilizational policies in order to overcome growing economic difficulties and deficiencies.

This was not the whole strategy; emphasis has been put on science-technology and improved management tech-

[23] See *23-ii S'ezd KPSS, Stenotchët* (Moscow, 1969), p. 141. Tolstikov, the exsecretary of the Leningrad party organization, was known as a conservative hard-liner. He became Soviet ambassador to China.

niques, as the 1973 reorganization amply illustrated. Obviously, an authoritarian-technocratic orientation is favored. Improved control capabilities of the center are sought through better information channels, more computers, more incentives for scientists, and so forth. Decentralization, autonomy of enterprise, new forms of incentives, new ways to rekindle support and initiatives, which the economic reformers would like to see, are not in the foreground for the moment.

Similarly, the leadership appealed for an alliance "of the working class with science" instead of seeking "alliances" with larger social groups. The latter would certainly demand concessions and rights, which the leadership was not ready to grant.

What the appeals to increase the party's involvement in economics might mean can be gleaned from the following example. Agriculture is the one field in which the Soviet government has achieved some notable results in recent years, not as a result of more interference of party organizations but rather as a consequence of more investments, better prices paid to producers, and improved standards for peasants. Still, the problem has not been resolved, and many troubles still lie ahead from these quarters. In July 1970, the Plenum, which dealt with agriculture, said to party organizations that since the *kolkhozy* would accumulate large sums as a result of higher prices, the party would be required "to take under its control the use of these means." Otherwise, presumably these sums would not be reinvested in an adequate way, as they are expected to be, with the highest possible efficiency.[24]

Why would the *kolkhoz* and its management fail to use the money in an "economic" way? How and why would the interference of the local party secretary make the system work better? These questions may be asked about the whole range of problems. The leadership wants better and faster introduction of new technology, and it expects the party

[24] *Partiinaia Zhizn'*, no. 15 (1969), p. 6.

apparatus once more to take control; the efficiency of industry and ministries cannot be improved without introducing new, automatic information-processing and management techniques, and the party is asked to deal with it; managers do not have professional skills and must be retrained, and the party is asked to interfere.

Familiar sermons remind industrial management that plan targets are the highest law and *kolkhozy*, and that state procurements are the supreme commandment. Other old, fairly discredited, even bankrupt recommendations miraculously reappear at a time when the Soviet press is as full as ever of details and disclosures about the continuing dysfunctions, defects, and losses in the economy and when all the signs exist that, as in Antonov's example, the workers continue to break bricks.[25]

If this is so, the new orthodox line may be inadequate to solve the problems of Soviet economy and society. Both the "growing homogeneity" and demand for monolithism, as well as the return to party-mobilization devices in order to solve economic problems, are no remedies. If this is what it relies on, can the party still be the appropriate agency to introduce automatic management systems, to retrain managers, or to supervise *kolkhoz* investment? And in what sense is a party engaging in such activity in a direct and detailed way a political party at all?

[25] This is no joke. Bricks are still being broken; see *Pravda*, 19 March 1970.

CHAPTER ELEVEN

The Party: A Look "from Below"

The Diminishing Role of the Rank and File

AN examination of the party organization at its lower levels reveals the phenomena that have contributed to the weakening of the party's control of economic and social processes. A crucial problem has been the diminishing role of the rank and file, and signs of crises in this domain. Lower party apparatuses too seem to become prone to "a crisis of identity," resulting from an unclear definition of their basic functions, their exact role *vis-à-vis* other administrations and social groups. Consequently, their capacity to do the job is not without its problems.

The rank and file, the basic party cells in factories, offices, and institutions, clearly have become a problem for the leadership. Usually, the ordinary citizen party member has been asked no more than "to behave"—to work zealously, to be a model to his coworkers, to be disciplined, and to induce others to do the same. He has also been asked to present criticisms and proposals for improvement of whatever drawbacks he has seen, but insuperable barriers often have been raised against his exercising such critical and creative functions. At best, his criticisms could be directed officially only against marginal phenomena, because the party has asked for criticism only to expose defects in the implementation of plans, not in the plans themselves, so that such criticism may be turned exclusively against nonpolitical officials. The party simultaneously has erected barriers against more effective and broader criticism. The critique the party is teaching should be "businesslike"; in other words, "constructive" proposals should be made without examination of principles and of the basic power structure. Otherwise the critic may risk being accused of "malicious faultfinding" (*zlobnoe kritikanstvo*). He has to beware of making generalizations, especially of venturing into independent evaluations of past or present party lines, because he either can easily become guilty of a "nihilistic attitude toward the history of Soviet society"or can slide into a sinful "maligning of everything and everybody" (*okhaivanie vsego i vsia*). There are convenient derogatory slots of this kind prepared for every possible seriously critical manifestation.

Some party members eventually propose some small-scale improvements or attack some unbearably inefficient bureaucrats, provided they are not too powerful. But, the power exercised by the administrations of factories is considerable. It is well shielded not only by the principle of "one-man rule" and the toothlessness of trade unions and workers' assemblies, but also by the fact that the managers, who are members of the same primary party organization as the workers, are at the same time their bosses. A very different situation must be created in Soviet administrations to enable a worker to criticize openly the bosses on whose goodwill his promotion, salary, and sometimes even his employment, depend. The phenomenon of "suppression of criticism" (*zazhim kritiki*) in party organizations, not only in primary organizations but also in larger units, is widespread and well documented by Soviet sources although they never engage in analysis of it. But the reasons for this timidity are obvious: the administrations have privileges and power, local and higher party *apparatchiki* support them, the rank and file in the party are too weak and they can only complain and wait for justice to be dispensed from above. They have no power to take things into their own hands.

The party cells, where the members debate how to fulfill their obligations, find themselves under heavy pressures of contradictory demands and tendencies. On paper, they are

279

supposed "to supervise the administrations" and to mobilize party members and the masses for the implementation of plans. However, it is quite obvious that they are not in a position to "supervise" because, in fact, they are asked simultaneously to support the administrations they are supposed to "supervise," to strengthen their authority, and to help them fulfill those plans by disciplining the workers. And this happens to be their real task. Furthermore, the directors of enterprises and offices are not only running the operation but also hold positions in party committees. At best, the secretary of the party cell is a junior specialist with little professional prestige and knowledge of the state of the enterprise, and his real function consists in helping the administration to fulfill the plans on which all premiums and advantages depend, including his own. In most cases, the secretaries become merely *tolkachi* who help the management to get resources or easier plans. Some may be more or less influential with higher party organs, and occasionally help in ousting a weak director. On the whole, they drift together with the administration. The proofs thereof are irrefutable: the presence of a party cell in every factory does not prevent management from hiding resources from higher authorities or from engaging in numerous semilegal or illegal practices; the secretary knows of these practices, but he would become unpopular if he were to hinder the practices that help obtain easier plans and better bonuses.

If cell secretaries are unable to exercise control over administrations, the rank and file's ability "to supervise" them is even more of a myth. Party members are asked to be diligent, to observe everybody's behavior, and to execute orders and policies in which they have no say. The activity of the cell, although sometimes "hectic," is absorbed in trivia. Since policies are defined at higher levels, the local party's prerogatives are unclear, weak, and formal; it may have difficulties in determining what exactly has to be done and how.

A document of the Byelorussian Central Committee states that the cells fail either to supervise the administrations or to organize the masses, as they have been asked to; they tend to neglect educating and guiding youth and *Komsomol* members, and trade unions. Or, alternatively, they forget the specialists, technicians, and administrative personnel. Severely criticized for poor results in the work of their institution, for lack of discipline, for sluggish performance, the committees veer from one extreme to the other; they tend either to engage in a wave of disciplinary measures, distributing fines and reprimands, or to slide into an "irresponsible liberalism and *laissez-faire.*"[1]

Swings of the pendulum from overmeddling to "liberal" undercontrolling have become a constant feature of the party's working style. The lower echelons of the party have been hard pressed from above to perform ill-defined, impossible tasks, and they have lacked the power to execute them. Administrations and technicians have been assigned and given power to do their job. Workers supervised by these administrations have tried to defend themselves from too much pressure, and the party cell has become a buffer between the two. In the last analysis, its function has consisted of trying to discipline workers and to help administrations.[2] Such a role is meaningless to ordinary members; there are other organizations that are better prepared to

[1] *Partiinaia Zhizn'*, no. 7 (April 1970), p. 41—but there are many sources on such phenomena.

[2] We still hear from the Soviet press that many factory administrators prefer to use a style of relations with subordinates that is characterized by rudeness, bullying, and shouting. This style is termed "tough leadership" (*zhëstkoe rukovodstvo*), and is still widespread, though it probably has been undergoing a considerable process of "softening." The party officially does not approve of it; this illuminates the thesis of this book: had party cells really controlled and educated the administrators, as it is claimed, such "style" and rude attitude toward workers could not be maintained over a long period of time. But it was because party cells followed, rather than controlled, the administrators—which was no secret to the central leadership. The primitive harshness of the administrators has been disappearing in the Soviet Union because of rising education standards of workers and the growing sophistication of managers, not because of the "supervision" by cells.

deal with activities of a technical and professional character, which the cells are constantly asked to consider, and
disciplining others and themselves is certainly not their main
worry. Other agencies exist for doing this job.

Agenda of the party cell in the Moscow Regional Soviet
—the important local government in the region that in-
cludes the capital—indicate the formal functions of such a
cell. The Central Committee has recently accused party
members of lacking or of having lost the necessary intransigence toward defects, so cell meetings now tried to deal
with them more efficiently, for example, with the low output
of the factories over which the executive committee
(*ispolkom*) presides; or the deficiencies in the style of work
of Soviet officials, especially their neglect of complaints
from the public (an old theme, incidentally, which thousands of meetings in thousands of cells never extirpated).

A typical agenda of the party members of the regional
executive committee (*oblispolkom*) was entitled: "The
Work of Communist Party Members in the Apparatus of
the Moscow Regional Executive Committee in Controlling
How Decisions of Higher Organs and of the Executive
Committee Are Being Carried Out." Such an agenda is in
itself revealing the subordinate role of the party member
in the general bureaucratic machinery. Another had the
title: "The Role of Party Members in the Apparatus of
the Moscow Regional Executive Committee in Organizing
the Improvement of the Quality of Goods Produced by the
Local Industry"—the members of this organization probably
have already heard and discussed this theme *ad nauseam*.

Other concerns of a party cell included "some results of
the economic reform in industrial enterprises subordinate
to the executive committee of the Moscow Regional Soviet,
and problems of Communist Party organization."

Not only are such topics typical, but also typical is the
explanation why this or that topic, notably the last one,
should be put on the agenda: the trouble is, says one document, that "some communists"—a euphemism in Soviet

282

terminology for "very many communists"—"perform but weakly the control of how decisions are carried out."[3]

Consequently, the party press is continuously complaining about two other widespread phenomena. First, the decisions of such meetings are purely formal and produce no results whatsoever; they are phrased in rather general terms or deal with technicalities that are of no concern to the cell. But the highest party organs have never admitted that the cell has been asked to do an impossible job, and the cells, therefore, could not be blamed for such failings.

Second, the leadership has been alarmed about the general apathy and boredom that party life and cell meetings have generated. It is not surprising. Outside the professional party apparatus, members have had little influence on policy, and the cell has become a place where workers and technicians chatter and speechify—such are the reactions of members themselves outside the professional party apparatus. The rank-and-file member is not allowed to engage in any deep analysis, economic or any other, of the enterprise, not only because he has been inadequately prepared for it but also because he has not been asked to do so. He also cannot afford to attack his superiors (*nachal'stvo*), because he knows from observation and personal experience that this can cause him trouble.

The rank and file inside the party, therefore, have behaved exactly like most of the members of their class (workers, low- and high-level officials), as general currents in Soviet life have attested. In economic activity or other spheres, the behavior of simple party members does not seem to be at all different from that of others. If Soviet life has bred masses of self-seeking individuals who strive "to get things" by any means, engage in drinking, or succumb to "Western influences," the party membership and hierarchy have not been immune to such sins. All these "pilferers," "merchants," or "embezzlers," ready to steal and to enjoy life on the cheap at the expense of the community and

[3] *Partiinaia Zhizn'*, no. 2 (1970), p. 93.

whom the press never stops denouncing, are present inside the party and include among them holders of important party jobs, although there is no way of knowing without reliable statistics whether such phenomena occur inside the party at the same ratio as in the general population.

The party has been helpless in dealing with the political apathy of its rank and file. Without substantive changes in the character of the party, the indifference and boredom plaguing party meetings cannot be remedied. The party has made a variety of proposals to enhance its "attractiveness," but it has exhibited the naïveté of an organization that is drowning in its own formalistic routines and that cannot sense their absurdity. For example, a party cell in one ministry tried to enliven its meetings with discussions of "theoretical" topics, which were supposedly "deeper" than those normally dealt with in this particular ministry. Thus, one meeting was devoted to the "lively" theme about "Lenin on the importance of competition in the building of communism," to which party members first objected because they had never dealt with such issues before, but finally the meeting was reported as having been successful,[4] which we very much doubt.

The Lower Apparatchiki

In examining some of the problems of larger party organizations and their apparatuses on the district, city, and regional levels, the predominance of the professional party apparatus and the lack of influence of the unpaid, voluntary, and elective members of the party committees of different echelons is quite apparent. The rather numerous so-called elected activists, even members of district and regional committees, have not counted for very much either in their own eyes or in the eyes of those whom they visit when doing their party assignments. One such activist frankly stated in a party journal that nobody has taken them seriously. Only the *shtatnye*, the full-time party offi-

[4] *Ibid.*, no. 3 (1970), pp. 75–76.

cials, have been taken seriously.[5] Thus, a general tendency in the organization is confirmed: power has been so unevenly distributed that only the real powerholders "count"; the others—masses and activists alike—have become an inferior category.

Undoubtedly the party apparatus is both powerful and quite active. However, its internal processes have tended to give real and meaningful decision-making capacity only to key sections and have left to the rest of the machinery the rather menial task of execution. This has crippling effects on the morale and activity of large parts of the party apparatus itself, especially on the lower levels. The lack of clearly defined functions and serious prerogatives, evident in the activity of the lowest cells, has been a problem for higher echelons as well. Not only the decisions of party cells but also the action of district party committees (*raikomy*) and regional party committees (*obkomy*) suffer from formalism and irrelevance. The central party press has never stopped demanding that these echelons acquire the "real Leninist style" and that they improve the quality of their work. Such officials have been drowned in details (*tekuchka*), have indulged in chatter (*zasedatel'skaia sueta*), and have applied "the pump" (*nakachka*) more often than not in solving their problems. This last method consists of calling the persons involved into the secretary's office for a personal interview or for a special meeting and to "pump" them with orders, warnings, threats, and exhortations. Many decisions of conferences and meetings have resulted in stern exhortations but very general and empty resolutions—which have sought "to demand the extirpation" (*potrebovat' iskoreneniia*) of defects, "to eliminate immediately" (*nemedlenno ustranit'*) deficiencies, "to launch on a large scale" (*shiroko razvernut'*) some activity, or even less explicitly, "to point to certain drawbacks" (*ukazat' na nekotorye nedostatki*) to those responsible, without out saying which drawbacks are meant. Repeating ver-

[5] G. Pavlov, *Kommunist*, no. 17 (1969).

batim the terms used by the Central Committee, these resolutions have urged officials "to raise the masses," "to
strengthen controls," and, "to reinforce exactness."

If all these decisions made sense, the Soviet Union would
have been not only a superpower, as it already is, but also
the most efficient country on earth. In too many cases these
dicta have been no more than routine orders and have not
produced the results desired by the party leadership.

A typical case of party involvement in solving production
problems may be seen in the following example. Worried
by the agricultural situation in its district, the local party
committee decided that milk production should rise. But it
fell. The higher party boss, quoting this fact, charged that
it was the customary lack of "control of execution of decisions," very common in the party, that accounted for such
results. And he offered his opinion on what should have
been done, which illustrates the *apparatchik*'s capacity for
organization. The *raikom*, says the high official, should have
followed the example of another *raikom*, which, facing the
problem of dropping milk-production in a certain *kolkhoz*,
convened specialists and several outstanding milkmaids
from other, more efficient farms and organized a study trip
to the deficient *kolkhoz*. After meetings and impromptu research, the cause for the deficiency was discovered: the
local milkmaids did not know how to use the milking
mechanism.[6]

Could not such a fact have been spotted and diagnosed
by the *kolkhoz* chairman, the party cell secretary, or the
agricultural services of the *raikom*? It is not known. However, it was proposed that the powerful intervention of the
raikom secretary was needed. This was how the secretary
had been advised to act in order to solve such problems.

Considerable evidence can be adduced to show that
much of the party apparatus is inefficient, weak, and poorly

[6] K. Fomichenko, in *Pravda*, 23 March 1970. He was the head of
the organization and instruction department of the Cheliabinsk Regional Party Committee.

organized. The Central Committee has constantly harassed the lower echelons, has admonished them to do their jobs better, and has claimed that its own organization is exemplary and should be taken as a model. While it could be granted that the organization of the Central Committee is superior, it has also been claimed that the whole party apparatus, as a result of recruiting specialists with university training, has become more effective. Still, an "organizational problem" is never simply a problem of organization or educational level, however important these factors may be. The definition of the functions, the conditions created or missing, for doing a job, and the meaningfulness and relevance of the task are indispensable preconditions for activity. In an article on party work in *Pravda*, a high-ranking party organizer has written about these problems and has offered his solutions. He dealt with the so-called instructors who are sent to visit and observe work methods, to gather information, and to help local organizations to improve things; they are the most numerous category on every level of the party apparatus.

Unfortunately, a survey undertaken by sociologists in several party organizations disclosed that these key officials of the machinery tended to waste 70 percent of their time at their desks in their offices, filling out forms and writing numerous reports and memoranda, whereas only 30 percent of their time was devoted to observation and inspection. The *Pravda* article described an *obkom* instructor who visited a factory, talked to the local secretary, and made decisions about production methods. A year later, another instructor, unaware of the previous inspection and recommendations because of poor record keeping, found the same defects and decided upon a new set of measures to be executed by the local secretary. There was no way for him to know what had been found and decided upon a year earlier. Thus, a year had been wasted—nothing had been done.

This could have been interpreted as the inefficiency of a subordinate in contrast to the efficiency of a highly placed

287

important critic. Unfortunately, the proposals of the critic would raise doubts about his ability. In order to avoid the obvious nonsense, he proposed that there be a diary in the places visited and in the party office from which the inspectors are sent. It seems remarkable that no other way of knowing who is doing what has yet been discovered in the *obkom* of a great industrial region of the Soviet Union![7]

The weak performance and unimpressive style of the party apparatuses have been well known to many people working in other apparatuses and have long been a source of derision. The same well-informed source has admitted it openly. In proposing his "revolutionary" suggestion of diaries, he attacked "opinions . . . about the boundlessness and accountlessness of the party apparatus."

The question of the essence of party activity, its exact role and methods, as they have been performed not only by unpaid activists but also by paid personnel, has often been raised and has revealed a malaise within some sections of the party apparatus. Criticism of the party and its membership from the outside has paralleled the doubts and signs of malaise inside. A deputy member of the Politbureau would not have found it necessary to deal with such problems at a party Congress had not such questions become widespread and disquieting. For him the trouble consisted of a "loss of party spirit" (*partiinost'*) among some party cadres. To judge from his speech, certain cadres felt that their jobs lacked meaning, especially in contrast to those of specialists working in other administrations: "it must always be realized that party work is not a spare-time occupation but a profession, more—it is a great art. Unfortunately, some people have lately begun to forget this."[8]

Undoubtedly, leadership functions, on the central and on the local levels, are highly complicated political ones, and

[7] *Ibid.*

[8] V. Mzhavanadze, speaking to the Twenty-Third Party Congress, *23-ii S'ezd KPSS stenotchet*, pp. 185–186.

demand experience and know-how. But this concerns only a small number of the leading cadres. At the same time, many executive functions are strictly bureaucratic supervisory jobs; even on a high level, such jobs seem to many party officials less prestigious than those of the specialists whom they supposedly supervise or instruct. Eventually, such specialists begin to feel that their party counterparts are inferior. Mzhavanadze tried to explain to all those party cadres who were not sure whether their jobs were important that the party methods differ from the ones applied by Soviet and economic agencies (the professional bodies dealing directly with the real jobs). "It is important for the party man to be a specialist in some branch of the economy, but . . . party spirit in the management of the economy means, above all, strengthening all political, organizational work among the masses."[9]

What does this mean? Propagation of policies, but not participation in decision making and policy formation? Supervision of the lesser fish, especially the "masses" and rank and file, but not of those who hold responsible jobs and have the capacity to perform them? If this is so, how interesting will the lower level party jobs look and how attractive will they be to able, creative, ambitious people?

The above observations point to certain tendencies in the party, some of which are already operative and others which are still in the making and will be felt in the long run; they follow from tensions arising from the social milieu and from the party's inner structure and self-image. The distribution of power and the bureaucratic character of the whole organization, in which the party membership is no more than an accessory to key sectors of the apparatus, is the crux of the problem. It contributes to an atrophy of the role of the rank and file and produces questions and doubts about the nature of the party job and the role of the whole organiza-

[9] *Ibid.*

tion as it is presently conceived. The prestige of party membership in the estimation of the Soviet population at large does not seem to be high; possession of a membership card may still be cherished by those who want party jobs or who have patriotic motives, but even for the majority of the rank and file inside the party, their membership seems not to be a very significant fact in their personal lives.

This is the organization that is being urged to raise the efficiency of the Soviet economy; to speed up the technological revolution; to help retrain management and technicians; to see to it that new management methods are promptly introduced, that *kolkhozy* spend their money wisely, that resources are efficiently used, and that scientific discoveries are assimilated more quickly into the national economy. Evidently, party secretaries write, as they should, hundreds of articles reporting that they have performed these functions, that they have organized meetings, consultations, and seminars to explain to the party apparatus what computers can do before they meet and inform managers on these problems.

But is the party really the proper agency today to busy itself successfully and meaningfully with this kind of function? Unless the party apparatus, at some stage, becomes what Khrushchev wanted from it, the retraining of managers, the introduction of automated management systems, and so forth is the business of governmental agencies. In any case, what are the millions of rank and file supposed to do in all this? The definition Mzhavanadze gave of the party's function does not include the kind of direct interference in economic problems that the leadership is asking the party to engage in, in order to help win the battle for efficiency and productivity. But when it does interfere, it is not equipped to do so. The dilemmas the party is facing in trying to define its own role in the economic sphere in modern conditions point to the roots of the current and future questioning about what the party is, and what it can and should do.

Arcana Imperii *Revisited*

The outline of changes in the functioning of the system and the party, the description of the current prevailing policies, which may continue for some time yet, and the sketch of selected problems recurring inside the party organization have pointed to accumulating difficulties in coping with new problems. The rigid and narrow-minded return to past slogans that have permeated the current line, the overcautious and unimaginative practical policy proposals, such as those produced by the last Congress, exhibited an overwhelming effort to preserve the *status quo* and to delay or thwart change unless administered in safe and inoffensive increments.

According to some political scientists, it is only the "incremental" approach to change that makes realistic and reasonably efficient policy. But such advice may all too often be fallacious. Some situations may require considerable reforms and "increments" in very massive doses. Systems must be able, when necessary, to rearrange and to restructure themselves, sometimes even so far as to alter their very identity. Delaying important reforms for too long a period may lead to crises. For example, some Soviet economists, such as Fedorenko and Novozhilov, proclaimed that the existing economic situation could be remedied only by introducing, after careful and thorough planning, far-reaching changes throughout the economic system almost at a shake. They may well have been right; procrastination may exact a heavy price from the country in terms of elemental, unpredictable outbursts, switches, and convulsions. But it is precisely the fear of sweeping changes—which is not a Soviet monopoly, of course—that has motivated the worn-out clichés of the post-Prague ideological "counteroffensive."

Although the Soviet system has been faced with internal dissension and has been at a critical juncture for some time, it would be fallacious to assume that the regime is crum-

291

bling. The system and its powerful leadership are apparently at the peak of success; even though one can discern disquieting trends, which work like rust and create menacing cracks. The party's *arcana imperii*, which proved successful in the past, and have not yet been abandoned, became to a large degree counterproductive. The party's situation, then, may be described neither as comfortable nor as a failure but, to paraphrase Deutsch, as rather "strained and partly overcommitted,"[10] bound in turn to lead to further tensions, which will force the system to undertake new efforts for reform. The monopoly of information, ideology, and communications, which still are powerful controlling devices, has hindered the modernization of economic and political life and severely thwarted the development of science, culture, and creativity in many spheres, as Sakharov and his comrades have indicated. The ideological straitjacket has proved especially damaging in the sphere of culture, and the imposition of uniformity concocted by party agencies was and continues to be pathologic. In fact, besides hampering the country's culture, ideological controls have never worked properly. Not surprisingly, they proved unable to prevent the development of subcultures, countercultures, opposing creeds, and ideologies, often if only in an inchoate state. The widespread hooligan subcultures, all kinds of "Western" influences, nationalism, xenophobia, religious beliefs, and mysticism—all possible and impossible trends of the past and brand new ones bred by Soviet reality—have continually frustrated the guardians of formalized schemes and have revealed the impotence of dogmas remote from reality and imposed by ideological monopoly. The distaste for *diamat*, the general lack of interest in *Pravda*, and the very common practice of listening to the BBC have been some of the fines the party has paid for adhering to a failing ruling device.

---

[10] K. Deutsch, *The Nerves of Government* (New York, 1966), p. 116. He offered here a general classification of situations and did not deal with any particular system.

Supervision, selection, and control of cadres—epitomized by the practice of *nomenklatura*, another source of the party's power—have also had dysfunctional results, which may turn out to be a growing liability to the country. There has been an unavoidable tendency for the cadres selected by party agencies to suit the taste of these agencies, to favor personality types that the ruling organization prefers, and to exclude others. The losses that this method may entail, in terms of the creativity and overall performance of a system, are incalculable unless the system learns to open the way for a larger variety of talent from a variety of sources. A favorable climate for creativity is created where there is tolerance of criticism and at least some encouragement for originality and open-mindedness toward the new and the unfamiliar; unfortunately, this has not been the preference of the party, which leans heavily toward uniformity, discipline, conformity, and docility.

The usual policy toward cadres and the insistence on the importance of its methods is the basis of a practice that seeks to solve problems by changing personnel, reshuffling, reorganizing, selecting, and sacking—a continuing but often futile, if not actually wasteful, exercise that the system has clearly abused. Such activity replaced thinking and caused a reshuffling of officers and a renaming of offices instead of an attempt to cope with problems. Antonov ridiculed the naïveté of this approach, and today's leaders, it is fair to say, seem to be less prone to use such devices than their predecessors. But the heart of the cadres policy—the *nomenklatura*—is far from having been scrapped.

Turning now to two other organizational tools of the party—the ubiquitous network of cells, present in every nook and cranny of society, and the regulation of the party's social composition—one can discover here too that these clever and efficient control mechanisms have begun to exhibit their limitations. As suggested earlier, the cells are in a state of stagnation, boredom being one of its symptoms.

The regulation of social composition is worthy of brief

293

comment.[11] To preserve its influence and control of society, the party has selected, in certain proportions that have been fixed by the leadership, representatives of all the classes and social groups. The criterion for such regulation has changed in the course of Soviet history from a clearly pro-letarian bias in the revolutionary beginnings to a clear preference for citizens who practice "leading professions" and are therefore able to play leading roles in various social activities. As a result of these policies, the party has taken into its ranks a high proportion of social groups that have been strategically important—scientists, technicians, teachers, artists. At the same time, to avoid too elitist a membership and a rift with the masses, which would cause a loss of influence among workers and peasants, the party endeavored to enroll a high proportion of the latter too. Nevertheless, people engaged in manual work have for some time constituted a minority inside the party, as the preoccupation with those who manage important spheres of life, and with preserving a smoothly functioning system, have pushed the party to care more for those who can lead.

However, in using this device to control and run society, the party unavoidably has reproduced in its ranks, although with a bias in favor of the intelligentsia, the whole structure of society. Inevitably, inside the party tensions could be expected to arise between, on the one hand, the different social groups trying to influence the party with their outlooks and interests and, on the other, the organizations' backbone —the *apparat*—trying to weld all these groups and individuals into disciplined organization men, ready to carry the word of the party to their respective social groups remaining outside the party.

Big organizations generally develop techniques for inspiring loyalty and zeal, and the CPSU has been a consummate master in this domain. Cutting across social groups,

[11] See T. Rigby, *Communist Party Membership in the USSR, 1917–1967* (Princeton, N.J., 1968).

294

classes, and mentalities, conditioning them so as to ensure that their primary loyalties are to the organization, to the exclusion of any other influence, is a very complicated operation. Such welding can work well so long as the organization masters economic and social processes, and preserves enough vigor in doing this. Otherwise, these loyalties will naturally turn to self-interest or group interests rather than to the interests of the particular organization.

The trouble has been that two additional important traits of party rule—its principle of "democratic centralism," which means, in the last analysis, a concentration of power and privilege at the summit of a hierarchically organized machinery, and the persistent claim of this machinery to control and run everything—have bred dysfunctional phenomena that weaken the capacity of the party to absorb the membership conveniently. Thus, a situation arises where the party may have to yield ever more to the differentiated social influences with their sectional outlooks, traditions, and values rather than dominating them. The party's obsessive fight for "monolithism" is in itself proof that keeping its unity and grasp intact has become a strenuous task.

The party's way of running the economy has already been shown to be crucial for the understanding of its internal structure. More than ever, the economy is still the main activity in which its efforts are heavily concentrated. A look at the organizational chart of the secretariat of the Central Committee, in which a majority of its departments are devoted to supervising branches of national economy, offers an additional reminder of this state of affairs. The party presided over the creation of the economic system and was itself deeply marked by the way in which the economy was run. An effort predominantly devoted to economic development transformed the party into a politico-administrative machinery, geared to supervision and intervention in the most direct and detailed way in every sphere of economic life; it reinforced the tendency of the party to keep all other

295

spheres under the most strict supervision, so that they neither impede its main effort nor produce diversionist tendencies.

Hence the party's appetite for supervising and dictating policies to all the important spheres of social activity has forced it to concentrate on controls that devour the best of its energies, often at the expense of other vital functions. It is precisely this appetite, now so vigorously reasserted as being the very essence of party rule and not open "to the slightest nipping" (*maleishee ushchemlenie*) that is the mainspring of the processes undermining the political capabilities of the party. By the very nature of the problems Russia is facing, the factors and forces to be controlled in a body of such scope and complexity grow more quickly than the possibilities of the organization to devise agencies to do the controlling. And, on the other hand, the bigger the effort to supervise, to check, to censor, and to curb, the stronger the factors that work to paralyze the very tools able to do the job. A phenomenon parallel to one in the economy has been operating in the system at large. In the economic field the self-perpetuating, but self-defeating, method of planning and controlling a multitude of details accounted for a situation in which the planning center, as it assumed wider responsibility, had to coordinate more agencies, absorb larger quantities of information, and counteract dysfunctions. Finally, these methods led to the loss of control and resulted in the drift of the economy into unintended and unwanted directions. There was also a subsequent slowing down of performance, which, among other factors, was caused by the jamming of central planning agencies.

The hierarchical bureaucratic structure of the CPSU is plagued by a similar phenomenon. Its thrust to control and to dominate has resulted in a loss of influence, control, and grasp of many fields, especially of the deep structural processes that have been working inexorably to produce elemental outcomes. In other words, its obsession with keeping all the cards in its own hands has made the game difficult. Incidentally, if the leadership has learned quite a bit about economics and technology, it has not learned how to handle complex social problems; there are no departments in the secretariat of the Central Committee to deal with them. . . .

The methods and habits of ruling acquired in the economic sphere have proved unsuitable for culture and other important areas of society; but allowing these areas to be managed in different ways, according to different principles, poses a threat to the unity of the controlling agency. A multitude of problems could have been solved if social groups, associations, and organizations had been permitted to take the initiative without the party's indispensable approval. Therefore, the party, facing accumulating backlogs of problems, has found that coordination has become ever more complex. Many problems cannot be handled by imposing uniformity when variety is indispensable or by imposing submission or discipline when a larger scope for initiative and action is the answer. In a situation where leaders feel that the accumulation of such actions may easily get out of hand, they more and more suspect any uncontrolled initiative. In such circumstances, imbalances in society cannot be tackled efficiently, especially since the party's social theories were, and still are, ridiculously inadequate to see clearly what is happening. Dealing with conflict and diversity, two main traits of a modern polity, has been difficult for an agency geared, one would say viscerally, to imposing uniform, easily manageable patterns. Had the party been ready to genuinely invent multiple forms of action and diversify its policies to suit the particular areas and milieus, it would have been a very different organization indeed. Unfortunately, the obsessive fear of "spontaneity" and the fervor to control society demand that the party—or rather the current ruling conservatives—

deny freedoms, censor publications, and hamper rather than release forces, or encourage initiatives, which can thrive only in the climate of tolerance and independence.

As long as this pattern continues, the internal self-propelling quest for ever more domination of the apparatus over the whole party and system and for the concentration of all power at the top, will continue. The self-defeating tendencies in this pattern are by now too obvious; to control a society and to instill it with values and behavior patterns wanted by the center, a huge party with a mass of rank and file membership, is an absolute must. But denying that rank and file, as well as the major sections of the apparatus itself, an independent role and meaningful participation in decision making, and asking them primarily "to behave" and to engage in executing details of policies as they come down from above do, in the long run, result in growing indifference and apathy among the membership.

With an indifferent and passive rank and file, the method of regulating the party's social composition by enrolling individuals from every social class who would become party emissaries to their respective social milieu has become less powerful and less effective. Instead of being a bearer of party images toward the outside, such a membership becomes a soft boundary between party and society through which society can press the party more than the party can counteract. Under these conditions, the mini-society within the party becomes more an agent of the environment inside than the party's agent outside.

Hence, the party's defense will tend to center around the apparatus alone; but the trends described above will assail this rampart ever more strongly and will cause additional erosion and division.

The power pattern that the party has been forced to perpetuate as long as it has been loath to relinquish any authority and begin to delegate responsibility will continue to contribute to the political underdevelopment of the party membership and of the citizenry at large without arresting the processes which are corroding the power and vigor of centralized authority. Already the homogeneous, monolithic unity of society, the party, or the entire apparatus has become an illusion. Behind the façade of a unanimous vote of a party congress some 4,000 strong, with members raising their hands as one man on every issue put to their vote, reality will continue to escape the party's grip; and the party will be pressed ever harder to yield to the dreaded "spontaneity." The numerous small, diffused, uncontrolled, and unwanted streams producing corrosive influences have been getting stronger; but bold political initiatives, programs for action, exciting new goals, and methods for conscious, rational change have failed to appear. Instead, fear of change has been the manifest mood—an ominous sign for any system. As the heavy crust of routines and *status quo* forces preserve more and more of the same, the malformations will continue unabated. If this analysis is correct, more conflict and even considerable tremors can be expected to haunt Soviet political life in the coming years.

CHAPTER TWELVE

The Inspiration of the "1920s"

IN this book the interpretation of the problems and topics raised in the economic debates by reformists and critical economists has centered on the historical aspects and meaning of these debates, and on the political aspects and ideas they contain. These two are interrelated in many ways, in particular because the term "historical" has been defined in two ways. The debates relate to history because they have raised some problems concerning past events and proffer opinions, openly or guardedly, about past controversies. But what concerns the past does not lie entirely within it, and much that was unresolved in previous decades remains on the agenda in the present. Thus, the debates have been historical since they have dealt with major themes that have recurred throughout the recent Soviet past and present, sometimes subsiding and going underground, at other times flaring up with considerable vigor, even fury, when political circumstances have made it possible. These historical themes are part of the current political scene; they can rally forces and form camps and are therefore potentially explosive. It is now possible to clarify how the historical debate is part of present politics.

A comparison of opinions and programs just prior to the first Five-Year Plan with those that have emerged recently, should begin by pointing out the difference in stages of development, particularly in the field of economics, in which the country found itself then and now. A predominantly peasant country with a backward agriculture, though endowed with a quite modern but small urban industrial sec-

300

tor, was seeking during the 1920s the way to industrialization and to modernization. This was crucial to the survival of the new regime, which felt insecure with regard to its own internal social basis and quite sure of the inevitability of a future clash with its highly developed and hostile neighbors.

Some forty years later, the problem is no longer how to industrialize but how to run an industrial giant. Security, on the internal social front and in the international environment, changed entirely in character. The hostile and obsessively experienced encirclement no longer exists, and Russia has become a superpower that cannot be seriously threatened, at least not in the immediate future.

Internally, there can no longer be any more talk, as was maintained previously, of hostile capitalist classes, a predominant ocean of petit bourgeois peasantry or kulaks and NEPmen ready to join forces with agents of subversion or direct foreign intervention. All these have disappeared, at least from the point of view of a rational analysis, although some people inculcated with views prevailing in the former situation still refuse to accept the facts.

Talent and cadres for the industrial establishment are today available or can be produced and directed into the areas in need of them, especially since the country has become urbanized and has a highly developed educational establishment and an impressive army of scholars and educators. The problems in this field are far from solved, but the state is no longer as desperately short of cadres as in the late 1920s.

Also, the technological level, the complexity of problems, and the scale of the economy of today bear little resemblance to the relatively small industrial establishment at the end of the NEP. The tools at the disposal of today's professionals, the sophistication of their economico-mathematical arsenal, is such that problems can be raised and solved, coefficients and aggregates measured, and trends followed

301

and extrapolated with a precision that was not available to the economists and politicians of the 1920s. Although it would be possible to list many more differences between the two periods, it is sufficient to say that we are clearly dealing with two different stages of historical development.

Nevertheless, it is also striking how considerable is the similarity (even straight identity of terms) of problems and concepts as they were debated during the NEP and in the 1960s. The resemblance is particularly pronounced with regard to the ideological contest just before the "big drive"; to many large and impersonal aspects inherent in the social and political setting that obtained in the NEP environment; and, more specifically, to the program of the right-wing leaders, especially Bukharin, who opposed the Stalinist conception and vision of the future.

What has happened recently was not learned directly from any particular person in the past. It was an independent discovery, a coincidence, of which a few of the older and more experienced personalities might have been fully aware but others did not see, and some did not (and still do not) care for the possible continuities with long-forgotten and seemingly irrelevant people from the past. However, coincidence opened the way to a growing awareness of such historical antecedents—of examples, models, inspirations, and personalities of the 1920s who might have been right and suffered for it.

This last personal-political point has been the most difficult to make in the Soviet Union for obvious reasons, although at a certain moment under Khrushchev significant "rehabilitations" seemed near. Abroad, to begin with, Imre Nagy was known to have declared privately that he was a "Bukharinite."[1] In the early 1960s, for the first time Polish economists discussed frankly and sympathetically the debates of the 1920s and came to new conclusions about the

[1] F. Fejto, *Histoire des Democraties Populaires. Après Staline* (Paris, 1969), p. 507.

positive contribution and the validity of Bukharin's ideas, explicitly citing the importance of his "Notes of an Economist."[2] In the Soviet Union Khrushchev was contemplating the official rehabilitation of Bukharin, and an important official, P. N. Pospelov, told a conference of Soviet historians in 1962 that "neither Bukharin nor Rykov, of course, were spies or terrorists,"[3] thus momentarily leaving open the question of what they actually were.

Yet there has been no official rehabilitation. But any such rehabilitation, or even the explicit mention of names, is of secondary importance (although not a matter of indifference) in the face of the remarkable reappearance of ideas, concepts, and terms as they were used in the old controversy and, in particular, by Bukharin and his associates, without names being mentioned.

Many pages could be filled with quotations from contemporary writers—mainly economists, some of them architects of the reforms, or at least of the revival of Soviet economics —who prove that arguments, injunctions, and, most important, the theses of "Notes of an Economist," "this muddled anti-party document" as Stalin castigated it, has been taken up or repeated almost verbatim.

Author after author has criticized harshly "the enticement with supertempos," one of the main bones of contention between Bukharin and Stalin, which, they added, has cost the economy so dearly. Others clamored against planning without preparing the necessary resources, as Bukharin had spoken out against planning "without bricks,"— a theme to which Khrushchev, among others, often returned. The relation between agriculture and industry in

[2] See E. Temkin, *Karola Marksa Obraz Gospodarki Komunistycznej* (Warsaw, 1962), pp. 277–278; Cz. Bobrowski, *U Zródeł Planowania Socjalistycznego* (Warsaw, 1967), p. 118; and W. Brus, *Ogólne Problemy Funkcjonowania Gospodarki Socjalistycznej* (Warsaw, 1964), pp. 78–110.

[3] Quoted in R. Tucker and S. Cohen, eds., *The Great Purge Trial* (New York, 1965), p. xxvi.

the process of industrialization has often been treated today in Bukharinian terms. Many have condemned the failure to allocate resources in the correct proportions between these two branches of the economy in order to achieve a healthy economic growth rate. Bukharin's advice not to move too fast regardless of resources and to constitute reserves as an indispensable lubricant for ensuring a smooth functioning of the economy and a steady growth have been repeated, and the neglect of this prescription in the past has been scathingly condemned.

Especially noticeable is the scarcely veiled endorsement by several modern authorities of the industrialization strategy recommended by Bukharin against Stalin's plans in 1927–1928. Efimov and Kirichenko have expressed their interest in, and preference for, the discarded approach by praising highly and by appealing to study the decisions of the Fifteenth Congress on matters of industrialization, which were and still are for them valid strategy. They praised the approach for being free of fetishes about the superiority of production means (sector A) over consumer goods (sector B); for having recommended long-run growth, not just maximum tempos; for having warned correctly that a different course would result in dwindling growth rates; for having proposed adequate growth for light industry and agriculture; and for having warned against maximum pumping of funds from agriculture to industry. The legacy of the Fifteenth Congress seemed the more valuable to the authors because it represented a sum of experience accumulated through ten years of planning and economic policy, and because of the sound "Leninist principles" in economic policy, such as "widespread use of market and market categories, putting into practice genuine cooperative principles in different forms," that the congress endorsed. The authors quoted the appropriate resolution of the congress, including a warning against freezing resources on an overextended front for industrial building sites.[4] These were familiar theses of Bukharin, Rykov, and Tomsky, which later were repeated in "Notes of an Economist" and during bitter infighting with Stalin's majority in the Politbureau and in sessions of the Central Committee's Plenum.

Another economist, V. S. Dadaian has also seen in the same resolution an example of an "optimal approach," and has underlined the following passage: "As far as correlation between *production* and *consumption* is concerned it is indispensable to bear in mind, that it is not permissible to seek simultaneously a maximum figure for the former and the latter . . . [nor is it permissible] to depart from . . . neither the unilateral *interest in accumulation* . . . nor . . . the unilateral *interest in consumption*. . . . In view of the fact that in the long term these interests, on the whole, coincide, it is indispensable to depart from an optimal combination of both aspects."

Novozhilov, too, has praised the same decisions, not only for correctly posing the problems but also for proposing the general direction in which correct solutions can be found. All have underlined the validity and modernity of these decisions.[5]

Yet these decisions represented the line that the majority on the Politbureau soon abandoned, leaving Bukharin, Rykov, and Tomsky to defend it as "a right-wing platform." Even if unintentionally, the problem of attitude toward "Notes of an Economist" is raised, and in fact the whole pattern or industrialization adopted against the advice of those judicious, optimal, and balanced views of the Fifteenth Congress is thus questioned, obliquely but quite transparently.

[4] A. Efimov and K. Kirichenko, in A. Efimov, ed., *Ekonomicheskoe Planirovanie v SSSR* (Moscow, 1967), chap. 4, pp. 112–114.

[5] V. Novozhilov, *Problemy Izmereniia Zatrat i Rezul'tatov pri Optimal'nom Planirovanii* (Moscow, 1967), pp. 22–23; V. Dadaian, *Ekonomicheskie Zakony Sotsializma i Optimal'nye Resheniia* (Moscow, 1970), p. 20.

The concomitant problems of market mechanisms, the methods and essence of planning, were rephrased in language similar to that of the condemned schools. The re-adoption of the concepts of market categories, the emphasis on the importance of pricing, attacks against those who were possessed by "a semi-*muzhik* fear of markets," numerous critiques of the unjustified neglect of money-and-commodity categories, which played havoc with the economy—all such conceptions, some accepted today quite officially, were rehabilitated, and views once fiercely persecuted as dangerous deviations were vindicated. But preserving markets and relying on market relations, particularly with regard to peasants, were also part of the same program of the opposition.

Bukharin's views on balanced growth and the postulate of proportionality in planning have become central themes in both the reformist thinking and the official line. The borrowing has not been acknowledged, and Nemchinov, who otherwise fought for such concepts without inhibitions, preferred, whenever possible, to borrow from other sources. "'The planning principle means proportionality consciously maintained,'" emphasized Nemchinov, using a quotation from Lenin. In this way a politically awkward situation has been avoided, and a host of economists and mathematicians can escape charges of heresy and yet promote one of their central theses, which they have seen as indispensable for mending the dysfunctions in the economy and correcting the numerous disproportions.

Nemchinov was one of the first to repeat in 1964—with hindsight afforded by bitter experience—the warning of Bukharin that thoughtless voluntaristic planning might cause no less chaos than capitalist anarchy. Others followed later. The old controversy on proportionality is back too, like, e.g., in the clash between two economists, one of them, Kronrod, contending that "society may, in certain circumstances, decide intentionally to maintain certain disproportions," the other, Shkredov, categorically rejecting it: "A plan which is assuming in advance disproportions cannot offer a genuine guidance to practical activity."[6]

The acceptance of the concepts of balanced growth and the role of markets vindicated not only Bukharin but also some brilliant economists, not members of the party, who wrote extensively during the 1920s, such as Groman, Bazarov, Flerovsky, and Yurovsky. They have to be acknowledged too as legitimate forerunners of modern thinking. Bazarov had given the following advice to the planner: "The national economy must be conceived of as a coordinated organic whole, a system of dynamic equilibrium with a maximum of stability, not only in the process of implementing the work of reconstruction, prepared by the general plan, but also at any single moment during the transition."[7] It seems plausible to assume that the best people in the Gosplan today know the work of this outstanding economist and planner, one of the best minds Gosplan ever had. This is the conclusion one reaches when seeing a competent planner quoting Bazarov in 1970 at long last in a matter-of-fact way, without the slightest malignity, on the important issue of cyclicity in planned economies.[8] Perhaps Yurovsky, too, who correctly maintained that the Soviet economy should be seen as "a special system of commodity relations" and who was the first to propose that the capitalist market economy was not the last market economy in history, will have his reputation restored. He prudently added that while classifications of this kind needed a longer historical experience, the existence of "a form of socialist market" had to be envisaged.[9]

---

[6] Both quoted in V. Shkredov, *Ekonomika i Pravo* (Moscow, 1967), pp. 72–73.

[7] V. Bazarov, "O Metodakh Postroeniia Perspektivnykh Planov," *Planovoe Khoziaistvo*, no. 7 (1926), p. 11.

[8] V. Krasovskii, in A. Notkin, ed., *Faktory Ekonomicheskogo Razvitiia SSSR* (Moscow, 1970), chap. 3, p. 80.

[9] L. Iurovskii, "K Probleme Plana i Ravnovesiia v Sovetskoi Gosudarstvennoi Sisteme," *Vestnik Finansov*, no. 12 (1926), p. 17.

Bukharin did not speak of "socialist" markets, but he was close enough to this school of economists to incorporate their and his own ideas into his program for controlled change and industrialization. In using equilibrium concepts and a systems approach already in his civil war writings, he was a genuine pioneer among Soviet Marxists.[10] He did not want "to skip stages," and favored the use of market categories as a way of running a planned economy for the historical period ahead. He even, as we have stressed, called for a combination of the plan with an anticipated impact of the market spontaneity—his own version of today's "plan and market" or "plan and *khozraschët*" approach, which helped an important Soviet school of economists to discover the validity of yet another Bukharinist intuition on the limitations of planning and the impossibility of implementing effectively, an all-embracing, overambitious central plan. This new realization, after some decades during which the plan was accepted as a fetish, has now been presented as the precondition for the formulation of a new economic theory of socialism and of socialist planning.[11] The antece-

[10] See *Teoria Istoricheskogo Materializma* (Moscow, 1921), chaps. 5, 6, and 7. Bukharin probably borrowed these ideas from A. Bogdanov. Lenin displayed irritation against anything taken from his former rival on the philosophical arena; he therefore mocked terms like "sociological," "systems," and "structure" (though not necessarily "equilibrium"). All of them today are very popular terms in the Soviet Union. For Lenin's remarks see *Leninskii Sbornik*, 11 (2d ed., Moscow, 1931), 348–403. These are his annotations to Bukharin's *Ekonomika Perekhodnogo Perioda* (Moscow, 1920).

Ideas such as "economic equilibrium" and "balanced growth" were quoted against their authors as proof of criminal intent during the trials in the early 1930s, which destroyed people like Bazarov, Groman, Yurovsky, and dozens of other experts.

[11] Additional examples for the "*plan i rynok*" approach are in A. Katsenelinboigen, I. Lakhman, and Iu. Ovsienko, *Optimal'nost' i Tovarno-Denezhnye Otnoshenia* (Moscow, 1969)—where the title itself expresses the orientation; see also I. Birman, *Metodologiia Optimal'nogo Planirovania* (Moscow, 1971), pp. 78–79, 99–103. For the term "socialist market" (*sotsialisticheskii rynok*), see *ibid.*, p. 99. See also A. Aikhenvald, *Sovetskaia Ekonomika* (Moscow, 1927), for the

dents of this approach in a historically relevant sequence—
Preobrazhensky in one version, and Bukharin in a different
one, quite akin to the spirit of modern reformers—are so
obvious, and the *plan i rynok* views so widely accepted today, that a worried conservative writer who shares these
views tried to mislead his readers by quoting Lenin and
Stalin as his sources. Bukharin has been shown to be the
opponent of it on the basis of a text . . . from 1920.[12] Unfortunately, the fraud, in this as in another point to be discussed, is only proof that some know very well what or
whom they would like to conceal.

The combination of the plan and the market—one of the
postulates of "Notes of an Economist"—was thus another
theme of the 1920s and of Bukharin that was discovered or
rediscovered. Among other themes, the related discussion
on "regulators" was also resumed by no less an authority
than Novozhilov. In his seminal book, he turned his attention to the forgotten debate and with the utmost serious-
ness discussed the problem in the same terms used in that
debate. For Novozhilov the idea of combining two regulators in one system was a very bold one, and he emphasized
that it was found and successfully applied at the beginning
of the NEP. During Stalin's regime, he explained, the idea

main lines of Bukharinist thought in the late 1920s, especially chap.
6, "Plan i Rynok v Sovetskoi Ekonomike" ("Plan and Market in the
Soviet Economy"), p. 229. On p. 289 he argued that plan and market
have to be seen as an entity and then explains, on p. 290, that even
without the existence of the peasant smallholders inside the state
sector money-commodity relations must still prevail. He called them
"socialist commodity relations" (*tovarnosotsialisticheskie otnoshenia*),
which may eventually disappear in full-fledged socialism (which was
too far away in the future to have any impact on the programs for
the day). Aikhenvald also explained Bukharin's "law of labor outlays"—with all the appropriate references to Marx. He was one of
Bukharin's "red professors," and an acknowledged Bukharinite. Bukharin wrote a short preface to this book.

[12] A. Pashkov, "Obshchie Voprosy Ekonomicheskoi Teorii Planirovania," in M. Fedorenko, ed., *Problemy Ekonomicheskoi Nauki i
Praktiki* (Moscow, 1972), pp. 25–26.

prevailed in Soviet thought that such a combination was impossible. But "plan and *khozraschët*" had already been used in Soviet history, and they were successfully combined and "passed the test in the most difficult conditions." Obviously, the two "regulators" were not easily coordinated, and a system could not run with such regulators uncoordinated. Historically, they had worked in the NEP and clashed in the years of industrialization, and their transformation into a combined and unified regulator would be difficult. But this should be the central task of the modern Soviet economy.[13]

Novozhilov's brief treatment reopened the debate and, without naming names, he hinted at the two different versions of the theme in the old debate: the idea of Preobrazhensky that the two factors, the plan and the market, were bound to collide, with the plan overtaking markets and private producers in the long run; and the idea of Bukharin that the two regulators were not and should not be mutually exclusive at all, but should be seen as complementary, and that the results of their interaction should be anticipated by planners.

Bukharin had tried to offer an explanation for the very possibility of such a combination. Behind the internal principle of the planned sector (productivity of labor) and that of the market (law of value) stood "the law of proportional labor outlays," which was common to all stages in historical development but operated through a differently functioning mechanism in each. This was another of the Bukharinist heresies that had later been heavily attacked, although it was based on very long and convincing (for Bukharin's purpose) quotations from Marx's *Capital*.

This "law of proportional labor outlays" also reappeared in the literature, in identical or slightly different terms; authors such as Strumilin and Malyshev came to adhere to it, and attracted much criticism from other, more dogmatic

[13] Novozhilov discusses regulators in his *Problemy Izmerenia*, pp. 28–31. See our summary of this debate in the 1920s in Chapter 4.

sources.[14] Novozhilov, too, although using a different wording, wrote about "the law of economy of labor which [has ruled all] history" but has its own form of expression in every economic system.[15]

In an obvious anti-Novozhilov sortie, a corresponding member of the Academy of Sciences, A. I. Pashkov, a conservative opponent, rejected both Preobrazhensky's "two regulators" and Bukharin's "law of proportional labor outlays" as bourgeois and petit bourgeois inventions; he particularly attacked Bukharin's formula as being some "eternal law of value." For him, characteristically, in opposition to the rejected notions, the Soviet economists should stick "to the Leninist theory on the decisive role of the state of the proletarian dictatorship in constructing a socialist economy."[16]

Thus, the old cleavages have reappeared today, and opposing camps, in many ways, have been formed along ideological lines similar to those of the 1920s. A number of big and small issues for which Bukharin and others stood, and on which they confronted Stalin, came back in identical terms in the form of criticisms of the past and proposals for change. One obvious reason for this is that Bukharin displayed considerable foresight about the course of Stalin's blueprint for industrialization. Many of his predictions were vindicated by events. He was right when he argued against overplanning, overinvestment, "taut planning" without appropriate reserves, the unilateral overexpansion of heavy industries at the expense of light ones and of agriculture and consumption in general. In the same vein, the facts

[14] See I. Malyshev, *Ekonomicheskie Zakony Sotsializma i Planirovanie* (Moscow, 1966), pp. 6–8; cf. A. Bachurin and D. Kondrashev, eds., *Tovarno-Denezhnye Otnosheniia v Period Perekhoda k Kommunizmu* (Moscow, 1963), p. 27, who outlined the debate on this question; E. Temkin, *Karola Marksa Obraz Gospodarki Komunistycznej* (Warsaw, 1962), showed Strumilin resuming Bukharin's "law."

[15] Novozhilov, *Problemy Izmerenia*, pp. 21–22.

[16] Pashkov, "Obshchie Voprosy," pp. 22–23.

of Soviet economic development confirmed his recommendations concerning artisans and small-scale enterprises and his insistence on market relations and pricing as indispensable complementary factors in planning—and the same theses also were argued by numerous modern writers. The statement therefore that some of the central assumptions of much of reformist economic thinking today sounds curiously "Bukharinian" should not astonish anyone.

But this is far from being the whole story. Another phenomenon—the fascination that the NEP period has for many people in different fields of intellectual and political endeavor—provides a more general explanation for the reappearance of old themes, or of new ones in an old garb, or for the resumption of opinions previously held as heretical, but without the names of the heretics.

NEP as Blueprint

The modern reformers have been painstakingly trying to remove many of the shackles of an implacable and powerful state, to force it to shrink, and to let society and the economy breathe more freely. They have been attempting to find a way to allow social and cultural plurality to express itself and flourish and to permit social groups to state their interests and to be able to defend themselves. Obviously, the nostalgic glance cast toward the NEP period in search for arguments and precedents may cause some excessive idealization and distortion of the history of that period. But the reasons for the fascination with this model are obvious and sufficiently warranted by reality. The intelligent Soviet reader and man of letters has been justified in pointing to the rather lively cultural life of the NEP period in contrast to the sterility of the subsequent one. In search of more flexible methods, less voluntaristic and arbitrary interference, an active role for the market, and application of mathematical and other tools of sophisticated planning, the planner naturally and justly has found inspiration in this

312

"golden age," just as the sociologist and other social scientists have extolled beginnings of many social sciences in the 1920s, which were later ruthlessly extirpated. The historian of social thought, culture, or political life can state that during this period—ideologically sanctified by Lenin's approval—there was considerable freedom of ideological and political debate, even within the party; cultural and political currents could exist, social groups could find forms of autonomous expression, legality and forms of due process were respected, and things moved relatively well. Rational political decisions prevailed, and crippling, arbitrary, primitive coercion was absent from the mainstream of society and politics. The observer of current Soviet culture and politics knows that every field or branch of activity, whenever it is experiencing a renaissance after a prolonged slumber, turns immediately to the 1920s for inspiration and for antecedents, even if such are sometimes not readily available. Under the conditions still prevailing in Russia, it is easier to appeal to roots in one's own history than to acknowledge openly one's own barrenness and to borrow from abroad. But in this case the previous stage actually had enough substance to attract attention when the search for a new blueprint was begun.

The NEP has served as a model, and there exists, in fact, a school of economists sometimes called "NEPmen."[17] Lisichkin, who wrote the well-known book *Plan and Market*, stated the problem quite frankly. For him, the NEP—the historical one, with its small peasants and merchants—was indeed a question of the past and rather less important. But there was another side to it, which, in Lenin's mind provided the strategy for a long historical period for the country on its road to communism. Lisichkin does not play with words and does not camouflage his thought in hints

[17] Cf. the conversation A. Werth had in Russia with a Soviet economist well informed on matters in his field, in *Russia—Hopes and Fears* (London, 1969), p. 146.

313

and recondite allusions. For him the NEP method was "the uniquely correct system of economic relations, till such times when full communism is built."[18]

This could plausibly imply that its outlines were still perfectly valid, and that the Stalinist period was only an aberration. The author has not used such sharp terms, but he had said enough to show how and why he disapproved of the "entirely new ways of running the economy"[19] that were installed in the 1930s and that, evidently, were not to his liking.

This text openly praised the NEP and directly condemned the policies of the 1930s, just as Novozhilov eloquently spoke about the bold and successful combination of "plan and *khozraschët*" principles in the NEP.

More important, certain major tasks that confront the country and the methods used to deal with them resemble those of the NEP period. The NEP was introduced at a time when a strongly centralized, militarized state found itself incapable of getting the country to move again without letting social forces recover and without appealing to them to act "from below" and to help instill a new life into the whole system. For this purpose, the state was forced to readapt the whole setting, to make concessions, to restrain itself.

It is in this sense that the resemblance of the past with the current situation and its central problem—as seen at least by Soviet reformers—is striking. Once more, although in different circumstances, in order to make events move more quickly and to lift Russia to a higher stage in its development, social forces must be given more opportunities for deploying their creativity, and the state must recede, adapt, and reform itself. But important differences in historical circumstances have to be stressed once more. First, the country, whatever its problems today, has behind it a long period of peace, and a renewed and strengthened society—in

[18] G. Lisichkin, *Plan i Rynok* (Moscow, 1966), p. 45.
[19] *Ibid.*, p. 48.

contrast to the exhausted and bleeding society of 1920. Second, Lenin's shattered polity has gradually been replaced with a powerful and efficient state; but later the state began showing signs of fatigue whereas the new groups and classes have acquired, however slowly, a self-assurance and a capacity to press it into reforms and transformation.

The recurrence of themes and even the identity of terms used have been particularly striking during transition periods, during the battles for or against the introduction of each of the two blueprints in question. Thus, from 1921 to 1923 the adherents of the NEP, with Lenin's backing, assailed the bureaucratic and administrative methods, dubbed them despisingly "glavkocracy" (*glavkokratiia*)—as it was done officially in the decisions of the Twelfth Party Congress in 1923—and struggled for more autonomy for enterprises, for juridical guarantees of such autonomy, and for granting of property rights to enterprises. The central tenet consisted of the application, on a large scale, of market methods and market categories. Hence, socialist enterprises had to pass the acid test of the market. Thus, autonomy for enterprise went hand in hand with acceptance of "market relations," and pressures for scientific methods, scientific freedom, intellectual freedom, and right to political debate were not far away, awaiting their turn.

The opponents of these methods defended their practices and counterattacked the "marketeers" and "denationalizers" as traitors to the idea of October, who undermined the role of the state and yielded planning to market chaos and to the sway of the elements.

The same themes, but with a diametrically different outcome, reappeared in the early 1930s, with a fierce onslaught on market categories, autonomies, balancing, equilibria, and other "capitalist" devices. This drive was conducted in the name of the superiority of the state, of its highly centralized structure, its planning in physical and natural units and amounted to the reemergence of the *glavkokra-*

315

tiia, or its equivalents. The glorification of state controls and state coercion, now being presented as the socialist principle *par excellence,* was accompanied by the establishment of monolithism in politics and ideology.[20]

An inconclusive interlude, with similar dilemmas and not dissimilar lines of clashing factions, occurred during the years 1933–1934, when efforts were made to end the pressures and to introduce a liberal policy on a large scale. This line has been associated with the ascendance of the "Kirov faction"; during this period, not surprisingly, Bukharin and many other ex-opposition leaders from Left and Right returned to the limelight. With the assassination of Kirov, liberalization was abolished and the centralizing and terroristic drive was resumed with murderous fierceness.

Finally, in the 1960s and 1970s, partisans of "administrative" and "voluntaristic" methods clash with proponents of cost accounting, market categories, scientific and "equilib-

[20] The topic is worth a special comparative study. Some sources can be helpful: S. Bratus', "K Probleme Khoziaistvenno-administrativnogo Prava," *Sovetskoe Gosudarstvo i Pravo,* nos. 11–12 (1930), p. 165, where he attacks two authors who asserted in 1927 that factories should be recognized as "subjects of law" and that their rights should be guaranteed by law. For Bratus' this was a pernicious attempt to undermine the state. Planning, in his view, is aiming at transforming market circulation of commodites into a direct product barter so that the production process comes nearer to and finally merges into a harmonious whole with "socialist distribution." The same Bratus', incidentally, was still professing the same views in the 1960s. Articles by L. Ginzburg, "Sovetskie Predpriiatiia v Period Sotsialisticheskoi Rekonstruktsii," *ibid.,* no. 2 (1930), pp. 90–114, and "O Khozraschete," *Revolutsiia Prava,* nos. 5–6 (1931), pp. 110–134, are a good source for following the significantly similar cleavages as they appeared in 1923 and 1930, as well as the battles of the opposing camps. The return to the same cleavages in the debates of the 1960s can be seen, for example, in the contribution by P. Krylov and M. Petrushin, in Efimov, ed., *Ekonomicheskoe Planirovanie,* chap. 2, p. 57. The two authors praise the decisions of the Twelfth Congress (in 1923) for having preferred "economic manoeuvering on the market" to the "glavkocractic administering" (*glavkokraticheskoe administrirovanie*) of the previous period.

rium" planning, and of freedom of creation and debate. With the appearance of these latter tendencies came a renewed interest in the NEP.

The Quarrel of Two Decades

If the NEP has served as a model for proponents of a mixed "plan and market" economy, their attitude toward the post-NEP era becomes a matter of great controversy for them. Lisichkin has rejected outright "the entirely different" system that followed the "quite natural" one. Some other writers, Novozhilov, for example, have tended to justify as temporarily unavoidable certain policies of the 1930s. A high degree of centralization with the corresponding restriction of market relations seemed to have been warranted by the international situation and by the strains involved in ambitious investment plans. But how much else, besides more centralization in the policies under Stalin would the different debaters be ready to defend in a genuinely free and frank discussion?

The answer is elusive, but almost all the characteristics of the Stalinist industrialization and many of the traits of the system erected under Stalin have been attacked piecemeal. The acerbity of the critique depends on current policies of the party leadership. But unquestionably, critics have severely condemned the destruction of cadres and the stifling of the intellectual life of the country under Stalin. Political economy has been inveighed against as hampering economic development; "supertempos" were attacked as the cause of "the disorganization of economic life."[21] The bulk of agricultural policy, including the impressment of peasants into *kolkhozy* by force and, particularly, the procurement policy that exploited the peasants by taking away the bulk of their produce without adequate payment, received sharp disapproval, as did, though less directly, the derac-

[21] S. Pervushin, V. Venzher, A. Kvasha, et al., *Proizvodstvo, Nakoplenie, Potreblenie* (Moscow, 1965), p. 20.

317

ination of the kulaks, because of this brutal action's trau-
matic results.[22]

Thus, it can be assumed that whenever conditions appear
more propitious for open debate of the Soviet past, the
opinions of numerous Soviet intellectuals about Stalin's
times are and will be highly critical or utterly negative. In
such a case, the role of the oppositions to Stalin, and particularly that of the Right with its program for alternative
policies, are up for reappraisal. Some questions and answers
in regard to crucial points in the old debate can be safely
anticipated. Bukharin's and Rykov's opposition to collectivization will have to be fairly examined. "No collectivization is possible without a certain amount of accumulation
in agriculture, because you cannot get machines for nothing, and you cannot assemble even one tractor from a thous-
and wooden ploughs," said Bukharin in June 1928; and
Rykov simultaneously warned that even with *kolkhozy* the
state would have to trade and to pay them a price, otherwise collectivization would not work.[23]

How would such opinions be evaluated today? Let us
consider the position of Mikoyan, who, in May 1930, referring to the opinions of Bukharin, declared: "How long ago
was it that we heard comrade Bukharin and the whole trio
of deviators declare [in February 1929] that 'the country
suffers from a penury of bread not because of the development of *kolkhozy*, but quite independently of this development. This penury will grow sharper, if we are going to
weld the successes of our policy in the countryside exclusively to the successes of the *Kolkhoz* movements.' " Mikoyan
went on to deride the prophecies that food shortages would
become acute in the near future and then boasted that the

[22] For sources on this trend see, in this book chapter 9, note 8, p.
220.

[23] F. Vaganov, *Pravyi Uklon v VKP(b)i ego Razgrom* (1928–1930)
(Moscow, 1970), p. 114, quotes Bukharin from party archives; and
Rykov's opinion, also from the archives, is in *16-aia Konferentsiia
VKP(b), Stenograficheskii otchet* (Moscow, 1963), p. 812.

THE INSPIRATION OF THE "1920s"

kolkhozy already helped to solve the grain problem in only one year.[24] What would be the choice of modern students when confronted with these two opposed statements?

Similarly, one could ask what would be the answer if researchers were confronted with two opposed opinions of Politbureau members on another crucial topic. In 1930 Kuibyshev claimed that the aim is to "[double] from year to year the investments in capital construction, and [reach] 30 percent of industrial growth each year"; Rykov opposed him, arguing that such talk was "naked arithmetic." Tempos did not have to rise each year; the "curve of investments may even be lowered" when necessary and, in any case, "it is by no means permissible to make a fetish out of tempos."[25]

A very embarrassing situation, even for a quite moderate Soviet historian, could arise if he is asked to make a statement about the following resolution of the Politbureau and the Central Committee passed in 1929: "Bukharin's declaration [in January or February 1929 on Politbureau meetings] that we do not have intraparty democracy, that the party gets 'bureaucratized,' that we institute bureaucratization, that there are no truly elected secretaries in the party . . . that the current regimen inside the party became unbearable, etc. . . . is deeply untrue and utterly false."[26]

But was it both "untrue and false," as the Central Committee reiterated with such outrage? The trouble, of course, is that Bukharin's declaration was exact, and soon results of this regimen would become unbearable for even the majority of the same Central Committee, when the so-called personality cult came to full blossom. Even today the conservative and dogmatic writers have continued to deny the truth

[24] A. Mikoian, *Ekonomicheskaia Zhizn'*, 3 June 1930.

[25] V. Kuibyshev is quoted from *Saratovskaia Partiinaia Organizatsia v Period Nastupleniia Sotsializma po Vsemu Frontu* (Saratov, 1961), p. 155; Rykov quoted in Vaganov, *Pravyi Uklon*, pp. 97–98 (from party archives).

[26] *KPSS v Rezoliutsiiakh i Resheniiakh S'ezdov*, 2 (Moscow, 1957), 561.

319

of Bukharin's assertions and to claim that everything was operating in accordance with the best democratic principles.[27] But then, how was the party transformed overnight into a victim of police terror, if it was "untrue and false" that there was no democracy in the party in 1929 or 1930?

There is only one correct answer to such questions as well as to another one, also quite significant, concerning the two opposing views of the character of capitalism and the role of the state in it. This time the opponent to Bukharin was Kaganovich. Bukharin committed the biggest possible error, Kaganovich thundered, by conceding an important point to social democracy "by admitting, first, the very possibility of an organized capitalism, and by admitting, second, that the imperialist state acquires a directly commanding role in the economy."

According to Kaganovich, who also expressed Stalin's thought, the opposite was true. The capitalist state does not play a leading role in the economy at all, and, moreover, it has even been losing what remains of its independence.[28]

With hindsight, the question of who was right in this controversy has been answered in numerous Soviet texts, which have fully understood that the growing role of the state in economic life in the West (and elsewhere) was one of the most important features of the political and economic reality of the twentieth century. Soviet economists know and today argue that the capitalist states have the ability to "program" many aspects of economic life, even if they have not conceded the term "planning" to them.

On these crucial points, as well as on many others concerning the rights and wrongs of the opposing factions in the party on the eve of the full Stalinist takeover, hindsight and some occasion to talk produced answers entirely different from hitherto accepted dogmas. Certainly, authors today have already clashed, although cautiously or by hints,

[27] Vaganov, *Pravyi Uklon*, p. 268.
[28] L. Kaganovich, "12 Let Stroitel'stva Sovetskogo Gosudarstva," *Revoliutsiia Prava*, no. 1 (1930), p. 15.

and have opted for one side or the other. But hesitations have been characteristic only of those who have endorsed the positions of Stalin's past critics. The ruling conservatives, or even more virulently, the neo-Stalinist trend, which is an extremely dogmatic faction inside the ruling coalition, have not hesitated at all. They have attacked openly and have explicitly used names to press forward their version of history. Only the critics, the objective historians, the party democrats, and the nonparty intellectuals have not been allowed to state their opinions openly. The other side knows the issues well and attacks without inhibitions—so long as power is on their side.

Since the ouster of Khrushchev, official spokesmen have never stopped their campaign on historical issues. They have tried to maintain a monopoly of right answers, because they have been fully aware of the politically explosive character of issues involved in discussing the respective merits and demerits of the anti-Stalinist programs and the light that subsequent events have thrown on the positions taken in that controversy.

The gravity and complexity of problems, which an open debate on these matters would reveal (as events elsewhere in Eastern Europe foreshadowed), have been well understood by conservatives. They have known that the whole edifice erected under Stalin to which they are still committed in many regards—the character of the social structure, the reality of its ideological links with Marxism, the character of its socialism, and the legitimacy of its rulers—could be easily shaken by an impetuous barrage of questions to which the only answer would be force. Such questioning, once intellectuals are allowed to conduct it, could easily spill over to larger groups of citizens with incalculable results for the present leadership.

Nevertheless, despite the difficulty of open debate, such a debate has been conducted by proxy, through various devices that have made its suppression almost impossible. The big, omnipresent, continuous controversy has taken on the

321

curious form of extolling "the 1920s" and criticizing the
1930s either directly, when possible, or by implication; for
example, by praising the decisions of the Fifteenth Congress on industrialization.

The more virulent conservatives comprehend well the
anti-*status quo* potential of the yearnings for the 1920s.
They have reacted sharply and have counterattacked on all
fronts. They defended and idealized the 1930s and the
whole Stalinist period, their main source of inspiration.[29]
Thus, the conservative literary crusaders, trying to stamp
out "pernicious" and "frivolous" trends in the cultural life
of the pre-Stalinist period, castigated the "nihilists" for ig-
noring and calumniating the literary and cultural creativity
of the 1930s and 1940s. They even bluntly demanded from
the "nihilists" recognition of socialist credentials and the
contribution to culture of the notorious Zhdanov decrees.
Such attacks have been especially prevalent in the party's
theoretical organ, *Kommunist*.[30] The official party historians, backed by powerful high authorities—and the appropriate organs of coercion when necessary—launched
venomous attacks against all those who "blackened the soviet past" and besmeared the party. "Blackened" referred
mainly to criticisms of the post-1930 period, which they
rightly considered the crucial formative period for the
existing state-and-party system. In the early 1970s, with

[29] Z. Brzezinski noted in 1964 that the years 1928–1952 are a
source of inspiration for Soviet conservatism. See symposium, D.
Treadgold, ed., *The Development of the USSR* (Seattle, 1964), p. 9.
Cf. also R. Judy, "The Economists," in H. Skilling and F. Griffiths,
Interest Groups in Soviet Politics (Princeton, N.J., 1971), pp. 216–
217. Judy depicted the struggle in Soviet economics between those
who were inspired by the 1920s and those who preferred the 1930s
and participated in making them. For a parallel development in the
(yet unresolved) fight for admitting political science as a legitimate
branch, see Paul Cocks, "The Rationalization of Party Control" in
C. Johnson, ed., *Change in Communist Systems* (Stanford, Calif.,
1970), p. 180.

[30] See article by Iu. Ivanov, *Kommunist*, no. 14 (September 1969).

more frenzy than at any time since Stalin's death, the regime proceeded to glorify the achievements of the party and its role in bringing about the great political trinity of the 1930s: collectivization, dekulakization, and "tempos." This comes, quite naturally, heavily seasoned with renewed attacks against the leftists, and especially the rightists, the "enemies of industrialization and collectivization," opponents of dekulakization,[31] and, incidentally, Stalin's adversaries.

This defense of party policies under Stalin was heavily undermined intellectually, in part even politically, by the blow that Soviet conservatism received from Khrushchev's de-Stalinization program, although the conservatives have recovered from it and have tried to heal the breach. By standards of elementary logic, the party could not have had any policies at a time when it was not asked what to do and was subjected to terror and assassination *en masse*. Therefore, claiming that the party was nevertheless healthy and clever and that the main pillars of policy were excellent amounted to a very thinly veiled defense of the essentials of Stalin's line, despite "some" admitted "excesses." Party propaganda launched its heavy artillery against those who thought that Stalin's policies were more than just "excesses," and who pressed for an exposure and detailed study of the whole period. Stalin's critics were assailed by party leaders as morally reprehensible, with a "predilection for the morbid"; as "calumniators of the glorious past"; as berators of the "heroic deeds of the working class," whose toil provided these intellectuals with bread; and as ingrates who repaid with insults.

Such themes have flourished in much of contemporary Soviet propaganda and have been best expressed by extreme Soviet dogmatists. The vehemence of their attacks

[31] See, for example, theses of the Central Committee published on the occasion of Lenin's centenary, which still serve as basic document in the national network of political education and propaganda, in *Partiinaia Zhizn'*, no. 1 (1970).

may be explained as a defense not only of the Stalinist era but also of the power structure of the present, since the majority of the older leaders in the party and the government joined the party during the Stalinist purges, obtained their first high-level jobs in the apparatus at that time, and reached top positions in the empire shaped by Stalin over which they now rule as a result of the methods and foundations laid down at that time.

It is thus understandable that defenders of the existing regime hate those who denigrate the methods and times that gave them their power and social position.

We are bearing in mind that the extent of changes that took place in the Soviet Union since the death of Stalin has been considerable. These changes have been studied in depth by Western authors, who often have concluded that the current system differs substantially from Stalin's totalitarian dictatorship. Underscoring the institutional transformations has been the massive development, accompanied by the emergence of a new social structure, and the leap into a new stage of economic growth that has imposed adaptations and reorganizations on the institutions. Such adaptations have been pervasive throughout the system and the party. The arrival of younger cadres, better educated and indifferent to many issues that seemed important in the past, has been an inevitable factor of change.

However, the institutional basis of the Soviet system, in particular the party, has not been completely transformed. The centralist dictatorial system, however rationalized, modernized, and mellowed, is still the main characteristic of the polity. Planning and the management of the economy, the hierarchical administrative structure, are still following the pattern created in the 1930s. The economic reforms tried to change it but the reforms are still in their initial stages, and even may be frozen entirely at this stage.

In the political system, law and its enforcement agencies, though better organized and more efficient than ever before, have retained their subordinate role to the will of the party. Since neither judge nor tribunal is independent, the party can manipulate them at will and frequently does so in prosecuting dissenters or even mildly critical citizens. The party was and is "extraconstitutional" and will not yield, not even on paper, to any limitations of its power.

The party monopoly of power, the arguments on which it is based, and the ways in which its power is exercised have retained so much of the previous system that it may still be classed as "Stalinist"—in particular, the adherence to the concept of social homogeneity in order to justify the monopoly of one party to the exclusion of freedom of political expression to any other factor. Moreover, the demand —nowadays voiced more loudly than during Khrushchev's reign—for monolithism in the party, "iron discipline," and the principle of "democratic centralism" has not abandoned the classical Stalinist interpretation: no unauthorized debate or political criticism; political decision making only by the top leadership. Any openly perceivable political tendencies and "fractional" activities inside the party are banned and considered treason, just as they had been in the "good old times."

It was during the 1930s that the Bolsheviks definitively lost their basic right to be political beings, to enjoy an ideological life, and to have some say in important problems of politics, ideology, and theory. They surrendered such basic freedoms to the party apparatus, and these have never been regained. The party leadership has denied information to the mass of party members in the same way as it has to other citizens; it has deprived the country of the right to a free political life and has claimed for itself total power over all activities, exactly as in the Stalinist era, including the manipulation of ideological life, dogmatization of party thought, selection of cadres, control mechanisms, and a whole series of "intangibles"—style, habits, moods, traditions, and thought patterns.

The student of Soviet political pronouncement after the invasion of Prague would be astonished by the enormous

325

campaign—intended for internal use and not just for some revisionists abroad—to propagandize the legitimacy of the party monopoly and to ban any political opposition. But opposition existed in the 1920s and made sense, thus intensifying the conservatives' dislike of the nostalgia for the NEP and their support of the activities of the subsequent period.

Considering, therefore, both the amount of change and the weight of the persisting traits of the system inherited from the past, in particular from the 1930s, it becomes clear why the battle of the two decades—the 1920s against the 1930s—continues to rage overtly and covertly in Soviet political, cultural, and ideological life. Both camps, the reformists and the conservatives, have good reasons for preferring "their own" period. This battle has been another manifestation of the unfinished phenomenon in Soviet social history of the alternation of two models: the authoritarian-monolithic versus the "mixed," liberal and pluralist. The student of Soviet history cannot fail to observe the recurrence of those models and to dwell on their role in the Soviet past, and their eventual significance for the Soviet future.

The supporters of the "mixed" model have remained very much in the minority, whereas those of the authoritarian-monolithic one have retained firm control; but they exhibit signs of nervousness as if they felt themselves assailed, not so much by any one intellectual who could be easily silenced but by the more menacing, implacable trends that conservatives fail to master and that could not be "jailed." These trends conceal several possibilities for the future, but the most probable are variations on the main themes of the past. Some form of the "mixed" model is still one of the contenders against the various authoritarian and "centralizing" versions.

For and Against Leviathan

As we have demonstrated, the clash of preferences and interpretations of past events, as in the case of the duel of the supporters of "their" respective decades, has often been a way of talking about politics in the present; controversies of the past have strongly influenced debates about the future, and diverging opinions on historical interpretations have revealed opposing conceptions and feelings on ways of doing things today.

Despite the very different international environment and the domestic setting, present controversies often parallel those of the late 1920s, and we can now quote several other factors to understand better the coincidence. At the end of the 1920s the last opposition tried to avert the development of what was very soon to become "Stalinism." The reformers in the later days saw it happen, and tried to get rid of the vestiges of "Stalinism." In both cases the target of criticism was common. Bukharin's outcry against building socialism by using mass coercion was based on a correct anticipation of where such a course would lead the Soviet system. The opponents of the "administrative methods," today, whether they studied past practices or present ones, faced phenomena against which their leaders were warned, and their critiques, often unwittingly, used the same terms to condemn the same target.

There was also a more far-reaching coincidence: in the late 1920s as in the 1960s and 1970s, the focus was on changing or preserving a whole model—a set of basic traits in the way of running and developing the economy, in the relationship of social classes to state power, and in the climate that permeated cultural life. The preservation of the NEP model was Bukharin's aim, and its main characteristics appealed to modern trends in Soviet thinking as a kind of blueprint for their own searches. Thus, there was a common ground for the opinions on methods of planning and on the whole "plan and market" syndrome. The reasons for nostalgia for the 1920s are understandable, although the historical NEP with its agrarian backward character, the *muzhiki*, petty traders, high illiteracy, and many other traits of a pre-industrial era has certainly not been the central object of interest.

The cultural plurality of the 1920s, whatever its limitations, has certainly represented an ideal for many Soviet citizens. In this regard, Bukharin, an advocate of cultural diversity, is no less interesting and appealing to them than he is as spokesman for "planning with bricks."

An affinity between the 1920s and the present exists also in the sphere of politics or, in larger terms, in the pattern of relations between the state and society. The NEP was a system that was not poised for mass coercion and repression. It was deeply interested in devising forms of legality and sociological theories of law, penitentiary practices, and procedures that would match the realities of a mixed economy and exclude crude coercion from economic life.[32] The party spokesmen in legal theory in those years, Pashukanis and Stuchka, were at that time avowed Bukharinites.

Preserving such a framework, whatever difficulties and crises might jeopardize it, was the central tenet of the Bukharinist credo when he and his associates clashed with Stalin's aspirations, and it was a battle between schools whose positions were contradictory on almost every important issue involving outlook, objectives, theories, and strategies.

Bukharin's belief in the very possibility of a more gradualist approach to industrialization—with his concomitant recommendations for balanced growth, rejection of unrealistic tempos, and concern with preserving small-scale industry and agriculture—was based on a more optimistic view of the potential for socialist development of the peasantry and other "small people" of Russia than other currents in Bolshevism then held. The opposite prevailing view declared the very forms to which the majority of the nation adhered to be not only the main target for transformation (this was legitimate) but also the main enemy. The strategy

[32] On the rule of law and legal theory in those days, E. Carr, "The Rule of Law," *Foundation of a Planned Economy 1926–1929*, 2 (London, 1972), 373–376. See also V. Bandera, "The Nep as an Economic System," *Journal of Political Economy*, June 1963, pp. 265–273.

of excessive speed could not succeed without coercing the masses into new social structures almost overnight—and this onslaught against the "small people" was accountable for the most reactionary traits in Stalinism and the obvious symptoms of morbid social decay that this system exhibited.

Forced collectivization was the epitome of Stalinist strategy and the antithesis to Bukharinism. Presented as an anticapitalist revolution conducted in the name of socialism, collectivization and the "beat-the-clock" approach in industrialization, instead of liberating people and production forces and instituting higher forms of social relations for what was then the bulk of the nation, blundered into mass oppression of "a military feudal exploitation of the peasantry" and made Russia pay a heavy price. A still notoriously weak agriculture, inferior to both industrial and some nonindustrial societies, has been part of this price.

Bukharin worried that the humanist side of socialism was being lost in this process and feared that a highly centralized, bureaucratized superstate would be installed for a much longer period than any emergency or passing crisis would warrant.

The specter of the Leviathan state was certainly raised during the debates between the "trio of deviators" and the Politbureau majority at meetings in January and February 1929. This majority rejected not only the opposition's platform but also all partial proposals to mitigate excesses, and it embarked upon a different course. The discussion of the realism of the alternative proposals or of the inevitability of Stalin's path has already begun in the Soviet Union and has been going on for some time in the West. Bukharin's fear of the "Leviathan state," his opposition to erecting an overcentralized bureaucratic giant, and his rejection of mass violence and police methods in social transformation and in the sphere of economics in the framework of the postrevolutionary Soviet system, certainly parallels in its spirit the modern reformers' support of democratization of economic and cultural life, their search for expanding social

329

autonomy through the unleashed initiative of the masses, and their efforts to curtail state power and the omnipresence of administrative methods.

The development of "socialism through different roads" and the whole syndrome of "liberal communism" in Eastern Europe, similar to the ideas in the Soviet economic debates to which we have alluded, have not arisen out of a knowledge of Bukharin's ideas, nor those of other people active during the NEP. But once the new ideas have appeared, and if conditions allow freedom of debate and of research, the affinity can and will be discovered and the continuity will be recognized openly.

Though current politics makes it impossible as yet to recognize such continuity openly, or even if some authors are genuinely unaware or uninterested in such continuities with the past, the historical parallels are striking quite independently of whether they are acknowledged or not. This becomes even more evident when still another present controversy is remembered and compared to one in 1929. This is the debate over "cooperative socialism" and the new approaches to "social interests" and ownership principles. Venzher and Shkredov, among others, as we already know, have argued strongly for combining state and cooperative principles (the latter, according to Venzher, being the "higher" one) and for (according to Shkredov) recognizing the legitimacy of individual, group, and state ownership. Shkredov has repudiated the monopoly of "some abstract owner" (the state) as detrimental and contradictory to social diversity. Recognition of this diversity and of the primacy of social interests led him to ask for the juridical expression of interests of social groups through their participation in ownership and the full recognition of the legitimacy of forms other than the state's ownership and supremacy. A text belonging quite clearly to this family of ideas recommends an approach that "assumes a most complex combination of personal, group, mass, social, and state initiatives. We have overcentralized everything in an exag-

THE INSPIRATION OF THE "1920s"

gerated way. It is time to ask ourselves if it is not appropriate to make a few steps toward the Leninists' 'Commune
state.' " But this passage has been excerpted not from Novozhilov or Venzher, but from Bukharin's "Notes of an Economist," and significantly it was Kaganovich, who quoted it in
a speech to party activists in November 1929, in order to
make it the main target of his attack, quite appropriately so
from his point of view. He scorned the "combination of personal, group, social, and state initiatives" and, in particular,
the very term "Commune-state" or rather the "few steps"
toward it that Bukharin wanted to make. "These are steps
to a petit bourgeois and, next, to a bourgeois democratic
state," he exclaimed, and he added that Bukharinites and
other enemies "joined hands against centralized management, against centralization, against the Leviathan."[33]

Here is, we believe, the crux of the debate, both in the
past and in the present, the real stake of a battle running
through Soviet history and as yet unfinished. The sortie of
Kaganovich the "statist," or the Stalinist, against Bukharin,
the proponent of "socialist pluralism," prefigured a realign-
ment of arguments and camps that would occur several
decades later and would be characterized in exactly the
same terms.

Mikoian (Kaganovich's pal in the old, hectic days when
together they destroyed the rightists) knew what he was
saying when he maintained that Bukharin represented "a
whole system of conceptions," "a consciously considered
theoretical and political line," that was, he maintained,
incorrect.[34]

Whether it was correct or not is a big problem. But
Mikoian was right in saying that this was a distinct political
program and, eventually, a stream that Stalin thought to be

[33] L. Kaganovich, *Sovetskoe Gosudarstvo i Revoliutsiia Prava*, no. 1
(1930), pp. 29–30.

[34] Vaganov, *Pravyi Uklon*, p. 38, brings this passage from party
archives. Mikoian spoke to the April 1929 plenum of the Central
Committee.

potentially dangerous. Stalin's anxiety was expressed through the efforts of prosecutor Vyshinsky during Bukharin's trial to negate and obliterate what Mikoian and others knew was true: that the oppositions, Bukharin's and Trotsky's alike, were political trends alternative to the ruling faction. This was the fact Vyshinsky was instructed to deny, to trample, and to forget. "The Trotskyites and Bukharinites, that is to say, the 'bloc of Rightists and Trotskyites' the leading lights of which are now in the prisoners' dock, is not a political party, a political tendency, but a band of felonious criminals, and not simply felonious criminals, but criminals . . . whom even ordinary felons treat as the basest, the lowest, the most contemptible, the most depraved of the depraved."[35]

No more contemptuous indictment could be imagined; but it has turned, by will of history, against this prosecutor himself. It is not easy to find strong enough terms to characterize the job Vyshinsky was doing. Obviously, his victims won an important moral point, because today the "felonious" part of the indictment has been dropped. But those among the victims who were not repressed Stalinists, but precisely "a political party, a political tendency," have not been rehabilitated and have remained under constant attack. The fact that they constituted an opposition inside the party is the real offense which still arouses the ire of powerholders. For a modern writer to recognize continuity and affinity with the opposition of the 1920s would be political suicide in the Soviet Union, and reformers, even if they want to, cannot afford to mention these names. But the conservatives, as we said, have no inhibitions. In book after book "the opportunists" of yesterday have been related directly to today's revisionist traitors to socialism, such as those in Prague who dared to demand "the so-called free play of political forces."[36] The accusing finger, reminiscent

[35] Tucker and Cohen, eds., *The Great Purge Trial*, p. 515. (This is the transcript of the trial in English.) He repeats the same on p. 517.

[36] This is what Vaganov is doing in his *Pravyi Uklon*, pp. 270–272.

of Vyshinsky's, has been pointed against "revisionists" in Prague and at the same time against anyone at home who wants to play "opposition."

Here lies the big difficulty for eventual rehabilitation or for some form of adoption, officially or only by some current in opinion.[37] To rehabilitate Stalin's opponents means also to endorse the very fact of an opposition inside the party, and the line of the current leadership consists precisely in nipping in the bud the slightest hint for the legitimacy of intraparty political groupings. As long as this is so, not an inch will be conceded to former leaders of a "political party, or tendency," even in regard to affairs solely concerning the past. Stalin's enemies have no rights in the Soviet Union, not until the next "thaw" at least.

[37] G. Katkov underlined correctly in his *The Trial of Bukharin* (New York, 1969), p. 191, Vyshinsky's (and Stalin's) main purpose— obliterating the oppositions as political trends. He may have a point also when he asserts that Bukharin, in the last analysis, failed in the trial because he gave up his position and lost "a unique opportunity to thrust his political ideas on future generations." In a free debate, I suppose, the rehabilitation by many historians of Bukharin for the period up to the end of 1934 is highly plausible. But is it possible to put back to the Pantheon of political leadership a man who did yield to the brutal force of a corrupt regime? This is more difficult to answer and to anticipate. In this sense, Stalin and Vyshinsky largely succeeded in making abject the personalities of their victims by the very way they used to crush them.

CHAPTER THIRTEEN

Conclusion

THE DEBATES among the economists and the opinions expressed by those of them interested in serious reforms have been significant in many respects for the study of the Soviet system. First, these economists, highly knowledgeable about the state of their country's economy, have played an important role in enlightening their public on this score. Many of them have been close to governmental circles and have mixed with administrators and top leaders. Sometimes they have held administrative positions, served as consultants and experts, participated in the arguments in the inner circles of power on the state of the economy and the different competing proposals for solutions.

At the same time, their role has been important for the intellectual and political development of their country. Not only have they created or re-created an important discipline, but they have also been instrumental in helping other social sciences to appear and in spreading among their own practitioners, as well as other social scientists and top administrators, a spirit of free inquiry, a distaste for dogma and empty propagandist claims, and a taste for debate.

No doubt their challenge to entrenched and obsolete propaganda-backed dogmas, and the way they helped to destroy some of them, has been a positive, intellectually liberating factor, either parallel to what has been done in other fields of inquiry or actually opening roads for others.

It is difficult to know how many of the million-odd people who have been listed in the Soviet Union as planners and economists actually have learned from the innovators or share their opinions. This study certainly concerned a minority, but it included some of the most prestigious names in Soviet economics. In the wake of debates in which they have had to carry the burden of impressing new ideas on a milieu that has not always been particularly open minded and could easily hide behind the bogey of "revisionism"—always ready to be launched at reformists—the economists that were studied have offered us new insight into some important facts of Soviet intellectual development. Economics has been in flux and has included a variety of schools of thought, not only on problems of economic theory or strictly technical aspects of their profession but also on larger aspects concerning their society and polity. Their divergences centered around programs for change and in many ways have overlapped or joined hands with streams of intellectual and political thought in circles much larger than just their own profession.

The critical economists, partisans of reforms, are part of the sophisticated and enlightened sector of the intelligentsia whose moods and opinions exercise influence on at least some high-level economic administrators and political officials. The development of such moods has been a relatively new post-Stalinist phenomenon in the Soviet Union, and it may be assumed that they have been growing in importance in society. Seen from this angle, the content of the debates among economists deserves careful scrutiny, both for the information they offered and for the opinions they expressed. The ideas generated by economic debates and reforms have been a major event in Soviet intellectual life, even if enhanced controls and censorship have recently blunted their edges. So long as unsolved problems remain and continue to accumulate, removing ideas from the surface by censorship or other forms of pressure and forcing them back under the surface may be good *real-politik* but poor politics. Under these conditions critical ideas will keep reappearing and presenting serious challenges to the existing ideology.

The critics, as we saw, showed that the existing model of

335

running the economy has become inefficient; that the official political economy was dead—but so were, at least by implication, many other official dogmas. The image of "society" to which the leadership has continued to adhere, a structure supposedly every day more homogeneous and thus ever better represented by the party, has been declared to be nonsense. Society is complex, multifaceted, and presents a pattern of often conflicting group interests. As this reality has not been properly acknowledged, the claim of the party to be the sole and best agent of "general interest" has been all too often unwarranted. The governmental and party administration, the leadership, have had their own interests too, and therefore nothing has been automatic about their ability to serve the general interests first or best.

The story of the Soviet economy told by the modern scholar has been simultaneously a story of tensions and accumulating contradictions among the state and social classes and groups, sometimes a straightforward chasm between state and society—a far cry from the pretended harmony between the centralized state and party guidance, and mass initiative and popular sovereignty. State property, the ideological mainstay of the whole model, has been questioned. It is far from being the very essence of socialism, as officially claimed; it may be the basis for expropriation by the state rather than a way of putting national wealth at the disposal of society.

All these ideas have led to serious questioning of the entire model and its ideology. For the first time many people have stated or implied that there are other models, too, and that the time was ripe for finding a new one in the economic sphere. The state, as omnipotent agency of total control and manager of economy, society, polity, and culture, has been trying to do too much with often disappointing if not damaging results. For the first time, relations among state, society, social groups, and economy were scrutinized.

A great debate was thus initiated, and out of it Soviet political science was born. In this process the very lynchpin of the system, the party, though not yet an object of study, certainly stopped being seen by debaters as the *sainte nitouche*, the depository of all possible virtues it has claimed to be. For a powerful organization that has put itself above constitutions, laws, and scholarly scrutiny, such criticism has not been easy to swallow, and it certainly has fought back. But it has been pierced with arrows, if only by ricochets; the process of "desacrelizing" the party in the eyes of scholars and the public at large and looking at it as a purely historical, time-bound phenomenon that evolves, performs, and may eventually become inadequate, has already begun.

It was no accident that the economic debate had to engage itself in problems other than the narrowly economic ones, because incentives and motivation in a state-controlled system cannot be understood in material and economic terms alone, nor can they be invented and imposed by administrative fiat or internalized only through action of the system's socialization agencies. Internalization of values and behavior patterns is a result of a complex interplay of conscious socializing with the sum total of experiences that individuals and social groups derive from the objectively constituted social system. If discrepancies or contradictions appear between values that are officially, or unofficially, sponsored by the state and the values and motivations that actually guide people in their activities, a discordance appears between the image of the system the state wants to impress on the citizens and the images that are actually formed in their minds. Such discord or contradictions between official and nonofficial values and perceptions of life is a normal and constant phenomenon in every system, but if it reaches deeply into areas that determine the system's vitality (such as the economy) or becomes generalized, the political system is under strain.

In the Soviet Union, with its state omnipresence and omnipotence, the accumulation of contradictions between officially expected behavior patterns and actual actions and

337

motivations of large social groups does reverberate more loudly on the state than elsewhere, and on the grip of its machinery on processes of social development. We are led to the conclusion that the Soviet system has experienced strains caused by phenomena of "discordance of motivations," which have worked differently in economics and in culture, among the popular masses and among intellectuals. Unfortunately there are no ways of affirming the intensity of such contradictions. But indifference toward official ideology has been one area where the phenomenon is widespread, and the economy is the other one.

The economists often stated what the clashes have been and what their results may become. The pernicious rift between "the plans" and "the market" should be closed, if the economy is to advance to a higher stage; otherwise factories will feel that fulfillment of plans will put them at a disadvantage, and the resulting disincentives will have the most crippling effects. There has been a lack of harmony between the motivations and rationale of higher administrations and those inherent in the actual working place. Such rifts constitute variations on the same theme: maladjustments and collisions between officially devised incentive schemes (themselves often uncoordinated and self-defeating) and those engendered by self-interest as conceived by crews or by managers of enterprises.[1]

Quite clearly, the whole intricate mechanism of relations between "the state" and "the economy" needs mending. Similarly, sociologists have observed the sluggishness of the labor force, or working class, its restless turnover, "lack of discipline," and escape in alcohol, which directly concerned the "state" as employer and the party as "guide."[2] Youth has

[1] Cf. S. A. Kheinman, in A. Notkin, ed., *Faktory Ekonomicheskogo Razvitiia SSSR* (Moscow, 1970), chap. 2, p. 70; I. Birman, *Metodologiia Optimal'nogo Planirovaniia* (Moscow, 1971), p. 79.

[2] M. Sonin, in Notkin, *Faktory*, chap. 4, pp. 106–107, reported that sales of alcohol in the Soviet Union grew 2.5 times in 1965 compared to 1950. Labor traumas and many other sequels go with heavy drinking.

been a multifaceted problem. The growing numbers of high school graduates are frustrated when they find themselves on jobs without adequate compensation and mechanization, the results of the slowness of economic development and inadequacy of industrial organization.[3]

These and other corrosive factors have been operating constantly and pressing ever harder on the seams of structures and institutions. In fact, the whole traditional power structure, based on the alleged monism of party-state-economy-society-ideology, has been subjected to pressure on all the joints. The concept of an "ideological monolith" certainly has become obsolete, but is still being maintained by powerful institutional arrangements, which have contributed to the perpetuation of both political and economic underdevelopment. Censorship continues to handicap scientific inquiry and cultural development; absence of political debate is depriving the country of the indispensable climate for the formation of creative leadership and for the abolition of the citizenry's political indifference.

The party (its relations to the state, to society, to its own membership) has no way of escaping erosion. As long as it perpetuates the dysfunctional factors in the cultural and political spheres, it is inescapably being corroded by its own secretions.

In summing up the tendencies that our scrutiny of the party disclosed, the party seems to have enclosed itself in a few ever-deepening contradictions. Its survival in the existing framework had demanded growing controls, which tend to be ever more elusive in a complex socio-economic system; hence the party leadership has been caught in an

[3] On frustrated graduates coming to workers' benches, see V. Zhamin, in Notkin, *Faktory*, chap. 5, pp. 117–119. On the other hand, too many young people still get only professional education, which means they do not finish high school and therefore are not awarded a diploma. As a result, they simultaneously work and try to complete their high school education, which takes years and which is irrational, says F. S. Goriachev, *23-ii S'ezd KPSS, protokoly* (Moscow, 1966), p. 160.

339

obsessive urge to reinforce its control, in order to preserve the existing patterns when the interest of the country's economy and society consist of finding adequate new policies, reshaping old institutions, and creating new ones.

A basic secondary contradiction breeding opposing tendencies inside the party consists of alienating or rendering indifferent the membership because of a growing discrepancy between the powerful and the powerless.

As this trend continues, the road opens more widely for a penetration into the party of the basic societal contradictions—between the privileged and underprivileged, the nationalists and the socialists, the conservatives and the democrats, the self-seekers and the idealists—and for the divisive influence of these forces on the apparatus and the leadership.

The hierarchical structure and disproportionate power distribution along the ladder contributed to the deepening of such internal contradictions and dysfunctional trends. As the rank and file and lower echelons of activists and even professional bureaucrats have been forced to act only as executives of policies decided upon elsewhere, and have been denied power and scope for initiative, nothing much of importance can be accomplished without orders from above. The whole organization has depended too much on guidance and pressure from above, and the leadership has behaved as if it were resigned to the fact that the lower echelons cannot be trusted and must be given orders, not to mention other nonbureaucratic factors that must be closely watched. Thus, the flow of information and reporting from below has flooded the center, and much superfluous, distorted, and unreliable data has contributed to the party's failure to cope with needs and events.

One more paradox has stemmed from the party's power structure. By denying social classes and groups the rights of political expression and open defense of their interests, the party has helped to perpetuate and deepen the existing class cleavage and contradictions. In conditions of declining economic growth and the weakening of social mobility, these contradictions are acquiring a more explosive potential, they penetrate the party, and complicate the already complex maze of factors subverting its capacity for leadership. Because the party has sought ever-widening control, any diminution of it seems troublesome to the now prevailing coalition in power. Hence, the indispensable innovation and political creativity is seen as the main danger, when they might just be the requisites for progress.

The difficulties the economy has encountered, as well as the obstacles that kept blocking the economic reforms and frustrating the reformers, are rooted to a large degree in the same general realm of politics that has been accountable for much of the lethargy and backwardness in state and party. The fact that the Soviet Union has rapidly undergone a technological revolution but has lagged behind its Western competitors in this respect, as well as what we call its "political underdevelopment," can be traced equally to the same excessively etatized and centralized patterns with their heavy and inflexible administrative machineries, which can be geared to perform important tasks but have difficulty adapting themselves quickly enough to new tasks and to tackling new types of phenomena. They therefore often have failed precisely where modern life is most exacting: accommodation of speedy changes, assimilation of new ideas, coping with diversity. On this score the Soviet political environment is particularly unfavorable. It is true that in the system over which the party is presiding, its role as a specific administration devised to coordinate different bureaucracies and to overcome their tendencies toward routine and narrow self-interest orientation (*vedomstvennost'*) was in the last two decades important and successful, but different symptoms have shown that the coordinator may be losing his grip: this is evident in phenomena such as the weakening of ideological vigor; the all too reluctant shedding of obsolete dogmas; poor political involvement of the rank and file of the party; and the hardening of privi-

341

lege and status patterns. The dynamic aspects of the initial revolutionary heritage have been watered down, and signs of an old-fashioned "Great Russian chauvinism," the specter that haunted Lenin's last days, have successfully reappeared and are not seriously opposed.

Hypertrophy of state action through state bureaucracies, atrophy of social activity and creativity—such has been a persistent source of malaise, differently perceived by different social strata but constantly creating blocks and slowing down the economic, social, and political development of the country.

Reformers of different kinds and some of the top leaders have felt that the system may be reinvigorated through an injection of a modernized *laissez-faire* package of measures, spread over society and inside the administrations, because with the omnipresent state trying to do too much, too much that is precious and necessary has been overlooked or stifled. Previous practice has shown that reduction of direct government interference has tended to produce almost immediate beneficial results, notably in the sphere of culture. Far from artists' ateliers, in fields and barns, less interference equally benefits plants and cows, which seem to be quite allergic to certain types of bureaucracy.

Freedom of organization and group initiative, outside and inside the ruling party, has become a frequent demand, in order to escape the impoverishing consequences of uniformity and the denial of freedom of action to those who would best take care of things that concern them directly.

So far, those who have advocated considerable changes on the line of such *laissez-faire*—a term for several possible versions of economic reforms and programs for political change—have been a minority. Quite understandably, the majority of the leadership has sought to avoid solutions that would entail a very considerable redesigning of institutions and the redistribution of power. They prefer to rely on science and technology, domestic or borrowed, in order to raise productivity in the economy, to improve the efficiency of its bureaucracies and managerial organization through streamlining and upgrading professional skills, to reinforce the capacity of the center with the help of modern mathematics, computers, and information technology. While such orientation has effected some improvements, mathematical economists and cybernetists have stated that these methods are insufficient to deal with current problems and that "pushbotton automation" and the "computopia" will not be able to save an overcentralized system.[4]

One should not, however, underestimate the existing regime. It has retained the capacity to maneuver, to rule, to control, to undertake change or yield to it, or to go on for a period without visible and important reforms, offering the ruling group powerful resources for its own defense and that of the *status quo*. The wealth of a huge country tightly controlled by the central government offers possibilities for reallocating and redistributing resources and even to waste some of them. But the very appearance and pressure of new needs and attitudes are difficult to control, to avoid, or to thwart.

The specifically Russian historical tradition, continued under the Soviet system, of authoritarian politics and weak or nonexistent democratic traditions and mass participation in the political process (this did happen, on a large scale, only during the revolutionary upheavals), as well as the relative youth of the modern segments of Soviet society, are the existing government's reserves for controlling the situation. Censorship and the powerful networks of compulsion —never as yet seriously tested by pressure of popular

[4] A. Katsenelinboigen, I. Lakhman, and Iu. Ovsienko, *Optimal'nost' i Tovarno-Denezhnye Otnosheniia* (Moscow, 1969), p. 20, derided the believers in "push-button automation." The term "Computopia" is used by E. Neuberger in his "Libermanizm, Computopia and Visible Hand: The Question of Informational Efficiency," *American Economic Review*, 16 (May 1966), 131.

forces—are also assets. The absence of vociferous public critics, so it seems at least, shelters the rulers from pressure and exposure.

The prestige of undeniable past achievements, the skillful appropriation by the party of the symbols of national grandeur, and the appeal to a deep-seated nationalism are additional buttresses. Furthermore, the depolitization of the masses plays into the hands of any leadership, to a certain degree at least, and enables it to manipulate social groups or to use one against the other.

Tactical concessions, selective material compensation, privilege to influential key sectors, and a large degree of freedom to exercise professional activity have been the weapons of the leadership. The party has granted freedom of research and scholarly activity (even some temporary privileges of a semipolitical character) to biologists, physicists, and other members of the scientific establishment in order to thwart the effects of previous meddling, which has resulted in damage to the economy, national defense, or other sensitive fields.

Many individuals and social groups can find full satisfaction in such sectional freedoms, which allow them the necessary latitude for professional activity, for exercising creativity, and achieving welfare and status. The party knows how to gain by this means the loyalty, or at least a nonhostile neutrality, of such professional groups.

The government of the Soviet Union is not inactive. But it has not yet found solutions to the problems in the economy. Massive proof can be mustered to show that the disquieting phenomena in the economy—the malfunctions and inefficiency stemming from a faulty structure and inadequate organization that forced the government, in the first place, to launch reforms—are still present and even flourishing; at the same time, substantive economic reforms have been shelved or replaced by a search for other answers. The basic problems to which critical economists addressed themselves (and the government accepted as valid)—slowness of technological innovation, inadequacy of incentives in the economic system to grow and to innovate, the inadequacy of many institutional arrangements of the economic administration—are all still on the agenda. The government, by making efficiency its central slogan, has acknowledged that it has been running an inefficient economy.

Yet slogans, minor adjustments, and changes have not eliminated the deleterious effects inherent in the system. Ministries have continued to behave in the old manner, using indicators and imposing targets that the reforms officially abolished; they have been disdainful of "economic methods." The material-technical supply system for producers' goods was left almost intact, as were all its defects. Despite all the changes, planning has been oriented to moving "from the previously achieved level," adding to what was done in the previous year the toughest possible target for increasing production in the next year.

As long as the administrative hierarchical framework to which the enterprises were subjected retain their basic traits, the latter use the same defenses: they hide resources and fight for the lowest possible production quotas, in order not to be caught unprepared for unfeasible quotas and not to find themselves deprived of premiums and penalized for nonfulfillment. Hence, the whole problem of incentives at the grass roots remains intact. In fact, authors have recognized that, for the moment, the various incentives devised with the intention of interesting enterprises in growing and innovating have not worked. Moreover, there have been no appropriate economic theory, no sufficiently viable pricing methods, and not enough managerial talent adequately prepared for a different type of economic activity.[5]

[5] These are summaries of statements from Soviet texts: M. E. Drogichinskii, in A. Rumiantsev and P. Bunich, eds., *Ekonomicheskiaia Reforma: Ee Osushchestvlenie i Problemy* (Moscow, 1969), chap. 11, p. 282, and Rumiantsev himself, chap. 2, pp. 44–55; see also Birman, *Metodologia*, pp. 86–99.

Perhaps an insurmountable "psychological barrier"—as one author put it—has been the major difficulty. But more is implied in another statement, which, pointing to "difficulties of growing up," could be easily reinterpreted as "difficulties of aging": economic science, organization of the economy, organization of planning and of management do not always "keep up with the growth of our economy, with the growth of our needs."[6]

Some of the reform economists knew and correctly predicted that reform would be a long and contradictory process[7] with alternate advances and retreats, thus accurately pointing to the larger aspects involved in the process. The causes of difficulty, which both the economy and the reforms encountered, have been "motivational, organizational, and institutional,"[8] according to a Western economist whose analysis is not very different from that of the previously quoted Soviet source.

Such statements have raised many complex questions about what should be changed. Obviously, the big problem of motivation is a formidable one, and the elaborate and intricate "incentive schemes" worked out in the planners' offices clearly have not eliminated the roots of negative phenomena.

The Soviet system was quite successful in motivating enough people to do things the government wanted them to do. It could sometimes be quite shrewd in its insight into what made different social groups tick, and offered them the necessary incentives. But now the dimensions of "moti-

[6] For "psychological barriers," see Drogichinskii, in Rumiantsev and Bunich, eds., *Ekonomicheskiaia Reforma*, chap. 11, p. 281, on institutions and science lagging behind the needs, and Birman, *Metodologia*, p. 10.

[7] See A. Efimov prediction in *Sovetskaia Industriia* (Moscow, 1967), pp. 325–326.

[8] G. Grossman, "Innovation and Information in Soviet Economy," *American Economic Review*, 16, 2 (May 1966), 127, which is not unlike what Birman was saying in the previous passage.

vation" have changed, together with the whole socio-economic environment, and the task has become much more complex.

The simple slogan of "efficiency" has hidden a task of monumental dimensions—the restructuring of the economic system and the changing of its internal proportions, including the elimination of vast areas of underdevelopment. Approximately 45 percent of the industrial labor force are unskilled, possess minimal skills, and work without mechanical aids. Such a serious handicap in industry has been complemented by similar situations in other sectors, especially agriculture, which made an impressive stride forward in the last decade, but it has not been "industrialized." About 70 percent of the huge agricultural labor force still perform their tasks manually. It has 8 tractors per thousand hectares of ploughland, against 34 in the United States and 129 in West Germany. It has one half the mechanical energy per laborer compared to the situation in industry, whereas American agriculture has twice the ratio of their industry. The USSR could afford only 40 kg of chemical fertilizer per hectare under cultivation compared to 198 kg in England and 313 kg in Germany. The yields are still extremely low —13 to 14 quintals per hectare, which is double the NEP or Tsarist figure, but still half of the American, and one-third (or less) of the German and English, not to mention the Netherlands. The comparisons look even more disadvantageous when it comes to animal foodstuffs.

Briefly, the technological revolution in agriculture that occurred in other industrial countries in the last decades has not yet come, or is only beginning in the Soviet Union. One central feature, which has concerned the perennial "proportions," has been underlined by scholars as a serious structural defect: in the United States 6 million people are employed directly in agriculture and 7 million more are employed in industrial branches working as suppliers for the farmers; in the Soviet Union 29 million are em-

347

ployed directly in agriculture and only 2 million work in industrial branches preparing machinery or other inputs for agriculture.[9]

Thus, in the 1970s agricultural output still constitutes a big problem, notwithstanding the social revolution to which agriculture has been subjected. Once more, as in the past, agriculture is said to be blocking the whole national economy. "Tempos of the whole economic development and the successes of communist construction in our country depend in many respects on improving agriculture."[10]

"Intensification," the slogan for agriculture and for the rest of the economy, will cost a lot in terms of resources, in addition to the large sums already invested in agriculture in recent years. Soviet agriculture seems insatiable, and it may well be that investments are not the whole problem.

Thus, agriculture, so long as it is not "intensified," will continue to occupy a huge pool of the labor force at a time when easily available reserves of labor for industrial development, construction, transportation, and services are exhausted, including the self-employed housewives who were recently very energetically induced to take up employment. Simultaneously, this labor force is quite restless, its turnover is great, and its discipline poor. To obtain higher productivity from labor, deeper interest, and motivation, workers have to be courted in some way, especially through a higher standard of living (not to mention training in skills or equipping them with better machinery). Similar inducements must be offered by the government to gain the goodwill and dedication of its technicians and administrators and the scientific establishment, without whom "intensification" and efficiency are unthinkable.

[9] All the data are from A. Emel'ianov, ed., *Ekonomicheskie i Sotsial'nye Problemy Industrializatsii Sel'skogo Khoziaistva* (Moscow, 1971), pp. 54–56, 59, 67–68. The comparisons with other countries are in a table on p. 54.

[10] *Ibid.*, p. 6.

Hence, a situation is created in which the government simultaneously needs its peasants, workers, technicians, and scientists. A whole nation must be induced to participate in order to succeed in the task. Can the government cope? Can this be done through the traditional methods of streamlining or reorganizing administrations, by the traditional bureaucratic ways—"apparatus-like methods" (*apparatnym putëm*) as a Soviet political term goes? Is the existing system appropriately constituted for such an immense operation of lifting itself up without substantially transforming itself in this process?[11]

Questions such as these have different answers, and the debates that were studied proposed some of them. But only

[11] According to recent reports available on the results in the economy during the years 1971 and 1972, the plan for 1971 achieved the big macroeconomic indicators, but neither productivity of labor nor the expected yearly averages for the quinquennium were attained. The plan for 1972 failed to reach all the important targets (however modest and reasonable), presumably because of a very bad year in agriculture. For the targets see *Gosudarstvennyi Piatiletnii Plan Razvitiia Narodnogo Khoziaistva SSSR na 1971–1975 Gody* (Moscow, 1972), pp. 75, 345. Fulfillment figures for 1971 and 1972 are in *Ekonomicheskaia Gazeta*, no. 5 (January 1972), pp. 3–6, and no. 5 (January 1973), pp. 5–8, entitled "Vypolnenie Gosudarstvennogo Plana Razvitiia Narodnogo Khoziaistva SSSR." The year 1973 was supposed to be crucial for the success of the whole plan, which was no more than an intermediary stage on the long road toward intensifying the economy. But results for 1973, published in *ibid.*, no. 5 (January 1974), pp. 5–8, do not show any breakthrough in comparison with the two previous years. Despite a fabulous crop—an all time record —which certainly helped to prop up the national income figure, important indicators did not reach the expected yearly averages for the quinquennium. Industrial production was heavily handicapped by the poor showing of the consumer goods; labor productivity in industry and construction, especially the latter, are well behind the expected averages. The same applies to animal foodstuffs and even the excellent crop of grain did not reach the growth targets and yields during the first three years of the plan. Thus, the main targets of the plan will not be reached, unless the next two years see some dramatic improvements.

events of the next decade or so will be conclusive. What can be known is the character of the problems involved. The economy creates the most complicated and urgent worries for the regime, but these are by no means the only ones. The general social structure adds some more complications, but also not a few props and forces that help to overcome difficulties or oppose far-reaching changes. If it is difficult to anticipate the outcome or the possible solutions for the economic ailments, it becomes almost impossible to predict the shape of things to come in a whole complex society and state. Economic activity—like industry, agriculture, commerce, and construction—nurtures big social classes and important professional groups, but important social groups and large strata of population evolve from noneconomic spheres. The state administrations, the educational establishment, cultural activities, and numerous noneconomic services make the social structure a complex system in which the problem of economic growth and technological advance interact with other needs of society. Cultural values, psychological needs, and political aspirations complicate the field enormously and warn against primitive economic determinism. If, in essence, the way of producing and distributing material resources often happens to be the source of problems, the solutions adopted are barely predictable, because they depend on the relative strengths of opposing social forces that clash on a stage larger than just the economy; and youth, bureaucracies, parties, and armies often play a crucial role. Programs finally adopted and systems emerging from the interaction can take on different shapes.

After all, such programs, plans, and blueprints for social transformation rarely depend on the logical or scholarly merits of texts and speeches. The constellation of forces, their compromises, and the quality of leaders who are fighting for the new solutions will decide the final outcome.

In the Soviet Union, as elsewhere, the remedies adopted for the cure of accumulating deficiencies and tensions therefore can take on different forms. The survey of other Communist countries offers a range of formulas adopted, for example, by Tito, Gierek, Mao, or Kadar. In the Soviet party, so strongly biased toward the techno-bureaucratic rather than the socio-political type of reform, some success in efforts to improve economic performance through reinvigorating the controlling capacities of the center and better management methods cannot be excluded. It is this line that obtains for the moment, since it seems to offer the most reassuring results for the supremacy of the ruling group without causing social upheaval.

The approaches to social problems of such a techno-bureacratic type are not confined to the Soviet Union, and not everybody, even at the top, believes in the validity of such strategies. For many thinking people in the Soviet Union as elsewhere, better efficiency through improved technologies, including techniques of indoctrination and manipulation, are not worth having at all.

Fortunately, progress on such lines is, at least, no less problematic, not to say utopian, than through democratization, for instance. If current policies do not work, as they plausibly may not, phenomena of stagnation and exacerbation of tensions will continue to produce new battles and clashes of camps and programs. The political potential of the different social forces, of which not very much is known yet, will manifest itself then and will be tested.

It is probable that what we learn from the economic debates, or from *samizdat*, are only announcements of future trends and political cleavages. So much is in fact happening in the depths of society, so much is brewing and maturing, that the existing façade of political unanimity and apparent simplicity is no longer identical with "Soviet politics."

The alternation between "thaws" and "freezes," which has characterized Soviet politics since Stalin's death, externally express the deeper tensions involved. If the system, in its current version, is in fact "overextended" and has difficulty coping with the growing maze of problems and social and

351

economic complexities, more revisions, turns of policy, "thaws," and "freezes" can be anticipated. Deriding or silencing open opposition, under these conditions, cannot be taken as more than a temporary success. Every "thaw" testifies anew to the deeper currents coming ever nearer to the surface, ready to burst forth. It is therefore quite legitimate to consider seriously the prospects in Soviet politics, among others, of a democratic stream that is trying, within the framework of a planned economy, to open the way for substantial changes in the Soviet system.

The body of opinion studied in this book, the personalities and groups promoting such opinions, are no more than an embryo, but an embryo that can be seen as a prefiguration of a growing trend, including scholars, administrators, and politicians, outside and inside the party, which may one day give leadership to a new coalition of forces. They, in any case, are the stuff of which parties, or factions inside parties, are made. They possess the intellectual capability, economic and administrative expertise, and enough allies in other intellectual disciplines to work out theories and programs of reform and modernization. They also can relate themselves to important and acceptable chapters and trends in the Soviet past and can propose solutions that are well in line with certain traditions inside the party. The "neo-Bukharinite" flavor of their thinking, especially in the way they criticize Stalinism, is, for the moment, no asset and is not acknowledged. But we have already had a foretaste of what may plausibly happen, in Khrushchev's debunking of Stalin, with victims and "traitors" becoming heroes overnight.

The Soviet political mind will need such heroes, and will need all the support it can get from an uncensored history of their country if it is to get rid of much dead weight and to advance to a new stage.

So long as admirers of the 1930s are firmly in the saddle, this is not yet possible. A fair trial for the anti-Stalinist factions inside the party, as well as other, nonparty trends, will occur when historical inquiry loses its fetters.

The crystallization and reinforcements of trends of a type we described here is one of the preconditions for such an "unfettering." What is already discernible is a quite articulate school, capable of offering alternative patterns not only for running the economy but also for the whole political system. If their analyses are correct, then this will become ever more apparent as the deficiencies of the current line grow and erode its vigor. It would be then quite reasonable to expect that the struggle will grow fiercer to force the party to relinquish obsolete and inefficient practices, to reform its own mechanism together with the whole nexus of relations between party, state, economy, and society.

Such deep changes rarely occur without difficulty and struggle, but reformers will have a chance to press their demands to bring the political system into accord with the growing complexity and modernity of society. This can be done, according to one line of reformist thinking, by transforming the rigid "administrative planning" of the economy into an optimal system relying on market techniques, with a flexible efficient "optimal plan," that grants a large place for autonomy and initiative for producers' units; by relinquishing an oppressive and utopian view of society as allegedly and increasingly homogeneous, and allowing social groups and group interests to express themselves and enter into the real and freer interplay of forces, from which an adequate political system will grow, permitting a better coordination and more leeway for social life; by emancipating the citizenry and creating conditions for their participation in political life; and, finally, by reducing the totalitarian ambitions of the party and transforming it into a political organization, either one among others, or unique, but with a free internal political play.

This last conception had already been anticipated in 1926 by another Bolshevik critic of the party, the relatively un-

353

known Ossovsky, who was severely punished for his heresy. Like many other heresies, this one may be able, under new conditions, to prove itself and may be adopted by many as a program. If the party wants internal unity, Ossovsky declared, it must allow the existence of other socialist parties in which different social interests will be able to find political expression; but if the party does not want to or cannot admit other parties, then it should allow political factions in its midst. Otherwise the price will be too high.[12]

During Ossovsky's lifetime, the granting of freedom to nonparty members appeared as granting freedom to enemies, to adverse social classes that would destroy the new social order. This stand against political freedom, which was developed and maintained in a situation of class polarity and enmity, still continues today. The question "who is the enemy now?"—when there are no NEPmen, no kulaks, no remnants of old ruling classes, no ex-Tsarist officers and gendarmes to be deprived of civil rights—is already being asked, and is a challenge because of its poignancy.

The price paid in the past for the excesses of dictatorship was heavy indeed, and if many would argue that it was unavoidable, it is difficult to argue the same today. Groups and interests keep forming subterranean streams and grope for expression and defense of their views. Without democratization, only forces that thrive on secrecy can benefit most. Democratization, on the contrary, would clarify the real political potential of Soviet society, awaken political life, let them recognize themselves openly in past streams and continue their traditions, or at least become known to

[12] Iu. Ossovskii, "Partiia k 14–tomu S'ezdu," *Bol'shevik*, nos. 7–8 (1926). The editors published this article of a member of the opposition to show what treasonable thoughts they entertained. Ossovskii's article was circulated through a kind of *samizdat* of those days before it was published.

At the present time Roy Medvedev, another, apparently quite lonely, voice has called for the same in his book on socialist democracy, *Kniga o Sotsialisticheskoi Demokratii* (Amsterdam, 1972).

the country for what they really are: socialists of different shades, communists, democrats, nationalists, chauvinists, racialists.

Ossovsky's assumption is today more true than ever. The new trend in Soviet political and intellectual life that has been studied shows the country the way to overcome the crippling consequences of a "civil war model," to drop the unrealistic monolithic cast, and to develop the regime into a direction that will allow Soviet society to enter an age of political reason, escaping for good the seemingly fatal bi-model pendulum.

Apparatchik: An official serving on the party administrative machinery, full time and paid. The term is used for any bureaucracy (*apparat*), but is normally reserved for the officialdom of the party secretariats on all the levels.

Apparatnym putëm: Using methods most characteristic of the *apparat*, through administrative pressure and commands rather than persuasion and bargaining.

Blat: From the jargon of the criminal world which became a widespread colloquial term; it is applied to the system of connections with and among influential people through which influence and material advantages can be exchanged, not normally available to ordinary law abiding citizens.

Chinovnichestvo: Officialdom. See *chinovnik*.

Chinovnik: Russian tsarist term for official. It is used in the Soviet Russian language in a pejorative sense.

Chuvstvo khoziaina: Sense of ownership, a feeling one may have that he is the owner of the place; party propaganda claims that this is how workers feel about the nationalized state industries. See *khoziain*.

Davai, davai!: A traditional Russian exhortatory exclamation of work supervisors urging their labor force to work more quickly. Often resented by workers who saw in this expression a symbol of the inferiority of their position in regard to bosses, whatever the social system in Russia.

357

Deliaga (plural: *deliagi*): Narrow minded, self-seeking individual, minding only his own business.

Diamat: Acronym for *dialekticheskii materializm*, dialectical materialism.

Glavk (pl. *glavki*): Acronym for *glavnoe upravlenie*, chief administration. The term has been used to denote the chief directories for managing different branches of industry inside the former Supreme Council of National Economy and later in the framework of industrial ministries.

Glavkizm: Pejorative term for bureaucratic, heavy-handed methods of management which characterized the *glavki*.

Glavkokratiia: Pejorative and mocking term denoting a system of "glavkist" methods.

GPU: Abbreviation for *Glavnoe Politicheskoe Upravlenie*, Main Political Administration, official term for the Secret Police.

Intelligent: A man belonging to the intelligentsia.

Khapun (pl. *Khapuny*): A strongly pejorative term for somebody who is ready to obtain anything he can, even if he has to steal.

Khozrashchet: Acronym for *Khoziastvennyi raschët*, economic calculation—a cost-and-profit accounting as well as an approach mindful of cost and profits in economic management.

Khoziain: (pl. *khoziaeva*): Owner or boss. Most often used for peasants running their own family farms, as opposed to peasants who work mainly as agricultural laborers or who have small and very poor farms.

Kolkhoz: *Kollektivnoe khoziastvo*, the Soviet collective farm in which the Soviet peasants are organized.

Kolkhoznik (pl. *kolkhozniki*): Member of the *kolkhoz*.

Kto-kogo?: Who will win?—used by Lenin and others as a slogan in situations where two camps are in sharp conflict with each other—in this context, the proletariat and the bourgeoisie, and their fight that, at least in the long run, must lead to the complete victory of one over the other.

Kulak: Fist. Term used for the richer peasants who exploited hired habor, or exploited their neighbors in other ways.

Kul'turno: In a cultural way. Educated, polite, or just literate.

Kul'turno upravliat': To manage institutions of the state, or any other, in a way modern professional people should.

Kustarnichestvo: From *kustar'*, a kind of craftsman (mainly peasant) working for the market together with the members of his family. *Kustarnichestvo* means the whole sector of such artisans in the national economy. In a pejorative sense, it refers to acting or running an enterprise or a whole branch of the economy inspired by the habits of backward, small-scale family enterprises.

Maleishee ushchemlenie: "The slightest encroachment" (on somebody's rights or some principle).

Mattekhsnab: Acronym for *Material'no-technicheskoe snabzhenie*, material and technical supply. The system of supply of materials and technology for industrial enterprises as it works in the Soviet economy.

MTS: Abbreviation for *Machinno-traktornaia stantsiia*, a state enterprise that concentrated and operated tractors and other basic agricultural machinery and appliances, which *kolkhozy* themselves were not allowed to own. The *MTS* was abolished in 1958.

Muzhik: Little man. A traditional Russian term for "peasant."

Nachal'stvo: The body of *nachal'niki*, a Russian Tsarist term for leading officials, which retains its meaning in the Soviet Union. Also heads, bosses. Denotes a whole class of industrial and other bosses.

Nakachka: The action of pumping. In the Soviet political and administrative informal terminology (sometimes used also in a pejorative sense), the term applies to the current method used by party bosses who summon their subordinates and "pump into them" tenets of doctrine or demands and orders for action. Critics, sometimes important party leaders, attack such ways of discharging their duties by party officials as undesirable because it is basically a one way boss-to-subordinate discourse, but not the more preferable method including exchange of information and analysis of the situation, followed by clear practical decisions concerning action to be taken.

Nariad (pl. *nariady*): A document prescribing some action or ordering disposal of some goods; a current term in Soviet administrative practice.

Nash brat: Colloquially, "one of us," e.g., "a worker like ourselves."

Nemedlenno ustranit': "To eliminate immediately." One of the most current clichés in party decisions when the superior officials end a resolution with an exhortation "to eliminate immediately" all shortcomings or negative phenomena.

Nomenklatura: The method by which the responsibility for nominations to important jobs is divided among the party hierarchy. More narrowly, just the list of jobs which cannot be filled without the approval of one of the appropriate party committees.

Ob'edinenia: Associations. The relatively recent term for groups of enterprises (sometime also called "firms"), organized under one administration which the current reforms promote all over the economy.

Obkom: Acronym for *Oblastnoi komitet*, the regional party committee.

Obshchestvennye nachala: Principles of social organization, based on self management, as opposed to the principles of organization directly by or under the control of state bureaucracies.

Ogul'noe okhaivanie vsego i vsia: Wholesale slandering of everything and everybody. Used often in Soviet official propaganda against those who do not restrict their criticism to drawbacks in the functioning of particular spheres of the system (the party prefers the latter and calls it "positive" and "businesslike"). Anyone who engages in criticism of a more general character incurs this type of accusation from the authorities.

Partiinost': Party spirit. An attitude that the party demands from everyone when dealing with political or other problems. Such an attitude is constantly required of writers. They have to write their novels in accordance with the views of the party.

Perekapitalizatsiia: Overinvestment.

Pererozhdenie: Degeneration.

Perestroitsia: To reorganize, to rearrange the institutions; to readapt.

Piatiletka: Soviet term for "five-year plan."

Plan i rynok: Plan and market.

Politekonomiia: Acronym for *politicheskaia ekonomiia*, political economy. Officially the ideologically approved branch of theoretical economics.

Potrebovat' iskoreneniia: To demand the extirpation (of malfunctions), used largely in party documents and decisions, and attacked for having become a cliché without any means to enforce such an action.

361

Pravomernost': Rightfulness, the quality of being in step with juridical principles.

Preodolenie: Overcoming.

Priamoi produktoobmen: Barter.

Prorabotka: Used in Soviet political practice for action taken against an opponent or otherwise undesirable consisting of "working him over," attacking him relentlessly, often behind his back, until the ground is prepared for his surrender or dismissal.

Rabochii narod: Working people. Used often by people working with their hands to distinguish themselves as a class from those who do not work, but give orders and enjoy privileges.

Raikom (pl. *raikomy*): Acronym for *Raionnyi komitet*, district party committee.

Raskhititeli: Embezzlers.

Rasporiaditel': The one who has the right to dispose of property.

Razgrom: Destructive or plundering raid.

Razreshitel'naia i razvërstochnaia sistema: System of allocations and quotas prescribed from above. It is a critical statement about a system where nothing can be done without permission or an order from a higher authority.

Razvërstka: Administrative distribution of quotas to be fulfilled, e.g., the amount of grain to be delivered to the state by every district and *kolkhoz*.

Razvërstochnyi azart: "A lust for imposing quotas," a pejorative term for a civil-war style of coercive action.

Rvach (pl. *rvachi*): A person inclined to grab goods for himself, rather than to mind the general interest.

Samizdat: The illegal, or informal, network of publications of pamphlets and books, typewritten and mimeographed, at the private initiative of individuals. Considering that most of the texts published in this way would not pass the censorship, this activity in the Soviet Union is illegal and is often prosecuted.

Samotëk: Spontaneity, uncontrolled action.

Shiroko razvernut': To unfold on a large scale. Used largely in party documents and one of the established clichés which are attacked as hollow by some party officials who prefer efficiency to such generalities.

Shtatnye: Employees on the approved payroll of an institution.

Snabzhenets (pl. *snabzhentsy*): Employees responsible for supplies in enterprises.

Sovkhoz: Acronym for *sovetskoe khoziaistvo*, a Soviet agricultural enterprise run by the state.

Sovnarkhoz: Acronym for *sovet narodnogo khoziaistva*, council for national economy.

Stikhiia: Spontaneity, elemental force.

Tekuchka: Soviet administrative practice where officials are all too often engulfed by current affairs and have no time for important long-term problems.

Tolkach: An employee, formally declared to exercise some approved profession but engaged informally as supply agent for the enterprises trying to "push through" goods that the administration does not expect to get through formal arrangements.

Tovarnik: Epithet applied to economists who believe that Soviet economy is a market economy.

Tovarno-sotsialisticheskie otnosheniia: Socialist market relations.

363

Tovarnyi: Commercial, pertaining to marketed products.

Tovaroobmen: Circulation of commodities.

Udarit' rublem: To beat with the ruble. Pertains to policies demanding from factory managers to mind the cost accounts and profitability under the penalty of losses, including loss of their premia. Hence the idea of "control through the ruble."

Udarnyi (pl. *udarnye*): Adjective formed from *udar*. Blow or shock, as in *udarnaia brigada*, a shock brigade. Used to denote enthusiastic and speedy action, first in military usage, and next on the economic front, particularly on priority building sites (*udarnye stroiki*, shock sites) worked on by highly motivated shock workers.

Ukazat' na nekotorye nedostatki: To point to certain drawbacks. Used in official decisions of party committees that are criticized for their vagueness.

Uravnilovka: The tendency to equalize salaries. This practice is attacked by the party as petty bourgeois. Also tendency of bureaucrats to apply the same criteria to different people and situations.

Vedomstvennost': Departmentalism. The tendency of officials to fight for the interests of their department to the detriment of more general interests.

Vrastanie: Growing into. Used by Bukharin to promote a policy which allows peasants, including the better-off, to get incorporated into the socialist economy.

VSNKh: Abbreviation for *Vysshii Sovet Narodnogo Khoziaistva*, Supreme Council of National Economy, a superministry which was responsible for Soviet industry before the establishment of specialized commissariats (ministries) for different industrial branches.

Zagotovki: Procurements.

Zalimitirovannaia sistema: A fettered system. Used by Nemchinov to criticize the methods of managing and planning the economy.

Zasedatel'skaia sueta: Flurry of committee meetings.

Zaiavki: Formulas used for presenting requests for supplies to higher administrative bodies.

Zazhim kritiki: The suppression of criticism. A well-known phenomenon in Soviet party life whereby administrators suppress criticism stemming from the rank and file.

Zlobnoe kritikanstvo: Malicious criticalness. Used by the party leaders against critics they do not like.